AF560220

THE JUNGLE KINGS

Ethnohistorical Aspects of Politics and Ritual in Orissa

STUDIES IN ORISSAN SOCIETY, CULTURE AND HISTORY

Editors: HERMANN KULKE and BURKHARD SCHNEPEL

Vol. 1: Jagannath Revisited: Studying Society, Religion and the State in Orissa, edited by Hermann Kulke and Burkhard Schnepel

Vol. 2: The Jungle Kings: Ethnohistorical Aspects of Politics and Ritual in Orissa by Burkhard Schnepel

THE JUNGLE KINGS

Ethnohistorical Aspects of Politics and Ritual in Orissa

BURKHARD SCHNEPEL

MANOHAR
2002

First published 2002

ISBN 81-7304-467-8

Published by
Ajay Kumar Jain for
Manohar Publishers & Distributors
4753/23 Ansari Road, Daryaganj
New Delhi 110002

Printed at
Lordson Publishers Pvt. Ltd.
Delhi 110007

CONTENTS

LIST OF ILLUSTRATIONS

ACKNOWLEDGEMENTS

In the writing of this work, I have come to owe gratitude to many people and institutions—too many to mention all of them here. But let me name at least a few. My research for this book was financed by the Humboldt Foundation from 1990 to 1992, and then by the German Research Foundation from 1992 to 1995, both based in Bonn, Germany. Without their financial support this book would not have been possible.

While doing library research and writing up my findings, I was a member of the South Asia Institute in Heidelberg and, from 1998 onwards, the Institute of Historical Ethnology in Frankfurt am Main. In these institutes I had many occasions, both formal and less formal, to discuss and present my ideas, and I was helped and inspired by the comments of many interested colleagues. I was also invited to give papers based on my research on jungle kings at various universities in Germany, to mention only Leipzig, Munich and Berlin, as well as outside Germany, namely Paris, Gothenburg, and Prague. Among the colleagues who invited me, I wish to mention only, with gratitude, Professor Göran Aijmer and Professor Jean Claude Galey.

In Germany, one of my main supporters from the very first days of my Orissan research, starting in 1990, has been Professor Hermann Kulke, of the University of Kiel. Although a historian, he has always shown great interest in my social anthropological and ethnohistorical pursuits, supporting my applications for travel grants and research money at all stages, and becoming a constant source of intellectual inspiration, both in personal communications and through his writings. In Heidelberg, it was especially Professor Klaus-Peter Koepping who supported my research in various ways, both intellectually and organizationally, last and not least by supporting my habilitation in 1997. I am very grateful to both of them.

The book was first published in German by the South Asia Institute of Heidelberg University (as volume No. 177 of the series 'Beiträge zur Südasienforschung' through Franz Steiner Verlag, Stuttgart) in 1997. I am grateful to the South Asia Institute for allowing me to publish an English version. I should like to thank Dr Robert Parkin, Oxford, for translating it, and even more so, for patiently considering my numerous wishes for changes, alterations and additions.

As far as Orissa is concerned, I am indebted to countless individuals for their help at all levels and of all kinds. In Orissa, it was Professor Gagan Dash, of the Linguistic Department of Berhampur University, and his wife who were among the first to help me get to know the country, its inhabitants and, last but not least, its language. In Bhubaneswar, at the

Department of Anthropology of Utkal University, I found a place of constant support, and I was often invited, at all stages of my research, to present and discuss my findings. I think with gratitude of many members and students of the Department, who were always encouraging, stimulating and full of good, intelligent advice.

In the field, I encountered many supportive and encouraging people who took a lot of trouble to answer my endless questions, discuss various issues with me at length, and even accompany me on my sojourns. In this context, let me only mention members of the family of the former royal houses of Jeypore, Parlakimedi and Daspalla. I am also grateful to Dr G. Nanda (Jeypore) and Sri J. Shroff (Koraput), as well as to many others whom I had the honour and pleasure to meet. I am also grateful to the Director and staff of the Orissa State Archives in Bhubaneswar, as well as to the many people, 'high' and 'low', in the numerous guest houses, government bungalows, hotels or private houses where I took my board. All of these people offered me something that money cannot buy: hospitality and friendliness.

Someone famous once said that fieldwork often only fails at home, namely when it comes to writing up. I have already mentioned some of the institutions and persons who helped me while doing so. But it should not be forgotten that there were many very important friends and relatives without whose emotional and other kinds of support nothing could have been done. Among these, I am especially indebted to my mother Margot and to my late father Max Schnepel, as well as to my wife Conny.

Last but not least, I wish to express my gratitude to Prasanna Kumar Nayak, Professor at the Department of Anthropology and Director of the Scheduled Castes and Scheduled Tribes Research and Training Institute in Bhubaneswar. I first met Professor Nayak in 1989, when he was in Berlin as a Fellow of the Humboldt Foundation. It was due to his invitation that I started my own research in Orissa one year later. Ever since, I have profited greatly from his great expertise in the anthropology of Orissa, his sincere scholarship and his genuine interest in the pursuit of knowledge. During my various stays in Orissa, Professor Nayak supported me in all possible ways, not only intellectually, but also in many everyday affairs and in emergencies such as stomach pain or lost money. Although he had many other things to do while I was around, he never once complained or hesitated to give his assistance, sometimes even accompanying me into the hinterland for weeks. I, therefore, wish to thank him specifically for his never-ending support and friendship.

June 2002 BURKHARD SCHNEPEL

Introduction

'The whole country is enclosed and broken up by many mountains, and the people who live in, on, or beyond the mountains know nothing of any king, or of Jahangir; they recognize only their Rajas, who are very numerous, and to whom the country is apportioned in many small fragments by old tradition. Jahangir, whose name implies that he grasps the whole world, must therefore be regarded as ruling no more than half of the dominions which he claims, since there are as many rebels as subjects.' So wrote the Dutch traveller Pelsaert, who visited the Indian subcontinent at the start of the seventeenth century (cited after Wink 1986, 191). Elsewhere, Pelsaert described the Mughal Emperor Jahangir (1605-27) as 'king of the plains or the open roads only' (ibid.). At a somewhat later period, an Italian traveller by the name of Manucci wrote that, apart from the Mughal ruler, there were over five thousand other kings living in the middle of the jungle. Similarly, the historian Bhimsen reported of the Mughal Empire in the early eighteenth century that, although Shah Jahan (1627-1658) and Aurangzeb (1658-1707) had admittedly conquered the greater part of the Deccan, there were 'still as many as one thousand forts in the possession of zamindars' in the area (ibid., 39).

This situation, of an Indian subcontinent overlain with many little kingdoms, can serve as our starting point. However, the focus of the discussion that follows will be less on larger political entities such as the Mughal Empire than on the politico-jural and social units of little kingdoms which, according to the statements cited above, constituted and put life into the Mughal Empire as well as other state organizations in India. To this end, I shall concentrate on examining certain little kingdoms in the south of the east Indian state of Orissa, my special interest being the kingdom of Jeypore, located in the forested upland interior, whose former sovereign territory is bounded by what has come to be known in modern times as Koraput District (see Map 1).

Central to my study, therefore, is the institution of the 'little kingdom', and especially the kind of 'little kingdom' I wish to qualify as 'jungle kingdom'. Of all the different ethnohistorical aspects I shall be examining, I shall concern myself first and foremost with those that refer to questions of politics and ritual, as well as the various interfaces between these two domains. The historical period I shall be looking at most closely is the pre-modern period of British colonial rule. However, references to earlier periods of the history of Orissa and its neighbouring kingdoms, as well as present-day manifestations and transformations of kingly authority will also enter the present study. It is therefore both historical, in the sense that it deals with the phenomenon of the Indian kingdom, which ceased to exist after about 1950, and anthropological, in that it deals with present-day politico-ritual phenomena that comprise my personal observations. Viewing the object of study less in terms of kings and kingdoms than in terms of the principle of kingly authority and the different manifestations of this principle in politics, ritual and ideology, it will be evident that I shall be dealing with a phenomenon whose history is continuing. In brief, India has known royal principles of organization and authority—or 'kingship'—which continue to exist and to be effective today, even when kings and kingdoms are gone.[1]

The present study requires some explanation at the outset, above all with regard to how it differs from many other studies on the themes of kingship, ritual and the state in India. The unit of the little kingdom has received relatively little academic attention so far, even though little kingdoms are to be found in great numbers in many regions and historical periods in India. If one takes the two most relevant academic disciplines in this area, it can be seen that historians have concentrated overwhelmingly on researching the history of regional phenomena, 'great kingdoms' and important states, while anthropologists have typically focused their attention on the local level of villages, tribes or sub-castes (*jāti*). Little kingdoms, which occupy the middle level of social and political organization, have been either ignored entirely by people working in the two disciplines or a negative significance has been attributed to them. Thus, in historiography, the existence of many little kingdoms, with their mostly 'rebellious' *rājā*s, is often interpreted as expressing the inability of Indian rulers or 'great kings' to carry into practice the central power and universal rule they proclaimed. In anthropology, little kingdoms have frequently counted as kingdoms that were crippled by the supposedly more important caste and tribal principles of organization. I shall go into these points in greater detail in sections 4.1 and 4.2 of Chapter I.

In the present work, I intend to counter the neglect and/or misinterpretation by academics of what has been a quantitatively as well as qualitatively significant unit of the political system and social order in India. In the course of my research, I was increasingly compelled to recognize that I could not simply ignore the silence and theoretical deficit surrounding research on Indian little kingdoms. With respect to other questions I soon realized that my own statements were always located against a background of protracted debates, above all controversies sur-

[1] For a similar argument, see also Galey (1989a).

rounding the character of the Indian state, the nature of the caste system, the relationship between politics and religion, the authority of the Hindu king, and the boundaries and transitions between 'tribe' and 'caste', and other related questions. I did not always see these debates as useful in the evaluation of my own material, and several times even saw them as leading to error. At the same time, they have so strongly dominated the general academic discourse that I could not ignore them completely.

I, therefore, saw myself faced early on with the task of tracing the origins and effects of the relative neglect of Indian little kingdoms as an object of study, even though this was a matter only indirectly linked to my actual object of research. This task is tackled in the first chapter, which looks at the history of theories concerning the state in India, and where I make explicit the models, theorems, sketches and ideas from which I diverge later in the evaluation of my own data. My critique will, therefore, be less deconstructive than constructive, even where (as in section 2) earlier accounts must in general be condemned as misdirected and 'orientalist' in character. Naturally, I also discuss those works (as in sections 3, 4.2, 4.4, 5.1, 5.2 and 5.3) in which the ground was prepared for the more intensive studies of little kingdoms which have emerged in recent years. Sections 4.3 and 5.4 also discuss those authors who quite deliberately make the little kingdom the political and geographical boundary of their research.

In turning towards this unit, situated at the middle level of the political and social organization of India, I am concentrating, as already indicated, on a terrain that is delicately poised between the local level of research, usually studied by anthropologists, and the regional and imperial level, usually studied by historians. It is, therefore, only to be expected that such a study will adopt a mode of research that renders the strict division between anthropological and historical questions, approaches and methods invalid, and in which the two disciplines will enter into a discourse in which each complements and inspires the other. The considerations and undertakings of the present study that transcend and merge these disciplines and that are expressed by the epithet 'ethnohistorical' in the title of my book will not be dealt with explicitly here. The close kinship between the two disciplines has been extensively documented since the dissolution of structural-functionalist ahistoricism in anthropology, as well as in numerous ventures into traditional anthropological areas of research from the direction of historiography in the last three to four decades. For the most part, therefore, I would like to confine my reflections on the methodological approach to this study when it comes to evaluate the data, only making them explicit where it seems necessary to discuss the nature of the sources examined, as, for example, in Chapter III, section 2, and Chapter IV, section 2.[2]

In this Introduction, however, at least one aspect should be discussed which is often forgotten in the usual pleas for closer co-operation between the disciplines of anthropology and history, namely that there are many different styles or schools in both. The representatives of these two disciplines speak in many different voices, having, to some extent, fairly different cognitive interests, approaches and ideas concerning the objects and methods of their disciplines. In addition, they regard other disciplines, for example sociology, literature or psychology, with different amounts of curiosity, and demarcate themselves from these more or less strictly. For this reason, in what follows, I would also like to present the contents of the different chapters of this work in the context of the types of anthropology and history that bear most pertinently on each one.

While the first chapter is directed towards a history of theories or ideas, the second offers an introduction to the history of Orissà and an overview of the little kingdoms of this region. Orissa's history has been well researched, although there are relatively few works which expressly undertake an analysis of the structure of power of the great kingdoms of the region. I, therefore, saw myself faced with the task of systematically evaluating the most important historical works on Orissa with particular reference to the question of the roles and positions that little kingdoms occupied within their different great kingdoms. One might describe this undertaking as an attempt to re-read the historiography of an Indian region, but with an anthropological gaze directed towards the social and political structure of the sort that has been applied by orthodox social anthropologists to the analysis of African kingdoms.[3]

Section 1 of this second chapter outlines the conditions that allowed royal authority to be established and strengthened in Orissa. Section 2 traces the reasons for the historical growth of some of these little kingdoms into sub-regional, regional and imperial kingdoms. Here, attention is directed especially towards the development, in medieval Orissa, of the relationship between the Gajapati or 'great king' and the presiding deity of the kingdom (*Reichsgottheit*), Jagannath, and his cult in the pilgrimage centre of Puri. The basic elements that shaped the ritual policy of the jungle kings of south Orissa can already be traced to this relationship between Gajapati and Jagannath. Section 3 examines the types of relationship the little kings of Orissa had with their respective overlords, and

[2] For an explicit discussion of this problem, see Schnepel (1999).

[3] See, for example, Evans-Pritchard and Fortes (eds. 1940).

the structures of the different historical kingdoms down the centuries, from the start of our era to the end of the British colonial period.

These first three sections of the second chapter profit considerably from existing research into the history of Orissa and lay the basis for an understanding of the most important data on the policy of the great kings, an understanding without which the history (or histories) of the little kingdoms of south Orissa cannot be understood. However, since the position of the little kingdoms in the overarching political system is given great attention in these sections, this means that I am already adopting the perspective which will characterize the present study overall. I believe that a perspective which takes the framework of the little kingdom as the basis for description and interpretation will lead to new insights. The second chapter, therefore, concludes with an overview of the little kingdoms of south Orissa in sections 4 and 5, as well as lays the groundwork for the study of the kingdom of Jeypore. This means that concepts crucial to the present study like the jungle and the jungle kingdom are also discussed.

Chapter III is concerned with the early history of the ruling dynasty of Jeypore, the period from about 1450 to 1570. At first sight, this chapter provides a traditional historical account, that is, a reconstruction of 'how it actually was' after the manner of the German historian von Ranke. Admittedly, this venture is being pursued with respect to a period and area for which there are hardly any facts that can guarantee 'historicity'. All that can be consulted are family chronicles and other documents, which, in part, were only commissioned by the royal house at the start of the twentieth century. The ideological or fictional content of these sources cannot be overlooked. The examination of earlier periods of Jeypore's history, thus, requires not only a critical encounter with the sources, but also some reflections regarding whether, and how, 'actual' history can be reconstructed in this case. I have dealt with the problem by attempting to show that ethnohistory is more than simply writing the history of an area hitherto studied only by anthropologists. In Chapter III, therefore, it will be shown how plausible historical conclusions can be reached when one consults sources which have so far been largely left to the anthropologist to interpret, such as myth and ritual. This is possible especially, as I wish to show, when anthropological approaches—for example, structuralist interpretations of myth or the examination of symbolic systems—are combined with historiographical methods and perspectives in a meaningful way.

Such a synthesis is called for especially in Chapter III, section 1, which probes the origin of the Suryavamsha dynasty of Jeypore. For on this point precisely, the emic sources are not sparing with legitimizing fabrications, when, for example, in family chronicles, a Rajput origin for the dynasty or the divine election of its founder are postulated. A more general disquisition on the problem of Rajput identity and the question of the 'Rajputization' of Indian royal houses is given in section 4. Section 5, in which I examine the period in which Suryavamsha rule was consolidated up to about 1570, is confronted with similar problems, although the 'hard' data for this period are richer. Section 6 summarizes the results of Chapter III and looks briefly at the historical period in which Muslim rulers replaced the Gajapatis of the collapsing great kingdom of Orissa as overlords.

In Chapter IV a new problem area is foregrounded in the discussion, a further step being taken inwards, or downwards, in that I place the relationship between the jungle king and a local governor within his kingdom at the centre of my account. In order to explain the structure and dynamics of this relationship, I look at the estate of the *thātrāja* of Bissamcuttack in north-east Jeypore. My account concentrates on a long-running dispute carried out between the king of Jeypore and the *thātrāja* of Bissamcuttack in the nineteenth century in the form of complaints, petitions, requests, etc. to the British colonial rulers. The documents in the Orissa State Archives, which I have evaluated in this context and which I present in section 2, offer interesting information on various questions and problem areas. For one thing, these sources make possible a reconstruction of 'actual events'. I go particularly into this matter in sections 5 and 6, where it is shown that the two parties produced their own 'histories' for the colonial courts during a legal dispute. Although these histories were written with legal and political ulterior motives, they contain valuable evidence which allows us to reconstruct the history of the relationship between the two protagonists. Furthermore, in matters that these quarrelling parties brought up again and again before the British colonial government, those points that were of decisive significance for their own understanding of themselves and for their strategies of action can be very clearly recognized. It thus becomes obvious that besides the material grounds of conflict (like the distribution of land or money), questions of prestige and honour played a decisive role, especially in either resolving or escalating the conflict. Since these matters of honour were mainly expressed in the idiom of ritual, the documents contain much valuable evidence of the ritual life of the people in this jungle kingdom and of the multiple connections between politics and ritual which prevailed there.

The discourse between the two parties took place in the colonial context. The mere existence of the British, who adopted a position comparable to that of kingly overlords in earlier periods, and whose legal organs decided the outcome of the conflict, led to the fact that the arguments brought forward in the actions and papers of the indigenous actors were already geared to colonial modes of understanding. I deal with this situation especially in section 3, using the example of a celebration held to honour Queen Victoria in Jeypore in 1877. However, it was not only by reason of their function as judges that the British dominated the content and form of the discourse, as well as the outcome of the dispute between king and 'feudal' retainer. Even when disputes continued to smoulder, such as those of 1877 or the conflicts of the following decades dealt with in section 4, the British played an active part in the negotiations through their own letters, position statements, warnings and edicts.

All in all, in Chapter IV it is less a matter of writing history in the conventional sense as of reconstructing the actual political and legal situation at the time of the dispute and of asking how arguments were used in order to influence and/or legitimize political and legal actions and decisions. An analysis of the discourse conducted between parties acting on different levels of the political system is therefore central to this chapter. It is also a matter of exposing the political, economic and ritual interests that lay behind the arguments and the discursive strategies. In comparison with the earlier chapters, therefore, a new type of perspective is being introduced and a new kind of problem is discussed. In this chapter my approach is most clearly in the tradition of postmodern anthropology, in which concepts like 'power', 'cultural hegemony', 'agency', 'negotiation' and 'multivocality' determine discussion and analysis. As regards the ethnohistorical approach used in this chapter, I see myself inspired by the work of Sahlins (1985) on the history of the Polynesian island world, the 'invention of tradition' school (Hobsbawm and Ranger eds. 1983), the history of mentality and the everyday or social history of Europe, as well as by the most recent reflections of historians like Greenblatt (1988) and other advocates of the New Historicism school of thought (see Veeser ed. 1989, 1994).

In Chapter V, the ritual policies of the jungle kings of south Orissa become the focus of my discussion. Here, my interest is in the royal patronage of locally rooted earth and mother goddesses, which represents one of the most important aspects of the ritual policies of the little kings of south Orissa. The fact that here I am relying mainly on my own observations demonstrates again my aim of bringing about a fruitful synthesis of anthropological and historical perspectives and forms in acquiring data. The concrete data I collected on the spot, through conversations, interviews and observations, lead me first of all to a general overview of the present-day cults of these goddesses which are presented in section 2. I then devote sections 3 and 4 to a detailed treatment of five goddesses, namely Khambeshvari, Mohuri Kalua, Budhi Thakurani, Majhighariani and Markama. In this way, I also arrive at an understanding of the historical significance of the establishment and legitimization of royal authority of the Hindu type in an area that was settled overwhelmingly by clan-based ethnic groups, whose belief systems and rituals can be called 'tribal' in character. My description of the cult of the tribal goddesses patronized by the kings of south Orissa, and my analysis of the political significance of this patronage, are led by considerations which can be labelled diachronic or developmental and which therefore again concern another sort of 'historical time' (Koselleck 1979). This is because, in order to arrive at a better understanding of the many-sided forms in the iconography, iconology and cults of these goddesses, I oppose 'tribal' religion to 'Hindu' religion, seeing both as ideal types. And as a result, my discussion of the different ways in which originally aniconic images of goddesses were anthropomorphized reveals the different possible developmental stages in the process of the Hinduization of these goddesses.

Chapter VI is devoted to the royal patronage of the great Hindu goddess Durga. Thematically, this chapter is linked to the foregoing in the sense that the south Orissan tribal goddesses increasingly converged with Durga during the process of their Hinduization—iconologically, iconographically and in areas of ritual practice. However, there was a point at which tribal goddesses and their devotees resisted being 'embraced' by Hindu little kings and their Brahman priests. In the first section of this chapter, therefore, the phenomenon of Hinduization is discussed again by explaining the points of contact, transitions and boundaries between the cult of the tribal goddesses and the Durga cult. Section 2 is concerned with the patronage of Durga or related goddesses like Kali and Manikeshvari by the little kings of the sub-region. Among other things, it is shown that possession of a metal Durga statue or *mūrti*, which is honoured in addition to the aniconic, immovable local goddesses, represented a most important status symbol and emblem of political power. As a source of power (*śakti*), Durga statues were highly prized trophies which individual kings of the region sought to steal from one another. This section also gives a historical overview of the relationship of the kings of Jeypore to 'their' Durga *mūrti* (supposedly stolen from the Gajapati) from the end of the fifteenth century to the modern period, a relationship which, over the course of centuries, was subjected to numerous trials. In comparison with the patronage of local goddesses, my discussion of the royal patronage of movable and spatially transferable Durga statues provides additional insights into the complex relationship prevailing in south Orissa between the politically understood sovereign territory of a king (*kṣatra*) and the religiously understood sovereign area of a divinity (*kṣetra*), as well as of the dynamic relationship between territory (understood as land and people) and politico-religious power.

Section 3 of Chapter VI offers a description and interpretation of an important centuries-old festival in the jungle kingdom of Jeypore, namely the *dasarā* festival. Here I refer to written eyewitness reports from the nineteenth and early twentieth centuries, as well as to my own interviews with elderly inhabitants of the royal capital of Jeypore and with members of the royal house. This information is supplemented by my own observations of the *dasarā* festival in present-day south Orissa. Although my sources and the phenomenon being examined may therefore be labelled ethnohistorical, my interpretation of the ten days of celebrations is rather ahistorical and structural-functionalist in style. However, it is also indirectly inspired by Kantorowicz's analysis of European theories of corporations (Kantorowicz 1957), Elias's analysis of courtly rituals (Elias 1983) and Canetti's insights into the dynamics of masses and power (Canetti 1980).

While important functions of the *dasarā* festival included the periodical renewal and strengthening of the political unity and military striking power of the kingdom, as well as the confirmation of the king as the highest political, military and ritual authority in the kingdom, it also provided a platform for the 'insubordination' and striving for independence of some powerful local governors of the kingdom, who repeatedly and ostentatiously kept themselves apart from the event in Jeypore and even held their own *dasarā* festivals. One such 'rebel *dasarā*' is described in section 4 of Chapter VI, particular attention being focused on the specifically tribal elements of the festival. In this section I am again relying on historical reports, but I also make use of my own enquiries, interviews and observations made on the spot. The structural-functionalist interpretation of the *dasarā* festival in the previous section, with its focus on the mechanisms that strengthen social and political cohesion, is thus significantly supplemented and relativized in this section, in which the centrifugal elements—the different perspectives of the various actors involved and the negotiability implicit in the *dasarā* festival—also receive expression and enter into the interpretation.

At this point, I would like to return to the question of the sense in which the present study is an ethnohistorical one. Anthropologists whose work is located in the tradition of British social anthropology usually see an intellectual watershed in Evans-Pritchard's Marett Lecture (Evans-Pritchard 1950) in which, to the consternation of many listeners, the ahistorical dicta of Malinowksi and Radcliffe-Brown, which up to then had scarcely been challenged, were fundamentally questioned. Evans-Pritchard characterized anthropology in his lecture as 'a kind of historiography' (ibid., 123). Recalling Maitland he maintained that 'anthropology will have the choice between becoming history or nothing' (ibid.). A decade later, Evans-Pritchard warned historians, too, to choose between anthropology and being nothing (see 1961, 20). Fortes, in his inaugural lecture as William Wyse Professor of Anthropology in Cambridge in 1953, referred back to Evans-Pritchard's statements of 1950, seeing the controversy they had triggered as to whether social anthropology should be regarded as belonging to the natural sciences or to the humanities or as being a branch of history as 'futile' and 'meaningless' (1953, 30, 36). Fortes agreed with Evans-Pritchard's ideas regarding certain parallels in the working methods and epistemological interests of historians and social anthropologists, but for him the specific task of social anthropology as a scientific discipline with its own themes and methods was fundamentally different from that of history. Social anthropologists should concern themselves mainly with the study of the synchronic structures of living societies and should examine how particular institutions and customs hold the total structure of a society together. According to Fortes, there are 'two roads in the study of social life' (ibid., 29). The historical method 'seeks to explain customs and institutions by tracing their antecedents in the past and the steps by which they came to be what they are where they are' (ibid.). The sociological method 'seeks explanations of contemporaneously interdependent customs and institutions, the significant connections being those that reveal the function of an institution in relation to the whole system' (ibid.).

Nearly fifty years after this discussion, it seems as if the history of social-anthropological thought has helped Evans-Pritchard's position to victory. By contrast, Fortes is seen today as someone who is outdated, at least as regards his position in the 1950s. From the perspective of the present, however, it is doubtful if the character of the interdisciplinary relationship between history and anthropology can be reduced to a vague paradigm of the merging or elective affinity of the two disciplines. It is precisely against the background of the often confusing and arbitrary multitude of methods, theories and perspectives which characterize the newer anthropology and other humanities that Fortes's call for 'disciplined disciplines' still has relevance. Yet, in my view, there are other reasons why, with respect to the relationship between anthropology and history, the orthodox 'either-or' of structural-functionalism should not simply be replaced with a 'both-and' or 'both-together'. Rather, one should make use of the heuristic value which arises precisely because of existing differences between the two disciplines. Within a field of productive or creative tension, each discipline may overstep its respective boundaries with specific questions and intellectual pursuits in mind, though in doing so, it might also find it necessary to stress differences and retain or even re-create distance.

The twenty-four months of research I spent in India for this study were distributed roughly equally in archives and in the field. The archival research was undertaken mostly in the Orissa State Archives in Bhubaneswar, where I was able to view the basic printed records of colonial historiography—district gazetteers, census reports, annual administration reports, etc. However, my greatest interest was in local documents of different types and lengths, from brief notes to dozens of pages of comprehensive court files, which from about 1850 to 1930, grew out of the written exchanges between the many little kings of Orissa and the colonial authorities. These documents, which are often written in English or are accompanied by an official translation by colonial officials, were transferred only about a decade ago from scattered local storage sites, where they were usually prone to deterioration, to Bhubaneswar where, professionally preserved, archived and catalogued, they are available for research. As for the several thousand documents from south Orissa, which are catalogued under the rubrics of 'Ganjam District Records' and 'Koraput District Records', in all likelihood I am the first person to have examined these documents. I found further material in the central Settlement Office and in some other government offices in Cuttack, another administrative centre of Orissa. Since the sub-region of south Orissa belonged to the Madras Presidency up to the founding of the province of Orissa in 1936, I found more documents in the Tamil Nadu State Archives in Madras/Chennai and the Andhra Pradesh State Archives in Vishakhapatnam and Hyderabad. For the most part, these stem from an earlier period of British colonial rule, which was officially exercised in the Northern Provinces of the Madras Presidency from 1765 onwards. In addition, I was successful in obtaining some material in local libraries and offices, for example in the private library of the Jeypore royal palace, the Settlement Office of Koraput District, the archives of the Collectors of this district, and the library of the Jagannath temple in Koraput.

As far as my 'fieldwork' is concerned, I place this word in quotation marks, so as to avoid the impression that I undertook fieldwork in the classic Malinowskian tradition. The little kingdom of Jeypore is no island, but a unit in a more comprehensive political structure and a wider cultural area. Yet, even if one were to identify and draw a boundary around this and other little kingdoms analytically as a separate unit (which is both legitimate and necessary), the differences from the classic units of anthropological fieldwork clearly emerge. Thus, for example, the population of Jeypore and Koraput District are not as internally homogeneous, nor do they possess such clear boundaries as an island population, like that of the Trobriands, or a 'tribe', such as the Nuer, were or at least were assumed for a long time to be. The little kingdom of Jeypore alone accommodates more than a dozen ethnic groups or important sections thereof, each with its own language or dialect as well as other peculiarities which, should one wish to research them thoroughly, would require a single-minded decision in favour of a long stay with just one of them.

Taking the unit of the little kingdom as the framework of reference to delimit and organize the acquisition of my data and their interpretation also enabled me to take a decision against fieldwork, strictly speaking. However, this decision did not mean opposition to fieldwork in the wider sense, understood as a move outside the study, the library and the archive, and into the field. I sought to obtain a view of the present-day and past lives and ideas of people on the spot, through conversations, interviews, observations, statistical investigations and other types of interaction. This still leaves unanswered the question of how one can—apart from interviews with increasingly elderly and, in terms of numbers, scarce eyewitnesses—carry out anthropological research into a kingdom that has not existed since 1951. In answer, I would like to recall what has already been established at the beginning, namely the fact that the principle of royal authority has continued to exist even after the kingdoms and their kings had been removed. Present-day manifestations of this principle are to be observed above all in the domain of ritual. In other words, rituals are not simply products of history. They incorporate history within themselves and thus they also accommodate the principles and structures of the actions and ideas that characterized earlier times. Alongside myths, legends, family chronicles and oral traditions, rituals, therefore, form important sources of information for ethnohistorical research. They supplement, to a significant degree, the inscriptions traditionally researched by historians and can replace them where, as in Jeypore, sources of this type scarcely exist. With regard to the process of data acquisition and research, I have, therefore, also sought to acquire knowledge less by pursuing first history, then anthropology and then the two together, as by moving within the overlapping border areas of the two disciplines and seeking to exploit the possibilities available to me there.

All in all, the present work differs from many other studies on the closely linked themes of state, kingdom, ritual and politics in India mainly by directing its gaze to the unit of the little kingdom and by its use of an ethnohistorical approach in researching this unit. In this sense, it stands quite clearly in the tradition of the pioneering work in this area, namely Dirks's *The Hollow Crown* (1987), which takes a south Indian little kingdom as its subject. The studies of Berkemer (1993) and Kulke (1979b, 1980, 1984c, 1992), which are dedicated to little kingdoms in Kalinga and central Orissa should also be named in this context. However, in contrast to these three authors and to other little-kingdom scholars who will be mentioned later, in Jeypore I have chosen a kingdom whose sovereign territory lay exclusively in an upland, forested interior. Because of its secluded situation and the fact that its population was largely of tribal origin, Jeypore differs in important respects from the little kingdoms of the coast and river plains. I have, therefore, characterized Jeypore and similar little kingdoms as 'jungle kingdoms', using this concept to draw increased attention to a hitherto rarely researched sub-type of the little kingdom, with its own specific phenomena and problems.

CHAPTER I

LITTLE KINGDOMS AND THE STATE IN INDIA: A HISTORY OF IDEAS, THEORIES AND MODELS

1. Introduction

Before 1947, modern India embraced an area of something over four million square kilometres. More than half the territory counted as 'British India', while somewhat less than half was occupied by the so-called 'native', 'feudatory' or 'princely' states. Altogether, in the period immediately before independence and the partition of the country that quickly followed, there were 565 princely states which were not directly subject to British colonial rule and were counted as sovereign as far as the regulation of their internal affairs was concerned, at least in principle. The princely states were of differing sizes. The two largest, Kashmir and Hyderabad, each covered about 220,000 square kilometres, while the smallest, Katodia and Lodhika in Gujarat, measured a mere 2.6 and 19.5 square kilometres respectively. Actually, most princely states were of modest size. The political and legal status of many was also so limited that the British classified them as 'non-salute states', whose rulers were not granted gun salutes on ceremonial occasions. In order to obtain a more exact idea of the number of kingdoms on the Indian subcontinent, it must also be remembered that in the two centuries before independence, numerous royal houses with ancient lines of descent and with prestige extending beyond their borders had been demoted to 'estate holders' by the British. In this degraded position they were deprived of their royal privileges and made subject either directly to colonial jurisdiction or to the sovereignty of the prince in whose territory their estates were located.[1]

The figure given above of 565 princely states, which occupied about half of the Indian territory, illustrates the extent to which traditional India was covered with kingdoms. Periods of history in which the country was dominated by only one or a few great powers, such as under the Mughals or the British in the late-colonial period, were the exception. Yet even when sovereign territories of regional, transregional or even pan-Indian size were established, many kingdoms often continued to exist, with their

[1] On these points, see Allen and Dwivedi (1984, 2-6); Imperial Gazetteer (1909, Vol. IV, Ch. 3); Mohan (1990, Chs. 1, 2).

sovereigns, as quasi-autonomous sub-units of the larger empires. Little kingdoms, however different they may have been in size, structure and function, thus represent a conspicuous factor in the history and political organization of the Indian subcontinent.

The aim of this introductory chapter is to examine some of the important studies on state and kingdom in India. Here, my discussion will be guided by, and limited to, the question of the position ascribed to little kingdoms. Of the large number of publications on this topic, only those in which the authors seek to arrive at statements which transcend their own concrete, spatially and temporally limited data will be dealt with. The focus of my discussion is therefore on *models* of state and kingdom in India.[2] The different models, or at least attempts to build models, are here described in a very abbreviated manner. The historical data that underlie them cannot, for the most part, be analysed thoroughly; in addition, later modifications of a model and the debates they have triggered must often remain unacknowledged or only be discussed in the notes. This is because, within the confines of the present work, I am concentrating on determining the character of the particular model itself (the model of the model, so to say) and on explaining the status that little kingdoms are accorded in it.

A retrospective examination of those studies in which little kingdoms are made the concrete focus of theoretical considerations need not detain us long. The study of little kingdoms as a *sui generis* object of research that might also possess theoretical and methodological relevance for the study of the Indian state as such is still only in its infancy, as far as both the collection of relevant data and the theoretical evaluation of these data are concerned. In view of the large number of little kingdoms on the Indian subcontinent in practically all periods of its history and almost everywhere, this lack of academic interest is hardly to be explained by the empirical situation. At least one reason for this failing must, therefore, be

[2] By 'model' I understand on the one hand a reduction or ideal-typical abstraction of concrete historical, anthropological or other sorts of empirical data. On the other hand, the heuristic value of a model also, and above all, lies in the fact that it is forward-looking and offers a guide or starting point, not a definitive explanation, for the understanding and investigation of those data which are not accounted for in the creation of the model itself. On the epistemological nature of scientific models, see Handelman (1990, 22-41). Where authors who have not built models in the strict sense are discussed, we are still dealing with 'founders of discourse' in Foucault's or Barthes' senses, that is, with authors who discuss relevant aspects or problems so concisely that they have had a lasting influence on later works. On this, see Geertz (1990, 25-7) and Inden (1990, Ch. 1).

sought in the nature of the preconceptions of both Western and Indian researchers who have investigated the themes of state and kingdom in India. This epistemological imbalance, therefore, also requires the inclusion of studies on the state in India in which little kingdoms are not considered at all or merely valued negatively. The classical models of Indian historiography, to which the next section is devoted, belong in this category.

2. The orientalist models

In this section, in order to structure my review of the literature, I shall begin by following Kulke, who identifies 'at least five distinct models of state formation and of the state in India between 1000 and 1600 AD' (1995a, 1-2). Of these, I shall deal in detail with the four classical models of 'oriental despotism', the 'centrally organized or unitary state', the 'feudal state' and the 'patrimonial state', reserving discussion of the newer model of the 'segmentary state' and other studies for later sections.

The four classical models from Indian historiography are all rooted in a Western or Eurocentric image of the state, which sees the state as being defined by the facts that the centre has a monopoly of power, that there is a hierarchically organized administrative structure and that we find clearly drawn territorial boundaries. In accordance with this Western model, different degrees of centralization and of the exertion of power by central elites over local and middle-level holders of authority are postulated. Diverging assessments of these degrees then provide these authors with important measures for the building of their models and for their demarcation from other competing ones.[3] Because the essential criteria for model-building are, thus, based on their supposed nearness to or deviation from Western ideals and because these models of the Indian state are essentially conceived as contrasts to or replicas of the Western model, I would like to characterize them as 'orientalist' in Said's sense (1978).

2.1 Oriental despotism

The European idea of 'oriental despotism' is old. Its first formulation is found in Aristotle in the fourth century BC.[4] In the Middle Ages, at the time of the crusades and the threat from the Ottoman Empire, as well as later in early modern debates in political philosophy for and against

[3] See also Kulke (1995a, 2-5).

[4] See Aristotle (1989, 188-200).

absolute monarchy,[5] it served as an ideological template which helped the idea of a genuine 'occidental' form of the state to take shape. The Eurocentric fiction of oriental despotism was reinforced by the reports of European travellers who visited India in the seventeenth and eighteenth centuries, so that the image of oriental despotism was henceforward based on observations made within the Mughal Empire.[6] The idea of oriental despotism received further academic elaboration in the colonial historiography and utilitarian political economy of the eighteenth and early nineteenth centuries by British authors like Jones, Mill and Smith. Here the attempt to legitimize British colonial policy by evaluating Indian sovereigns as 'despotic' is unmistakable.[7] In the German philosophy of that period the notion of oriental despotism merged with Hegel's reflections on the philosophy of history, where it underwent further Eurocentric definition.[8] The various characteristics ascribed to the institution of oriental despotism by these authors, with their different emphases, were shaped or, better, transmitted by Marx's expositions on India into a synthetic and formal whole.[9]

Apart from his reading of the authors just mentioned, Marx's conception of oriental despotism was also based on parliamentary papers and the reports of British colonial officials available in London. For example, he accepted the data and 'bourgeois-colonial' conclusions of the *Fifth Report* of 1812, whose data he adopted without much questioning them, at least when it came to assess the nature of the Indian state. The influence that Marx's image of orientalism was to exert subsequently was, therefore, based less on any deep or original investigation of the material as on an ability to think in terms of a model and to argue polemically, as well as on the significance ascribed to his expositions in other philosophical and political contexts. It was only because of Marx's numerous interpreters and exegetes from science and politics—'Marxists' as well as 'dissidents'—that his expositions concerning India acquired the

[5] See Machiavelli (1986 [1514], 29-37) and Montesquieu (1965 [1748], 128-37, 160-6, 192-3, 200, 266-7, 284, 300-1, 367-8).

[6] Of the authors of these reports, Bernier (1914 [1710]) exercised the greatest influence on the fantasies of those at home.

[7] See Jones (1831), Mill (1858 [1821]) and Smith (1778).

[8] See Hegel (1961 [1848], 211-47).

[9] Marx never brought his remarks on India together in a systematic fashion. His statements, scattered throughout newspaper articles, notebooks, letters, manifestos, academic treatises and books, can be found in Marx (1972).

character of a model which has apparently lost none of its attraction right up to the recent past.[10] In addition, in the political economy of Marx, Engels and other authors, oriental despotism was integrally associated with a mode of production characterized as 'Asiatic' to the extent that the idea of the 'Asiatic mode of production' widely became congruent with that of 'oriental despotism', not infrequently replacing it without fundamentally altering the essential features and elements of the model.[11]

For Marx, as for other authors before and since, the village community represents the basic unit of Indian society. According to these thinkers, the social atom of the 'village' is internally held together through a type of caste system that is not political or legal but merely social and religious in character. In the model, village communities form closed worlds or 'little republics', within which a division of labour, spread among the different castes, leads to wide-ranging social self-regulation and economic autarchy.[12] Placed over these village communities, and hardly linked with them organically, is the state. The sovereign is regarded as the highest and sole landowner, who—supported by numerous bureaucrats—receives land rents from individual village communities and recruits his army from them. In addition, according to this model of oriental despotism, the sovereign functions as the master of large, state-controlled irrigation projects, without which neither extensive agriculture nor the much desired extraction of a high surplus would be possible. ('Asia' was conceived of as consisting of large, arid stretches of land.)[13]

In this model, the oriental despot is a totalitarian ruler uncontrolled by any other institution. Yet, he and his legal institutions interfere only marginally in the social life of the village. This life, according to another

[10] Wittfogel (1977 [1957]) must count as an outstanding later representative, and Bahro (1990) as a more recent example.

[11] Detailed studies on the intellectual history of the concept of oriental despotism and critiques of aspects of the concept can be found in P. Anderson (1974, 462-549), Bailey and Llobera (eds. 1981), CÉRM (1969), Gunawardana (1976), Habib (1962), Krader (1973, 1975), Kulke (1995a, 3), O'Leary (1989), Thorner (1966) and Wink (1986, 186-9, 377-9).

[12] The idea of the isolated autarchy of the village is stressed especially by Hegel and Marx. Cf. also the critiques brought forward by Dewey (1972), Dumont (1966) and Inden (1990, ch. 4).

[13] This 'hydraulic' aspect is a decisive characteristic of oriental despotism in the explanations of Mill and Smith, who use geographical and climatic factors to buttress their arguments. This is also true of Marxist representations of 'Asiatic' modes of production and in Wittfogel's 'hydraulic state'.

central idea of the model, goes its way unaffected by dynastic changes or imperial wars and is characterized by stagnation and passivity. The autarchic unit of the village, enclosed within itself, then stands antagonistically opposed to the changing historical despots who, apart from hydraulic management, simply seek to cream off an agricultural surplus without giving anything in return. In India, however, this situation did not lead to class war or 'history' in the Enlightenment sense but was passively tolerated by the subjugated and accepted as inevitable. Individual dynasties changed repeatedly, but the structure of the state as a whole and life within village communities remained untouched by them.[14]

In the model of oriental despotism, therefore, the village is at the lowest level in which a natural, organically grown, stable community of farmers is opposed to the higher and stronger but artificial and purely parasitical, exploitative level of the state. The sovereign only appears as the ethnocentrically distorted type of a despot qualified as 'orientalist', characterized by opulence, decadence, lasciviousness, and insatiable lust for the enlargement of his personal wealth. In the occidental view, he is a monarch beyond any control, feeling obliged to no common well-being. Furthermore, his behaviour is tolerated and made possible by the slavish mentality of the farming community.

The difference between great and little kings has no relevance in this model of a single-centre state. The state and village community form not only the two poles of the political system, they represent the only levels that exist at all, between which no further levels, such as that of governors or a land-owning nobility, let alone sovereign kings, are identified.[15]

[14] Jones, Montesquieu and Mill stress the 'ahistoricity' of Indian village communities, an idea that also has great relevance with Hegel and, through him, Marx. According to Marx, the stagnation of the village and the despotic character of the sovereign determined one another: '…we must not forget that these idyllic village communities, inoffensive though they may appear, had always been the solid foundations of oriental despotism…. We must not forget that this undignified, stagnatory and vegetative life, that this passive sort of existence, evoked on the other part, in contradistinction, wild aimless unbounded forces of destruction, and rendered murder itself a religious rite in Hindustan. We must not forget that these little communities were contaminated by distinctions of caste and by slavery, that they subjugated man to external circumstances instead of elevating man to be the sovereign of circumstances…' (Marx 1972, 36-7).

[15] Jones, Machiavelli and Montesquieu especially saw the decisive difference between occidental and oriental monarchs in the lack of a territorially anchored nobility and in the state monopoly of landed property. For Marx, this lack of private property in land and soil counts as 'the greatest desideratum of Asiatic society' (cited in Thorner 1966, 43).

Thus, all in all, complex political systems in which several levels of administration or a number of hierarchically linked kingdoms exist cannot be grasped with the model of oriental despotism. Here, kings oppose one another merely as the sovereigns of territories, strongly demarcated from one another, acting in a totalitarian and mostly antagonistic manner. They are great or little merely according to their respective power. Often, however, oriental despotisms are little, since (as Marx writes) 'just as Italy has, from time to time, been compressed by the conqueror's sword into different national masses, so do we find Hindustan, when not under the pressure of the Mohammedan, or the Mogul, or the Briton, dissolved into as many independent and conflicting States as it numbered towns, or even villages' (Marx 1972, 35).

In this model, therefore, little kingdoms are taken notice of, if at all, merely as being the remnants of an oriental despotism in decline. Within these despotisms, the 'superstructure' (state) and 'base' (village communities) only have existence without a 'middle structure' (nobility, governors), and even the two poles hardly seem linked to one another as a functional whole. Points of contact are only provided by the supposedly necessary state control of the irrigation system and by taxation measures. Internal differences within the idyllic village community on account of caste, class or other criteria only enter into the model in so far as the resulting division of labour makes possible the autarchy of the village. All in all, the model is based on long outmoded data, whose acquisition and evaluation was always distorted by the preponderance given to 'Western' political, social and intellectual concerns and questions. There are no aspects of this model which have not been rejected by more recent studies. The model of oriental despotism can, therefore, be laid to rest as an element in European 'intellectual history' which has no relevance for an understanding of actual Indian history and politics.

2.2 The centralized state

A further model of the state in India is that of the centrally organized, i.e. 'central' or 'unitary state', which closely corresponds to the Western image of the ideal state. It, thus, represents an image which seeks to level out or make even, rather than oppose (like the model of oriental despotism), 'own' and 'other'.[16] This model proved so popular in the historiographical assessment of Indian states that it can be characterized as

[16] Since the two models mutually supplement and define one another, they ultimately do not contradict one another.

'conventional'.[17] The model of the central state sees the state in India as a construction that is administratively organized in top-down fashion, and with fixed territorial boundaries. A strong central authority is assumed and this authority is believed to possess a monopoly of power, with means of control and fiscal organs acting effectively right into peripheral areas. Governors who are appointed by the centre and can be recalled at any time preside over the subordinate, hierarchically related administrative levels and territorial segments of the state.

The central state is also unicentred. Within it, there is no king other than the great king, for subordinate persons of authority in the same system count not as kings but simply as functionaries or officials of the centre. The rise and fall, growth and contraction, of a given kingdom, thus, do not represent the structurally immanent properties and dynamics of the Indian state as such: as with oriental despotism these processes are explained as being merely the result of changes of dynasty and of wars. With the idea of the Indian central state, therefore, the pejorative model of oriental despotism is disposed of. However, this only happens if one also adopts the Western ideal of the state, which continues to lay down the norms and measures against which Indian historical manifestations of the state are measured. Nevertheless (or perhaps precisely for this reason), different historical kingdoms of the subcontinent are readily ascribed a unitary character by modern Indian academics. Moreover, for many of these scholars the ancient Mauryan Empire became *the* paradigm for such a state. In this way, the young Indian nation state was equipped with the dignity of having a long tradition of geographical, cultural and political unity. The relatively recent model of the European nation state certainly remained important, but it lost its superior lustre in the face of the (assumed and postulated) ancient origin of the Indian nation state.[18]

[17] Kulke writes: 'No generally accepted name of this model has yet been found. Various designations are used in this context, e.g. "bureaucratic" … "unitary" … "imperial" … or "conventional" …. The term "Indian historiographical model" is used here, as the overwhelming number of early and of contemporary "conventional" contributions of Indian historians are depicting the pre-modern Indian state in the line of this model' (1995a, 2).

[18] See also Wink (1986, 9-12, 19-21). Kulke characterizes the historical background of this model as follows: 'This "imperial model" emerged particularly during the time of the Indian freedom movement, when, at the height of British Imperialism, Indian historiography became a major prop of the national claim that classical Indian culture and civilization had produced political and social institutions which were equal if not superior to those of their imperial masters' (1995a, 4). For examples of the conventional model of the central state, see Altekar (1958) and Nikalanta Sastri (1955).

2.3 The Indian feudal state

A controversial model, one which has great influence even today in the historiography of India, is the model of the 'feudal state' of a particularly Indian kind.[19] The entry of this model into the modern historiography of India took place against the background of an emotional debate, burdened by political ideology, over the value of the Marxist concept of the 'Asiatic mode of production'. In this debate, the feudal state model represented an attempt to replace the model of oriental despotism with a more dynamic, Indian variety of feudalism that was easier to integrate into the teachings of historical materialism. Again, it was a Western model, that of the West European state of the Middle Ages, that served as a reference point for European and Indian historians seeking to establish this model, even when Indian characteristics were being emphasized. Once this model had been established intellectually, it offered—now once more in harmony with Marxist teaching—a historiographical and political platform for allocating India a place in the world of class wars and progress, and to place it on the threshold of socialism.[20] Not infrequently this led to completely outdated attempts to construct evolutionary taxonomies. The heuristic value that might have been found in a comparison of Indian data

[19] Assessments of Indian political systems as 'feudal' go back to the colonial historiography of the early nineteenth century and are exemplified by Tod (1920 [1829-32]). As with the idea of oriental despotism, this notion of early feudalism also helped legitimize the British takeover of power in India, as Cohn (1983), Dirks (1987, 332, 385) and Inden (1990, 172-90), among others, stress. In the modern historiography of India, the standard works are Kosambi (1956a, 1956b) and Sharma (1965). In 1985 an edition of the *Journal of Peasant Studies* appeared under the title 'Feudalism and non-European societies' (Byres and Mukhia eds. 1985), in which the essays by Habib, Mukhia, Perlin, Sharma and Stein (all 1985) make reference to the debate on feudalism. Further developments of the model can be found in Jha (ed. 1987), Sharma and Jha (eds. 1974) and Yadava (1973). For criticisms and commentaries, see Kulke (1982, 239-47), Mukhia (1981), Rothermund (1970a) and Sircar (1966). For an overview of the modern history of ideas regarding the model of the Indian feudal state, see Kulke (1995a, 3, 6-18). In characterizing the dominance of the idea of the feudal state in the modern historiography of India, it should not be forgotten that numerous detailed historical studies often use terms like 'feudal' or 'vassal' without questioning them.

[20] For Marx, the supposed 'history-lessness' of Asia had been the one reason for not extending his concept of feudalism to this continent. Ironically, therefore, in the model of the Indian feudal state, Marx had to be overcome in order to be able to find a use for the Marxist philosophy of history for India.

with those emerging from feudal formations of the European Middle Ages was not sufficiently realized.

The existence of many little kingdoms became conceptionally relevant in the feudal state model as it was assumed that formerly great kingdoms—the ancient Gupta Empire often served as a paradigm[21]—collapsed into many smaller units in the course of history. The existence of numerous little kingdoms and princedoms in the feudal state is, thus, mainly seen as resulting from the weakness and decadence of a once strong central power. This central power attempted to arrest its loss of power and decline through 'feudalization', that is, through land grants or the granting of fiefs to priests and military or administrative functionaries enjoying fiscal and legal immunity or other advantages. Ultimately, however, the formerly strong state emerged weakened from this process because, with time, the vassals succeeded in strengthening their positions, appropriating their own royal dignities and establishing themselves as a new class of landowners at the middle levels of the political organization, where they appropriated the agricultural surplus at the centre's expense.[22] In the feudal state model, therefore, there is a diachronic component which relates to the collapse of power and the fragmentation of the central state, and also to the waning of mercantile, urban powers and of money at the expense of the growing importance of an agricultural subsistence economy.

According to this model, the effective exercise of royal authority is limited to the nuclear royal domain. Alongside it exist numerous secondary centres of power, each with its own jurisdiction and extraction of surpluses, as well as its own authority within its own hereditary lands. In contrast to the model of oriental despotism, therefore, in the feudal state model the nobility are ascribed a strong position, comparable to the position of the nobility in the Europe of the Middle Ages, where the relative freedom of this group, it is assumed, led to 'history' and progress. And as in Europe, so too in India, the relationship of the aristocracy to the formerly strong central power was 'feudal', in the sense that subordinates performed military and ritual services for their overlords as well as made tributary payments to them. Basically, however, at this middle level, the

[21] Though, as Chattopadhyaya (1995, 201) and Mukhia (1985, 284) remark, from the third century BC up to the Rajputs in the early nineteenth century, there was hardly any period of Indian history that has not been ascribed the title 'feudal'.

[22] Sharma (1995, 56) identifies up to five levels of infeudation and sub-infeudation.

land-owning hereditary aristocracy were internally autonomous and externally only nominally subject to an overlord.

Though little kingdoms have been seen as integral to the Indian feudal state and were thus somehow integrated into the model, the evaluation made of them has been overwhelmingly negative: not only did they symbolize the loss of power, human capital and territory on the part of a formerly powerful unitary state, they were also seen as the cause of its collapse. Therefore, with regard to the Western model and ideal of the central and unitary state, the model of the Indian feudal state represents merely a degenerate and unstable version of the same. Nor does the positive significance of the existence of little kingdoms—for example, as integral components in the structure and dynamics of a larger political polity embracing it, or as factors securing the continued existence of a powerful empire, or even its achievement of imperial greatness—occur in this model. In the vision of the feudal state, little kingdoms embody decadence and collapse. They are regarded as historically necessary elements on the way to socialism and freedom, but as elements which still need to be overcome.[23]

2.4 The patrimonial state

The model of the 'patrimonial state' stems from Weber's sociology of power, in which patrimonial domination is categorized as traditional among the three pure types of legitimate rule, with charismatic and bureaucratic/rational domination being the other two.[24] According to Weber's classification, the legitimacy of traditional rule is based 'on an established belief in the sanctity of immemorial traditions and the legitimacy of those exercising authority under them' (Weber 1968, 130). The ruler is not a detached superior but a personal lord, and it is not the objective rational-legal duties of office but personal links that determine the relationships of the administrative staff with him. Patrimonial rule, which Weber represents as *the* basic form of traditional rule, has its germ in the patriarchal authority of a single person, which was extended beyond his original dominion to extra-patrimonial areas (that is, to weaker

[23] However, the possibility of interpreting the role of little kingdoms in the framework of a feudal state model more positively or more 'organically', and thus as basic to the Indian state, is suggested by Kosambi's concept of 'feudalism from below'. This is also envisaged by Chattopadhyaya (1995, 201-7, 227-30) and Kulke (1982, 1995a), who ascribe an integrative role in state-building to land grants and infeudations. Cf. also section 5.3.

[24] On Weber's model of the patrimonial state in general, see Bendix (1977, 329-59), Rösel (1986, 118-36) and Weber (1976, 130-6, 580-625).

patriarchal households of the same sort). Through this process domestic power developed into political power, patriarchal power into patrimonial. According to Weber, patrimonial rule is, in its own understanding of itself, not based on tradition but is guided solely by the ruler's personal discretion. In practice, however, limits to the personal arbitrariness of the ruler are fixed by the sanctity of tradition. Where, out of this mixture of traditionalism and arbitrariness, it is the latter that predominates, Weber speaks of 'sultanism' as an extreme form of patrimonialism and as a form of the state that is related in type to oriental despotism.

Weber argues that in actual history patrimonialism frequently formed the basis of political constructs of extraordinary size. In these political systems, the domain of the patriarch functions as the core around which newly attached extra-patrimonial domains of the same sort are grouped. This results in the fact that the overall political system is in form almost identical, though in a tremendously enlarged version, to the rule of the patriarch in his own smaller domain. The patrimonial ruler, typically for Weber a king, therefore organizes his political power as he organizes control of his household, and the division of office functions under patrimonial rule usually follows a pattern which stems from the household administration and continues to be linked to it in terms of personnel. For Weber, therefore, the patriarchal household and patrimonial state are constructs of different size, though homologous to a high degree structurally and in respect of their principles of organization and authority.

Now, according to Weber, the spread of patriarchal power into extra-patrimonial realms confronts the rising patrimonial state with organizational problems which make it a labile political form in itself. The destabilizing factors arise especially from the recruitment and provision of military and administrative coercive staff necessary for the process of extending power. The constantly increasing prebendalization—i.e. the appropriation of sinecures and power by the military and other functionaries as a return for their services—that occurs with the growth of the realm ultimately leads to an increasing decentralization and loss of patrimonial power and to the emergence of independent local powers seeking to split themselves off from their patrimonial lord. There is, according to Weber, a permanent battle between patrimonial lords and local dignitaries. The basic paradox of patrimonial rule, therefore, lies in the fact that with an ever-increasing extension of power the central control of patrimonial rulers becomes fragmented and weakened through the delegation of power that becomes necessary.

Another structurally immanent weakness of the patrimonial state for Weber consists in the personalized nature of the relationship between the patrimonial ruler and the various dignitaries or functionaries. Patrimonial rule is described as a form which is rigid and cannot adapt easily to new situations and duties. It represents a stark contrast to the effective and impersonal rule of rational-bureaucratic domination. Instead of being based on objectivity and rational ideals of administration, without consideration of personal ties and standing, in patrimonial rule everything rests expressly on personal relationships and on personal demonstrations of mercy, promises and privileges (cf. Weber 1976, 604-5).

According to Weber, all this gives rise to a situation in which the local fief holders, the further they are away from the seat of the ruler, the more they seek to escape his influence (cf. ibid., 611). A centre–periphery scheme therefore emerges in Weber's characterization of patrimonial rule: first there is the core area of the patriarchal household and domain; then come the outer provinces, with their own patrimonially acting governors, who, with increasing distance from the centre, become progressively more independent; finally, in the remotest areas the dignitaries are only nominally dependent on the patrimonial ruler and only pay tribute under pressure. The Weberian patrimonial state is in this sense a labile political conglomerate. Internally, one finds various degrees of dependence on the patrimonial overlord, from strongly dependent officials in the patrimonial household to tributary fief holders right through to semi-independent or only nominally dependent patrimonial lords or kings (cf. ibid., 613).

The extent of patrimonial power depends not least on the personal ability of the lord to make his will felt (cf. ibid., 605). This ability, according to Weber, should not be based exclusively on his military strength, since such a situation would leave him in great dependence on the military, which could turn against him, as happened all too often under sultanism. In order to strengthen the loyalty of the subjects and provide additional legitimacy to the ruler, the erection of a 'community of understanding' between the ruler and the ruled is, therefore, required. Another strategy of the patrimonial ruler against progressive decentralization, and against the military, dignitaries and functionaries becoming too dangerous, consists in ideologically imbuing the kingdom and the king with an aura of sanctity. On the political level, the duplication of office, and the strategy of giving offices complementary or even overlapping functions, prevents individual office holders from drawing too much power into their own hands. The personal nature of patrimonial authority, according to Weber, also makes it necessary for the ruler to be permanently on the move, personally monitoring administrative affairs on the periphery of his realm. He also requires the periodic appearance of his officials at court or demands the permanent presence of their sons or other family members in his physical proximity, using them as security in order to counteract possible misuse of office or overstepping of authority.[25] Last but not least, functionaries and dignitaries can be tied by a feudal type of vassal loyalty. Weber thus treats feudalism as a variety of patrimonialism. For him feudalism is a 'border case' of patrimonial domination, in which the relationships between lords and vassals have become stereotyped and fixed (cf. ibid., 625). In this sense, feudalism is a routinized form of patrimonialism. Patrimonial dignitaries and functionaries differ from feudal office holders in not being organized corporatively into status groups of noble men; rather, their loyalty is personal and often expressed through face-to-face oaths. In comparison to patrimonial functionaries and dignitaries, feudal vassals have greater independence and power in relation to a weak lord. Thus, according to Weber, feudalism is the historical result of a weak patrimonial state.[26]

Weber's statements concerning the patrimonial state are located on a high level of abstraction from actual historical manifestations of this type of state. Where these are looked at concretely for reasons of illustration, they emerge either from Europe (frequently characterized by Weber as the 'Occident') or from the 'Orient' (phenotypically opposed to it), the latter being represented mainly by the Islamic sultanates of the Near East, the Egypt of the Pharaohs and ancient China. Indian states seldom emerge as concrete historical examples of patrimonialism in Weber's sociology of power, though he characterizes Indian political forms as patrimonial states in his so-called 'sociology of religion'.[27] All this makes one suspect that Weber is discussing oriental patrimonialism not in order to understand better Egypt, China, India, etc., but, antithetically, in order to elucidate the nature of a supposedly 'occidental' ethics and rationality.[28]

[25] Rösel comments on these strategies as follows: 'This "personalistic" strategy of centralization is archaic, because there is a physical limit to any King's personal movement, concentration and control.... As this strategy implies a constant series of face-to-face encounters, it puts extraordinary emphasis on purely personal traits, the "strength of the individuality" of the King.... This "showcase" type of government, this rule by display, therefore puts a large premium on...the myth of the personality' (1986, 128).

[26] In this view, Indian feudalism is, therefore, not a variety of occidental feudalism; rather, the latter is merely a special case of universal patrimonialism. The occidental bias which is attached to the feudal state model is therefore turned on its head in Weber's model of the patrimonial state, at least in this respect.

[27] See Weber (1988).

[28] On this, see also Kulke (1995a, 39), Rösel (1986, 139-40), Schluchter (1984) and Schnepel (1987a).

Weber's model of the patrimonial state finds some echo in the historiography of India, especially with regard to the Delhi Sultanate and the Mughal Empire, though this reception is relatively new: Kulke characterizes Blake's study of 1979 as a 'pioneering work' (1995a, 37). Blake comes to the following conclusion from his assessment of the Mughal sources known as *Āin-i-Akbarī*: 'In its depiction of the emperor as a divinely aided patriarch, the household as the central element in government, members of the army as dependent on the emperor, the administration as a loosely structured group of men controlled by the Imperial household, and travel as a significant part of the emperor's activities, the *Āin-i-Akbarī* supports the suggestion that Akbar's state was a patrimonial-bureaucratic empire' (1979, 94). This view of things is explicitly opposed by Blake to those interpretations which describe the Mughal Empire as a central state organized administratively, fiscally, jurally and militarily. down to the last detail, in hierarchical fashion. Blake's additional qualification, 'bureaucratic', also indicates that he regards the Mughal Empire under Akbar as being in a state of transition between the patrimonial and rational-bureaucratic forms of the state.[29]

As regards the problem of the little kingdom, the basis of the model of the Indian patrimonial state, like that of the feudal state, lies in the idea that the existence of many little kingdoms is to be traced back to a lack of power on the part of the central authority. According to this model, the strong centrifugal powers of the sub-units can only be slowed down if the ruler has personal power and charisma, and so long as the personal loyalties of the governors tied to him endure. The control of the patrimonial ruler is, therefore, often restricted to his hereditary lands and,

[29] Blake (1979, 79-80) distinguishes between patrimonial kingdom and patrimonial-bureaucratic empire. For him, the first marks a point in Weber's evolutionary scheme for the extension of patriarchal power in which the household is still functioning without the decentralization and paradoxes that occur with a further extension of power. This distinction is not found in Weber himself, and its application to actual Indian kingdoms does not seem very sensible to me, since even in the case of most little kingdoms, the area to be controlled is so large as to go way beyond the character of any extended household or beyond the possibility of personal, all-pervasive control by patriarchs. On the patrimonial state in India, apart from Blake (1979) and Kulke (1995a, 36-9), see also Bayly (1992, 187-9), Hardy (1987), Perlin (1985b), Rösel (1986, 137-44) and Stein (1980, 408-11). The latter (1985b, 1985c) categorizes the south Indian Vijayanagara kingdom of the fourteenth to sixteenth centuries as a transitional form between the segmentary state (dealt with in section 3) and the patrimonial state. Rösel sees regional kingdoms especially as 'structurally akin to Weber's concept of patrimonialism' (1986, 137).

within the whole kingdom, to the most important social groups, administrative functions and branches of the economy. Indian little kings—'tributary princes' (*Tributärfürsten*) and 'part kings' (*Teilkönige*) in Weber's terminology—thus possess relatively great internal autonomy, their policies being characterized by continual efforts to make their subordinate position purely nominal or to throw off completely the supremacy of the patrimonial ruler.

Weber's emphasis on the personal character of the relationship between the lord and his dignitaries, functionaries and subjects (although 'orientalist' in character) provides a route to a better understanding of the emic view concerning the nature of the relationships just mentioned. We are dealing with a situation in which the ruler not only views everything personally, he himself is seen by everyone and presents a sensorially tangible image of the perfect ruler.[30] Simultaneously, against the background of Weber's explanations, the inability of the ruler to control renegade governors can be analysed as a problem structurally immanent in the exercise of patrimonial rule and as causally springing from the paradox, already mentioned, of an external extension of power with a simultaneous fragmentation of central control. Structural antagonisms, conflicts and plural forms of power are ultimately presented as integral elements of the model. Weber's model is, thus, in a better position to handle the relativity, dynamics and dialectics of political action than the other models presented so far.

Nonetheless, a further shift in focus is required to advance the ethnohistorical study of the phenomenon of the little kingdom in India. Attention should be directed less, as with Blake, on the transition from the patrimonial state to the central or the bureaucratic state as on the transition indicated by Weber from patriarchal to patrimonial authority. Moreover, if, in doing this, instead of patriarchal power (which in Weber's thought is very much akin to the 'origin' fantasies of nineteenth-century ethnology),[31] one places local or tribal institutions at the start of the analysis, the study of little kingdoms as intermediaries between the micro and macro levels of political organization could be advanced further.

[30] This personal character of Indian politics, which can be noticed up to the present day, leads McLane too (1993, 13-16) to characterize the situation in eighteenth-century Bengal as 'patrimonial'. Mines and Gourishankar (1991) stress the significance of personal charisma in the acquisition of political power in modern south India.

[31] Cf. Kuper (1988, Ch. 2).

3. The segmented state

The foregoing discussion has made it clear that in order to obtain a better understanding of the Indian state, it is necessary to question critically the dominance of Western ideas, concepts and criteria concerning what a state is and, as far as possible, to supplement or replace them with indigenous ones. Certainly the 'occident–orient' comparison should not be thrown overboard in doing so. Rather, Western perspectives and cultural comparisons accompanying them should be explicitly brought into the discussion and allowed to contribute to the clarification of both sides.[32] As regards the analysis of emic ideas and cultural manifestations of the state in India, with increased concentration on the Indian view-points, it should not go unremarked that these are not necessarily more representative of the whole than Western models. Such an assumption would again represent a Western prejudice, namely that of the uniformity, all-pervasiveness and totalitarianism of 'oriental' (and 'primitive') thought. In most cases, even emic ideas and practices only reflect view-points expressing the specific social, historical, political, intellectual or personal lived-in-worlds and perspectives of the authors or actors. Thus, the *Dharmaśāstras*, for example, convey a better understanding of how certain Indian groups regarded the (ideal) state than, for instance, many philosophies of the early modern European era. However, at many points the *Dharmaśāstras* represent only the view-point of the priestly class, not that of the holders of political power, let alone the general population or even subaltern groups.

Following these basic remarks, in the remaining sections of this chapter I turn to the works of those authors who seek to understand the Indian state largely from the actors' own points of view and who no longer deserve the epithet 'orientalist'. In the case of the authors discussed in this section, namely Cohn, Stein and Wink, we are also dealing with scholars hoping to arrive at a better understanding of the state in India through a synthesis of historical and anthropological perspectives and theories. Thus, Cohn characterizes himself as 'an anthropologist among the historians' (1987),[33] and in his analysis of the south Indian Chola kingdom, Stein uses an interpretative framework borrowed from the British school of social anthropology.

[32] In Dumont's words: 'There are two ways of looking at any piece of knowledge, a superficial one that leaves the knowing subject out of account, and a deeper one that includes him' (1986, 5). Cf. also Schnepel (1987b).

[33] Cohn focuses on the problematic relationship of these two disciplines in some of his writings (1962a, 1980, 1981).

3.1 Cohn

Let us begin with Cohn, to whom goes the credit for having introduced the concept of the 'little kingdom' for the first time into academic discourse, in an article published in 1959.[34] Here, the little kingdoms of the Benares region in the eighteenth century are already being represented as those 'political-judicial units' in which the pre-colonial 'prestige and power system' of the region found its most important delimitation. One year later, Cohn took his thoughts further in this direction,[35] before formulating them succinctly in a 1962 article entitled 'Political systems in eighteenth-century India: the Banaras region',[36] to which I turn in what follows.

Cohn distinguishes four levels in the political system of eighteenth-century India. The imperial level of the Mughals embraced nearly the whole sub-continent, leading Cohn to stress that, even after the collapse of its actual power towards the end of the seventeenth century, Mughal rule served other rulers far into the eighteenth century as the most important source of political legitimacy. Political systems on the secondary level were formed by the so-called successor states which grew out of the territorial dissolution of the Mughal empire. The authority of the sovereigns of these kingdoms, which were often congruent with the boundaries of cultural and linguistic macro-regions, was mostly of imperial origin. Thirdly, Cohn identifies the regional level where authority-holders were appointed by the respective imperial or secondary rulers and legitimized through royal grants (*sanad*s). According to Cohn, the incorporation of regional rulers into the empire or into states on the second level was achieved by oaths of loyalty and implied financial and military obligations. On the fourth level, the local level of the smallest political units, Cohn sees a number of different authority-holders in action: lineages, adventurers or tax officials who progressed to becoming chiefs themselves, and indigenous chiefs. These local authority-holders were subject to rulers on the regional level, though they often drew their legitimacy from the secondary or even imperial levels.[37]

Levels three and four, which are obviously also the levels of relevance to the study of little kingdoms, are central to the further discussion of Cohn's article. The ruler on the regional level, the *rājā* of Benares, was

[34] See Cohn (1959).

[35] See Cohn (1960).

[36] See Cohn (1962b).

[37] On these points, see Cohn (1962b, 485-6).

originally a functionary of the *nawāb* of Oudh, the ruler on the secondary level, by whom he was granted land and the title of '*rājā*' in recognition of his successful work as a 'tax-farmer'. Certainly, the internal sovereignty of the *rājā* was not absolute, since troops from the imperial and secondary levels were still stationed in some fortresses in the area, and important administrative officials of the region continued to be subject directly to the *nawāb*. The *rājā* was also obliged to pay tribute to the *nawāb*, to give him gifts on particular ritual occasions and to supply him with troops if required. In return, he received a turban and a sword from the *nawāb* as emblems of authority. The relationship between *nawāb* and *rājā* is described further as follows:

> The Raja of Banaras at every opportunity tried to avoid fulfilment of these obligations; and on several occasions the nawab sent troops to try to bring his subordinate to terms, if not to capture and kill him. On these occasions Balwant Singh would retreat with his treasure and army to the jungles of Mirzapur. After a time the nawab, distracted by similar behaviour in other parts of his state or by his intervention in imperial politics, would compromise with Balwant Singh and withdraw, at which Balwant Singh would resume his control of the zamindari. [...] A balancing of relative weakness appears to have been central to the functioning of the system. The nawab could not afford the complete chaos which would result from the crushing of the raja. On occasion the raja could be forced into paying some revenue and providing some troops to support activities of the nawab. On the raja's side was the need for legitimacy. [...] Power the raja had; but he needed authority as well. (Cohn 1962b, 488-9)

What kind of picture of the eighteenth-century Indian state is being presented here? Cohn's analytical distinction of four levels in the political system seems at first sight to be drawn from the idea of a hierarchically ordered structure in which power was delegated downwards from emperor via *nawāb* and *rājā* to local chief. Cohn further attributes the weakness of the centre and the insubordination of subordinate authority-holders to this construct. Thus, at first sight, Cohn seems to be hanging on to the orientalist model of the central state (together with the apparently typical Indian inability to have this state function without problems).

However, if the passage quoted is examined more closely, it can be seen that Cohn is making precisely the apparent lack of functioning and the conflict between the different authority-holders central elements in his interpretative approach. The remark in the passage quoted above, that 'a balancing of relative weakness appears to have been central to the functioning of the system', refers back to methodological statements by Cohn in the introduction to the same article:

> The integrity of the larger group, paradoxically, is usually maintained through internal conflict and competition among the groups in the society. [...] Consensus and balance are achieved through conflict and through the awareness that there are always other groups ready to step in. [...] Although these societies are segmentary in their structure, culturally there are often rituals, traditions, myths and histories through which the political order is legitimized and maintained. (Ibid., 484)

These statements of Cohn's, which relate to 'pre-modern societies' in general, are reminiscent of central tenets in the theory of segmentary lineage societies, which dominated the social anthropological thought of the time.[38] Just as in studies concerned with the analysis of African 'stateless societies', so too phenomena that can be characterized by concepts such as 'conflict' and 'feud' are accorded great weight in Cohn's analysis of the political systems of pre-modern India. And because, in his case, these phenomena now count as important structural elements and principles of state organization, the state no longer appears as merely a deficient version of the Western model. In addition, Cohn links his new approach to the questioning of a specifically Western perspective which Geertz was to characterize aptly some years later with the words, 'impressed with command, we see little else' (1980, 121). Cohn seeks to counter this Western bias with his distinction between 'power' and 'authority'. In the sentence from the passage quoted above, 'power the raja had; he needed authority as well', he makes it clear that in interpreting the Indian state, relations characterized by the power to give orders and to receive obedience should not be placed at the centre of the analysis so much as questions of legitimacy and honour.[39]

[38] See, for example, Evans-Pritchard and Fortes (1940).

[39] Here, Cohn is probably being guided by Weber's distinction between power and domination. Power signifies the 'chance' to prevail with one's own will even against opposition and even if this is based on sheer force (see Weber 1976, 28). Domination, on the other hand, signifies the chance to secure the obedience of appropriate persons to a particular order with a particular content (ibid.). Thus, domination is always associated with a certain degree of organization and legitimacy (ibid., 28-9, 822-3). Certainly, the decisive point in Weber's sociology of domination consists not in the difference between power and domination but in the distinction of different grounds of legitimacy (ibid., 122-4). So far as I understand this point, the distinction drawn by Cohn between power and authority is meant to differentiate between domination as a relationship characterized by

If we return to a direct examination of the text we see that Cohn is not yet using the concept of the little kingdom for the regional level of the *rājā* of Benares. Only on the local level of the political system does he identify 'three main types of political structures or "little kingdoms"—rajadoms, *jagirs* and *talukas*' (ibid., 489). *Tāluk*s are represented as areas controlled by Rajput patrilineages of dominant status. The relationship of these lineages downwards to the population and upwards to the regional king was comparable with the corresponding relationships of the local kings. Local kings and dominant lineages of the *tāluk*s received taxes and services from the rural population, merchants and artisans, and both were similarly obliged to transfer a proportion of their income to the *rājā* of Benares. According to Cohn, the difference between lineages and '*raja-doms*' consisted in the fact that the latter 'differed from the talukas in one major structural feature: there was an acknowledged head, the raja. Inheritance of control of the land passed on in one family and in this one family to only one person at a time, usually the eldest son of the previous raja, who was recognized as the raja' (ibid., 492-3). This difference casts doubt on whether the *tāluk*s controlled by the lineages can be described as little kingdoms. The concept of a kingdom generally refers to an institution characterized by the sovereignty of a single person, whereas the *tāluk*s of the Benares region were presided over by 'corporations aggregate'.[40]

Nor, in my view, can Cohn's *jāgīr* type be characterized as a little kingdom, although the criterion of sovereignty by a single person is applicable here. Cohn writes: 'the jagirs, like the rajadoms, often had a single head rather than a corporate body or lineage as the dominant internal political power, but the jagir was usually held as a revenue-free holding, the state's share of produce or the revenue going to the jagirdar' (ibid., 493). And: 'Jagirs were usually not granted in perpetuity' (ibid.,

orders and obedience, and domination from the point of view of grounds of legitimacy and, thus, authority. However, Cohn also often uses the term 'power' only in the sense of 'force', so that ultimately there is no clarity on this point.

[40] On the *tāluk*s of the Benares regions, see Cohn (1962b, 490-2; 1959). The distinction made here between *tāluk* and '*rajadom*' admittedly reifies what was a fundamentally flexible situation. As Fox (1971) clarifies, lineage-controlled *tāluk*s could turn into local kingdoms ruled by monarchs, or vice versa, if the constellation of power between the lineages of an area changed or if the respective position in the 'developmental cycle' of a given dominant lineage favoured the formation of one or other organizational form. Chattopadhyaya (1976; 1995, 213-21) and Thapar (1984) stress that lineages have often formed the starting point for state-formation in India.

494). *Jāgīrdār*s were, therefore, not kings but at most relatively autonomous functionaries and governors whose services were rewarded by a given king from the surplus of an exactly demarcated estate. The fiction of the continuity of their office was also quite definitely absent. Without being able to go into an anthropological theory of corporations,[41] here I would like to argue that the ideologically important fiction of continuity counts as the constitutive characteristic of corporations. While for me, therefore, *tāluk*s do not represent kingdoms because they are not corporations sole, *jāgīr*s do not qualify for the title of 'kingdom' because they are not corporations.

Regarding the '*rajadom*' on the local level, the last of the three types of little kingdom put forward by Cohn, we learn that the local *rājā*s derived their legitimacy through a transfer of authority from the secondary or even imperial level. The source of legitimacy for local *rājā*s was, therefore, the same as for regional rulers, though their direct obligations mostly existed in relation to the *rājā* of Benares. The main tasks of the *rājā*s on the local level were tax collection, maintenance of internal order, and the construction and maintenance of local infrastructure (roads, irrigation systems, bridges, rest houses, etc.). Cohn also stresses that in many cases the '*rajadoms*' of the Benares region lay on the boundaries of the kingdom, in jungle and hill areas, in which tribal groups dominated numerically.[42]

While I have conceptually excluded *tāluk*s and *jāgīr*s from being characterized as little kingdoms, kingdoms like that of the *rājā* of Benares, which Cohn describes as a regional kingdom, could still be included in the category of little kingdom. Certainly, criteria like marginality and restricted territorial size do not apply to the Benares kingdom, which is centrally situated in the fertile valley of the middle Ganges and had a number of little kingdoms subject to it. However, it will be remembered that the periodic insubordination of the *rājā* of Benares was strategically backed by an important geopolitical element, namely the jungle. The *rājā* was repeatedly able to defy the *nawāb* because in the event of punitive action he could flee with his family, followers and treasure into the distant and inaccessible woods of Mirzapur. The policies of this regional king, characterized by a great drive towards independence, were, therefore, based essentially on his ability to withdraw for a particular period to a marginal and 'little' position in the event of a threat. In other parts of India, too, as is shown by many historical examples, the

[41] On this, see Fortes (1970), Kantorowicz (1957), Schnepel (1990).

[42] On '*rajadoms*', see Cohn (1962b, 492-4).

survival of regional kings not infrequently depended on their ability to transfer their base to marginal areas and to shrink their domains accordingly. Thus, the Indian state was not only faced with attempts by peripheral and subordinate units to split themselves off from the centre and even to encroach on its sovereign area, even superordinate centres reduced themselves to peripheral and 'little' positions when the constellation of power demanded this. In the context of Indian politics, movements between centre and periphery, great and little, valley and jungle, went in both directions.

3.2 Stein

One of the most significant of the more recent models of the state in India is that of the 'segmentary state'. This originated in the anthropology of Africa, where it was developed by Southall (1953) in his analysis of the political system of the east African Alur. Stein transferred the model from there to the medieval south Indian kingdom of the Cholas.[43] Of all the models dealt with so far, the model of the segmentary state is that in which the control and exercise of power by the central power is seen to be at its lowest level. It is, therefore, opposed implicitly, as well as in explicit theory, to the concept of the unitary and centralized state in which central control is believed to be strongest.[44]

[43] The idea of the segmentary state first appears in the context of research on India in Fox's study (1971, 56-7) of the pre-colonial political community of the Rajputs in north India. In a symposium in 1973 (Fox ed. 1977), the concept became the focus of a debate between historians of India which is still continuing. Among the articles arising out of this symposium, it was Stein (1977a) who most emphatically put forward the model of the segmentary state, while authors like Cohn, M.S.A Rao and Stern (all 1977) opposed it critically or rejected it. In Stein's major work (Stein 1980), the conclusions concerning the Chola kingdom already arrived at in 1977 are explained in greater detail and the model is also applied to the historically later Vijayanagara kingdom. In further articles, Stein revises some of his positions, especially as regards the interpretation of the Vijayanagara empire, whose type of rule he there regards as 'military fiscalism' or 'patrimonial' (Stein 1985c), as 'proto-patrimonial' (1985b) or, again, though with some reservations, as a 'segmentary state' (1985a, 1989, 1991). Here I will concentrate mostly on Stein's article of 1977, in which the model is presented paradigmatically. An initial criticism of Stein's model by myself, which will be revised and extended in the present section, can be found in Schnepel (1994a, section 3).

[44] The model of the central or unitary state was questioned by Stein in his 'The State and the Agrarian Order in Medieval South India' (1975), when he writes: 'The Indian king was an overlord, not a manager; he demanded submission to his claim of superiority, rather than obedience to his orders' (ibid., 77). There is no

Stein makes clear the object of his attack by saying that the central state is defined by 'territorial sovereignty, centralized government, specialized administrative personnel, and a monopoly of legitimate force' (Stein 1977a, 6). According to Stein, these four elements are also present in the segmentary state, though their effectiveness is restricted to just the core area of a central dynasty. Political authority and control of this dynasty are most marked in the centre of the kingdom but vanish as one moves towards its periphery. According to Stein, the segmentary state is a pyramidally ordered political system composed of several politico-administrative centres of similar type. Of these centres one has ritual hegemony, but it does not exercise any political power over the others. The other centres or 'peripheral foci' are smaller replicas of the primary centre lying at a lower level of the system. Their rulers enjoy political authority and autonomy in their respective segments, while also acknowledging the ritual sovereignty of a common overlord. The segmentary state is, therefore, characterized as a political system consisting of many simultaneously existing royal segments held together by ritual ties. Its central segment exercises symbolic and custodial functions, not political or administrative ones.[45]

In Stein's own words, 'there may be numerous "centers" of which one has primacy as a source of ritual sovereignty, but all exercise actual political control over a part, or segment, of the political system encompassed by the state' (ibid., 10). Stein then brings the concept of the little kingdom into his model: 'In the segmentary state, executive authority is the same at the prime center and at any subordinate segmental center except that it is exercised over fewer people. In the Indian context this principle is expressed in terms of "little kingdoms" and "little kings", where a local ruler possesses "kingly" authority equal to that of any great king, but more limited in scope' (ibid., 11). According to Stein, in contrast to this arrangement of the segments, which is described as 'pyramidal', a hierarchical structure is characterized by the fact that 'at successively subordinate levels of the system there are *different* kinds of executive authority' (ibid., 11, emphasis in original).

Stein's perspective, new in the south Indian historiography of the time, leads him to reinterpret some current assumptions. By evaluating data on the Chola empire which he obtained from contemporary inscriptions and

---

systematic development of an alternative model in this 1975 article, though this is announced for the future (see ibid., 88).

[45] On these points, see Southall (1953, 248-9), Stein (1977a, 9-10; 1980, 274; 1985a, 75).

normative texts Stein concluded, for example, that Chola strike forces were not the sub-units of a central army but independent militia groups, locally recruited and retained. Further, the territorial units of the Chola kingdom, known by the Tamil term *nāḍu*, represented not the subordinate administrative units of a hierarchically ordered kingdom but rather autonomous politico-territorial units stemming from pre-Chola times, each with its own ethnic and ecological character. Thirdly, although those chiefs mentioned in the inscriptions as heads of the *nāḍu*s certainly fulfilled significant administrative functions in relation to the whole, they should not be seen as either the functionaries of a central bureaucracy, nor as officials appointed or nominated by the king: rather, they were the representatives of the dominant groups in their locality, from which their power and legitimacy stemmed. Fourthly, in their stereotypical preambles (*praśasti*s), the many thousand Chola inscriptions of the macro region indicate less political control than ritual sovereignty on the part of the Chola kings. The *praśasti*s promulgate 'a standardized message of a great kingship' (ibid., 17), not royal directives or orders. According to Stein, therefore, all in all the attempts of the Chola kings were directed less towards establishing an administrative and coercive apparatus over the hereditary dynastic lands in the Kaveri delta than towards erecting an ideological superstructure (in the religious idiom of the time), through which the numerous local segments, with their princes, could be subsumed under a common Chola patronage.[46]

While Cohn's understanding of the Benares region was based on the conceptual difference between 'power' and 'authority', Stein seeks to grasp the character of the medieval Chola kingdom through the difference between 'political sovereignty' and 'ritual sovereignty'. The oppositions presented by Cohn and Stein respectively only correspond to one another in a limited way. Let us recall that by the concept of 'authority', Cohn wishes to stress a specific aspect of domination—legitimacy—and to lend it greater weight in the analysis of the Indian state, which was generally defined in terms of structures of command only. Stein's model, by comparison, is based on an opposition between religion and politics as two semantic fields, to which, moreover, he attributes different degrees of effectiveness. Thus, with Stein, ultimately, a 'merely' symbolic or nominally existing ritual sovereignty is conceptually opposed to a form of political rule exercising actual control.[47]

[46] On these points, see Stein (1977a, 12-17; 1980, 90-140).

[47] Stein uses a variety of other oppositions, which somewhat confuses the matter: 'political sovereignty' and 'ritual sovereignty'; 'political control' and 'ritual

As regards the role of the little kingdoms, local chiefs were important in recognizing the ritual sovereignty of the great kings. This was the precondition for the rise of the segmentary Chola state. However, for Stein the relationships between the ritual overlord and his little kings were dialectic in nature. Concerning the position of the little kings, we learn that 'recognition and emulation of this great kingship by lesser local chiefs conferred upon the latter the symbolic credentials of legitimate "little kings"' (ibid., 17). By recognizing the ritual sovereignty of the Cholas, the local chiefs could claim for themselves the status of kings, although of a 'little' type. In Stein's words: 'It was precisely as a result of the Chola ritual sovereignty that these *nāḍu* leaders gained and maintained their "little kingly" status' (ibid., 44). Elsewhere he writes:

> While chiefs of the Chola age were complete rulers in the practical sense, chieftaincy as a moral condition, as authority, depended upon the existence of an anointed king. The pragmatic competence of Chola period chiefs sprang from being part of the dominant people of the nadu, called *nāttār*, through the idiom and the fact of kinship; royal competence, alternatively, sprang from the homage offered by a chief to an anointed king, through the idiom and the fact of service. [...] Such service extended to the chief the obligations and the privileges of *rājādharma*, the responsibility and power for protecting the diverse groups of a chiefdom, not only the chiefs' kinsmen, but all of the locality. It meant, further, the support and protection of Brahmans and gods. In short, it obliged the chief to fulfil royal tasks within his mini-realm and to enjoy there, as a consequence, a near royal status. This linking, through sacred actions, of great and small chiefs to Chola kings made of the polity a state, and this alone. (1985c, 394-5)

For Stein, therefore, the political power of the local rulers of the Chola kingdom sprang from local roots and was based on traditional criteria like kinship, descent or territorial belonging. However, the little kings or *rājā*s acquired their royal status and dignities from above, through a king anointed according to Vedic rites, whom they served. In this service,

---

suzerainty'; '*kṣatra*' and '*rājadharma*'; 'political power' and 'sovereignty'; 'appropriate power' and 'full, royal sovereignty'; 'political authority' and 'royal sovereignty'; 'pragmatic' and 'merely symbolic'; and 'power' and 'authority'. However, the essential dichotomy in the model, between the realms of politics and ritual, which are seen as being of differential effectiveness, remains untouched. Cf., inter alia, Stein (1977a, 10; 1980, 48, 274; 1991, 219). There are numerous criticisms of this point in Stein's model: see, for example, Dirks (1987, 403-4), Inden (1990, 208), Kulke (1982, 248, 253-5) and Sharma (1989).

Stein, therefore, sees not only that element that makes a king a great king and his kingdom a state of the segmentary type: service also makes a local chief partake in the sovereignty of the anointed king and thereby turns him into a little king. In this dualistic picture of the state, Stein also points to inherent structural oppositions or contradictions which elsewhere he describes as 'contradictions in political principles and processes between the lowest level of political organization and the highest' (1975, 65).[48]

In the 1977 model of the segmentary state, two further types of opposition are attributed great significance for the pyramidal segmentation of the Chola kingdom. First, Stein distinguishes between those *nāḍu*s where the caste principle of social organization prevailed and those dominated by tribal principles of organization.[49] Stein extends this observation by differentiating three zones within the macro region, which he sees as being defined by ecological, economic and demographic characteristics. For in the Chola kingdom there was first of all a 'core zone' of river valleys, thickly settled and sufficiently provided with supplies of water; then came an 'intermediate zone', of areas in which sufficient water reserves were not available to provide regular and controlled irrigation for agriculture; and finally, Stein identifies a 'peripheral zone', which was not very suitable for settled agriculture and in which agriculture had to rely on variable rainfall.

In *nāḍu*s of the central zone, according to Stein, the caste principle of organization usually prevailed; they were characterized internally by vertical stratification and a marked division of labour. Political control within the *nāḍu*s of this zone was mostly exercised by assemblies of the dominant agrarian or Brahman castes. The influence of the Cholas was greatest in this zone. *Nāḍu*s of the middle zone were less strongly hierarchical as far as their internal social and political organization is concerned and mostly fell under the leadership of a chief or *rājā* from the oldest or best established group in the locality. The political power of the Chola did not have such a strong impact on the intermediate zone as on the core zone. Tribal characteristics of organization were most strongly marked in *nāḍu*s of the peripheral zone, whose members felt they had a common ethnic identity. Social hierarchy and the internal division of labour were only weakly developed. As in the *nāḍu*s of the intermediate

[48] On these points, see also Stein (1977a, 17-26, 44-6).

[49] For Stein (1977a, 38), the terms 'tribe' and 'caste' mark a dimensional, not categorical distinction, as in Bailey's sense (1961).

zone, in the those of the peripheral zone we mostly find strong chiefs or little kings as governors.[50]

To the opposition between *nāḍu*s which were shaped by the caste principles of organization and *nāḍu*s in which the tribal principle predominated, Stein adds another, namely the opposition between agricultural groups and mercantile or artisan groups.[51] In this context, Stein also explains the opposition already mentioned between the local levels and the level of the state or between the little kingdoms and the great kingdom: 'For the state as a whole, the oppositional tension inhered in the relationship between the primary center of ritual sovereignty and all of the constituent, segmental parts' (ibid., 44). Elsewhere, Stein even identifies two types of kingdom in India: 'On the one hand, there was a form of kingship which was universalistic, absolutistic, fiscally and extractively oriented; on the other hand, there was a form of lordship, very like kingship, but localistic, relativistic, or collegeal, and redistributivist' (1985c, 408).

If we critique Stein's model we would have to emphasize that it is certainly not enough to see the segmentary state in India as being characterized merely by the fact that it consists of a number of segments. That would be banal, since there would be no state anywhere that was not 'segmented' in this sense. Furthermore, it would be too short-sighted to see the fundamental principle of state formation in the recognition of the ritual sovereignty of a central segment by the peripheral segments. After all, Stein adopted the model from African anthropology, where it had been developed by Southall against the background of the theory of segmentary lineage societies and of the dichotomy, already inherent in this theory, between acephalous and state-organized societies.[52] To be able to

[50] On these points, see Stein (1977a, 27-40; 1980, 136-40; 1985a, 57-8).

[51] See Stein (1977a, 40-2; 1980, 173-215). In south Indian terminology, this opposition is often expressed in terms of the distinction between right-hand and left-hand castes. On dual classification in south India, see also Appadurai (1974) and Beck (1970).

[52] The history of the theory of segmentary lineage societies in anthropological thought is a long and controversial one. In very broad terms, it starts with Durkheim's 1893 treatise on the division of labour (cf. Durkheim 1933) and reaches its high point in the work of Evans-Pritchard and Fortes in the 1940s (cf. Evans-Pritchard 1940; Fortes 1945; Evans-Pritchard and Fortes 1940), which provided a model for later monographs. Starting in the 1950s, a great number of theoretically oriented works also appeared, until (outside Indian historiography) the theory lost its intellectual attractions in the early 1980s. Studies relevant to the

apply the epithet 'segmentary' to the Indian state, and thus to establish the 'Afro-centric' model convincingly for India, Stein had to show that organizational principles were at work in the Chola kingdom similar to those which counted as constitutive of segmentary societies in Africa. In addition, he had to show that these processes and principles established a state. Stein was aware of this double burden of proof, though it escaped most of his critics.[53]

One element in the theory of segmentary lineage societies is the principle of the opposition between structurally equivalent groups. Stein thinks he is rediscovering this principle in medieval south India: 'The Chola system was segmentary in that it consisted of a multiplicity of structurally equivalent segments: *nāḍus*' (1977a, 43). We also learn that 'the equilibrium of the entire segmentary system (i.e. the Chola state) and its constituent parts (i.e. the *nāḍu* segments) rested upon these various oppositions' (ibid., 44). It is clear that the constitutive elements of African segmentary societies, namely unilineal descent groups, only find a limited correspondence in the south Indian *nāḍu*s. Only if *nāḍu*s belonged to just one of the three zones identified by Stein could they be regarded as 'structurally equivalent' as the theory requires. The principle of structural opposition which is so important in the theory of segmentary lineage societies and which resurfaces in Stein's work rather vaguely as 'these various oppositions', then, cannot be transferred so easily from

---

theory include Dumont (1979), Gough (1971), Holy (1979), Kelly (1985), Kuper (1982), Middleton and Tait (eds. 1955), Sahlins (1961) and Sigrist (1968).

[53] In what follows, I will concentrate on viewing Stein's model in the light of the social anthropological theory of segmentary lineage societies. Critiques and commentaries by authors like Berkemer (1993, 19-21), Champakalakshmi (1981), Dirks (1987, 403-4), Hall (1980), Heitzmann (1987, 358-61), Inden (1990, 206-11), Kulke (1982), Ludden (1989, 204), Mukhia (1985), Perlin (1985a, 123-9), Ramasvami (1982), Rudolph (1987, 738-40), Sharma (1995, 81-4), Shulman (1985, 19-20), Subbarayalu (1982) and S. Subrahmanyam (1986, 358-61), which deal with historiographical as well theoretical aspects of the model, must be set aside here, even though they are relevant and have influenced the critique being presented here. Southall (1988) approved of the transfer of his model to India, yet his statements are not very helpful, for they mix up different conceptual levels, as when he tries to link the political form of the segmentary state with the Asiatic mode of production. This, in turn, compels Stein (1977, 227-9), who is sensitive to the problematic of the 'Asiatic mode of production', to distance his version of the model from Southall's explanations (and not only in this respect). An overview of the controversies surrounding this model, which continue up to the present time, can be found in Kulke (1995a, 18-31).

Africa to India. What, in the model of segmentary lineage societies, was still an opposition between structurally equivalent descent groups changes with Stein into a collection of qualitatively different types of relationship between functionally different groups on different levels of social and political organization: between left-hand and right-hand castes, between tribe and caste, between *nāḍu*s of the same zone, between *nāḍu*s of different zones and between primary centre and peripheral foci. The opposition between the universal and the local concept of kingship also enters this picture somehow.[54]

Even when one compares Stein's *nāḍu*s with African lineages in the model and regards the many-sided conflicts of interest that predominate between these groups as 'structural oppositions', one misses statements concerning how all this forms an overarching political system of the segmentary type. Apart from the principle of structural opposition, no principles of organization or processes are uncovered by Stein comparable to those which count as basic to the maintenance and functioning of the whole in the theory of segmentary lineage societies. What, in the Indian material, for example, would correspond to the continuous processes characterized by concepts like 'fusion' and 'fission', or to the situationally determined relativity and dynamism of political action? What, in short, corresponds to the system of unilineal descent groups, dynamically interlocked with one another and ordered pyramidally, whose segments either unite with or oppose one another on different levels along lines of descent criteria, responding ad hoc to the particular situations at hand?[55]

Stein's remark, that 'the system was pyramidal in that each segment was led by men who shared a quality of legitimacy in substantial part derived from the Chola kings through the operation of Chola ritual sovereignty' (1977a, 43), does not provide a satisfactory answer to these questions. In the light of the theory of segmentary lineage societies, the transfer of the model of the segmentary state to India is, therefore, ultimately not convincing: none of the basic units, processes and principles attributed to segmentary lineage societies in modern anthropological theory finds correspondence in south India. Stein's model of a segmentary society merely corresponds to Durkheim's theoretically outdated picture,

[54] Elsewhere (1985a, 62-6), Stein sees the different oppositions as being effective only *within* any given *nāḍu* unit, not *between* them, which further confuses the picture.

[55] With Stein, *periyanāḍu*s appear not as the next highest levels of co-operation but merely as later historical developments.

in which the whole is simply composed statically of worm-like segments laid next to one another.[56] Stein's Chola state is certainly segmented, but not 'segmentary' in the sense in which this term has been used in anthropological theory.[57]

[56] See also my more comprehensive account of the anthropological theory of segmentary societies in Schnepel (1994a, 18-25). Middleton and Tait characterize the difference I am referring to between Durkheim and modern social anthropological researchers as follows: 'The term "segmentary" has been used with reference to several types of social systems, but the essential features are the "nesting" attribute of segmentary series and the characteristic of being in a state of continual segmentation and complementary opposition. This usage of segmentary is different from that of Durkheim (1893), in which segmentary systems are those formed by the repetition of smaller segments (clans). [...] Here neither the nesting attribute nor that of a continual process of segmentation need be present. All that is necessary is an exhaustive series of equal units. In this type a unit can be subtracted from the total series without disorganization: a segment is merely lopped off' (1955, 7-8). The fact that Stein attributes ritual sovereignty to one segment in his model may turn Durkheim's worm into a cephalopod, but it does not make the Chola kingdom a segmentary state.

[57] Stein is aware that, from the point of view of establishing the model of the segmentary state, it is not enough to deconstruct the concept of the unitary state and contrast it with an apparently less integrated type of state with relatively autonomous segments. Kulke (1982, 255-63), for example, faults Stein with not sufficiently emphasizing the integrative principles of the segmentary state. However, Kulke himself sees the segmentary state as being different from the centralized one mainly by virtue of a limited degree of integration and social cohesion, not because it has different organizational principles. Stein answers this criticism in a 'Postscript' to Kulke's article: '[The issue] is not segmentation *versus* integration, but segmentation *and* integration' (in Kulke 1982, 263, Stein's emphasis). And in 1991 Stein remarks: 'To find the segmentary political concept valuable merely for noting the peripheral attentuation of central rule is to reduce a segmentary political system to an imperfect manifestation of centralized authority' (1991, 220). Here, though he holds fast to his model, the initial flourish of 1977 has softened into a weaker and more awkward position: 'The purpose here is to clarify my present position on segmentary political relations in pre-modern India while maintaining an openness about its final definition, hence it is an interim report' (ibid., 217). Stein also recognizes that, in his transfer of the model from Africa to India, the structural opposition of lineages became problematic, because he did not make a clear enough analytical distinction between a political type of segmentation and a social one (ibid., 218-19; 233). However, not even this intellectual shift is of much use when one remembers that the theorists of segmentary lineage societies wanted to show precisely that what appeared to be 'merely' social criteria, such as kinship, could constitute political systems of quite a large size.

Stein's statements concerning structural oppositions in the Chola kingdom perhaps indicate the boundaries of the model most clearly. Yet they also contain important insights concerning the institution of the little kingdom, which should not be ignored here. Stein claims that 'oppositions explain why the political order of the Chola period and later in South Indian history did not collapse into a fragmented system approximating statelessness' (ibid., 42). However, it was not the oppositions as such to whom was attributed the binding effect (as is argued in the theory of segmentary lineage systems), but a qualitatively different type of integration, which held together the localities and made them function (*despite* the existing oppositions and the conflicts and centrifugal powers resulting from them): 'A kind of kingly legitimacy was necessary for the management of the two kinds of oppositional tensions present in every part of the macro-region' (ibid., 46-7). And: 'The sharing by local chiefly figures of the rule competence of the Chola rulers, as the source of ritual sovereignty in the Chola system, provided each with the minimal kingly credentials necessary for coping with the fundamental oppositions in the society of the macro-region' (ibid., 49). Hence, when it comes to finding the bonds that held everything together, Stein's statements refer less to the principle of opposition than to a monarchical principle of rule.[58]

Stein's model forms 'an immensely powerful deconstructive tool' (Dirks 1987, 403), which brings into question the traditional model of a centralized state and its unquestioned orientalist maxims. In comparison with that model and others in which the presence, often realized only hesitantly, of many small sub-units of royal type are regarded as being merely fragmentizing, Stein succeeded in creating an awareness that the social and political cohesion of Indian political systems is reached not despite but because of their segmentary character. Thus, both the feudal state and segmentary state models see the state in India as multi-centred in character. However, as Chattopadhyaya points out, they differ through 'their respective notions of "parcellized sovereignty" and "shared sovereignty"' (1995, 223), with the latter type of sovereignty being ritual not political in type.

On account of his shift of paradigm, Stein was no longer guided in his analysis of the Chola kingdom by the misleading conceptual dichotomy between state and village community and focused instead on an inter-

[58] Stein, later, accepted this position, too: 'Chieftainship in medieval India cannot be taken as either a complete system of authority or as adequately theorized; for that the principle of monarchy is crucial' (1991, 223).

mediate level of corporate life, that of the *nāḍus*.[59] The units established at this level of social and political organization, including many little kingdoms, gain greater significance in the assessment of the overall system, which is now understood as being multi-centred and multi-layered. If one accepts for the moment Stein's distinction between actual political rule and merely symbolic ritual sovereignty, the *nāḍus*, *periyanāḍus* and little kingdoms appear as the largest possible politico-legal units in which political control can effectively be exercised. However, Stein's view of the whole, like Cohn's view of four levels, is still a top-down one: the understanding of the structure of the Indian state is not sufficiently approached from below, from the perspective of its constitutive elements. Ultimately, it appears that the *nāḍus* in Stein's model sometimes simply assume the structural role which in other models was held by the encapsulated 'village republics'. *Nāḍus* are seen mainly as being directed inwards in their activities and as being somewhat opposed to the state, linked to it only ritually, while economic, political, cultural and other types of relationship between the *nāḍus* and the state (at least in the model) are ignored or appear as 'merely symbolic'.[60]

One aspect that might prove useful in the study of little kingdoms is Stein's sub-division of the macro-region into different zones, in which he shows the influence of Subbarao (1956).[61] However, the latter's distinction between 'areas of attraction', 'areas of relative isolation' and 'tribal areas' (or 'areas of isolation') might prove more useful than Stein's distinctions between central, intermediate and peripheral zones, in analysing the effectiveness and extent of political control by a superordinate great kingdom over its little kingdoms. This is especially the case when one also understands 'attraction' and 'isolation' as manifestations of different strengths of political charisma in Weber's sense. In any case, the opposition between the denominations 'little' and 'great' in the characterization of Indian kingdoms should also be linked to the polar concepts of 'centre' ('strong attraction') and 'periphery' ('isolation') and their intermediaries ('intermediate zone', 'relative isolation'), as well as to other relevant cultural, ritual, demographic, economic and ecological criteria. Such an approach would allow little kingdoms to be determined more exactly in their relation to the centre and differentiations between

[59] Here, Stein owes a great deal to Subbarayalu's study of the *Political Geography of the Chola Country*, which appeared in 1973.

[60] See Inden's critique (1990, 207-9).

[61] Subbarao's study had proved important for Stein in an earlier article (Stein 1969), in which he takes over from Subbarao the concept of the 'nuclear area'.

the little kingdoms themselves to be established, as the present work will seek to do later, by formulating the concept of the 'jungle kingdom'.[62]

The significance that Stein also attaches to ritual and to the ideological function of religion in establishing, consolidating, legitimizing and exercising kingly rule as well as in shaping the relationship between great and little kings, opens up important insights and perspectives, even though the distinction, so basic to the model, between ritual and politics (including the different degrees of effectiveness attributed to these two domains) remains questionable.[63] Stein's own statements might even lead to the model of the segmentary state being replaced by a model of the ritual or sacred kingdom, conceptualizations that Stein himself suggests.[64] In this sense, Stein also indicates the direction which the study of the Indian state should take in his view: 'The opening from the present conception of the segmentary State and of State formations more generally in pre-modern India must be of another sort: it must be in the direction of culture and ideology' (1991, 229). And when he adds: 'as never before, the scholarly resources for this line of enquiry into modern states are adequate to that task. All bear critically upon the segmentary State concept and all, being the work of anthropologists, are centrally concerned with culture' (ibid.), he is referring to Dirks and his 1987 study of a little kingdom, which I will discuss shortly.[65]

[62] See especially Ch. 2, section 5.

[63] Already in 1982, Stein had begun to react to criticisms of his model on this point: 'I reject the idea of ritual "as a weak substitute" and do see it as a genuine political means, as you put it' (in Kulke 1982, 263). In the 'Interim Report', he explicitly distanced himself from this separation: 'It is necessary to reject Southall's proposition that "the spheres of ritual suzerainty and political sovereignty do not coincide". [...] In India, I am now convinced that distinction is incorrect; lordship for Hindus always and necessarily combined ritual and political authority. That is, the practice of political authority, or appropriate power, made it incumbent upon any lord to foster and to be involved with ritual action and services, whether this was in relation to gods or to their subjects. And, this is true whether we are speaking about great kings or minor chiefs' (1991, 233-4). It is also worth noting that Stein's own analysis of royal ritual politics concentrates, from an early stage, on the economic and political significance of south Indian temples. See, *inter alia*, Stein (1977b, 1977c; 1980, especially Ch. VI).

[64] See, for example, Stein (1985a, 80).

[65] See section 4.3.

3.3. From structure to process: Wink

Wink's analysis of the policy of the Marathas in the eighteenth-century Mughal Empire represents a further development of the insights presented by Cohn and Stein.[66] In the introduction to his work, Wink refers to the fact that interpreters of Indian political history have often sought to explain the repeated acts of insubordination—such as the constant unwillingness of the *rājā* of Benares to pay tribute—by using a 'mentalistic jargon', i.e., terms like 'treason', 'corruption', 'disloyalty', etc. forming a standard explanatory vocabulary. 'There is at best', says Wink, 'an acknowledgement of a different system of "ethics" but never of a different political system' (1986, 6).

Wink opposes this picture of a political system characterized by chaos, disorder, treason and imperfect cohesion to what at first sight seems a paradox. According to this new picture, the 'insubordinate' and autonomous behaviour of Marathas, Rajputs, Jats, Sikhs and other 'gentry groups' represented a necessary element, indeed a basic precondition, for the success of Mughal expansion. According to Wink, it was only when the expansion of Mughal power began to encounter the natural frontiers of the Indian subcontinent at the start of the eighteenth century that an involution of the system occurred. The office-holders and landowners at the intermediate level of the political system, who had become strong and independent through the Mughal expansion, now shifted their expansive energies inwards.[67] There these powers had already been at work, but they were largely hemmed in by the Mughals and/or directed outwards, towards the peripheries of the empire. The same politico-military groups which had come to power under the Mughals and had made possible the steady expansion of the Mughal Empire led its fall in the eighteenth century. Hence, the intermediate groups were the authors of the Mughals' fall as much as their rise.

This assessment of Wink's recalls the paradox of patrimonial rule analysed by Weber, according to which the territorial expansion of power must always bring with it the waning of central control. However, Wink explains the nature of the political processes and dynamics being questioned not by recourse to Weber's sociology of power, but by examining indigenous theories of political action. Here, on the one hand,

[66] Cf. Wink (1986, especially 9-65, 157-82, 377-88).

[67] The reference here is to landowners and imperial governors of various types and origins, generally characterized under the Mughals by the Persian term *zamīndār*, which included not a few little kings. On *zamīndār*s, see Fox (1971, 10, 49), Gordon (1969, 407-8), Hasan (1969) and Neale (1969).

he uses Kautilya's *Arthaśāstra* as a model, while on the other he examines the notion of *fitna* derived from the Perso-Arabic thought, which forms the actual key to his analysis.

Originally, according to Wink, *fitna* was imbued with religious significance because in the early Islamic world the term was mainly used to address the split in and decline of Islamic 'world rule'.[68] The fiction of universal sovereignty also prevailed among the Mughals and the pejorative meaning of the notion of *fitna* continued, although it was increasingly applied to the field of politics. *Fitna* became synonymous with a semantic field circumscribed by concepts such as rebellion, intrigue, separation, schism, uprising, unrest, disorder, chaos, conspiracy, revolt and civil war. Wink stresses that these negative connotations of *fitna* only make sense if one starts from the idea of an universal Islamic rule, transcendentally understood, or from the perspective of an equally universal Hindu concept of *dharma* transcending everyday *realpolitik*. Western interpretations of the state in India also adhered to a negative view of the processes characterized as *fitna* because of their Eurocentric ideas of the nature of the (nation-)state, which, for them, was defined by fixed territorial boundaries and the centre's monopoly of power. If, however, one looks beyond the idealizing, transcendental-imperial and Western-centralist interpretations of Indian political history and turns to a prejudice-free analysis of actual political mechanisms and processes, a new picture emerges. Wink stresses that 'in the Islamic world *fitna* was the normal political mechanism of state-formation or annexation. [...] Objectively *fitna* implies no more than the forging of alliances' (ibid., 26).

Fitna, thus, describes a process marked by the continual entering into, as well as dissolving or renewing of, alliances, loyalties, dependencies, rivalries and enmities. While from the standpoint of the notion of universal rule, *fitna* represents a subversive power which is destructive of order, in the domain of actual political action, it represents that positive power which maintains a fragile but extremely dynamic and flexible system of mutually balancing forces and counter-forces. It is *fitna* that lends the political system its own vitality and expansive force. Thus, seen positively, *fitna* appears as 'the pivotal element in the political system of the period' (ibid., 250). We also learn that 'it was always the incorporation of disorder, or rather the complementarity of order and disorder, which made possible the establishment of sovereignty' (ibid., 194) and that 'the state organized itself around *fitna*' (ibid., 196). As a

[68] The 'great' *fitna* of 657, which culminated in the killing of the third caliph, Uttman, in Medina, represented the *fitna* par excellence.

permanent forging and breaking of alliances and allegiances, as the permanent stirring up and exploitation of conflicts, inheritance disputes and revolts, *fitna* occurred at all levels of the Mughal Empire: at the court and in the family of the imperial ruler; between the Sunni Mughals and their powerful Shiite adversaries in the Deccan; between the Mughals on the one hand and the Marathas, Rajputs and other status groups, office-holders and warrior bands on the other; within Maratha or Rajput ruling houses or dynasties; between Maratha kings and their powerful Brahman *dīwāns*; and not least, on the level of the little kings, *zamīndārs*, local governors, clans and tribal societies.

According to Wink, *fitna* was determined less by the actual use of military power as by the 'political use of military power' (ibid., 27). Despite the skirmishes, raids, border engagements and sudden offensive actions, matters rarely came to the deployment of whole armies in medieval and pre-modern India. Often, the mere display and fame of a 'sword' was enough to attain a politico-military goal. 'As opposed to a purely military operation', writes Wink, '*fitna* was at least a mixture of coercion and conciliation and characteristically implied intervention in and making use of existing local conflicts' (ibid., 27). Thus, the conquests and territorial gains of the Marathas were usually 'conquests on invitation' (ibid., 75) and 'always at one stage or another supported or invited by Mughal governors who, through a Maratha alliance, attempted to boost their own independence from the imperial centre and to secure more solid local roots. In all cases the Marathas also found support from Hindu clan leaders, local chiefs or *zamīndārs*' (ibid., 41). *Fitna* was, therefore, primarily not rebellion or war but 'a matter of "political arithmetic", assignments or grants of land revenue, gifts of cash or the bestowal of other "monetized honours"' (ibid., 33). In this game of power, *zamīndārs* and little kings rooted in their localities provided a decisive role:

> *Fitna* by intervention in the conflictive structure of vested rights was essential in state expansion as it was the gentry whose co-operation was needed to gain access to the agrarian resource-base without which no state could survive. Without it not even an army could maintain itself in the field. [...] In reality conquest is 'drawing' *zamīndārs*. (ibid., 160)

This view of things, which derives mainly from the situation of the Islamic state in eighteenth-century India, Wink attributes to other periods of Indian history too: '*Fitna* can be equated with the political expedient of *upajāpa* of the Indian *arthaśāstra*, comprising conciliation, gift-giving, sowing dissension among and "winning over" an enemy's local supporters, and involving the use of force only secondarily' (ibid., 27). In the context of medieval and pre-modern Indian history, political sovereignty therefore appears overwhelmingly as a question of alliances and allegiances. Sovereignty is understood as showing itself as open to all sides and adaptable to changing constellations of power: it does not depend on the questions of whether one's territory is maintained intact and/or whether one has monopoly of power, as was the case with sovereignty in European nation states.[69] The 'fall' of the Mughal Empire in the eighteenth century thus also represented not the decline of a previously centralized and despotically acting power, but at most an increased localization and gentrification, a coming to prominence of forces at the intermediate level of the political system, belonging integrally to the empire and formerly responsible for its extension of power.

Against the background of such an interpretation of the state in India—an interpretation which, like Cohn's and Stein's, questions the central premises of many earlier interpreters and forces the intermediate level of political processes to the centre of attention—one phenomenon that Western observers commented on with increasing astonishment becomes more understandable, namely the fact that, even after the decline of their power, the Mughals counted well into the eighteenth century as nominal overlords, worthy of allegiance, for the fundamentally stronger Marathas and other independent powers. The fiction of Mughal universal rule or patronage was to a great extent maintained by the Marathas as well as by the various rulers of the successor states and other powerful persons. In a related ideological shift, one not infrequently stressed one's own *zamīndāri* status and actively sought the imperial sanction of the Mughal ruler.[70] What the Marathas and others strove for was not 'universal dominion' but 'sovereignty'. For this, however, the position of the little king was obviously not subordinate or secondary in type but very much the key position from which politics was pursued.

In his work, Wink hardly takes any notice of Cohn or Stein, nor does he adopt the concepts of 'little king' or 'little kingdom'. He talks mostly of 'gentry groups', 'intermediate gentry', 'intermediate sections of society' or, using the generic concept of the Mughals, of *zamīndār*s. Where processes are to be demonstrated, he often uses the term 'gentrification'. This lack of intellectual adherence to Cohn and Stein is astonishing, for the correspondence between Wink's insights and the insights of these authors is clear and not only in the common rejection of assessments of

[69] See Wink (1986, 27-8).

[70] See Wink (1986, 39-46).

the Indian state as unitary or feudal. Wink's basic distinction between a static 'universal dominion' and a hotly fought-over '(political) sovereignty' also recalls Cohn's and Stein's distinctions between 'power' and 'authority', or 'ritual sovereignty' and 'political sovereignty'. As with Cohn, so too with Wink, conflict and feud are accorded a state-founding and state-bearing function.[71] The many-layered and segmented character of the state in India is integrally included in the analysis of all three authors who, therefore, all recognize the great significance of an intermediate level of holders of political power. Wink most clearly brings out the important role of the agents at this level for the continuance and dynamics of the political system as a whole. More than Stein and Cohn, Wink succeeds in analysing the processes and dynamics that are at work within Indian political systems and that determine their dynamic and open character. Wink provides insights into precisely those processes of 'fusion' and 'fission' which Stein ignores and whose consideration, in the context of model-building, could have established a 'segmentary' state out of Stein's 'segmented' state.[72]

Finally, however, Wink's analysis implies a turning away from Cohn's and Stein's models of a hierarchically layered multiple kingdom consisting of many royal segments. For these models are still indebted to a relatively static and organic idea of a corporation composed of monolithic blocks and rooted in territory. Wink mostly avoids talking about structure and the state. Instead, he shifts processes and a dynamically understood political sovereignty so much to the centre of the analysis that these become the object itself: 'the various actors should not be seen as hierarchically graded authorities holding power from the Mughal Emperor downwards, but rather as incumbents of concurrent rights. These

[71] Shulman (1980a) also sees the nature of the south Indian state as 'founded on the principle of inherent internal conflict', with the king representing the 'focus of a delicate balance'. Appadurai (1981), similarly, places the analysis of conflicts, which for him are 'lenses into the key principles of the social and cultural order and focuses for the study of change' (1981, 2), at the centre of his study of south Indian temple politics. However, for Appadurai, the 'moments of disruption' and 'social dramas' in Turner's (1974) sense are merely exceptional situations that do not appear, as with Cohn, Shulman and Wink, as elements of political action that—a paradox only at first sight—constitute the state.

[72] However, as with Stein, Wink runs the risk of locating the cohesive effect and political function of ritual at the centre alone, while most actions and forces outside the transcendental and ritual centre appear as *fitna* and *realpolitik*. In other words, neither author sees ritual clearly enough as being important and effective at all levels of the political system.

concurrent rights evolve in a mesh of intertwined rivalries kept together through *fitna*, shifting relationships, in other words, through double or multiple alliances and cross-alliances' (ibid., 154). Wink's Indian state is not a harmonically acting body or a fixed form but 'a form of institutionalized dissidence' (ibid., 386), a multi-stranded tangle of dynamic processes and loose ends.[73]

4. Village, caste, little kingdom and ritual kingdom

As an object of study in and for itself, the unit of the little kingdom was discovered relatively late. Since this neglect can hardly be ascribed to the empirical insignificance of the object itself, the gap between the historical, political and social significance of the phenomenon and the sparse academic attention accorded it must be sought in the researchers' own prejudices. Without going any further into the Indian variety of the debate on orientalism, which is presently being pursued in a lively manner,[74] we can suppose that—apart from the Eurocentric bias of most state models—the conceptual dichotomy between state and village, as well as other intellectual premises and theorems that have guided anthropology, have negatively influenced the study of little kingdoms. In addition, the academic division of labour has led to little kingdoms frequently falling out of consideration altogether when it came to devising and/or subsidizing research projects. In this section, therefore, we will attempt to review and problematize the study of little kingdoms more intensively against the background of anthropological theory-building and with

[73] Appadurai and Breckenridge (1976) had already emphasized that royal authority in (south) India was exercised less over a territory than over a process. See Wink (1986, 158). As a confirmation of Wink's insights, one can consult Kolff's study of the 'military labour market' in Hindustan from 1450 to 1850 (Kolff 1990) in which the author illustrates the agonistic character of the state in the north of India at that time. His focus is less on the *zamīndāri* stratum of society than on the well-armed and battle-hardened farmer stratum, that is, on those 'almost ungovernable tens of millions of people protected by mud forts, jungles and ravines all over the plains of Hindustan' (ibid., 7), who were 'as free to become rebels as they were to turn auxiliaries' (ibid.). However, in Kolff's scenario the *zamīndār*s and little kings are attributed a decisive role as intermediary 'dealers in manpower' (ibid., 65). S. Bayly (1989) and Berkemer (1993) adopt Wink's analysis in studies focused respectively on south and east India.

[74] See Breckenridge and van der Veer (eds. 1993) and Inden (1990), but also Ahmad's critique (1991) of Said and Inden in particular and of the debate on orientalism in general.

respect to such units as village, caste, tribe and kingdom. In the present section I would like to concentrate on three authors, Dumont, Dirks and Hocart. Before doing so, however, it is worth comparing anthropological and historical approaches with one another with regard to their interest or lack of interest in little kingdoms.

4. 1 Historiographical and anthropological perspectives compared

If one sketches the typical research areas and activities of academics from the disciplines of the history and anthropology of India, the following picture emerges. Historians typically concentrate on the history of great kingdoms and state formations, in which the most important sources of data collection are inscriptions, copper-plate grants and edicts. By contrast, anthropologists traditionally concentrate on villages, tribal societies or local caste systems, their data being obtained through participant observation in the field and interviews on the ground. Cohn's statement that 'research in history is based on finding data; research in anthropology is based on creating data' (1962, 6) may, therefore, be extended to the conclusion that the former finds data that relate to regional and trans-regional frameworks, while the latter creates data regarding local and sub-regional phenomena.

Regardless of this difference in methods, interpretative frameworks and contents, both history and anthropology have habitually neglected the historical existence of little kingdoms both descriptively and analytically. As regards anthropology, this discipline seems to have been led by the long-current paradigm of the autarchy or encapsulation of the village or of local or tribal groups, to such an extent that the presence of little kingdoms has been ignored. Royal principles and elements (that could also be traced) were then merely seen as having been imposed on to the local level without any mediation. Thus, although the royal paradigm did not remain unnoticed in anthropological research, it was generally regarded as a foreign element in local life, whose research counted for little as far as the elucidation of local phenomena was concerned. In historically oriented studies of great kingdoms or state formations, the existence of little kingdoms was long regarded as merely the result or expression of an orientalist inability to conceptualize anything similar to the unitary state of Western provenance, or at least to transform it permanently into practice. According to important premises of this research tradition, little kingdoms symbolize a failing of the state and they, therefore, were taken into account when it came to explaining the assumed fragility of Indian states.

This division of labour and the theoretical premises associated with it have repeatedly been questioned by representatives of both disciplines, so that the picture sketched above immediately needs qualifying. Among historians there are not a few who stress the necessity of turning more strongly to the analysis of an intermediate level of social and political organization and thus combining 'microscopic' and 'macroscopic' perspectives.[75] In addition, studies of little kingdoms or of different thematic aspects located at an intermediate level of the socio-political organization have regularly been put forward in this discipline.[76] However, only occasionally does one find in these studies an explicit discussion of the methodological and theoretical relevance which the choice of the politico-territorial unit of the little kingdom as an object of research provides.

As regards anthropology, it can be seen that in the study of Indian tribal societies colonial ways of acquiring knowledge, especially the census activities of the British,[77] and the holism long predominant in anthropology have both contributed to the reification and encapsulation of the phenomenon of the 'tribe'. However, in the wider anthropology of the 1960s and 1970s a shift of perspective occurred which influenced the anthropology of India too, as a consequence of which the view of a tribe as defined by clear boundaries and being totally isolated came to be questioned.[78] This change in perspective was supported by the situation on the ground, for any study of Indian tribal societies involved not only the question of boundaries and transitions between tribe and caste, but also the problem of the integration of tribes into the domain of Hinduism. Scholars sought to understand this thematic field by using concepts like 'Hinduization', 'Sanskritization', 'universalization' or 'Rajputization'.[79] The pragmatic interest of the modern Indian state in ways to incorporate tribal societies into the structures of the nation state also led to increased research activity with reference to the relationship between tribe and state.[80] However, ethnohistorical research on the relationship between

[75] Apart from Cohn, Stein and Wink, already dealt with, Bayly (1983), Fox (1971), Frykenberg (1963, 1965), Metcalf (1979) and Subrahmanyam (1986) should be mentioned.

[76] For examples, see Baker (1976), Calkins (1970), Hasan (1969), Henningham (1990), McLane (1993), Naveen Patnaik (1991), Rana (1987), Rao (1977), Rudolph (1963), Sakalani (1987) and Thusu (1980).

[77] See Appadurai (1993), Cohn (1987) and Ludden (1993).

[78] See, for example, Béteille (1980), Fried (1975), Godelier (1978a) and Southall (1970).

[79] See Urhahn (1985).

[80] On this question, see Oberdieck (1991).

tribal units and the little kingdom or the development of tribal societies into little kingdoms is still the exception today.[81]

In the so-called 'village studies', which shaped the anthropology of India especially in the 1950s, attention was focused explicitly on the many-sided social, economic, ritual, political, cultural and kinship cross-connections between the inhabitants of the different villages of an area.[82] Though the old idea of the village as the basic unit of Indian life somehow continued to live in these studies, the complementary idea of the village as an autarchic and unchangeable 'little republic' was challenged on the basis of new data acquired on the spot. Marriott's statement, that 'both little communities and greater communities are mutually necessary conditions of each other's existence in their present forms' (1955, 191), states in a nutshell the position of this branch of research. Yet, even when scholars saw their analytically isolated object of study, the village, as embedded in a wider network, they rarely followed this through with the necessary change of focus from the unit of the 'village' to the unit of the 'little kingdom' as an alternative politico-territorial framework of analysis. Relationships between persons or groups belonging to different villages (characterized in these studies with concepts like 'exchange', 'network' or 'transaction') were still regarded as *intra-village* relationships and, characteristically, not as *inner-little kingdom* relationships.

4. 2 Dumont

The situation is rather more complex when it comes to examining the role little kingdoms have played in studies of the Indian caste system. Certainly, the most important corporate group found within the caste system, the endogamous sub-caste or *jāti*, is anchored within the village (though differently weighted in south and north India). However, it could not be overlooked that, as the elements of a system of hierarchically ordered sub-castes, *jāti*s clearly extend beyond the village framework. It is, therefore, not surprising that Dumont, a leading theorist of the Indian caste system, accords the village only secondary methodological significance.[83] Instead, Dumont identifies the territorial framework that

[81] As examples, Chaudhuri (1993), Guha (1974), S. Singh (1974), Sinha (1962); (ed. 1987) and Wills (1919) might be mentioned.

[82] See, for example, Gough (1955), Mandelbaum (1955), Marriott (1955), Opler (1956), Singer (1956), Srinivas (1955, 1975) and Srinivas and Shah (1960).

[83] See Dumont and Pocock (1957) and Dumont (1980, § 74). Similar objections against the village as a framework for interpretation are found in Burghart (1985), Fuller (1992, Ch. 6), Inden (1990, 151-4) and Mayer (1960).

delimited the Indian caste system 'on the ground'—and within which it should be analysed—as the unit of the little kingdom.[84]

However, in his work *Homo Hierarchicus* (1980), Dumont discusses the territorial anchoring of actual caste systems only after having subordinated the empirical to the ideological, power to status, and politics to religion in the previous chapters, which are devoted to the ideology of caste. Dumont formulates his most important thesis in this context, a thesis he had already presented in 1962 in an evaluation of classical texts on the theme of 'Kingship in Ancient India', as follows: 'Concretely, the relation between the functions of priest and king has a double aspect. While spiritually, absolutely, the priest is superior [...] he is at the same time, from a temporal or material point of view, subject and dependent. And conversely the king, if spiritually subordinate, is materially the master' (1962, 290).[85] Dumont, therefore, acknowledges that the territorial demarcation of actual caste systems on the ground frequently corresponds with little kingdoms, but he interprets this fact from the perspective of caste ideology. And since, according to Dumont, this ideology not only ignored territorial size and unity but directly caused fragmentation, the ideology of caste is, in his view of things, ultimately responsible for the fact that there were many little kingdoms in India rather than a few great ones.[86]

As regards the exercise of political authority in the village, for Dumont the village head is basically a representative of the dominant caste, whose authority replicates that of the little king. The authority of the little king himself, on the other hand, is only a manifestation of the royal authority handed down in Hindu ideology over centuries, which is itself subordinated to the ideological principles of purity and hierarchy.[87] Similarly, Dumont accords kings and their executive organs great influence on the order of (actual) caste systems at particular periods. However, this influence, Dumont argues, only occurred at local levels, and then only in

[84] Dumont explicitly adopts the term 'little kingdom' from Cohn. See Dumont (1980, § 72).

[85] Like Stein, Dumont uses a series of oppositions, which do not make his position any clearer, as for example, when he contrasts 'spiritual authority' with 'temporal authority', 'ritual status' with '(secular) power', and 'theory' or 'ideology' with 'fact'. The responses, both positive and critical, to Dumont's work are too numerous to be mentioned here. A reference to Quigley's book (1993), which summarizes the debate neatly, must suffice.

[86] See Dumont (1980, 154).

[87] See here Dumont (1980, 160-4).

the form of refined evasions and distortions of the all-embracing and important caste principle, according to which kingly power is subordinated to priestly status and religious values and is 'encompassed' by them: 'Power, devalued to the advantage of status at the overall level, *surreptitiously* makes itself the equal of status at the interstitial levels' (Dumont 1980, 153; my emphasis).

Therefore, Dumont too does not ascribe little kingdoms and their rulers the role of autonomous agents. He acknowledges that little kingdoms typically formed the territorial frameworks for actual caste systems on the ground, but power for Dumont remains subordinated to status, the royal paradigm to the caste principle.[88] However, once they have achieved power, kings threaten to pervert the caste principle in order to further their own selfish, materialistic and political interests. Given this assessment of things, it cannot be said that Dumont neglected the importance of the little kingdom, as did most anthropologist, but he takes over from historiography the typically negative evaluation of this intermediate unit of political organization.

4.3 Dirks

Many of the paradigms and much of the knowledge of traditional historical and anthropological research addressed here begin to break down as soon as the frame of reference that directs the acquisition and interpretation of data is circumscribed by the unit of the little kingdom. My retrospective has reached a point at which it can finally turn to studies that focus directly on little kingdoms. Central in this regard is the work of Dirks.[89] He not only examines little kingdoms because they form an element in the political structure of India that could hardly be ignored any longer, an important concern for him was to throw fresh light on certain much discussed 'white elephants' of research on India by focusing on the little kingdom. The nature of the Indian state and the character of the caste system represent two such hotly debated problem areas for Dirks. Similarly, the type of authority that Hindu kings possessed and the relationship and interdependence between the domains of religion and politics define for him another problem area of this sort.[90]

[88] See Inden's critique (1990, 152-4).

[89] See Dirks (1976; 1979; 1982; 1986; 1987).

[90] With regard to the debates surrounding these two last-mentioned questions, Heesterman (1978) and Trautmann (1981) speak of the central 'conundrum' in the Indian philosophy of the state and in research on India. Among the numerous studies devoted to the nature of royal authority in different contexts in Hindu

Here I concentrate on Dirks's magnum opus of 1987, *The Hollow Crown*. At the centre of attention in this book is the little kingdom of Pudukkottai, with an area of some 1,100 square miles in the midst of the Tamil-speaking region of south India and which had around 200,000 inhabitants at the start of the nineteenth century. Dirks characterizes the wider theoretical problem, to the clarification of which an assessment of the Pudukkottai data was to contribute, as 'the relationship between the Indian state and Indian society in the old regime, and the transformation of this relationship under British colonialism' (1987, 5). On the one hand, the material used consists of a type of source that is usually central to historiography, the inscription. However, Dirks also consults oral traditions which recall the deeds of local chiefs and kings and which represent for him elements of 'the poetics of power' (ibid., 6). Of these texts, the most important ones are ballads, family chronicles (*vaṃśāvali*s), temple *purāṇa*s and genealogies collected at the turn of the nineteenth century and kept as the Mackenzie Collection in Madras and London. In addition, Dirks consults colonial reports and administrative files as well as his own data collected through fieldwork. He himself describes his research as 'ethnohistory'.

Dirks's statements on what little kingdoms are, unfortunately, appear quite unsystematic and scattered throughout the book. In an initial characterization, he opposes little kingdoms to 'large, transregional kingdoms' (ibid., 5). He also describes them as 'political regions which constituted the lowest level of the late pre-colonial state' (ibid.). Later, when he turns to the actual object of his research, he equates the concept of *polegar* (which stems from colonial historiography) with that of the little king. Thus he can report: '"polegars"... were in fact *pāḷaiyakkārar*-s (chieftains, lords), here called "little kings", over domains (*pāḷaiyam*-s, literally armed camps) that varied greatly in size and description' (ibid., 19). Hence, an important criterion for the little kingdom of Pudukkottai and others of its type consists, for Dirks, not in its territorial size but in its position at the lowest level of the political system.

Dirks sees a further characteristic of pre-modern little kingdoms, at least those of the *polegar* type, in the long-lasting resistance they maintained against their incorporation into the wider politico-economic order of the time. This power of resistance, which reminds us of *fitna*, found its

---

India are Appadurai (1983), Appadurai and Breckenridge (1976), Burghart (1987), Coomraswamy (1942), Fuller (1992, Ch. 5), Gonda (1969), Heesterman (1971, 1978, 1979), Inden (1978, 1990, Ch. 5), Mayer (1981, 1991), Richards (ed. 1978), Schnepel (1996) and Shulman (1985).

most conspicuous expression in south India in the so-called 'Polegar Wars' against the *nawāb* of Arcot and the East India Company in the second half of the eighteenth century. Only in the early nineteenth century, we learn, did the British succeed in establishing politico-legal, military and fiscal control over the *polegar*s, who, in the course of this process of subjugation, were either turned into landowners without political rights or expelled entirely from their hereditary estates.[91]

Dirks's first and probably most important, even if not entirely convincing, point of criticism against Dumont comes in the context of these historical considerations. Several Indian institutions, ideas and usages, which Dumont sees as traditional, are for Dirks simply the outcome and constructs of colonial policy. Thus, Dirks stresses that 'many of the things we assume to constitute Indian "tradition" are in curious ways the products rather than the predecessors of colonialism' (ibid., 324).[92] Consequently, the theories put forward by Dumont and other authors, for example, that of Brahmanic superiority, are specific to particular periods of Indian history only. Indeed, the theories of Dumont and his followers are themselves largely 'artifacts of colonialism' (ibid., 9). In order to counter this type of error, Dirks demands that 'the old regime must be studied' (ibid.), by which he means the period from the late middle ages to the early nineteenth century. As regards the little kingdoms of south India during this period, according to Dirks, they incorporate the ancien régime in themselves, for the resistance that the *polegar*s maintained for so long against new forms of political rule went along with 'the obvious persistence of the local social structures' (ibid., 23). Little kingdoms, thus, represent for Dirks 'the last and most vigorous survival of older social and political forms' (ibid., 28).[93]

[91] Dirks (1987, 22; 1986).

[92] Elsewhere (1989b), Dirks speaks of the colonial 'invention' of caste, which, in turn, is criticized by van der Veer (1994, 19).

[93] Dirks's warning of a possible confusion of colonially determined constructions and social realties with traditional Indian institutions must be taken seriously. However, his claim that little kingdoms embodied older, indigenous social and political forms of organization in themselves seems dubious to me. For, if these statements create the impression that little kingdoms represent traditional India, and if this is seen as a characteristic of the institution as such—which occasionally seems to be the case, for example, when Dirks describes little kingdoms as 'vestigial polities' (1987, 53)—then one is simply heading in the wrong direction again. The history of south India is so rich in conquests and in accompanying ideological and organizational influences over conquered peoples that south

With respect to the historical background of the little kingdoms of the Tamilnadu region, we learn that many of them appear for the first time with the emergence of new transregional Hindu kingdoms in the late Middle Ages. Dirks also shows that the ability of some of these kingdoms to extend their dominions into the central kingdoms was basically a phenomenon of the seventeenth and eighteenth centuries. Altogether, Dirks sketches a picture in which the little kingdoms of south India originally arose under the protective power of Hindu great kingdoms. These great kingdoms needed little kingdoms with military strike power for various strategic reasons: to serve as a vanguard in raids, as guardians of the borders or simply as allies who, in an emergency, could offer aid and possibilities for retreat. However, the more the little kingdoms gained in power and military strength, the more their *rājā*s felt that the patronage of the great king (which had formerly aided their rise) now overshadowed their own lustre and fame. The little kings then turned increasingly against their own former overlords with their *fitna*-like unruliness.[94]

If one takes this picture as a starting point, one finds that the little kingdoms of south India are characterized less by their old and traditional internal structures than by the fact that they had to adopt appropriate forms of military organization in order to be able to fend off external threats and invasions successfully or to attack effectively and undertake raids themselves. Little kings, who did not have the means to oppose great kings with equivalent military and administrative apparatuses, had to maintain tight affinal, agnatic, tribal, ritual and caste networks with their subjects in order to be able to administer their kingdoms effectively and to raise soldiers rapidly. Dirks's insights on this point should, therefore, be more sharply formulated and turned upside down: little kingdoms were not little because they contained traditional forms of social and political organization; rather, they organized things traditionally because they were little.

A further characteristic emphasized by Dirks, one which is connected indirectly with the ability of the *polegars* to defend themselves successfully for long periods against invasions and external influences, is the peripheral situation of their kingdoms. Dirks interprets the aspect of marginality as basically economic and ecological in character and concludes that the little kingdoms of the region he is examining lay

---

Indian little kingdoms can hardly be said to represent ahistorical islands embodying traditional India in its pure form.

[94] On the history of the little kings of Pudukkottai, see Dirks (1987, 19-54, 139-99; 1982).

mainly in 'dry and mixed economic zones' (ibid., 115). Marginality is also defined as a relation to a centre:

> Much as these little kings might like to occupy the center, they cannot. First, their social base is in areas that, for irreversible ecological reasons, can never be central. Second, the very nature of little kingship as depicted in vamcavalis derives from the recognition and grace of the overlords whom the little kings serve and worship and from whom they accept gifts. And yet, even where the texts sing the praises of overlords, the principal motive is to proclaim the greatness of the honors that the little kings receive from their overlords. Thus, the texts enhance the prestige of the little king, for the greater the overlord the greater the little kingdom under him. (Ibid., 95-6)

In this passage, Dirks indicates the relative position of little kingdoms in a vertically (super- and subordinate) and horizontally (central and peripheral) ordered system of relationships between kings dissimilar in type. According to Dirks, these relationships are shaped mainly in an idiomatic field characterized by prestige, ritual, honour, prestations and services. Thus, elsewhere, Dirks arrives at the important formulations (which appear to represent a further development of Cohn's and Stein's insights) that 'one of the features which distinguished great kings from little kings was that little kings were given some, but not all, of the titles of the great king, whom we can now see as a king who possesses all titles' (ibid., 65) and that 'honors must not only be identified in relational terms, but these relations are necessarily hierarchical' (ibid., 87).

However, the historical dynamics and changeability of the hierarchical relationships between Indian kings and chiefs threaten to get lost in Dirks's perspective because, ultimately, he traces his definition of marginality back to an irreversible ecological situation. Like Stein, he runs the risk of falling victim to an economic and ecological determinism according to which different ecotypes each necessarily produce different social and political structures. According to Dirks, even though little kings wished to move into the centre and become great kings themselves, this was not possible for unalterable ecological reasons. Against this point of view one could put forward the thesis that the criterion of marginality in the study of Indian political systems only makes sense if it is understood as a politico-ritual criterion and not as an unalterable ecological property, i.e. if it is grasped as a dynamic and relational component and not as the absolute and permanent essence of a phenomenon or thing.[95]

[95] This view of things keeps open the possibility of taking historical dynamics into account, in the course of which little kings became great ones despite their

Dirks's statements on what makes a kingdom a little kingdom and on how the Indian state is itself to be understood, ultimately, remain undeveloped. None of the characteristics of little kingdoms gathered here from different places in his work—that they are on the lowest level of the political structure, their attitude of resistance, the persistence of traditional forms of organization within them, their ecological and economic marginality—are developed theoretically. This deficit is all the more astonishing, as Dirks is very ambitious in his studies regarding the treatment of far-reaching methodological and theoretical questions, for example, when he discusses the idea of 'ethnohistory'.[96] His actual analysis of the history of Pudukkottai is also meant to address wider problems, for example, when he seeks to grasp the effects of the early colonial regime on the 'old regime' in south India more generally.[97] And not least, he discusses questions of the nature of the Indian state and caste system in a 'grand' manner.[98]

Dirks always arrives at his most succinct formulations when he is concerned with the relationship between religion and politics and with the 'conundrum' of kingly authority. To begin with, this aspect of his work takes the form of a critique against Dumont, who, like Marx, Maine, Weber and others before him, is blamed for regarding the state as an epiphenomenon detached from the caste system. Dumont's idea of the caste system as purely religious in character and as shaped by Brahmanical superiority over the king is also attacked. Dirks argues, instead, that in south India, before the British seizure of power, 'kings were not inferior to Brahmans, the political domain was not encompassed by a religious domain' (ibid., 4). He is also convinced that the social order cannot be regarded as autonomous and untouched by political conditions: 'Indian society, indeed caste itself, was shaped by political struggles and processes' (ibid., 5) and 'caste was embedded in a political context of

peripheral positions, for example, by widening their original basis of power or by shifting it to a more central area. Similarly, this view allows us to grasp historical changes in which centrally situated great kingdoms became little kingdoms after defeat, either by remaining in a subordinate position in their former domains or by shifting their bases to a peripheral area. Chattopadhyaya also stresses that 'a nuclear region is finally a chronological and not a geographical region' (1995, 222), and he provides some historical examples of the possibilities addressed above. Further examples from Orissa will be discussed in the next chapter.

[96] See Dirks (1987, 10-16, 55-9, 401-6).

[97] See Dirks (1987, Ch. 11).

[98] See Dirks (1987, Chs. 1, 8, 13).

kingship' (ibid., 7). Explaining this point he adds: 'The prevalent ideology had not to do, at least primarily, with purity and pollution, but rather with royal authority and honor, and associated notions of power, dominance, and order' (ibid.).[99]

Dirks seeks to arrive at a better understanding of Indian society and at a critique of the theory of the relationship between religion and politics formulated by Dumont by placing greater weight on the political significance and function of ritual or, in other words, on the symbolic aspects of power. For him, ritual practices and beliefs at all levels of social life cannot be detached from the politico-economic domain but are linked to it in complex ways. Here, Dirks is also placing himself explicitly in the tradition of Stein, even as he clearly dissociates himself from Stein's assessment of ritual as 'merely symbolic' and of politics as 'actually effective'. Thus, Dirks argues, with reference to Stein: 'The analytic separation of state structure from state ritual ignores the diffusion of ritual forms associated with kingship throughout all modes and levels of political relationships' (Dirks 1979, 172).[100] As regards this 'diffusion', Dirks attributes great significance to ritual transactions in the village, as well as to royal gifts in the form of honorary titles, symbols of authority, money and land as important means in the formation of power.[101]

[99] For a critique of Dumont, see also Dirks (1987, 3-10; 249-61; 324-40; also 1989a, 1989b). The influence of the Hindu king over the caste system is discussed in historical and anthropological detail, *inter alia*, in Greenwold (1975), L.K. Mahapatra (1984) and Maynard (1917).

[100] See also Dirks (1987, 403-4).

[101] Here Dirks is following in the footsteps of Gonda (1965), Heesterman (1957a), Marriott (1968), Mauss (1967), Sahlins (1972) and, again, Stein (1980). Generally speaking, this approach to the study of Indian ritual and politics is characteristic of the work of a group of authors whom one can describe as the 'Chicago School', in which, apart from Dirks, Appadurai, Breckenridge, Cohn, Inden, Marriott, Shulman, Singer and Stein can also be counted. Raheja, too (1988a, 1988b, 1989), to mention at least one further 'member' of this circle, criticizes Dumont's distinction between a ritual domain of values and a non-ideological, politico-economic domain of facts. British-colonial (and Dumontian) interpretations of Indian society are based on an essentialization of relatively late colonial constructions. According to Raheja, in the colonial assessment of things, 'royal patterns of ritual and gifting', especially, were ignored, misinterpreted and reworked in such a prejudicial direction, that 'a complex indigenous transactional logic, informed by ritually elaborate notions of sovereignty, was replaced, in the colonial conceptualization of the situation, by a purely instrumental logic' (Raheja 1988a, 499). The significance of the gift as an institution capable of constituting polities is also emphasized by McLane (1993, especially Ch. 5).

In this regard, Dirks sees a historical change taking place in the royal ritual politics of south India, which started under the Pallavas of the sixth century and was carried through right into the ninth century, and which also radically influenced later dynasties. In these periods, the 'great gift' (*mahādāna*) appears for the first time in place of the old Vedic sacrifice as the central ritual constituting royal authority.[102] This ritual development, we learn further, went together with the expansion of the political system. Indeed, it was the central ritual role that gift exchange acquired in that period that permitted this form of political expansion, because it allowed the king 'to establish hierarchical relations with individuals who had previously been either rivals or allies' (Dirks 1987, 29).

According to Dirks, therefore, the rise and exercise of the little-kingdom rule of the *polegar* kind was only made possible in a political system in which gift exchanges placed kings and chiefs of different categories in a hierarchical relation to each other and in which the 'hierarchical solidarity' that thus emerged was expressed, henceforward, in the idiom of gift exchange: 'The expansion of the political system developed in concert with a transactional network that extended the province of the gift as a mode of statecraft beyond the borders of single localities' (ibid., 31). Dirks identifies 'a number of short circuits' (ibid.) in this system, which reach down into the exchange system, known as *jajmāni*, between sub-castes on the local level. Thus according to Dirks, kingdoms in pre-colonial India were 'the jajmani system writ large, if by jajmani we mean nothing more than the exchange and redistribution of goods and services in the context of a hierarchical system of social relations' (ibid.). Elsewhere Dirks deepens this insight as follows:

> The king's emblems not only signify his own sovereignty, but their presentation to lesser kings and nobles marks and establishes a special relationship, a substantial bond. The bestowal of emblems and titles ... has the symbolic effect of sharing part of the sovereignty of the king with one of his subjects. The subsequent acceptance of these emblems completes the act of service/worship and serves to acknowledge that it is a great honor for the recipient to share, as a subordinate, part of the king's own royalty. Through this transaction the king not only shares part of his sovereign substance, but incorporates the 'servant' into his own sovereignty, or lordship. (Dirks 1987, 86)

As regards Dirks's analysis of rituals conducted in the temple, for him these are closely linked to the phenomenon of the gift. Gifts to temples

[102] On this point, see Dirks (1976).

and Brahmans counted as 'the sine qua non of kingly activity' (ibid., 29) Moreover, 'the shift from the Vedic sacrifice to the great gift as the central constituent activity of ritual kingship' (ibid., 38) was only one element in the 'more general transition from the ritual worship practised in sacrifice to the devotional worship, or *pūjā*, of puranic Hinduism' (ibid.). Thus, temple rituals were, according to Dirks, also political by nature and fell into the ambit of kingly power:

> The kinds of honors that constituted authority in the old regime were those received as shares of worship in local temples as well as those granted as emblems and titles (pirutus) by kings. The authority to arbitrate disputes concerning honor in temples, and the gifts and privileges upon which these temple honors were necessarily predicated, came from the Raja. Indeed, the honors received in temples from deities were at another level privileges accorded by the king. The deity was not so much the paradigmatic sovereign as worship was paradigmatic exchange. (ibid., 289)

In this context, Dirks arrives at one of the central tenets of his work: 'Puja was a root metaphor for political relations' (ibid.). Going further, he regards *pūjā* not only as a metaphor, but as a 'cultural mechanism' (ibid., 102) in the establishment of political relationships. He concludes: 'We see that service and worship are indissolubly combined in political relationships, that gifts of "symbols" can determine political and economic relations. […] Worship as a form of transaction and mode of relationship pervades the political process' (ibid., 106-7).[103]

These excerpts make clear how closely, for Dirks, the political and religious elements of culture and domination were intertwined in precolonial India. Consequently his assessment of the character of the Indian state, the nature of the relationship between the king and his functionaries and the nature of royal authority, and how the relationship between religion and politics was envisaged, leads to a very different conclusion as compared to Dumont. Dirks also 'deconstructs' the models of the bureaucratically organized unitary state and the feudal state: 'Acting on behalf

[103] Further discussions of temple ritual and gift exchange are found in Dirks (1987, Chs. 4; 9; 12). Like Wink, Dirks is especially indebted to Appadurai and Breckenridge (1976), who first worked out the homology between god and king analytically, and who stress that south Indian temple deities rule less over a domain than over a 'redistributive process'. See also Appadurai (1981, 18-22). In this context, other ethnohistorical works that make the temple the focus of discussion are: Appadurai (1977), Béteille (1965), Breckenridge (1977), Dumont (1986b, IIIA), Fuller (1979; 1984; 1985), Presler (1987), Preston (1980a), Shulman (1980b), Spencer (1969) and Stein (1977b; 1977c).

of one's lord thus does not constitute the realization of a relationship rationally structured by bureaucratic form and normative prescription' (ibid., 103). And: 'In fundamental contrast to the western European world of feudalism, the order, and therefore the relational significance, of land and service was reversed. In Europe lands were held by vassals on the condition of service. In south India, however, service was offered first, with the hope/expectation that gifts…would follow' (ibid., 44).

Overall, therefore, Dirks sketches a picture of the state in pre-colonial India in which great and little forms of royal authority determined one another. According to Dirks, little kingdoms could only arise because the new transactional system, based on ritual gifts and *pūjā*, granted them important positions within the extended hierarchically ordered political system. But even the great kings needed the little kings for reasons of their own constitution: exchange of gifts and temple-centred *pūjā* could only create and renew royal authority if the ritual lord and all-embracing sacred king had a receiving and serving little king standing by his side.

4.4 Hocart

Next to Stein, Cohn and Marriott, among the most important intellectual precursors that influenced Dirks's thought in the direction of the ideas and theories discussed here is one whose impact on more recent research on India has been altogether so great that his work must be examined now, namely Hocart.[104]

The basic hypothesis running through Hocart's work is that all human institutions, activities and achievements, whether money, war, kingship, monotheism, medicine, agriculture, prostitution, metallurgy, democracy or even the Indian caste system, are of ritual origin. They are develop-

[104] Hocart's major work was done in the 1920s and 1930s, though published much later in some cases (1933, 1950, 1954, 1969, 1970a, 1970b, 1987). The fact that Hocart only came to the notice of anthropologists from the late 1960s may well be due to the fact that his historicizing style of thought belonged to a period of intellectual history in anthropology in which the evolutionist and diffusionist speculations of the nineteenth and early twentieth centuries were seen as having been superseded by the ahistorical British school of social anthropology shaped by Malinowski and Radcliffe Brown. Moreover, the 'scale' of Hocart's statements, which often referred to humanity as a whole and not to the socially and culturally determined individual of a single, analytically isolated society, was diametrically opposed to the trend of his time. It was only as a result of Needham's (1970) publishing activities and his critical appreciation of Hocart's oeuvre that Hocart began to be read and reassessed in the light of his own paradigms. The following discussion of the main elements in Hocart's thought paraphrases my more detailed discussion in Schnepel (1988).

ments which can only be understood as coming from this origin and which, despite all changes, have not totally lost their ritual nature. Further, for Hocart, man's quest for life is 'the ultimate spring of all his actions' (1933, 133). This 'life' means not simply survival, or life as opposed to death, but vitality, well-being and fertility, in short, a 'full' or 'rich' life. For Hocart, ritual is man's attempt to attain, retain or improve this well-being: it is 'a life-giving method' or 'a technique of living'. To fulfil this purpose, the lord of the ritual or 'principal', as Hocart calls him, is equated with the object to be acted upon through a series of symbolic transformations. For, according to Hocart (as against Frazer): 'Ritual is action, not mere speculation. It does not just note resemblances but produces them for a practical purpose' (1954, 160-1). Ritual is, thus, introduced as 'a kind of creative syllogism' (1970a, 64) whose goal is 'to make one thing equivalent to another so that by acting on one you can act on another' (ibid., 69).[105]

According to Hocart, therefore, humans beings first co-operated in ritual: only here do they first experience a corporate social existence. When Hocart writes that 'ritual is a social activity and so requires an organization' (1970b, 59), he is referring to the central hypothesis of his thought, already mentioned, according to which ritual organizations preceded all other social, cultural and political activities, institutions and structures, before being transformed in the course of history, though retaining their true nature and their most important characteristics. Thus, Hocart writes at one point:

> The machinery of government was blocked out in society long before the appearance of government as we now understand it. In other words the functions now discharged by king, prime minister, treasury, public works, are not the original ones; they may account for the present form of these institutions, but not for their original appearance. These were originally part, not of a system of government, but of an organization to promote life, fertility, prosperity by transferring life from objects abounding in it to objects deficient in it. (1970a, 3)

The position of the king also developed out of the position of ritual leader or principal. For, with the increasing complexity of society, the ritual organization extended its sphere and took over new functions, including the important one of co-ordinating all the activities of the community. Originally, according to Hocart, on the ritual level there were

[105] On these points, see Hocart (1933, 133-4; 1954: 86-9; 1970a: 32-7), Needham (1970, xxxiii-xxxiv) and Schnepel (1988, sections 2,3,4).

many autonomous but interdependent ritual communities, each controlling only one part of nature with their principals. In the course of evolution, however, the formerly autonomous rites merged into a single complex, through which the whole of nature could be influenced. This evolution from a 'piecemeal ritual' to an 'all-embracing ritual' (Hocart also speaks of 'totemic rites' and 'cosmic rites') led to the formerly independent principals sooner or later falling under the authority of a single, superordinate and central figure, namely the king, who now controlled the 'world' and incorporated all other principals, with their parts of nature. Parallel to these developments in the ritual domain, processes took place on the political level that led to the centralization of power and the substitution of a horizontal order by a vertical one. In the centre of this society stood the sacred king, who had evolved from being a *primus inter pares* to the actively coordinating central authority of a hierarchically ordered community. However, the differentiation between local chief and king that emerged from this process is not fundamental for Hocart: 'both are merely varieties of the principal' (1970a, 86), and, therefore, simply manifestations of different stages of an evolution which has both its starting point and its permanent nucleus core in the ritual leader.[106]

As regards the Indian caste system, for Hocart this represents only one historical species among many of the genus 'ritual organization for life', a stage in evolution in which the king has already acquired a central role incorporating everything. However, according to Hocart, it is not only the king, priest and nobility who take part in ritual. Rather, all the members of the community are related to one another through a certain division of ritual labour, whose organs are the hereditarily constituted *jāti*s. For Hocart, therefore, caste groups like those of barbers, washermen, drummers, carpenters, cooks or potters do not represent occupational groups carrying out different technical tasks; rather, their *raison d'être* lies in fulfilling their distinct, but complementary, services within an all-embracing ritual complex governed by the king: 'In India, every occupation is a priesthood' (1950, 15-16). The caste system represents a ritual organization centred around the king as sacrificial lord. The most important duty of the king, as the embodiment of the god Indra, according to Hocart, is the performance of sacrifices, through which he intervenes in the eternal battle between the powers of light and darkness, seeking to influence it to the benefit of his ritual community. As well as being the cosmic warrior Indra, the king is also Varuna, the god who regulates the

[106] On these points, see also Hocart (1970a, 35-9; 72-81; 297-8) and Schnepel (1988, Section 5).

world and protects law and order: 'He is consequently a judge as well as a warrior, and remains so throughout Indian history. The whole prosperity of his people depends upon his *dharma*—that is, his observance of the established order of things' (ibid., 37).

4.5 The 'conundrum' of royal authority

Hocart's statements concerning the 'conundrum' of royal authority in ancient south Asia are a clear contrast to the picture sketched by Dumont in 1962, although both make use of the same sort of classical text. For Hocart it is the king, not the priest, who is the central figure of the Indian community, because of his role as sacrificial lord and ritual principal.[107] Castes do not swallow the kingdom, as Dumont argues: they simply exercise subordinate ritual offices in the state. On the state itself, Hocart writes: 'The Church and the State are one in India. The head of this Church State is the king' (1950, 67). And with reference to our problem of the little kingdom, Hocart argues that 'the king's state is reproduced in miniature by his vassals; a farmer has his court consisting of the personages most essential to the ritual' (ibid., 68). In Hocart's evolutionary schema, therefore, the local sub-units, out of which a kingdom first arose by means of incorporation, form miniature replicas of the sacrificial system of the great king, which they belong to simultaneously as subordinate elements carrying out complementary ritual services. On the whole, Hocart's theory is, as Quigley argues (1993, 15), 'an explanation of caste in terms of kingship', showing that it is possible 'to have a theory of caste which combines considerations of power with those of ritual' (ibid.).

The influence of Hocartian ideas on Dirks is obvious at many points.[108] For both writers, society and state, the social and the political, local and

[107] Certainly, Hocart admits that 'sometimes a priest may be the sacrificer' (1950, 37), but the priest is 'first and foremost the man who officiates for the sacrificer' (ibid.).

[108] In research on India, as far as I can see, Hocart is positively received for the first time in Dirks's article of 1976. Even though Dumont and Pocock (1958) discuss Hocart's interpretation of the caste system positively, they finally reject his key ideas, as Dumont also does in *Homo Hierarchicus*; see Dumont (1980, xlvi-xlvii; 29-30; 48-9; 67; 90-3; 365). Claus (1978, 18-21) views Dravidian cults from the Hocartian standpoint. Stein is also inspired by Hocart at several points in his main work (e.g. 1980, 276-81), and he arrives at the insight that 'kings were essentially ritual figures' (ibid., 24). Yet, only from the late 1980s did Hocart decisively enter the consciousness of scholars on India; see Galey (1989a), Inden (1990, 74-5; 217-18; 228-9), Quigley (1993; 1995), Raheja (1988a; 1989) and Schnepel (1995a; 1996), apart from Dirks (1987).

state structures, as well as caste and royal authority, are closely intertwined with one another. For both, ritual activities and beliefs count as the most important integrating metaphors and mechanisms, and therefore it is also ideas of 'service' and 'lordship', not of 'purity' and 'pollution' (as for Dumont), that represent the most important principles of order and organization. For both, politics and ritual represent domains that can hardly be differentiated from one another, the king in his exercise of ritual functions counting as the central figure of the community.

Certainly, with Dirks it is the gift and temple service, not sacrifice (as for Hocart), that represent the most important ritual forms constituting royal authority. Dirks also modifies Hocart's 'incorporative' model into the model of a 'shared' kingdom, in which the great king does not encompass the little ones so much as allowing them to partake symbolically and ritually in his authority and substance, thereby binding them to himself.[109] In terms of the theoretical approach, too, Dirks modifies important Hocartian maxims: 'Following Hocart, I analyse political systems in the same terms as ritual systems' (1976, 127); however, by regarding these systems as 'analytically homologous rather than as evolutionally derivative' (ibid.), he is reinterpreting Hocart's 'historicism' (ibid.) synchronically. Furthermore, as regards the relationship between ritual and politics, Dirks recognizes the heuristic value of explaining political structures from the perspective of ritual. Yet, he qualifies this: 'It is important to understand that ritual, though susceptible to an autonomous analytic, is itself situated in larger social and cultural fields' (ibid.). In *The Hollow Crown*, too, Dirks initially emphasizes, in words recalling Hocart, that 'ritual and political forms were fundamentally the same' (1987, 5) and that 'the realms of the "religious" and the "political" cannot be separated' (ibid., 107). He also speaks of 'Indian political-ritual communities' (ibid., 121). But this perspective undergoes a fundamental shift, when Dirks notes plainly (arguing against Dumont): 'I must stress the political both to redress the previous emphasis on "religion" and to underscore the fact that caste structure, ritual form, and political process were all dependent on relations of power' (ibid., 5).

Thus, in his attempt to distance himself from the notion of the great spirituality of the Indian mind (regarded as 'orientalist' in character), Dirks falls into another typical Western trap which distorts Indian conditions. As with Stein and Cohn, in Dirks's 'Machiavellian' approach, ritual activities and beliefs are seen mainly as a means to the achievement

[109] Dirks (1976, 128, 145-6). Wink also (1986, especially Ch. 2) uses the concept of a 'co-sharer' in seeking to understand the place of subordinate office-holders and landowners.

of political power and the enforcement of political aims. Ultimately, rituals are not really seen, under this primacy of politics, as independent, irreducible forces capable of motivating human thought and action by themselves. Visualized as politics by other means, rituals become dependent variables, which are subject to politics and the striving for power as the supposedly chief stimuli of human action and thought.[110] One suspects that Dirks only unites politics and religion in Hocart's sense in order to be in a better position to argue against Dumont's distinction of the two spheres and to be able to encompass the domain of religion by that of politics. Without wishing to accuse Dirks of dull materialism or to argue in favour of a naïve idealism, it must nonetheless be stressed that Dirks ultimately fails to take up the intellectual challenge provided by the Hocartian dictum of the ritual origin and nature of all human institutions, including political ones.

Finally, it must be affirmed that Dirks arrives at a fruitful re-evaluation of many controversial points precisely because he places the investigation of the institution of the little kingdom at the centre of his interest.[111] Certainly, this does not always occur decisively enough, not even in *The Hollow Crown*, because the insights provided by the Pudukkottai material are used all too often and all too quickly to criticize (a misrepresentation of) Dumont by using (a misrepresentation of) Hocart. In his eagerness to attack Dumontian ideas, Dirks, for all the light he throws on the institutions of the little kingdom and the Indian state, in the last instance does not put forward his ideas with sufficient sharpness.[112]

[110] Fuller's (1992, 81; 255) and Peabody's (1991, 745-8) criticism of Dirks and Raheja run on similar lines.

[111] Other studies centred round the analysis of the politico-ritual aspects of little kingdoms confirm, on the whole, Dirks's position and the heuristic value of his approach. See Bayly (1984; 1989, Ch. 1), Breckenridge (1977), Galey (1989b), Kölver (1993), Mayer (1985), Peabody (1991), Price (1979), Rao, Shulman and Subrahmanyam (1992) and Toffin (1993).

[112] Berkemer (1993, 23) and Stein (1991, 231) also find fault with the fact that Dirks does not arrive at the systematic model of the Indian state in *The Hollow Crown* that was initially promised in Dirks (1979). This omission may be due to the fact that the postmodern Dirks sees his task rather in deconstructing than in the tasks of defining, typologizing and model-building that are so frowned upon today. In doing so, it may be escaping Dirks, like many other campaigners against this alleged evil, that the problem lies not in definitions etc. as such, but merely in exaggerated and misdirected ideas of what definitions can and should achieve epistemologically.

5. Other approaches

This review of ideas, theories and models of the Indian state and little kingdoms must be brought to an end, without any claim of completeness being made for it.[113] A brief discussion of other relevant models, studies and theories will nonetheless be added here, to round off the picture.

5.1 Tambiah's galactic state

For a better understanding of the political theologies embodied in India's classical texts and ancient rituals, a consideration of Indological studies would be required. Apart from Drekmeier (1962), Dumont (1962), Gonda (1969) and Heesterman (1979), there are a number of studies which turn to the indigenous 'archive' from the point of view of textual criticism and linguistics.[114] This approach is especially interesting in the case of those authors who attempt to combine a study of classical texts and rituals with the analysis of historical kingdoms.[115] A greater focus on Muslim concepts of sovereignty and forms of rule as provided by Hardy (1986) and S. Bayly (1989) would also be necessary for a full analysis of Indian kingdoms.[116] However, it should be remarked that India's classical texts tend to paint a picture of the ideal king encompassing the entire world with his power, so that the historical existence of little kings, let alone their significance, is not reflected at this idealizing ideological level.

Tambiah's model of the 'galactic polity' cannot be ignored in any discussion of indigenous ideas concerning the state in India.[117] With

[113] It should also be noted that research for this book was completed with its publication in German (Schnepel 1997), on which this English translation is based. Since then numerous relevant publications have appeared, of which I would like at least to mention Brara (1998), Frenz (2000), Heitzman (1997), Price (1996) and the articles in Kulke and Schnepel (eds. 2001).

[114] See Derrett (1976), Hara (1973), Heesterman (1957b), Hoffmann (1953) and Lingat (1973).

[115] Inden (1981; 1990, Ch. 6), Mayer (1991), Rao, Shulman and Subrahmanyam (1993), Rudolph and Rudolph (1985), Sharma (1965), Shulman (1985), Stein (1975) and Wink (1984) can be mentioned as examples.

[116] As Hardy shows (1986, 48-51), the transitions and boundaries between Hindu kingdoms and Islamic sultanates, with their respective concepts of authority, were fluid in India. In the case of little kingdoms, and thus on the level of relatively direct interaction between the rulers and the population, these borders are even more difficult to fix, especially where the rulers were Muslim but the population overwhelmingly Hindu or a mixture of Hindus and Muslims.

[117] See Tambiah (1976; 1985b; 1985c).

reference to the traditional kingdoms of Southeast Asia, Tambiah's thesis is that these empires, with their dependencies and sub-units, were arranged in a galactic pattern, corresponding to the ancient Indo-Tibetan conception of *maṇḍala*: 'What emerges is a galactic picture of a central planet surrounded by differentiated satellites, which are more or less "autonomous" entities held in orbit and within the sphere of influence of the center' (1985b, 261). As regards the relationship between the centre (embodied by the king, his residence and the palace) and its satellites, according to Tambiah the former is exemplary in two senses: in the cosmological sense, since it represents the sacred universe, and in the ritual-performative sense, since it derives its centripedal force from the performance of significant rituals regenerating the cosmos and from its function as a source of the most important symbols of authority. The components, located in different orbits around the centre occupied by the *cakravartin* or 'universal ruler', faithfully copy the centre, multiplying themselves into many smaller replicas of the model according to the 'principle of bifurcation and duplication of similar units' (ibid., 276). As in Stein's segmentary state, therefore, the galactic state contains a centre essentially exercising ritual sovereignty, whose sun-like aura and attraction with respect to many little kingdoms of the same kind become increasingly weak the further one goes towards the periphery.

In the galactic state, forces of attraction and repulsion stand in fragile balance. The relatively autonomous satellites (to which one may apply the term 'little kingdoms', without doing violence to Tambiah's model) reveal a tendency to split off from the system in order to attach themselves to another galaxy or to form centres themselves. Tambiah speaks, in this context, of the paradox of a 'divine kingship … dialectically conjoined with perennial rebellions and succession disputes' (1985c, 324). In Tambiah's model, therefore, the fact that there exist several multi-centred galaxies next to each other, each with its own exemplary centre and with a number of little-kingdom replicas belonging to it, is the reason for the specific political dynamics within these states: 'If we introduce at the margin other similar competing central principles and their satellites, we shall be able to appreciate the logic of a system that as a hierarchy of central points is continually subject to the dynamics of pulsation and changing spheres of influence' (ibid.). Altogether, Tambiah develops a model for the Buddhist states of Southeast Asia which resembles Stein's framework, but which, as a model, is in a better position to account for political dynamics and changes and has the advantage of relying not on concepts from Africa (or rather, from the British anthropology on Africa), but on indigenous ideas. Since these ideas, revolving around the concept of *maṇḍala*, also belong to the

Buddhist, Hindu and tantric systems of thought in India—as expressed, for example, in Kautilya's *Arthaśāstra* or in the arrangement of districts in the Chola empire—the model offers a fruitful approach to the analysis of the historical kingdoms of south Asia.[118]

Tambiah stresses that, as a whole, the sovereign territory of a galactic polity is to be understood as a 'centre-oriented space'. This view presents a welcome alternative to the Western concept of the state as 'bounded space'.[119] However, the individual little-kingly components which constitute the galaxy themselves have over-rigid boundaries in Tambiah's model, appearing like the clearly bounded planets of a sun or like billiard balls. Inden hints at this fact when he accuses Tambiah of a 'lingering naturalism' and proposes a 'scale of forms' as an alternative (1990, 238). He suggests, further, that we 'think of the agents making up a polity as overlapping classes of agents, instruments, and patients' (ibid., 160). He sees in Indian kingdoms 'relatively autonomous agents' (ibid., 187) and 'complex, interrelated polities that could unite through pacts as well as "force" within a single imperial formation and create new centres not determined by a fixed military topography' (ibid.). Elsewhere (ibid., 267), he argues that India 'was neither a unitary administered polity, an empire or nation-state, nor a system of atomistically conceived, formally equal sovereign states. As an imperial formation, it consisted…of one (or more empires) and a number of other kingdoms. It was a scale of polities, of rulerships that overlapped one another'. Without delving further into Inden,[120] it is clear that it is not only the boundaries of the galaxy that should be regarded as 'porous' but also the boundaries and transitions between the individual little-kingly satellites.

5. 2 Geertz's theatre state

The model of the 'theatre state' developed by Geertz using material on Balinese kingdoms should also be mentioned here. Like the model of the galactic state, that of the theatre state is built upon the notion that the

[118] In their analyses of north Indian politics, Wink (1986) and Kolff (1990, 194-7) also repeatedly see a 'circle' of conflict and alliances, which recalls Tambiah's dynamic model of the galactic state, though these authors prefer to invoke Kautilya and omit any reference to Tambiah.

[119] In his distinction between 'dynastic realms' and 'nations', Anderson (1991, 19) also stresses that 'kingship organizes everything around a high centre' and that, 'in the older imagining, where states were defined by centres, borders were porous and indistinct, and sovereignties faded imperceptibly into one another'.

[120] For a critique of Inden, see Ahmad (1991, 154-7; 162).

central kingdom, as manifested in the *negara* court, represents an exemplary centre. For Geertz this centre is not merely the heart or motor of the state, it *is* the state: 'The ritual life of the court, and in fact the life of the court generally, is thus paradigmatic, not merely reflective, of social order' (1980, 13). However, according to Geertz, what the royal residence, the court and courtly ceremonial actually represented was the higher cosmic order of the gods. Explaining these ideas, and introducing his concept of the theatre state, Geertz characterizes the Hindu state of Bali in the following way:

> It was a theatre state in which the kings and princes were the impresarios, the priests the directors, and the peasants the supporting cast, stage crew, and audience. The stupendous cremations, tooth filings, temple dedications, pilgrimages, and blood sacrifices, mobilizing hundreds and even thousands of people and great quantities of wealth, were not means to political ends: they were the ends in themselves, they were what the state was for. [...] mass ritual was not a device to shore up the state, but rather the state...was a device for the enactment of mass ritual. (Ibid.)

Hence, Geertz, too, stresses that power is not simply decorated by cultural and ritual elements, but is in essence established through them. He couples this view with the express statement that symbolic activities and paraphernalia do not serve functionally to support political power by blinding the people or instilling fear into them. The dramas of the theatre state did not have any subordinate or derivative function with respect to the maintenance and exercise of power; rather: 'They were the thing itself' (ibid., 120) or 'they were what there was' (ibid., 136). Geertz even argues that the state and power served the ceremonial, or the theatre: 'Power served pomp, not pomp power' (ibid., 13).

This reversal of accepted politico-economic maxims concerning the constitution of power places Geertz within the Hocartian framework. Dirks congratulates Geertz for having freed the symbolic aspects of power from the odour of being 'merely symbolic'. Yet, Dirks follows Geertz's subordination of power to pomp as little as Hocart's subordination of politics to ritual. All in all, Dirks is 'left to wonder what Geertz really means by power', and concludes that Geertz 'raises more questions than he answers'.[121] And indeed, Geertz's image of the theatre state and of the king, statically understood as 'an icon, a figuration of the sacred, in itself sacred' (Geertz 1980, 108), offers little scope for the analysis of the political conflicts and power battles that decisively shaped Balinese

[121] See Dirks (1987, 401-2).

history too. Non-ceremonial relationships of power between kings and various office-holders are excluded from the model of the theatre state. The relationship between the people and the exemplary centre degenerates into an apparently artificial drama, outside of which actor and audience, elite and people, have hardly any points of contact. And ultimately, despite his reversal of the relationship between 'power' and 'pomp' and his stress on the power of the symbolic, Geertz cannot escape the problematic distinction between politics and ritual, which is certainly stood on its head, but not abolished. In addition, using a dichotomous logic recalling Stein, the pomp of the exemplary centre is, problematically, categorized as expressive-ritual, while the exercise of practical politics and purpose-directed economy is attributed to the local level of the *desa*, that is, to the rural area surrounding the *negara*.[122]

5.3 Kulke's processural model

Although most of the studies discussed here so far incorporate historical (evolutionary) processes and changes into their respective models, with Kulke we must now take a closer look at the '"non-aligned" contributions which emphasize processes of state formation rather than the state as a given entity' (Kulke 1995a, 40).[123] These studies address different sub-problems, for example, the development from tribal chief to *rājā*, the expansion of central administration into the hinterland, or the integrating role of urban temples in the ritual politics of expansionist medieval states. Kulke (1995b) forms this emphasis on indigenous, structural developments into a model which he calls 'processural' and which seeks to abstract itself from all too narrow historical cases.[124]

122 For a critique of Geertz in which these and other points are more extensively elaborated, see Schulte-Nordholt (1993), Tambiah (1985c, 316-22) and Walters 1980). Hunt (1994, 105-6) and Spiegel (1994, 170-1; 194-5) criticize Geertz's de-politicizing and aestheticizing of culture, which, they claim, maybe useful for conservative aims. Chartier (1992b, 59), mindful of Elias's work (1983), also stresses that courtly etiquette definitely counts as an instrument of power and can be interpreted 'politically'.

123 In this context, Appadurai and Breckenridge (1985), Burghart (1984), Chattopadhyaya (1995), Fox (1971), Gordon (1969; 1979), Heitzman (1987), Leach (1970), Perlin (1985b), Rudolph and Rudolph (1985), Singh (1974), Sinha (1962), Stein (1985c), S. Subrahmanyam (1986), Subrahmanyam and Shulman (1985) and Thapar (1984) should be mentioned.

124 The essential features of the processural model can already be found in Kulke (1978a; 1979a, 9-16; 1982, 255-8; 1985) and in Kulke and Rothermund (1991, Ch. 3, Section 2).

According to Kulke, prototypically, the formation process of early medieval Indian states began in locally limited core regions or nuclear areas which gradually grew from their bases into states through continuous agrarian expansion into the hinterland and through the political integration of neighbouring areas. Spatially, according to Kulke, these developments took place in three concentrically ordered geographical zones: 1) in the core region and starting point of state formation; 2) in the peripheries surrounding the core region; and 3) in the core regions of formerly independent neighbours or *sāmanta*s. Chronologically, these three zones corresponded to three stages in state formation that followed on from one another, from 'chiefdom' to 'early kingdom', and finally to 'imperial kingdom', each with their own leading personality: *rājā*, *mahārājā* and *mahārāja-adhirāja* ('supreme king of the great kings').

In the first phase of the chiefdoms (again, one may use the term 'little kingdom' without doing violence to the model), according to Kulke, the main concern of rulers was first of all to consolidate their authority within the nuclear area and to legitimize themselves with respect to their subjects. It is only in the second phase of the process, towards becoming an 'early kingdom',[125] that we find an intensification of political control within the core region through social and administrative hierarchization, an extension of this control into the peripheral areas of the kingdom, and a stronger politico-economic and ritual tying of these marginal areas to the centre. Here, we also encounter initial attempts by the *mahārāja*s of these early kingdoms to make neighbouring chiefs and *rājā*s tribute-paying. The last aspect of the extension of the sovereign territory leads to originally independent neighbouring kings (*sāmanta*s) being first conquered, then reinstated over their territory as regents owing tribute and loyalty. In the *sāmantacakra*—that is, the circle of subordinate but semi-autonomous royal neighbours with which every ambitious kingdom of the period sought to surround itself—a new type of political institution arose which was characteristic of the second phase of the process and which, according to Kulke, represents an 'Indian variant of feudalism'. The more *sāmanta*s and *mahāsāmanta*s a king could gather round him at receptions at his court, the greater his prestige.[126] The third phase, towards becoming an 'imperial kingdom', was characterized by a merging of two or more 'early kingdoms' with their intermediate zones into a new, considerably expanded core area. This development, according to Kulke, often went

[125] This concept is adopted from Claessen and Skalnik (eds. 1978).

[126] On the theme of the *sāmanta*, see also Chattopadhyaya (1995, 205-7), K.K. Gopal (1964), L. Gopal (1963), Sharma (1965, 20-4) and Yadava (1973, Ch. 3).

together with the original political centre moving into a new, more productive core region, which the central administration now sought to penetrate completely. Simultaneously, increased efforts were made to strengthen the legitimacy of the new imperial centre through ideological and ritual measures.

In this context, Kulke stresses that not even the comparatively well-administered imperial kingdoms could count as unitary states:

> The core regions were often surrounded by quite an amorphous conglomerate of autonomous polities (often 'successors' of the earlier sāmantas), allies and independent kingdoms which lay in the intermediary zone separating the next imperial kingdom. The differences in definition between tributary states and allies and independent kingdoms fluctuated continuously. The partial instability of the political system of the imperial kingdoms had its origin mainly in these geographical intermediate and peripheral zones. Incursions which could also have an effect on the stability of the central core region took place here through a change in alliances and through the striving for independence of dependent kingdoms. Most of the fights between imperial kingdoms therefore aimed at the control of these 'forefields'. (Kulke 1995b, 256)

Clearly, Kulke's model is not only seeking to do justice to the historical dynamics that led from chief to little king, from little king to great king, and even to emperor or 'king of kings'. Viewing matters synchronically, he also accounts for the presence of little kingdoms in the intermediate zones between the 'galaxies', with their changing alliances and their constant attempts to gain independence. And like Tambiah, Kulke sees in the events that occur in, and because of, these intermediate zones an important element in the political dynamics of the whole.

Like Wink's model discussed earlier, the processural model of state formation makes it clear that many interpretations of the state in India have been too static and too tied to the essentializing survey and description of structures: they did not take into account the constant changes that historical Indian kingdoms were subject to, even from the structural point of view. In addition, Kulke's model can accommodate a change of perspective through which the whole can be illuminated either from above, that is, from the point of view of the imperial centre, or from below, that is, from the point of view of local affiliated units. The processural model, then, has points of contact with the model of the segmentary state as well as with those of the feudal state, the unitary state and the patrimonial state, without improperly mixing their different premises and paradigms. Generally speaking, Kulke's approach is distinguished from other approaches above all in that, with him, important phenomena that are usually seen as fragmenting, decentralizing and thus ultimately as hindering state formation—such as granting land to Brahmans or the *sāmanta*-ization of peripheral areas—are interpreted as integrative and even indispensable in the creation of great kingdoms.

5.4 Little kingdoms in Kalinga: Berkemer

Reference to a study which touches on the present one at many points and which intersects with it on occasion, namely Berkemer's *Little Kingdoms in Kalinga* (1993), should not be omitted. Here, I would like to concentrate on the theoretical statements regarding the theme of the little kingdom with which he introduces and concludes his study.[127]

As the very title of the book suggests, Berkemer explicitly deals with the notion of the 'little kingdom' as shaped by Cohn and made more popular by Dirks. Interestingly, as a region of research, Kalinga lies between the 'Indo-Aryan' north, which provided Cohn with his material, and the 'Dravidian' south, studied by Dirks, that is, between the two great areas which have commonly determined the division of labour in research on India. Viewed historically, too, Berkemer seeks to apply the notion of the little kingdom to a period (AD 600-1700) which goes beyond the narrower limits of the pre-modern period which is the focus of attention of Cohn and Dirks. For Berkemer, little kings are all those persons described as (according to historical period, regional tradition or the ideological orientation of the interpreter) 'tribal chiefs', '*sāmanta rājā*s', *zamīndār*s, *ināmdar*s, '*polegar*s', '*rājā*s' or 'landlords'.

Berkemer, therefore, endows the terms 'little king' and 'little kingdom' with a heuristic value which is more comprehensive, both in terms of the time-space dimension and epistemologically. For Berkemer, these terms are etic technical terms[128] by means of which the analysis of deeper structures and general trends in the history of Indian kingdoms can be uncoupled from too short-lived historical and over-narrow situational and personal viewpoints. In using the term 'little kingdom', Berkemer is also seeking to avoid Western terms like 'prince' or 'chief', which are already burdened with different meanings and value judgements. He also warns us against a Eurocentric idea of the state involving substantialist politico-economic categories and seeing the state as being defined by rigid borders:

[127] See Berkemer (1993, 1-24; 319-23). On Berkemer's study in general, see also Schnepel (1995c).

[128] The category 'little king' has no direct correspondence in Sanskrit or any other Indian language, in contrast to terms like 'king', 'great king' or 'greatest king', which can easily be translated into indigenous terms.

> In modern Europe ... statecraft tries above all to acquire and maintain a monopoly of power in an area bounded absolutely clearly from its neighbours, in order to exercise power within it. In traditional India, as in medieval Europe, the effort goes into the acquisition of a share of power. [...] A monopoly of state sovereignty is not striven for at all. Rather, it is rule over holders of other shares of power that makes possible the aspired status of 'king of kings' (*mahārājdhirājā*) and that underlines one's own position as the head of as great a hierarchy as possible. (Berkemer 1993, 10-11; my translation)

Against this background, the phenomenon of the little kingdom is characterized as follows:

> A political system whose ruler can regard himself as independent as regards internal politics—for example, maintaining his own army, collecting taxes, receiving tribute from smaller kings and chiefs, and bestowing titles on them—and who, in addition, pursues an independent ritual politics within his own territory, but who at the same time must recognize a politically, ritually and militarily superior overlord over him, whose authority he shares and whom he needs to legitimize his own internal rule, is to be described as a 'little kingdom'. (ibid., 13; my translation)

Berkemer distinguishes himself from Dirks in that he makes one of the middle levels, not the lowest level of the political system, the paradigmatic location of the little kingdom. He takes over from Dirks the concept of 'shared authority', while his reference to the need for legitimation links him to Cohn. Yet, Berkemer is different from Cohn in his idea that this overlord may also be militarily superior. The idea of *fitna*, introduced into the discussion elsewhere in Berkemer's study (ibid., 21-3), does not sufficiently leave its mark on Berkemer's attempts at definition, although it informs his actual historical analysis quite positively.

As regards the 'middle' level, Berkemer describes it not substantially, as an intermediate level of a rigid hierarchical order, but in terms of the relativity and dynamics of political relationships:

> In the special case of Kalinga, this middle category of political institutions stands in structural opposition, on the one hand to still smaller little kingdoms and the territories of local elites and tribal clans, right down to individual villages, and on the other hand to the politically dominant kingdoms on the imperial level. [...] It can be concluded that relations of power between the little king and his different political partners had to be supported by a permanently changing basis of legitimation that was determined by the particular social context of those taking part. (ibid., 13-14; my translation)

Elsewhere, therefore, Berkemer also speaks of the 'double role' of the 'social category of the "little king"' (ibid., 2).

6. Closing remarks

In considering the concept of 'little king', we are necessarily dealing with a person who is a king. A king is a person who proclaims royal authority for himself in conformity with the generally accepted collective ideas of the nature of royal authority and of the preconditions regarding the assumption of office and the holder of this office, as generally expressed through ideology and ritual. Furthermore, this person also requires the recognition of an important part of the population that is subject to his rule.[129]

If such holders of royal authority are specified as little kings, kings of superior rank inevitably come into the picture. For, the additional qualification of a king as little cannot, in practice, refer primarily to measurable units like the territorial size of his sovereign territory or the number of subjects or villages in his possession. Doubtless, these criteria may be indications of whether a king is great or little, but basically the description of a king as little acquires heuristic value only when it is used in understanding the dynamic network of relationships between kings of different ranks. The identification of a kingdom or king as little is, therefore, based not on absolute, clearly measurable criteria, but rather on relational, abstract, politico-ritual criteria, which can change rapidly historically and are often subject to contradictory interpretations by those involved. Moreover, these interpretations depend on the social and political points of view of the respective actors and the respective situations in which they make their value judgements. In brief, a king is little only in terms of a changeable, tense relationship with another king, who, in this very same relationship, counts as 'great'.[130]

A king is (or becomes) great less because he is the lord of a clearly marked and rigidly bound territory within which other royal persons subject to him possess similarly bound properties or sovereign areas;

[129] If not: 'In sleep a king, but, waking, no such matter' (Shakespeare, *Sonnets* 87).

[130] A great king may, obviously, himself be little in another relationship, just as the king standing to him in the relationship of a little king may count as great in relation to other kings. This situational relativity and dynamics is also subject to historical processes, in which, within any given relationship, the epithets 'great' and 'little' may be changeable.

rather, he is a great king because he commands the distribution of land, offices, titles, hereditary relationships and other gifts which symbolize and constitute royal authority. In this way, he allows other persons to partake of his 'universal' royal authority and binds them into a system of hierarchical solidarity, a system which also involves conflictual negotiations. Doubtless, the great king also acquires hegemony over redistributive processes through power factors, such as the size and economic potential of the area he effectively controls or the number and strength of his warriors. However, his supremacy in relation to other kings is expressed *and* constituted primarily in and through the religious idiom of the gift and *pūjā*, and can therefore only be exercised by establishing a specific closeness to—or symbiotic relationship with—one or more deities. It is, therefore, basically ritual in form.

The totality of politico-ritual relationships between a great king and the little kings subject to him form what one might call a 'state' if one is prepared to abandon Western premises regarding the nature of the state. In India, the state is, typically, not a unitary construct with just one centre and rigid territorial boundaries. Rather, it is a network of politico-ritual relationships stretching out in many directions, fraying at the edges and overlapping into neighbouring and even more distant states. Ultimately, this network and, therefore, this type of state extends over the whole continent, with the geographical foci constantly changing. Although located on several levels, the many centres, or points of departure and goals, of these relationships are ultimately all of the same type, i.e., royal. Thus, all in all, the model of a dynamic, multi-centred, multi-layered and permanently expanding or contracting ritual kingdom in which conflicts play a positive and vital role is applicable to many historical states in India. And one essential element in this type of state is the little kingdom.

CHAPTER II

ORISSA AND THE LITTLE KINGDOMS OF THE REGION

1. Introduction

In the last chapter I dealt with several of the models and theories that will form the background to my discussion of the jungle kingdoms of south Orissa in the following chapters. In this chapter I would like to provide an overview of the actual situation in Orissa and of its little kingdoms, focusing no longer on theories, but on the ethnohistorical 'facts' themselves. Here we shall see Kulke's 'processual model', already treated more abstractly earlier, being enriched with the concrete historical details and data which led to the model's construction.[1]

Three questions will preoccupy me. In this first section, I shall go into the question of what were the most important foundations and preconditions in establishing and consolidating royal authority in Orissa on the local and sub-regional levels. The main question pursued in the second section will be how some *rājās* of Orissa were able to develop into *mahārāja*s and even *mahārājādhirāja*s. In the third section, I examine the question of how the relationships between the Gajapatis or great kings of Orissa and the region's little kings were shaped historically. In the fourth section I shall turn to south Orissa in order to present a bird's eye view of the little kings of this sub-region. The fifth section will introduce the kingdom of Jeypore, the focus of the present work, and will seek to free the concept of the 'jungle' from the taint of orientalism. Taken together, therefore, this chapter represents an attempt to re-read and filter the work of Kulke and other relevant authors with particular reference to the institution of the little kingdom and to arrive at an understanding of the role little kingdoms played in the political structure(s) of Orissa as a whole down the centuries.[2]

[1] See Kulke (1978a; 1978b; 1978c; 1978d; 1978e; 1979a).

[2] Few studies concern themselves explicitly with the administrative arrangements and political structures of historical Orissa kingdoms, namely Berkemer (1993), Biller (1986), Panda (1986) and Ramachandra Rao (1976). The works of Kulke focus on the relationship between the Gajapati kingdom and the Jagannath.

To begin with, three peculiarities of the region should be noted: a) Orissa is quite decisively shaped by the geographical division of the country into the lower levels of the coast and the river valleys and estuaries on the one hand, and the hilly and forested hinterland on the other. The hinterland is defined by a mountain range called the Eastern Ghats (or 'passes'), which run parallel to the coast at a distance of twenty to fifty kilometres. The plains themselves are also covered with woods and marshes.[3] b) In Orissa, by comparison with the rest of India, there were and still are (despite heavy 'Hinduization') a relatively high proportion of tribal population groups which are traditionally organized on a clan basis and not as hierarchized castes. In general, the further one pushes from the coast and river valleys into the hinterland, the higher the proportion. c) Orissa's deities and their cults have very strong local roots, which Kulke (1979a, 8) characterizes with the term 'territoriality'.[4]

The geographical situation described here is responsible for the fact that, in the history of Orissa, not even the most powerful kingdoms ever succeeded in bringing the little kingdoms of the hinterland, which were easily defended using guerrilla tactics, totally or permanently under their control, even when they lay near the centre. In Orissa, therefore, for a long time, a little kingdom's distance from the influence and control of the centre that exercised overlordship was of the structural type in Evans-Pritchard's sense (1940) rather than of a type that could be measured in kilometres. Thus, a jungle kingdom like Ghumsur, lying close to the Mahanadi delta but in the hinterland, lay at a greater structural distance from the centre than, for example, the coastal kingdom of Tekkali, which lay further south on the periphery of the great kingdom. Determining the degree of marginality of a given kingdom and its closeness to (and control by) the centre is also complicated by the fact that parts of the dominions of many of the coastal little kingdoms also lay in the impassable hinterland, or at least had fortresses, strategic refuges and allies in this hinterland. Thus, for most little kingdoms of the region, even those along the coast, there was some room for manoeuvre in their strategic interactions with the central power and when the need arose, many could create a situation of the greatest possible marginality.

[3] See Map 2.

[4] On these points, see Kulke (1979a, 6-9). Orissa's geographical and demographic situation is described in detail in the *Census of India* (1961a, 13-16; 1961b), Maddox (1920), O'Malley (1984), Roy (1933) and Sinha (1980; ed. 1987).

Therefore, instead of military operations and direct politico-administrative measures of control and compulsion, the different historical centres of power in the plains had to try and tie the kingdoms of the hinterland to the empire ideologically and to 'indoctrinate' their predominantly tribal inhabitants with Hindu ideas concerning the legitimacy of their rule. To be effective, such attempts to integrate the jungle kingdoms and pacify their warlike tribal populations had to take the most important elements of the pre-existing tribal cultures—especially the cults of the local goddesses—into account. Altogether, this constellation of different sorts of political, geographical, ritual and demographic factors led not only to the Hinduization of tribal worlds and world views, but also to the 'influencing of Hinduism by elements of tribal culture in such a way that, within the framework of the entire process of Hinduization, one can definitely speak also of the tribalization of Hinduism' (Kulke 1979a, 18).

The first of the three questions formulated at the start is, thus answered: even in establishing and consolidating kingly authority on the local or sub-regional levels, any contender for royal status, whether an adventurer coming from the outside or a tribal upstart, had to seek and find legitimacy in the eyes of the indigenous population.[5] Kingly rule in Orissa could not be built up or maintained on a long-term basis only through the military power of a standing army that was difficult to feed or lacked acceptance by the indigenous population and possibly even opposed it. However, if a king possessed the loyalty of his subjects, or their active military support, it was not only the internal agricultural surplus that could be profitably siphoned off, with the help of indigenous warriors, a ruler could also considerably extend his wealth and his landed property through raids. Such plundering enterprises constituted an important source of income in a region which was suitable for intensive rice cultivation to only a limited extent. Most important, however, was the fact that a king was in a position to defend his kingdom against the outside attacks of competing kings only if he had the active help of indigenous warriors who were familiar with the rigours and characteristics of their difficult natural environment.

The strategic advantage that little kings possessed in their impassable and jungle-covered kingdoms, therefore, was effective only if they succeeded in obtaining not just the passive loyalty of the tribal population

[5] In this context, Kulke (1979a, 26) makes an important distinction between the internal or vertical legitimation of a *rājā* in relation to his subjects, and his external or horizontal legitimation in relation to other *rājā*s.

but their active military co-operation too. And the best access to the trust of the population lay in the policy of paying tribute to the ritual beliefs and practices of the tribal 'autochthons' or *ādivāsis*. Only then could a king demand material and military tribute from his subjects in return.[6]

2. The rise of the Gajapati empire

We now turn to the second question, that of 'state formation'. First, it must be stressed that for most periods of its history Orissa had a large number of little kingdoms in the plains as well as in the mountainous hinterland. At the end of the first millenium AD, Kulke sees an 'almost confusingly large number of small, isolated principalities' (1979a, 11) and adds that, 'for centuries, the topography of the centres of these principalities remained practically unaltered' (ibid.). Even in the plains, these kingdoms were separated from one another by forests, marshes and warlike tribes.[7]

2.1 The nuclear areas of Orissa and their unifications

As can be seen from Map 3, in the first millennium of our age some of the most important nuclear areas of Orissa, which formed the starting point of the 'early kingdoms', were to be found in the valleys and estuaries of the rivers Mahanadi, Brahmani and Baitarani, which flowed through west and central Orissa. Up to the eighth century the area known at that time as Toshali and located in the common delta of these rivers was divided by

[6] On the relationship of the kings of the Orissan plains to the tribes of the hinterland, see, especially, Kulke (1978a; 1979a, 17-26). The many forms of the integration of tribal groups into Hindu society are discussed in Kulke (1976 and 1984b), while the ritual policy of the little kings of the hinterland of central Orissa in the establishment and consolidation of their rule is discussed in Kulke (1979b and 1984c). Elsewhere (1980), Kulke deals with the rise and consolidation of the rule of little kings in the tribal hinterland of Orissa so systematically that one might consider it as a sub-model of the first stage of his processural model. The determinants of the rise of such rule in Orissa and the structural characteristics that occur in the early development of state forms out of egalitarian tribal societies are dealt with by Bailey (1957; 1960) and Biller (1986, 61-123).

[7] Sharma describes this situation as follows: 'At a time when communications were primitive, the mountainous nature of the greater part of the region helped to sustain numerous kingdoms comfortably nested in reasonably defensible areas. Their existence was perpetuated by the predominance of aboriginal tribes, passionately fond of their independence' (1965, 227).

the Mahanadi into the two nuclear areas of North and South Toshali. Up river, in the middle section, lay the smaller nuclear areas of Khinjali Mandala and Khijjingakotta, ruled by members of the Bhanja dynasty. Further west, in the present-day Sambalpur–Sonpur region, then known as South Koshala, lay the hereditary land of the Somavamsha dynasty. South of the Mahanadi delta, in present-day Ganjam district, on the estuary of the Rushikulya river, was another nuclear area called Kongoda, the hereditary land of the Shailodbhava dynasty. Still further south, on the estuaries of the Vamshadhara and Nagavali rivers (in the present-day Srikakulam District of north Andhra Pradesh), was the original nuclear area of the Gangas, known as Kalinga.

As regards the unification of these principalities into 'early kingdoms' and 'imperial kingdoms', the Shailodbhava dynasty was first able to bring two of these nuclear areas together as a sub-regional kingdom when it conquered South Toshali early in the seventh century and united it with Kongoda. In the first half of the ninth century, the Bhauma Karas of North Toshali conquered the nuclear area of South Toshali and Kongoda, thus bringing together the three nuclear areas of the region that occupied the greater part of the Orissan coast. In the early tenth century the Somavamshis of South Koshala succeeded in extending their hereditary lands in the west of Orissa up-river into the smaller nuclear areas of the middle Mahanadi and linking them with the sub-regional kingdom on the coast. Thus, the first regional kingdom in Orissa was founded. At the beginning of the twelfth century the Gangas finally united their hereditary land of Kalinga with the different sub-regional parts of south, central and west Orissa (in the meantime Somavamsha rule had collapsed) and thus founded their own imperial kingdom.

Kulke describes this unification of the various nuclear areas of Orissa into larger kingdoms as 'feudalism from below', a phrase coined by Kosambi (1956a, 1956b). As regards the different supra-local kingdoms, we are faced with polycentric kingdoms arising through the stepwise, concentric unification of several smaller units (quite like the processes envisaged in Kulke's processural model), and not through the fragmentation of a formerly larger unit (as in the feudalism model). In addition, Kulke stresses that in Orissa the development of local kingdoms into sub-regional kingdoms and into the imperial kingdom of the Gangas, like the earlier rise and consolidation of the local principalities themselves, was characterized by the integration rather than expulsion or extinction of the tribal population, even though the conflict between the Hindu *rājās*' constantly increasing need to expand on the one hand and the hereditary land rights of the original inhabitants on the other never quite came to an end. Kulke also emphasizes the significant role of Brahman priests, who were settled in the region by means of land grants, in the 'internal colonization' and administration of the newly established dominions.[8]

2.2 Jagannath and the Gajapatis

In the ritual policy of Orissan kings on the regional and transregional levels the cult of the deity of Puri, honoured today under the name of 'Jagannath', acquired a predominant position. The historical development of Jagannath's royal patronage, which according to Kulke was aimed at promoting internal as well as external legitimacy, is well summarized in the following sentence: 'Kingship became part of the cult and the cult became part of the Orissan kingship and its main source of legitimation' (Kulke 1978b, 139). Historically, how did this symbiotic relationship between religious cult and political legitimacy arise and develop?

In the early twelfth century, after failing to conquer the Krishna-Godavari delta south of Kalinga due to the resistance of the powerful Cholas, the Ganga king Chodaganga (1078–1152) conquered the fertile Mahanadi delta. In order to consolidate his rule in central Orissa, Chodaganga transferred the administrative centre of his extended kingdom from Kalinganagara in the south to Cuttack in central Orissa. Moreover, Chodaganga, personally a great worshipper of Shiva, began to support the autochthonous god of Puri, who already enjoyed regional significance. For this Vaishnavite deity, then already being honoured in the form of a wooden effigy, Chodaganga had built the temple of Puri, known today all over India and visited every year by tens of thousands of pilgrims. These ritual measures, through which the Puri deity was raised to the status of a state deity (*rāṣṭradevatā*), decisively promoted the ideological and administrative unification of the different nuclear areas and little kingdoms of the region. Since the Puri temple was one of the highest of its time, in building it Chodaganga was also making a claim to the status of the highest Hindu *mahārāja* in the macroregion in this period.[9]

The rule of Anangabhima III (1211–1238) provides further evidence of the intensification of the relationship between king and cult. In an inscription of 1230, Anangabhima symbolically transferred his entire kingdom to

[8] On the points addressed in the previous three paragraphs, see Kulke (1978a; 1979a, 9-16; 1982a, 255-8; 1985). The integrative role of the Vedic *śāsana* Brahmans is dealt with by Pfeffer (1978) and Singh (1993).

[9] On these points, see Berkemer (1993, 154-68), Dash (1978a, 157-61), Eschmann, Kulke and Tripathi (1978, 176-7; 182-4), Kulke (1978b, 139-50; 1979a, 27-48) and Stietencron (1978a; 1978b; 1978 c).

the god of Puri, naming him the supreme king of Orissa and declaring that he himself would only rule as the deputy (*rāuta*) and son (*putra*) of the god, to whom alone belonged sovereignty (*sāṃrājya*) and the right of command (*ādeśa*). In order to support his own military victories ideologically, Anangabhima's son and successor Narasimha I (1238–1264), who extended the kingdom considerably towards the north, adopted the title that was to be associated with the rulers of Orissa henceforth, namely 'Gajapati' or 'Lord of the Elephants'. He also went a step further with the 'deputy ideology' (Kulke) of his father by proclaiming himself Jagannath's *military* deputy, only carrying out his conquests and political decisions at the express command of the god.[10]

The cult of the god itself developed in the thirteenth and fourteenth centuries in such a way that important Tantric, Shaktic, Buddhist and Shaivite deities, with their patrons and worshippers, were incorporated into the tribal-Vaishnavite cult in Puri.[11] Along with the increasing power of the Gajapatis, the political connotations of the name 'Jagannath' or 'Lord of the World' replaced the earlier philosophical-religious title 'Purushottama' or 'Highest Being'. In this period, Jagannath also acquired a reputation as the ninth incarnation (*avatāra*) of Vishnu, and Puri developed into one of the most important pilgrimage centres in India (as it is today). The wealth, reputation and (religious) legitimacy of Jagannath's earthly deputies, who appeared in spectacular roles at the yearly temple festivals, grew simultaneously with the splendour and greatness of the royal god.[12]

The year 1434 marked the end of Ganga rule over Orissa. Because the new Gajapati, Kapilendra Deo (1434–1465), was initially no more than a usurper of doubtful family origins and other *rājā*s in the region were very hostile to his rule, he required another kind of ritual legitimacy. While Kapilendra's predecessors merely counted as the god's 'deputies', he proclaimed that he had been chosen by Jagannath personally. All hostile actions against Kapilendra could therefore be represented as direct attacks (*droha*) on the god himself, while Kapilendra's own actions appeared to have divine sanction. In a further ideological development, the Gajapati

[10] See Eschmann, Kulke and Tripathi (1978, 190-3), Dash (1978a, 161-8) and Kulke (1978b, 150-5; 1979a, 48-66). On the ideology of the *rāuta*, see also Berkemer (1993, 168-72).

[11] As Rösel emphasizes (1980, 13-15), the present-day Jagannath temple complex houses 107 subsidiary shrines devoted to different deities.

[12] On these points, see Kulke (1978a, 133; 1978c, 200-4; 1979a, 50-70).

was now described as the god's 'first servant' (*ādya sevaka*). Ritually, this kind of ideology was expressed in a rite within the car festival (*ratha yātrā*), which takes place every year in June/July, in which the Gajapati sweeps the platform of the car at the feet of Jagannath's effigy with a golden broom. This sweeping rite, known as *cherā pāhamrā*, in which the Gajapati expresses not only his devotion (*bhakti*) and his awareness of his royal duties (*rājadharma*), but also his special relationship with the deity in front of tens of thousands of pilgrims, became the central rite of the car festival, as it still is today.[13]

In 1568, the Afghan troops of the Sultan of Bengal first conquered Cuttack, the residence of the Gajapatis, who had been weakened by numerous palace intrigues, and killed Gajapati Mukunda Deo. Shortly afterwards they took Puri, where they plundered the temple and then took the effigy north and burnt it on the banks of the Ganges. Orissa, up to the north end of Chilika Lake came under the control of the Kararani dynasty of Bengal, which, however, soon crumbled in battles with the Mughals and had to give up overlordship of Orissa around 1590. After some confusion, which mostly played itself out in the Godavari delta and the Deccan, south Orissa fell under the sovereignty of the Sultan of Golkonda.

The Afghans' simultaneous destruction of Gajapati rule and the Jagannath cult continued for over two decades until, under the Mughal emperor Akbar (1565–1605), a more tolerant religious policy and a more long-sighted diplomacy of winning over indigenous allies made possible the restoration of both kingdom and cult. The new Gajapati, Ramachandra Deo, was able to rise from the relatively modest position of *rājä* of Khurda to that of Gajapati because, in this favourable political climate, he succeeded in drawing the priests of Puri on to his side, convincing them of his ability to restore their cult and protect it from fresh attacks. This he underscored, first by having a new effigy of Jagannath made and consecrated in Khurda around 1586–7, and then by installing it in Puri in 1590. Against the competing claims of other *rājā*s in Orissa, who had similar Jagannath effigies installed in their residences, it was asserted that only the Puri effigy contained the inner core of the old one that had been destroyed by the Afghans and which is considered to be endowed with special vitality. According to the temple chronicles, this core substance of the effigy, known as *brahmapadārtha*, had been secretly rescued by one of the god's Oriya worshippers from the charred wooden effigy on the

[13] On these points, see Kulke (1978c, 204-8; 1979a, 71-5) and Dash (1978b, 209-221).

Ganges and brought to Kujang, a little kingdom in the middle of the Mahanadi delta, where he had buried it. Two decades later, Jagannath is said to have revealed the location of the holy core to Ramachandra in a dream. Using this trope of the 'lost and rediscovered figure', which had already once served the Somavamshis in Orissa, the priests of Puri claimed that 'it was Jagannath personally who had placed Ramachandra's personal charisma above the hereditary charisma of the other pretenders to the throne of the Gajapatis' (Kulke 1979a, 129, my translation). The 'deputy' and 'servant' ideologies were supplemented by what Kulke calls a 'successor ideology', which proclaimed Ramachandra to be the only legitimate heir of the earlier imperial Gajapatis.[14]

During the next century and a half, first under the rule of the Mughal emperor Aurangzeb (1658–1707) and his governors and then, after the collapse of the Mughal empire in the early eighteenth century, under the *nawābs* of Bengal, the temple in Puri was repeatedly plundered by Muslim forces. Yet, kings and priests succeeded again and again in fleeing with the Jagannath effigy, or at least with its *brahmapadārtha*, across the Chilika Lake and bringing it to safety from its assailants in the mountains of south Orissa, where the cult was continued secretly. Despite all these adversities, the cult and the kingdom were able to do more than merely survive in the seventeenth century. In the more peaceful periods in between, a series of ritual measures were introduced which further deepened the relationship between the 'Lord of the World' and the 'Lord of the Elephants'. A significant step was the building of a second royal palace in Puri by the Khurda *rājās*. In addition, the king's personal Brahman priest (*rājaguru*) took over the important function of the highest temple administrator (*baḍa parīkṣa*). This meant that royal influence over the affairs of the temple and royal control of its treasury could be strengthened and the power of the hundreds of temple priests reduced. In this period, the king began to evolve from being the 'deputy' and 'first servant' of the god into being his 'high priest'.

From the end of the sixteenth to the middle of the eighteenth century superordinate foreign powers were no longer interested, as the Afghans had been, in the destruction of the Jagannath cult or of the Gajapati kingdom. Rather, the efficient administration of the country allowed them to siphon off the considerable pilgrimage taxes and they contented themselves with restricting the politico-economic power of the Gajapatis,

[14] On these points, see Kulke (1978d, 321-9; 1979a, 76-133). On the 'Indradyumna legend' of the lost figure, see Geib (1975).

while their ritual position, on which the existence of the cult had meanwhile come to depend, remained largely untouched.[15]

In 1751, the Marathas of Nagpur decisively defeated the *nawāb*s of Bengal after a decade of incessant warfare. This led to Orissa coming under the control of a Hindu dynasty, which not only had an economic interest but also a strongly religious and ideological interest in building up its influence over the affairs of the temple at the expense of the Gajapatis. In 1803, however, the British were able to defeat the Marathas and occupy Orissa, providing the possessions of the East India Company between Madras in the south and Calcutta in the north with a strategically important land connection. The British sought, first, to draw the management of the Jagannath temple into their own control. The Gajapati of the time, Mukunda Deo II, who had fallen into disgrace, was twice taken into custody in the first two decades of the nineteenth century. The British also annexed his remaining estates, which had already been considerably reduced under the Afghans and Marathas. However, each time Mukunda had to be released to bring order back to the temple affairs and to preside over the cult again, which was incomplete and badly run without the Gajapati participation. Furthermore, protests within Britain, which forced the East India Company to refrain from too direct a participation in the 'idolatry' of the god of Puri, now notorious all over Europe as 'Juggernaut', also led to the restoration of the Gajapati.

In the meantime, however, the Gajapatis had lost all their economic and military power. As 'Puri *rājā*s', the 'kings without kingdoms', as Kulke aptly calls them, now lived permanently in the temple city. Temple and palace rituals were increasingly aligned with one another in terms of both timing and content, and linked yet more closely by the king's daily visits to the temple. On the ideological level, the Gajapati ultimately acquired an even more spiritual role than that of high priest. Henceforward, in a new interpretation of his position which Kulke characterizes as the '*pratimā* ideology', the 'Lord of the Elephants' came to be seen as a movable image of Jagannath and as a *calanti* Vishnu.[16] The Gajapatis

[15] On the points in the last two paragraphs, see Kulke (1978d, 329-42; 1979a, 133-204). The internal organization of the Puri temple is dealt with by Rösel (1980). Further information can be found in Mahapatra (1981), Mishra (1971) and Patnaik (1977).

[16] *Calanti pratimā*s are movable representations of the major deities, which are often brought out of the temples for processions and so on, instead of the often large and hard to move main images of the gods.

have been able to remain at the head of the socio-religious hierarchy in Orissa right up to the present day, solely on the basis of their ritual position in the Jagannath cult.[17]

3. The little kingdoms of Orissa and their Gajapati overlords

We now turn to the third question posed at the beginning of this chapter, which concerns the historical relationships between the Gajapati centre and the little kingdoms of the Orissa empire.

3.1 The early kingdoms

The existence of several independent little kingdoms in what is today west and south Orissa and north Andhra Pradesh is already certified in the Allahabad inscription of the Gupta emperor Samudragupta I, in which reference is made to his expedition to the south in the middle of the fourth century AD. Some of these little kingdoms were on the coast. Others lay in the 'great woodland' (*mahākāntāra*) of the area which in modern times is known as the Koraput and Kalahandi Districts; Samudragupta describes these kingdoms as 'jungle' or 'forest kingdoms' (*āṭavi-rājya*). While isolated little kingdoms in Orissa can, therefore, be assumed to have existed in the first centuries AD at the latest, a wider manifestation of royal rule conceptualized as 'Hindu' will only have come about in Orissa after Samudragupta and, to begin with, only at the local and sub-regional levels. The first indication of an alliance of little kingdoms, the 'eighteen forest kingdoms' (*aṣṭadaśa-āṭavī-rājya*), which lay in South Toshali, is found in an inscription from around 600, though the number eighteen should be understood as symbolic rather than factual.[18] In the seventh-

[17] On the points discussed in the last two paragraphs, see Kulke (1979a, 204-22). The synchronized palace and temple rituals are also described by Marglin (1985, Chs. 5, 6) and Ramachandra Rao (1976, 96-100). Marglin (1985, Ch. 4) offers an interpretation of the sacred role of the Gajapati different from Kulke's. In my *Twinned Beings* (Schnepel 1995b) I treat the Gajapati–Jagannath relationship in a cross-cultural perspective, in which the ritual role of the effigy is the focus of an analysis inspired by Kantorowicz's discussion (1957) of the fiction of the king's two bodies in European medieval political theology. On the role of the Jagannath cult in the creation of modern Orissa and the legitimation of its contemporary, democratically conceived political power, see Dash (1978c) and Tripathi (1978).

[18] Berkemer points out that, 'In the system of ritual sovereignty, the number 18 is to be understood as the symbolic expression of a harmonic unity of sub-units' (1993, 264, my translation). He also indicates that in Orissa, besides 18 the

century inscriptions of the Shailodbhavas, *sāmanta*s and *mahāsāmanta*s are mentioned, for the first time in Orissa, not as hostile neighbours, but as conquered kings who had been restored to their offices and owed ritual visits to the court of the conqueror. It is at the time of the Bhauma Karas and Somavamshis of the ninth and tenth centuries that we encounter grants from individuals who count as independent kings within their area of sovereignty, but who testify to the overlordship of a greater king.[19]

All this leads to the conclusion that, along with the rise of sub-regional and regional kingdoms from the middle of the first millennium, the numerous military leaders, tribal chiefs and *rājā*s of the region evolved as little kings—that is, as kings with a politico-ritual relationship with a superordinate great king—and into permanent elements in Orissa's overall political structure. Hence, under the Shailodbhavas, Bhauma Karas and Somavamshis, little kings and their realms represented indispensable elements in the continual growth of their politics. Certainly, the development of well-organized royal administrations and the systematic extension of central control can be discerned in the inscriptions of this period, which lasted to the end of the millennium and marked the rise of 'early kingdoms'. However, as soon as efforts at state formation extended over the original nuclear area of a given dynasty, the creation of little kingdoms out of adjacent chiefdoms or local kingdoms which had been *sāmanta*-ized and tied to the centre through land grants as well as gift exchanges in the court became an important element in the politics of expansion.

In addition, the titles used in the inscriptions of this period, like *sāmanta*, *mahāsāmanta*, *mahārājanaka*, *rānaka*, *rājaputra* or *bhūpati*, allow us to conclude that, in the process of state formation during this period, the hierarchization and the separation of functions among the different little kings of the region increased. The fact that the kingdoms of the Bhanjas, Shulkis, Tungas and Nandas, autonomous but under the Bhauma Karas, formed a semi-circle in the mountainous hinterland

---

numbers 9, 36 and 84 are also known from inscriptions. See also Acharya (1949) and Berkemer (1993, 265-8). The number 18 plays no role in Tambiah's *maṇḍala* scheme, where the starting point is geometric constellations of 5, 9, 17 and 33 units (1985b, 253-6).

[19] On the points in this paragraph, see Berkemer (1993, 83-112, 321), Biller (1986, Chs. 4, 5), Joshi (1967), Kulke (1979a, 6-10, 22), Panda (1986, Ch. 1), Rajaguru (ed. 1958-1966) and Sircar (1953).

around the Mahanadi delta and were described as *maṇḍalas*[20] also pérmits us to conclude that a '*maṇḍala*-ization' of the little kingdoms of central Orissa was taking place. I use this term to describe ties formed by the different *sāmanta*-ized little kingdoms among themselves, politically, ritually, militarily, and through kinship and marriage. It describes processes of synthesis that probably appeared for the first time in Orissa in the *aṣṭadaśa-āṭavi-rājya* or 'eighteen forest states' of the sixth century.

3.2 The Ganga period

A more definite terminology emerged in the copper-plate and temple inscriptions of the period of the eastern Gangas, from the turn of the millennium to 1434. An increasing number of official titles appear which describe different sorts of holders of functions and honours—on the level of the 'royal council'[21] as well as at province, district and village levels—of an increasingly unitary, hierarchically ordered administrative system controlled directly by the centre.[22] The Ganga era, thus, not only represents a period in the history of Orissa in which the territorial size of the kingdom reached a size hitherto unknown; the degree of centralization and the influence of the central administration beyond the hereditary lands, which the Gangas were able to achieve at least at the zenith of their power, had not been attained before in Orissa. While a central- or feudal-state model, therefore, underlies the accounts of many historians investi-

[20] See Panda (1986, 64 and 149).

[21] Thus, around 1100, under Chodaganga, there was a five-man royal council comprising the *mantrin* (minister), *purohita* (royal priest), *senāpati* (military leader), *dauvārika* (chamberlain) and *yuvāraja* (crown prince). Following administrative reforms under Bhanudeva I (1264-1278), the inner royal council was increased to sixteen, after which terms like *pātra, mahāpātra, pradhāna, mahāpradhāna* and *amātya* as titles for ministers of different types and significance appear frequently in the inscriptions. See Panda (1986, Ch. II). Rajaguru (1968-72 [vol. I], 210-214) also offers a list of titles under the early Gangas.

[22] According to Panda (1986, Ch. III), the Gajapati kingdom was divided into five provinces (*maṇḍalas*), which were further sub-divided into districts (*viṣayas*), sub-districts (*khaṇḍas*; in Kalinga *nāḍus*), village groups (*pañcālis*) and villages (*grāmas*), each with their respective administrators and heads, for example *viṣayapatis*. The fact that Bhanudeva I changed the *maṇḍalas* into *daṇḍapāṭas*, whose heads were no longer quasi-autonomous 'lords' or 'masters' (*maṇḍaleśvaras*) but 'administrators' (*daṇḍaparīkṣās*), indicates greater centralization under his rule.

gating the Ganga era almost without question,[23] we may ask, with Panda, 'What does the long list of official titles and administrative units that we can find in the inscriptions mean …, and what conclusions do these informations allow us to come to regarding the structure of the Ganga kingdom? Does their naming justify the conclusion that the Ganga kingdom was a centralized, bureaucratic state?' (Panda 1986, 7).

More appropriate than such an assumption, questioned by Panda, is probably the view that the Ganga kingdom represented a polycentric system whose most important components, apart from a strong and well-organized centre,[24] were a large number of militarily powerful and loyal, but semi-independent, little kingdoms. The long-lasting political and military greatness of the imperial Gangas was also based on their direct control of a relatively large hereditary territory in the Mahanadi delta, whose agricultural surplus was sufficient to feed the numerous 'unproductive' officials and courtiers required. Even a large standing army, whose core, apart from a numerically dominant infantry, was formed by a powerful cavalry and a large number of war elephants, was supplied from this source. The different function-holders in the administration and military were generally chosen for their political and military skills, and not on a hereditary basis. Their duties encompassed civilian and military affairs, which resulted in the militarization of the administration, as well as in its increased efficiency.

The centrally administered Mahanadi delta itself was protected militarily by a ring of twenty to thirty 'fortress-dwellers', who controlled all strategically important access points to the plains in the fortresses of their *gaḍajatā* kingdoms. The assembly of the 'eighteen forest states' in the sixth century, and the *maṇḍala* kingdoms that existed under the Bhauma Karas, probably formed the basis of a political system in central Orissa under the Gangas that can be described as a *sāmantacakra* or 'galaxy' in Tambiah's sense. In addition, Ganga power was based on an attempt to tie the most important little kingdoms on the coast—through

[23] For example, Banerjee (1930-1, 226-88), Rajaguru (1968-72, Vol. 1) and Ramachandra Rao (1976).

[24] When talking somewhat abstractly of the 'centre', I am thinking also of the king as a personal ruler. In Orissa, the king who was endowed with Jagannath's blessings was the final and sole source of all decisions. This 'personal' nature of the exercise of power, which recalls Weber's theory of the patrimonial state, is perhaps expressed most clearly in the fact that the Gajapatis personally commanded their armies and not infrequently joined in battles themselves.

which ran the connecting routes between the centre of the kingdom and its borders on the Hooghly river to the north and the Godavari delta to the south—as tightly as possible to the centre, or to control them directly through its own officials. The original hereditary territory of the Gangas in Kalinga, which came under the control of a governor (*mahāmaṇḍaleśvara*; *Kaliṅga-parīkṣa*, following the administrative reform of the mid-thirteenth century) appointed by the centre but having vice-regal powers in effect formed, as before, a strong, directly controlled bastion of power. The removal of the capital from Kalinganagara to Cuttack produced little change. This original hereditary territory of the Gangas was similarly surrounded by a *maṇḍala*-style ring of loyal local magnates. In the east, the sea provided protection from intruders while in the west the impassable Eastern Ghats, with their numerous jungle kings who were loyal to the Gajapatis but on the whole enjoyed a fair degree of autonomy, offered cover and shelter.

Panda's observation that the success of the Gangas was based on 'a unique "double rule" in Kalinga and central Orissa' (1986, 2) is noteworthy in this context, for it leads us ultimately to the conclusion that the kingdom of the imperial Gangas consisted of a unique bond between *two* well-organized *sāmantacakra*s. These formed a multi-centred state based on an effectively administered, fertile hereditary territory, and also a loose alliance with numerous other, more or less firmly controlled little kingdoms. The cohesion of the whole was also supported by the great ritual prestige that the Gangas were able to acquire through their promotion of Jagannath and, as Berkemer (1992) has shown, through their patronage of the temples of Simhachalam and Srikurmam in Kalinga.

In this context, the consolidation and even sacralization of genealogical links which, unusually for medieval India, spared the Gangas succession disputes and wars, is also noteworthy. The great prestige of hereditary charisma, focused on the eldest son, also indicates a reduction in the power of the little kings, whose houses not infrequently formed branches of the central dynasty and who were, until the period of the Bhauma Karas, used to joining in questions of succession when these were disputed, and even to influencing them militarily. Moreover, in the south of the kingdom, the local potentates who safeguarded the Kalinga hereditary territory on its borders were, for quite a period, not little kings but *nāyaka*s. For this southern region of the kingdom, therefore, one should speak of a *nāyaka* system rather than of a *sāmantacakra*, especially in the period from about 1100 to 1400.[25]

But who were these *nāyaka*s, who, according to all available indications played such a decisive part in the building up of the little Ganga kingdom into a transregional kingdom?[26] Originally, they were probably local warrior princes and Telegu chiefs whom the Gangas recognized officially as the governors of their home areas. In order to define more exactly the social and political position of the *nāyaka*s under the imperial Gangas, we must first of all, following Panda, distinguish them from the status group formed by the bureaucracy:

> The political and legal position of the Nāyakas differed fundamentally from that of the provincial governors and the high office-bearers subject to them. The latter acted as representatives of the king and thus provided a link between the central administration and the local Nāyakas of Kalinga. The Nāyakas, on the other hand, were military 'vassals' and as such had military, administrative and supposedly also certain fiscal tasks to perform on behalf of the central administration, for which they were recompensed with landed property or the tax revenues of specific estates. In their estates, which mostly consisted of one or more villages, they enjoyed an almost autonomous status. (Panda 1986, 105; my translation)

In addition, there are indications that administrative officials were replaced frequently, to keep them from creating an independent basis of power for themselves locally, while the replacement of *nāyaka*s, who often had traditional links with the people of their estates, was not the rule. Inscriptions also provide evidence that *nāyaka*s themselves endowed temples, in which they acquired prestigious positions as a consequence. From this, a quasi-royal status can be assumed for many *nāyaka*s.

While the *nāyaka*s are comparable to military vassals and must therefore be distinguished from administrative officials, they must, as Berkemer (1993) stresses, also be distinguished from the little kings of

25 Naturally, here, four centuries of considerable change as well as important territorial differences must largely be glossed over. Berkemer (1993, Ch. VI) and Panda (1986) give a more detailed picture of the administration and political structure of Ganga rule.

26 On the *nāyaka* system of the Gangas, see especially Berkemer (1993, 116-53, 256-7) and Panda (1986, 95-106; 125-34), whose insights form the basis of the following paragraphs.

the region. In appointing *nāyaka*s in areas that were formerly ruled by little kings, the Gangas sought to reduce as much as possible the power of the latter, who were certainly indispensable in the structure of imperial rule, but always focused strongly on their own legitimacy and tried to wrest the greatest possible degree of sovereignty. In contrast to the little kings of the region, to begin with, the *nāyaka*s had no royal legitimacy of their own, their powers of office being conferred on them. Also, the areas the *nāyaka*s governed were usually smaller than the little kingdoms of their predecessors and neighbours. Following Berkemer (ibid., 146), therefore, one can suggest that through the *nāyaka*s the central government established more direct contact with local warrior groups and tribal chiefs, while circumventing the little kings who had traditionally been the rulers of these groups. The acquisition of power by the *nāyaka*s meant a thorough militarization of society on a level below the unit of the little kingdom. Despite a far-reaching homology of functions regarding the services to be performed for the overlord (which, for both groups, basically consisted in providing taxes and, if necessary, warriors), the dynastic prestige and power of the *nāyaka*s was more restricted than that of the little kings.[27]

However, the differences and boundaries between the *nāyaka* and little king were not unbridgeable, as is indicated by the already mentioned endowment of temples by *nāyaka*s and other royal activities on their part. *Nāyaka*s, then, tended to become little kings themselves, as Berkemer (1993, 147-8) especially points out. Ironically, at the end of such a process, the *nāyaka*s—exactly like the little kings before them, whose powers they were originally meant to curb—not infrequently became a destabilizing factor themselves in the labile equilibrium of the divided, multicentred power around the Gajapatis. These two alternating processes in the history of Orissa, namely the reduction and replacement of the powers of the little-kings by office-holders of the central administration, and the attainment of independence by vassals and officials, could be described as the '*nāyaka*-ization of little-kingly domains' and the 'royalization of the administration' respectively. In this way, two sub-processes within the larger cycle of centralization and 'feudalization', which has determined Orissa's history for long periods, can be pinpointed and distinguished.

[27] The equivalence of functions also made it possible for some little kings to be conferred additionally with the function of *nāyaka*s of strategically important fortresses outside their own little kingdoms, or with the function of generals (*senāpati*s) of the central army. See Berkemer (1993, 46, 179).

3.3 Orissa under the Suryavamsha Gajapatis

Just as the rise of Ganga power was based on the support of the *nāyaka*s, so too was their decline associated with members of this increasingly insubordinate and independent status group, who were well on their way to developing into little kings. Kapilendra Deo, who usurped the throne in 1434 thereby ending Ganga rule, came from a *nāyaka* dynasty. The first serious uprising of the *nāyaka*s and little kings of Kalinga and south Orissa had already occurred under Gajapati Bhanudeva II (1305–1327), though the Gajapati general Rama Senapati was able to crush it.[28] Further sporadic revolts and insubordination on the part of the *nāyaka*s continued to occur up to 1434. The independence of this status group had increased to such an extent that one might speak of a far-reaching 'royalization' of areas subject to the *nāyaka*s. Some of the little kings in the south of the kingdom—among them probably the Shilavamshis of Nandapur, the dynastic predecessors of the jungle kings of Jeypore—are also said to have declared their independence as the power of the Gangas declined, so that they progressed from being little kings to being independent kings or became little kings in another galaxy.[29] Among the royalized *nāyaka*s of the kingdom, Kapilendra's grandfather, described in an inscription as the 'crown jewel of the *nāyaka*s' ('*nāyaka mauli ratnam*') and as '*mahārāja*', had already acquired a leading position as little king. Kapilendra used this position, probably 'at the head of a league of the dissatisfied' (Berkemer 1993, 192), to bring about the fall of Bhanudeva IV (1409–1434), then on a campaign in the south of his kingdom.

The manner in which Kapilendra seized power was unprecedented in Orissa's history, in that, while previous dynasties had extended their rule outwards from a core area through stepwise military conquest and concentric integration of new areas, the founder of the Suryavamsha dynasty came to power through a coup. Admittedly, Kapilendra's '*coup d'état*'

[28] The general described himself as *komddumarddanna* or 'vanquisher of the Kondh' in a 1321 inscription in the temple of Simhachalam. Since the Kondh are a tribal group found primarily in the hinterland of Ganjam and in Koraput, some of the jungle kings of south Orissa may well have been involved in the uprising. This uprising was linked with the simultaneous invasion of Telingana, lying to the west of Kalinga, by troops of the Delhi Sultanate, which some of the rebel little kings supported, indicating a change of galaxy. On these points, see Berkemer (1993, 180-2).

[29] As late as 1436, the last Shilavamsha ruler placed an inscription in the temple of Simhachalam claiming that he had washed his sword in the ocean. See Berkemer (1993, 191).

was only possible against the background of an already highly beleaguered Ganga power, which had to battle against expanding great kings and sultanates on all its borders, and saw itself weakened internally by great dissatisfaction on the part of the little kings, *nāyaka*s and, not least, a large part of the rural population suffering under an ever-increasing burden of taxes. Apart from Kapilendra and other *nāyaka*s, some ministers of the royal council also defected. The influential priests of Puri too, had turned against them so that this important status group did nothing to oppose the change of power.

The fact that this gigantic empire did not fall apart after Kapilendra's coup shows, according to Kulke, 'that during the previous centuries territorial integration had taken place which had led to the erosion of the autochthonous political power of the former nuclear areas' (1982, 259). It is certainly the case that Kapilendra inherited a relatively well-established imperial structure of power which, despite being weakened and despite changes in the central dynasty, did not collapse. But in order to relativize Kulke's statement it must be stressed that, outside the core region and beyond the strategically important coastal strips, this structure was based not on the erosion of local power bases and nuclear areas but on their continuing internal strength, with *sāmanta*-ization and *maṇḍala*-ization simultaneously taking place. Nor would anything change under Kapilendra. Indeed, Kapilendra left the administrative structure and the politico-military organization of the kingdom basically as he found it, so that our evaluation concerning the Ganga kingdom's structure of rule and the significance of its little kings also applies to the Gajapati kingdom under the Suryavamshis. Nonetheless, it is noteworthy that under Kapilendra it was possible to extend the kingdom considerably to the south. The southernmost province of the greatest Hindu empire of that time was now not Kalinga but a province known as Kondavidu *daṇḍapāṭa* in the Krishna-Godavari delta. Hamvira, Kapilendra's son, famous for his military campaigns, and Dakshina Kapileshvara, Hamvira's son, were the governors (*daṇḍaparīkṣā*s) of this province.

However, along with the Ganga empire's power structure, Kapilendra also inherited a political dynamics which was viewed with suspicion by the central rulers, namely the fact that the local magnates, whether officials, *nāyaka*s or little kings, made constant attempts to strengthen their autonomy against the centre. The centrifugal powers of these persons, to whom Kapilendra had himself belonged before his accession, was in no way removed by the change of imperial dynasty and claimed a large part of the energies of the new Gajapati, especially in the first decade of Suryavamsha rule. An inscription of Kapilendra's from 1436 states: 'All the kings in my Orissa kingdom should work for the good of the (paramount sovereign), should keep virtuous ways, should not remain in bad ways. If they act boldly towards the sovereign they will be expelled from the kingdom and all their property confiscated' (quoted in Subrahmanyam 1957, 34). This inscription was probably directed towards the little kings of central Orissa. However, among the rebellious kings of the time were also some of the jungle kings of south Orissa—a source from 1441–2 tells of Kapilendra's victory over the south Orissan little kingdom of Parlakimedi—and some of the local rulers of Kalinga.[30] Even towards the end of his more than thirty years of rule, Kapilendra was confronted with a rebellion of little kings, this time in Kondavidu, as he complains to Jagannath in an inscription of 1464. Especially bitter for him was the fact that this revolt was led by the 'vice-king' of the region, that is, by his eldest son. No doubt this treason was one reason why, a little later, Kapilendra selected not Hamvira, but his youngest ('illegitimate') son Purushottama (1467–1497) as his successor. Thereupon Hamvira is said to have allied himself with the Sultan of Bahmani against his brother, before probably being able to establish a new power base in the little kingdom of Parlakimedi. Thus, even at an early stage of Suryavamsha rule, questions of succession, which under the Gangas had raised hardly any problems, led to considerable conflicts and a loss of power within the imperial house.

Despite these difficulties with princes, little kings and *nāyaka*s loyal to the Gangas or those thinking about their own independence, Kapilendra and Purushottama temporarily succeeded in consolidating their kingdom internally as well. In this context it can be noted that most of Orissa's little-kingly dynasties that have continued into the modern period had their historical origins during the rule of these two warlords. The strategically important little kingdoms of the *sāmantacakra* on the Mahanadi delta and the little kingdoms on the coast of south Orissa, especially, were given to trusted followers by Kapilendra and Purushottama. In addition, some of the royal houses that had existed under the Gangas were conquered, reinstated and made personally tributary to the new lord. In other cases, kingdoms like those in the Krishna-Godavari delta or

[30] See Subrahmanyam (1957, 36). In this initial period, the Matsyas of Oddadi, the Chalukyas of Elamanchili and the Shilavamsha dynasty of Nandapur also fought against Kapilendra, whether from loyalty to the Gangas or to defend their own independence won in previous years. All three dynasties disappear in the middle of the fifteenth century from the historical records of Orissa, though the first two resurface elsewhere or under other names as surviving branches of the original dynasties. See Berkemer (1993, 184-92; 216-26).

Telingana, which before had either been independent or had belonged to another galaxy, now fell under the overlordship of the Suryavamshis. In yet other areas—especially in the mountainous hinterland—dispersed princes, local potentates, tribal chiefs, warrior princes, and paramilitarily organized merchants had been able to 'carve out' their own dominions in the confusion and the power vacuum that initially arose with the change of dynasty. But even they found themselves under Gajapati sovereignty at the zenith of Suryavamsha power. Or, they themselves symbolically offered their services—which are often stereotypically glorified in family chronicles as consisting of clearing the jungle and the pacification of its inhabitants—to the Gajapatis, in order to lend the blessings of a great king to their own strivings for royal dignity.

Under the early Suryavamshis, therefore, an extension and deepening of the central power took place, going beyond anything that had occurred before, as a consequence of which large areas of the kingdom were *sāmanta*-ized and *nāyaka*-ized. However, in many places the appointed administrative officers and military men soon succeeded in freeing themselves from the all too direct control of the Gajapatis and in placing their rule on a hereditary footing. In this way, in the course of time, the houses founded by these persons were able to appropriate royal dignity for themselves, which many retained into the modern period. The initial process of *nāyaka*-ization was, therefore, followed by a renewed process of royalization, which gained in strength especially after the defeats suffered by Prataparudra (1497–1538) in the south of the kingdom at the beginning of the sixteenth century. Towards the end of Suryavamsha rule, a revolt of little kings occurred in which the *gaḍajāta* states of the Mahanadi hinterland were again involved. Gajapati Govinda Vidyadhara, who himself had come to power through a bloody palace intrigue, complained to Jagannath in a (partly damaged) inscription of 1549: 'O Jagannātha! Without my becoming to behold Thy Lotus Feet, all is hell. In regard to the gift of pilgrims, whether belonging to this country or to a foreign country up to the vicinity of the Vindhya and Udayagiri mountains (...) the *Gaḍajāta* kings (...) should observe (...) He who violates this, rebels against Lord Jagannātha' (quoted in Kulke 1979a, 78). Govinda's son is said to have become the victim of the subversive machinations of a little king in the south of the kingdom. However, Mukunda Deo from Telingana, who usurped power in 1560, could never secure his position, because other little kings of central Orissa, especially members of the Bhanja dynasty, never gave up their claims to the Gajapati throne until the Afghan takeover.

All in all, therefore, far-reaching dynastic changes took place in Orissa under the Suryavamshis on the level of the great king as well as the little kings, although the little-kingly basis of the state's structure of rule and the cyclical dynamics of centralization and decentralization or 'feudalization' remained unchanged. As a result, the Suryavamsha period between 1434 and 1568 shows more clearly than any other period of Orissan history that a weakening or even change of power in the imperial centre was often answered immediately by the little kings with the suspension of tributary payments and services and sometimes even with rebellion or a change of galaxy. Only the position of the Gajapatis in the Jagannath cult and the oft-threatened wrath of the god to rebels against the centre seem to have exercised control over the centrifugal elements in periods of collapse and change. However, in the middle of the sixteenth century the little kings of Orissa were not yet directly parts of a system of ritual division of labour in the Jagannath cult; this would only happen under the later *rājās* of Khurda.[31]

3.4 Past 1568: Orissa under the Muslims, the Marathas and the British

Following the destruction of the Gajapati empire by the Afghans in 1568, and in the wake of the Mughals' assumption of power a short time afterwards, the most fertile parts of the central Orissan coast and the Mahanadi delta became directly subject to Mughal rule as so-called *moghulbandi* estates. The regents of over a hundred little kingdoms and estates in the hinterland of the region were given self-governing status, which guaranteed them great internal autonomy and relative independence with respect to the powerful Mughal governor (*subahdār*) in Cuttack, in return for nominal recognition of the overlordship of Akbar in distant Delhi and the regular payment of tribute. Towards the end of the sixteenth century, however, most of the little kingdoms lost the privilege of self-government. Only the most important and largest of them, like Khurda, Mayurbhanj, Keonjhar and Sambalpur, were able to retain their semi-independent status, while the *gaḍajāta* states of the hinterland were distributed among these greater kingdoms as fiefs. Ramachandra Deo, whose hereditary territory around Khurda alone measured 1,350 square miles, was able to increase the dominon he controlled tenfold through such enfeoffments with about thirty *gaḍajāta* kingdoms and neighbouring

[31] More detailed information on the history of the Gajapati kingdom under the Suryavamshis can be found in Berkemer (1993, 192-219), Kulke (1978a, 204-8; 1979a, 70-9), Mukherjee (1953, 25-47), Panda (1986, 132-9), Ramachandra Rao (1976) and Subrahmanyam (1957, Chs. 3-6).

estates.[32] Ramachandra's position as Gajapati, which hė had already acquired earlier through his role as Jagannath's highest patron, was thus also strengthened vis-à-vis other *rājā*s of the region both economically and territorially. In addition, Akbar raised him to the privileged status of *mansabdār* and thus gave him precedence over the other kings of the region. All in all, therefore, in the sixteenth century Orissa's Gajapatis changed from being transregional *mahārājādhirāja*s, first, into local little kings, and then into sub-regional *mahārāja*s. Certainly, they were now the respected overlords of their own *sāmantacakra*s, but in contrast to earlier times they themselves were subject to the rulers of a still greater galaxy. Furthermore, they had to tolerate other *sāmantaçakra*s of the same type in north and west Orissa, as well as influential Mughal governors in Cuttack, who were constantly trying to extend their own power.

In the seventeenth century, the battle for power between Khurda, other important Orissan dynasties and the Mughal *subahdār*s took the form of a struggle over who had precedence in the Jagannath cult. As we saw in the previous section, the *rājā*s of Khurda had been able to win this position for themselves early on, though in the period that followed they had to watch the rulers of Mayurbhanj, Keonjhar, Sambalpur, Parlakimedi and other Orissan kingdoms establish Jagannath cults of their own in their residences. In addition, Mughal governors and generals repeatedly intervened violently in the affairs of the temple. Nonetheless, by the second half of the seventeenth century the *rājā*s of Khurda succeeded in regaining the exalted position that the powerful Gajapatis of the Ganga and Suryavamsha dynasties once had. Despite their relatively small hereditary possessions, the Gajapatis of the seventeenth century assumed a position so similar to that of the imperial Gajapatis that a Mughal general described his adversary, Gajapati Mukunda Deo (1659–1689), as a ruler 'whom all the other zamindars of the country worship like a god and disobedience of whose orders they regard as a great sin'.[33]

[32] Among the most important *gaḍajāta* kingdoms that Khurda received as fiefs were Angul, Athagada, Banki, Banpur, Baramba, Baudh, Daspalla, Dhenkanal, Dompara, Hindul, Khandpara, Nayagarh, Narsinghpur, Ranpur, Talcher and Tigeria. From south Orissa probably came Athgarh, Khallikot, Ghumsur and Tekkali, although the status of these little kingdoms, which lay in the galaxy of the Sultan of Golkonda, is unclear. Slightly differing lists of *gaḍajāta* kingdoms under Khurda are found in Motte's travel report of 1766 (Motte 1953) and in Stirling (1904 [1822]). See also Map 4.

[33] Quoted in Kulke (1979a, 155). On the ideas in the previous two paragraphs, see Berkemer (1993, 220-6), Kulke (1979a, 104-17) and Sarkar (1916).

During the decline of Mughal rule, up to the beginning of the eighteenth century, as well as in the period which followed, under the Bengali *nawābs* and Marathas, Khurda was again gradually reduced to the status of a little kingdom. In the period following Akbar, which was one of less religious tolerance, the Gajapatis fell increasingly under the direct control of the Mughal *subahdārs* in Cuttack. Around 1730 Khurda's fiefs south of the Chilika Lake went to the *nizām* of Hyderabad. Simultaneously, the Muslim *nawābs* of Bengal, who controlled central and north Orissa in the 1730s and 1740s, subjected the Gajapatis to a more direct form of control. In 1760 the Marathas, who had come to power in 1751, abolished Khurda's feudal power over the *gaḍajāta* kingdoms and also subjected the temple administration in Puri to their own supervision. Thus, the central kingdom of Orissa, towards which the other little kingdoms of the region had oriented themselves for about 170 years, was very much reduced in terms of territorial power and ritual status by the middle of the eighteenth century. It now also had to face the powerful dynasties of the Chauhans, who ruled Sambalpur and Sonpur in west Orissa, and the Bhanjas, who controlled Keonjhar and Mayurbhanj in north Orissa as well as the powerful jungle kingdom of Ghumsur in southwest Orissa. Moreover, in the intervening period the smaller *gaḍajāta* princes of the hinterland had also entrenched themselves in newly built, stronger, mountain fortresses and had thus also gained in independence vis-à-vis the Gajapatis.[34] With the lifting of their status as Khurda's fiefs by the Marathas, the increased autonomy of these *gaḍajāta* kingdoms received appropriate expression.[35]

In the two decades before the Marathas came to power, the Gajapatis no longer sought to defend their 'galactic' sovereignty over the surrounding little kingdoms by declaring rebel kings to be enemies of Jagannath and threatening them with the god's anger, as the Gangas and Suryavamshis had done. To bind the little kings of Orissa more firmly to themselves they endowed them with privileges within the Jagannath cult, which they could enjoy during their visits to Puri. This 'diplomacy in the original sense of the word' (Kulke 1979a, 199) is historically documented by a number of royal letters (*chāmu ciṭāus*) to the highest temple supervisor (*baḍa parīkṣa*) of Puri. In these letters the Gajapati announces the

[34] Thus, Khurda's attempt to annex the little kingdom of Banki in 1728-9 did not succeed, which ended all further attempts by the Gajapatis to expand their state at the cost of neighbouring little kingdoms. See Kulke (1979a, 185).

[35] See Kulke (1979a, 141-68; 180-215) and Wink (1986, 107-15).

visit of each little king, gives detailed information about the intended gifts (consisting mostly of cloth, money and food) to be made by these individuals to the temple, and lays down exactly the counter-gifts they should receive from Jagannath and the rights (*ādhi*s) and privileges (*upādhi*s) they should be granted upon visiting the temple.[36]

For example, the *rājā* of Banki, was granted the hereditary privilege of entering the temple of Jagannath with the status and honour of a temple supervisor in a diploma of 1746. The priests were instructed that during his visit the entire temple should be 'cleansed' (*śodhā*) of other pilgrims, a fan with a golden handle should be provided for the 'fanning service' (*cāmara-sevā*) in front of the effigy, and a turban (*śāṛhi*) formerly worn by Jagannath should be tied round the head of the *rājā* afterwards. Other presents that the *rājā* and his family should be given from the temple treasury after the *pūjā* for Jagannath were also listed. In a letter of 1736, the *rājā* of Athgarh,[37] whose family had repeatedly given refuge to Gajapatis fleeing from Muslim armies in earlier decades, was granted the privileges of driving up to the temple in a carriage and, when doing so, of wearing a turban decorated with a silver elephant. In addition, the letter promised that he would be presented a symbol of royalty which till then had been almost monopolistically associated with the imperial Gajapati honour—an elephant. Furthermore, the Gajapati grants this *rājā* the freedom to conduct the worship of Jagannath with presents for the god that the *rājā* could select freely. However, the exhortation that 'You shall remain ever loyal at our feet with care' (quoted in Kulke 1979a, 203) is not forgotten. One year later, the *rājā* also received the right to have a drum beaten and a particular flag carried when riding out on the elephant.

[36] The *chāmu ciṭāu* diplomas, written on palm leaves, date from between 1654 and 1913. Information on the archiving of these letters can be found in Kulke (1987, 149-54). The greatest part of the royal orders were written between 1730 and 1750 by Ramachandra II and his son Virakeshari, that is, in the two decades before the Marathas seized power. Those they are addressed to are largely identical with the rulers of those little kingdoms that were granted to Khurda as fiefs by Akbar, so that, as Kulke emphasizes, 'these ritual relationships also corresponded geographically with the political structure of power in Orissa' (1979a, 200). Evaluations of the letters can be found in Kulke (1978d, 338-42; 1979a, 197-204; 1984a, 145-7; 1992), and, as regards south Orissa, in Berkemer (1993, 250-1). A collection of the letters, edited by Dash and Kulke, is in preparation.

[37] Here I am using the alternative, anglicized spelling 'Athgarh', in order to distinguish this kingdom in the north-west of Ganjam District from the identically named kingdom of Athagada in central Orissa.

In addition, he was named supervisor of the Jagannath temple, receiving a house and estates in Puri as a reward. In letters of a somewhat different nature, granting duties rather than privileges, the *rājās* of Athgarh, Banpur, Daspalla, Dhenkanal, Ghumsur and Ranpur are asked to supply wood, iron and ropes for the vehicle that carries the effigies of the gods at Jagannath's car festival (*ratha yātrā*). Virakeshari also specifies the type, quality and number of gifts from the temple treasury or of food offerings (*mahāprasāda*) that the *rājās* are owed as recompense for their services.[38]

Thus, in the first half of the eighteenth century, the Gajapati's hitherto monopolistic hold on the Jagannath cult was loosened. Yet, he did not lose his supreme position in Puri. By allowing other little kings greater participation in Jagannath's cult, he granted them a limited share of his own authority. However, by establishing a ritual division of labour which admitted other kings as subordinate members and servants in the cult, the Gajapati, as the 'first servant' (*ādya sevaka*) of the god, succeeded in constituting an 'incorporative' kingdom shaped by hierarchical solidarity; a 'sacred network' of political integration was created.[39]

The examples quoted make it clear that the granting of minutely specified ritual privileges and obligations not only secured the over-lordship of the Gajapatis; it also established internal differences in rank among the little kings by arrangements graded in the smallest ritual detail. Should the handle of the fan provided for the *cāmara* service be made of gold, silver or cotton? Should a royal visitor leave the various insignia of his royal status, such as his litter or his sword, at the main entrance to the temple or only in the vestibule? Was he allowed to carry out the 'sword and dagger service' (*churi-kaṇḍa-sevā*)? Where exactly should the viewing (*darśana*) and worship of Jagannath take place? What should be the quality of the cloth taken from the temple treasury as a counter-gift? Had the cloth been touched earlier by Jagannath? Had it served as a temple banner? All these and a number of other small ritual differences that were endowed with great significance threw light on (and determined) the prestige and status of the kings who visited Puri.

In this period of Orissa's history, we, then, find a *sāmantacakra* which was constituted, and expressed itself, ritually in the idiom of the practices

[38] On these points, see Kulke (1979a, 199-203).

[39] The 'network theory' of sacred places was first put forward in research on India by Cohn and Marriott (1958) and then developed for south India by Appadurai (1977), Preston (1980b) and Spencer (1969) before Kulke (1984a) also used it for Orissa with reference to the *chāmu ciṭāu* diplomacy of the Gajapatis.

and symbols of the Jagannath cult. At the centre of this circle of kings stood the Khurda *rājā*s, while its other components were formed by little kings of differing 'greatness' and prestige. Among the little kings, who consisted mostly of the 'castle-dwellers' of central Orissa, there were internal differences of rank in which the *rājā*s of Athgarh, Banki and Khandpara held more dominant positions. In remoter orbits (in the sense of structural distance) were kingdoms which were politically independent of Khurda and themselves partly superordinate over other kingdoms or even possessed their own *sāmantacakra*s. These kingdoms, amongst whom the important were Mayurbhanj, Keonjhar and Sambalpur in north, central and west Orissa as well as Parlakimedi and Jeypore in south Orissa, were effectively independent of the Gajapatis from 1568, being 'little' only in relation to the changing Muslim overlords and to the Marathas. Even ritually, being patrons of their own Jagannath cults, their rulers only oriented themselves to the Gajapatis to a limited extent, although the attraction that Puri exerted as the sacred abode (*kśetra*) of the wooden god never quite faded.[40]

Under the British, the overall situation changed yet again. Mukunda Deo II, who had come to power in 1799 as Gajapati, initially supported the East India Company in their fight against the Marathas, no doubt in the hope that the *gaḍajāta* kingdoms of central Orissa, taken away from him by the Marathas, would be transferred back to him as fiefs. Following the seizure of power by the British in 1803, this expectation was quickly destroyed for in the very same year eleven of the little kingdoms of the hinterland were accorded the status of 'feudatory states' or 'princely

[40] From time to time additional strategies of legitimation were used in order to enhance the status of one's own cult in relation to Puri. Thus, for example, the Parlakimedi *rājā*s of the period claimed that the original *brahmapadārtha* part was embodied in their effigy of Jagannath. For this reason and by virtue of dynastic claims linking them genealogically with the Gangas, they regarded themselves as the legitimate successors of the imperial Gajapatis and the actual patrons of the Jagannath cult. In 1753, Jagannath Narayana Deo, the *rājā* of Parlakimedi, supported by some 2,000 soldiers, is said to have climbed to the top of Jagannath's car at the *ratha yātrā* festival. His attempt to carry out the *cherā pāhamrā* ritual and thus declare himself Gajapati failed only because of the opposition of the priests. In 1759, the warriors of Parlakimedi took Khurda from Virakeshari, who fled to the Marathas in Cuttack, though the former were prevented from marching to Puri by the combined efforts of Virakeshari and the Marathas. See Berkemer (1993, 201-2; 306-9), Kulke (1979a, 210; 1987, 152) and Rajaguru (1968-72 [vol. 2], 116-18).

states', which granted them a relatively large degree of freedom from the British in their internal affairs and complete independence from the Gajapatis. The proclamation of other little kingdoms as 'feudatory states' followed quickly. The obligations the *rājā*s entered into with the British, namely to ensure 'peace and tranquillity' in their regions, to preserve 'perpetual friendship and loyalty' to the East India Company, to make regular payments of tribute, to guard the mountain passes leading to the valleys against penetration by hostile forces and, if necessary, to provide troops, reflect a catalogue of political, economic and military obligations which had already determined the relationship of the *gaḍajāta* kingdoms to the Gajapatis in earlier centuries.[41]

During a 'rebellion' in 1804 by Mukunda against the new colonial power, the fortress of Khurda was taken by the British and destroyed. The victors then confiscated the remaining territorial possessions of the Gajapatis and imprisoned Mukunda outside Orissa. Following his reinstatement as 'superintendent' of the temple in 1809, the Gajapati found himself as a king without any little kingdoms subject to him and even without any territorial possessions of his own: all that remained was his ritual position in the cult of Puri. In this period of political, military and economic powerlessness, Mukunda fell back on the practices of the Gajapatis from the heyday of the Orissa empire and reasserted the predominance of the Gajapatis in the Jagannath cult. Thus, for example, on their visits to Puri the *rājā*s of Parlakimedi, Khandpara and Sambalpur learned that access to the Jagannath temple had been refused them at the behest of the *rājā* of Puri and that they had been deprived of their hereditary ritual privileges in the worship of the god. Only the intervention of the British 'collector', the local representative of the new galactic centre around whom the little kingdoms of Orissa were now arranged, could slow down any further monopolization of the cult by the

[41] The 'princely states' of Orissa consisted mainly of the *gaḍajāta* kingdoms of central Orissa and the important kingdoms of north and west Orissa that were independent of Khurda, i.e., Angul, Banki, Athagada, Athmalik, Baud, Baramba, Daspalla, Dhenkanal, Hindul, Khandpara, Keonjhar, Mayurbhanj, Narsinghpur, Nayagarh, Nilgiri, Talcher, Tigeria and Ranpur. On the history of these kingdoms under the British, see Aitchison (1930, vol. 1), Cobden-Ramsay (1982), S.C. Padhi (1986), J. Patnaik (1988) and Samal (1988). Individual kingdoms or aspects of their history and political organization are dealt with by L.K. Mahapatra (1987), Mazumdar (1925), O'Malley (1908) and H.C. Panda (1985), as well as in *Feudatory and Tributary States* (1907) and *Twenty-five Questions* (1861).

Gajapati, who, it will be remembered, in this period was moving towards becoming the personal incarnation of Jagannath.[42]

4. The little kingdoms of south Orissa

In the two sections that bring this chapter to a close, I would like to provide a brief sketch of the little kingdoms of south Orissa and their ruling dynasties. By south Orissa I mean the sub-region in the south and southwest of the federal state of Orissa occupied in modern times by Ganjam and Koraput Districts. To begin with, I shall devote my attention to the little kingdoms of Ganjam, while the kingdom of Jeypore, corresponded broadly to the Koraput District, will be introduced in the next section as a paradigmatic jungle kingdom.

As already mentioned, between 1568 and the end of the sixteenth century, the little kingdoms of south Orissa gradually came under the sway of other overlords and their galaxies. Initially, they became subject to the sultans of Golkonda and their successors, the *nizāms* of Hyderabad, whose sovereignty and tributary powers on the coast of northern Andhra Pradesh were exercised by relatively autonomous governors (*sābahdārs*, *faujdārs*).[43] These Muslim governors also appointed some of the warrior princes they found in their baggage train as little kings and made them responsible for the collection of tribute from other *rājās* in their sub-region.[44] In the eighteenth century first the French and then, from 1766, British officials who ruled from the coast became the leading powers in the sub-region. In this period the kingdoms of south Orissa became administrative units of the Northern Circars, the northernmost administrative district of the Madras Presidency, while those of central and north Orissa were assigned to the Bengal Presidency and those of west Orissa to the Central Provinces. Despite this political, military and administrative separation of the little kingdoms of south Orissa from the rest of Orissa, the Gajapatis and Jagannath continued to draw them into their 'orbit', at

[42] On the *chāmu ciṭāu* diplomacy of the Gajapatis in this period, see Kulke (1978e, 350-2; 1979a, 216-18; 1992, 62-5).

[43] On the conquest of south Orissa by the sultans of Golkonda, see Kulke (1979a, 94-8).

[44] For example, the kingdom of the Pusapatis of Vizianagaram which, along with Jeypore and Parlakimedi, had a leading position among the kingdoms of south Orissa and north Andhra, originated towards the end of the sixteenth century. See Berkemer (1993, 227-316).

least on the cultural, ideological and ritual levels.[45] The attempts of many Oriya-speaking little kings of south Orissa, at the beginning of the twentieth century, to separate their kingdoms from the Madras Presidency and to align them with the administrative and linguistic province of Orissa that was being created at the time clearly shows their lasting orientation towards the north. These efforts were crowned with success in 1936, the founding date of the modern federal state of Orissa.[46]

This short glimpse of the history of south Orissa must suffice here.[47] Let me now give a brief summary of the most important statistical and historical data regarding the different little kingdoms of south Orissa, in order to provide an overview. We shall follow Map 5 and proceed from north to south.[48]

a) The kingdom of Khallikot formed the northernmost border of Ganjam. It is recorded as having an area of 238 square miles and around 350 villages, including 38 *inām* villages.[49] The yearly tributary payments (*peśkaś*) owed by the kings of Khallikot to the British, fixed at the start of

[45] On this, see also Berkemer (1993, 216-38; 250-1).

[46] On the history of the creation of the federal state of Orissa, see Berkemer (1993, 105-6), Padhi (1985, 277-304) and Patro (1981).

[47] The history of south Orissa is discussed by Das (1985), Maclean (ed. 1987, 64; 71-8), Maltby (1918, Chs. V, VI, VII) and Misra (1980). Scattered information can also be found in various works on the Gajapatis and their adversaries in the south which have already received mention in previous sections, for example, Berkemer (1993) and Subrahmanyam (1957, 315-22). Thousands of historical documents on the history of south Orissa, which still require systematic evaluation, can be found in the state archives of Orissa in Bhubaneswar, of Tamil Nadu in Madras, and of Andhra Pradesh in Hyderabad, catalogued respectively as *Ganjam District Records (New Series), Ganjam District Records (Old Series)* and *Vizagapatam District Records.*

[48] For the information that follows, I am drawing mainly on Behuria (ed. 1964). The historical frame of reference is the period from the 'permanent settlement' in 1802 to the absorption of the kingdoms by the governments of Orissa and, in some cases, Andhra Pradesh around 1950. The data available in Maclean (ed. 1982), Maltby (1918) and Taylor (1862, 144) are only given where they deviate considerably from Behuria's. Overall, I am concerned less with statistical exactitude, which can hardly be achieved anyway, than with using the figures to indicate the relative size of the different little kingdoms of south Orissa.

[49] *Inām*s are tax-free or tax-reduced estates, possession of which required the exercise of administrative, police, religious or other duties.

the nineteenth century in the course of the so-called 'permanent settlement', amounted to 18,482 rupees. Khallikot was divided into three *muṭṭhā*s or sub-divisions. In their family chronicle the royal family traces its origins back to a certain Rama Buya, who is said to have cleared and settled the jungle for which Gajapati Purushottama Deo appointed him governor of the area. Later, the *rājā* of Khallikot was given the title 'Mardaraja Deo' by the Gajapatis, in recognition of his having kept the Marathas out of the district.[50]

b) Athgarh, in the mountains west of Khallikot, had an area of 293 square miles and almost 300 villages including 71 in the *inām* category. The yearly taxes amounted to 59,919 rupees. The kingdom was divided into three *muṭṭhā*s. The founder of the old and established Athgarh royal family is said to have been a hermit called Jagga Daso. In 1854 the British auctioned off Athgarh to the *rājā* of Khallikot because of its tax arrears.[51]

c) Biridi, on Lake Chilika and bordering Khallikot, had an area of about 60 square miles and 83 villages of which 12 were of the *inām* type. Its yearly tributary payment was 4,275 rupees. Purushottama is said to have placed the territory under the control of one of his generals (*sirdār*s), named Balaram Sur, in 1489.[52]

d) Like Biridi, the kingdom of Palur lay on Lake Chilika. With only 29 square miles, it was one of the smallest of all the little kingdoms of south Orissa. Of its 20 villages, 4 were *inām*. The taxes amounted to 18 rupees. This territory is said to have been awarded to one of Purushottama's military commanders in 1489, a man called Darasathi Sur.[53]

e) With 6.5 square miles and 8 villages, two of them *inām* villages, Humma was the smallest little kingdom in Ganjam. Its taxes came to 637 rupees. Humma is said to have lain in the middle of an impenetrable jungle, the refuge of raiders and thieves. In order to give protection to the

[50] On Khallikot, see Behuria (ed. 1964, 74), Maclean (ed. 1982, 246), Maltby (1918, 16), Pattnaik (1982), Subrahmanyam (1957, 190) and Vadivelu (1984, 98-124).

[51] On Athgarh, which we have already encountered in earlier sections as the refuge of the Gajaptis when faced with Muslim incursions, see Behuria (ed. 1964, 74-5), Maclean (ed. 1982, 46), Maltby (1918, 16-17) and Subrahmanyam (1957, 190-1).

[52] See Behuria (ed. 1964, 76), Maclean (ed. 1982, 97) and Maltby (1918, 17-18).

[53] On Palur, see Behuria (ed. 1964, 76), Maltby (1918, 18) and Subrahmanyam (1957, 187).

population and to travellers, Gajapati Kapilendra Deo is said to have installed one Madana Mohana over the territory as *sāmanta rājā*.[54]

f) With an area of 1,350 square miles of which some 500 were in the hills (*māliahs*), Ghumsur in northwest Ganjam was one of the largest kingdoms in Ganjam. The kingdom had some 800 villages, which were administered by being divided among 18 valley and 24 hill or jungle *muṭṭhās*. In 1836 Ghumsur was annexed by the British who, after heavy fighting, removed the royal house which had ruled for over 850 years, from power. Yearly taxes amounted to 65,000 rupees.[55]

g) Aska was dissolved by the Mughals at the beginning of the seventeenth century and divided among the kingdoms of Ghumsur, Dharakot and Athgarh. There is no information on the size of its territory. Under British administration taxes amounted to 8,449 rupees.[56]

h) The kingdom of Mohuri, with 521 square miles of territory, lay mainly in the coastal region of central Ganjam though it also possessed 20 square miles of territory in the Kerandi Hills, foothills of the Eastern Ghats. Mohuri had 410 villages, including 65 *ināms*, and its tribute amounted to 60,000 rupees. The royal family traced its origin back to a general or *sirdār* called Somaraja, who was granted the territory by Purushottama Deo as reward for his success in a campaign. The British annexed Mohuri in 1844 after it had fallen into arrears and 'rebelled'.[57]

i) The kingdom of Dharakot, east of Ghumsur and north of Aska in the valley of the Rushikulya river, had a territory of 125 square miles with 207 villages of which 42 were *inām* villages. The kingdom was divided into three *muṭṭhās* and the yearly taxes amounted to 23,470 rupees. Originally Dharakot, together with Surada, Bodogoda and Sheragada, formed part of the kingdom of Khidisingi which, however, was divided between

[54] See Behuria (ed. 1964, 76), Maltby (1918, 18) and Subrahmanyam (1957, 187).

[55] See Behuria (ed. 1964, 73), Maclean (ed. 1982, 323-4) and Maltby (1918, 15). On the history of Ghumsur, see also Behera (1984 and 1987), *Reports on the Disturbances in the Zamindary of Goomsoor* (1836-7, vol. 2), Russell (1856, vol. 2), Stevenson (1916) and W. Taylor (1838). The situation in the Ghumsur *māliahs* is described in H.D. Taylor (no date, 22-7; 120-6)

[56] See Behuria (ed. 1964, 73; 82-3), Maclean (ed. 1982, 46) and Maltby (1918, 15; 28).

[57] Maltby's information (1918, 9) relates to the *tāluk* of Berhampur, an administrative unit which somewhat larger than the kingdom of Mohuri. On the history of Mohuri, see also Das (1978).

brothers in 1476 and fell apart into the kingdoms already mentioned. Surada later became a part of Ghumsur.[58]

j) The area of the kingdom of Bodogoda, west of Dharakot at the foot of the Eastern Ghats, was mostly hilly and covered with jungle. It occupied 167 square miles with 143 villages, including 16 of *inām* type, divided between three *muṭṭhās*. Taxes amounted to 3,770 rupees. Attached to the kingdom were roughly the 300 square miles of the Bodogoda *māliahs* or hill territories.[59]

k) The kingdom of Sheragada, southeast of Dharakot, was small in area but endowed with fertile land. It had an area of 29 square miles and 29 villages, ten of them in the *inām* category. Tribute payments came to 4,950 rupees.[60]

l) Sanakimedi, also known as Pratapagiri or Cinnakimedi, was the smallest of the Kimedi kingdoms found in south and central Ganjam. Lying to the west of Mohuri, it had an area of 180 square miles and its 180 villages, including 51 *ināms*, were divided among five *muṭṭhās*. The kingdom paid 19,104 rupees tribute. Sanakimedi traced its origin back to its separation from Badakimedi in 1776, when two hostile brothers, Moni and Jagannath Deo, went their different ways. The Sanakimedi *māliahs* attached to it embraced some 1,975 square miles; they were annexed by the British in the middle of the nineteenth century.[61]

m) Badakimedi, also known as Vijayanagaram or Peddakimedi, lying southwest of Sanakimedi, had an area of about 224 square miles and 228 villages, 50 of them in the *inām* category, divided between four *muṭṭhās*. Taxes amounted to 22,464 rupees. In 1607 the *rājā* of Parlakimedi gave the area, which later split into Bada ('great') and Sana ('little') Kimedi, to a younger son, the oldest retaining the hereditary territory of Parlakimedi. The Badakimedi *māliahs*, with an area of 377 square miles, were administered by the *rājā* of Badakimedi.[62]

[58] See Behuria (ed. 1964, 77), Maclean (ed. 1982, 269-70) and Maltby (1918, 18).

[59] See Behuria (ed. 1964, 78), Maclean (ed. 1982, 99-100) and Maltby (1918, 19). The Bodogoda *māliahs* are described in Taylor (no date, 20-1; 110-19).

[60] See Behuria (ed. 1964, 78). Maclean (ed. 1982, 821) and Maltby (1918, 19) mention amounts of 5,555 and 5,822 rupees respectively.

[61] See Behuria (ed. 1964, 78-9), Maclean (ed. 1982, 173) and Maltby (1918, 19-20). The Sanakimedi *māliahs* are described in Taylor (no date, 8-18; 90-108).

[62] See Behuria (ed. 1964, 79-80), Maclean (ed. 1982, 672) and Maltby (1918, 20-1). The Badakimedi *māliahs* are described in Taylor (no date, 30-5; 128-63).

n) Chikiti, to the east of Badakimedi, had an area of 110 square miles consisting of open, well-watered country. The 151 villages of this kingdom, including 27 *ināms*, were divided between six *muṭṭhās*. The yearly taxes came to 30,045 rupees. According to tradition, one of the Gajapatis granted the territory to a *sirdār* named Kasano, after he had conquered it from the *ādivāsis*, settled there and erected a fort.[63]

o) Surangi, a kingdom lying south of Badakimedi and Chikiti, had an area of about 82 square miles and 129 villages, of which 12 were *inām* in type. The taxes came to 3,628 rupees. The inaccessibility of the country enabled the kingdom to function, into the period of British rule, as a refuge for what Maltby called 'evil-doers'. The Surangi *māliahs* bordered the kingdom on the west.[64]

p) East of Surangi lay the little kingdom of Jarada, which had a hilly, jungle-covered territory 48 square miles in area. Seven of its 59 villages were *ināms* and the taxes it owed the British amounted to 1,951 rupees. The kingdom is said to have been founded in 1449 by one Veera Bhadra Singh, after he had succeeded in conquering the local *ādivāsis*.[65]

q) Parlakimedi, the largest and most important kingdom in the south of Ganjam, had over 639 square miles of territory with more than 500 villages divided among 24 *muṭṭhās*. Its taxes came to 87,825 rupees. After the founding of Orissa in 1936, the area remaining in Ganjam consisted of 201 square miles containing 248 villages, including 60 *ināms*. Taxes amounted to 38,371 rupees. Attached to the kingdom were the Parlakimedi *māliahs*, with an area of 354 square miles. The Parlakimedi *mahārājas* regard themselves, till today, as the descendants of the imperial Gangas.[66]

[63] See Behuria (ed. 1964, 80), Maclean (ed. 1982, 161; ed. 1987, 60) and Maltby (1918, 21).

[64] See Behuria (ed. 1964, 80-1), Maclean (ed. 1982, 382) and Maltby (1918, 21-2). The Surangi *māliahs* are described in Taylor (no date, 36; 174-5).

[65] See Behuria (ed. 1964, 81) and Maltby (1918, 22). On the Jarada *māliahs*, see Taylor (no date, 38; 180).

[66] On Parlakimedi, see Behuria (ed. 1964, 81-2), Berkemer (1993, 200-2), Maclean (ed. 1982, 417; ed. 1987, 60), Maltby (1918, 25-8), Rajaguru (1968-72, vol. II), N. Patro (1981), P.S.N. Patro (1981), Rao (1928), Russell (1856, vol. I) and Trikhy (1989, 126-47). The Parlakimedi *māliahs* are described in Taylor (no date, 39; 184-252).

r) Jalantra, a kingdom bordering Jarada and Chikiti, had an area of barely 100 square miles and 78 villages, with taxes amounting to 7,384 rupees. It is said to have been founded by Purushottama Deo. According to local tradition, after he had conquered the Soras, tribal aborigines of the jungle area around Mount Mahendra, he installed his son Govinda Chetroy Deo as *rājā* over the territory.[67]

s) Butrasingi, a little kingdom at the foot of Mount Mahendra, south of Jalantra, had hilly territory, known to be unhealthy, of about 22 square miles. Yearly taxes amounted to 525 rupees. The founder of the Butrasingi ruling family is said to have been a Sora chief named Damodra Nissunko.[68]

t) The kingdom of Mandasa, which lay at Mahendragiri and south of Butrasingi, had an area of 132 square miles and 166 villages. A part of the territory lay within the *māliahs*. The yearly taxes came to 14,035 rupees. The founder of the royal family is supposed to have come to Mandasa from the Punjab following a vision.[69]

u) Tarla, south of Mandasa and west of Parlakimedi, was some 52 square miles in area; its taxes amounted to 4,000 rupees. The founder of the royal family is said to have been a member of Purushottama's army.[70]

v) Tekkali was the southernmost of the kingdoms of the old Ganjam District before the founding of the federal state of Orissa in 1936. The ruling dynasty, which originated at the time of the first Suryavamsha Gajapatis, came to an end when the last *rājā* died without a successor and a branch of the family of the *rājā*s of Athgarh took over the estate.[71]

The five last-named kingdoms were allocated to Andhra Pradesh in 1936, where they now form part of Srikakulam District.

The data presented so far allow us to make some generalizations about the little kingdoms of south Orissa. For example, many of the ruling houses mentioned here trace their origins back to the middle or end of the fifteenth century. According to local traditions, their founders were military officers in the armies of Kapilendra and Purushottama, who were

[67] See Maclean (ed. 1982, 378) and Maltby (1918, 22).

[68] See Maltby (1918, 22-3). Maclean (ed. 1982, 101) records an area of 43 square miles. The Budrasingi *maliah*s are described in Taylor (no date, 37, 178-9).

[69] See Berkemer (1993, 206-7), Maclean (ed. 9182, 524) and Maltby (1918, 23). The Mandasa *māliah*s are described in Taylor (no date, 37; 177).

[70] See Maclean (ed. 1982, 878) and Maltby (1918, 23).

[71] See Berkemer (1997), Maltby (1918, 15) and *Tekkali* (no date).

appointed by one of these two Suryavamsha Gajapatis during or after a campaign.[72] Their initial military function also finds expression in the fact that the names of many of these kingdoms ended in 'fortress' or 'fort' (*gaḍa, garh, goda, kot*)[73] and that they were often located at strategically important points such as a river crossing, a pass through the Ghats or an isthmus.[74] If one envisages the military situation at the time of the first Suryavamsha Gajapatis, it becomes clear that during their repeated campaigns in the direction of the southern Krishna–Godavari delta Kapilendra and Purushottama wanted to march as far as possible through areas controlled by loyal followers. From these the Gajapatis expected not only passive loyalty and securing of the route, but in many cases they were also obliged to take part personally in the campaigns and to provide soldiers, provisions and equipment. These little-kingly dynasties, founded by the Suryavamshis, therefore, were initially bastions founded by military vassals.

The emphasis laid in some chronicles on the heroic clearing of the jungle by the founders of these dynasties makes us assume that, right from the start, these individuals strove to base their rule within their territory less on robbery and exploitation than on the regular siphoning off of an agricultural surplus and the setting up of an everyday kind of administration. Maltby also remarks in this context that these little kings were granted their land by the Gajapatis 'on the condition of ... keeping in check the wild aboriginal tribes of the hills' (1918, 15). It can be gathered from this observation that the Gajapatis sought to do more than just establish military vassals to secure routes and provide military aid. The installation of local governors, whose task was also to develop agriculture and trade within their territory and to protect the population from tribals and marauding raiders, indicates that the Gajapatis closely linked their attempts to expand their empire militarily with its pacification and internal colonization.

[72] For example, the founders of the little kingdoms of Khallikot, Biridi, Palur, Humma, Mohuri, Chikiti, Jalantra and Tarla. See also Berkemer (1993, 192-208, 325).

[73] For example, Khallikot, Athgarh, Dharakot, Bodogoda, Shergada.

[74] For example, in the south the kingdoms of Jalantra, Butrasingi and Mandasa were located on the Mahendragiri isthmus, while in the north Khallikot, Biridi, Palur and Humma lay on Lake Chilika and at the Khallikot Ghat, which separates south from central Orissa.

However, the fact that many of the ruling dynasties listed above trace their foundation back to the time of the first Suryavamsha Gajapatis does not mean that the kingdoms themselves were founded in this period. In most cases it was merely a dynastic change that took place in the wake of the replacement of the imperial Gangas by the Suryavamshis. In this first period of Suryavamsha rule, also, the new rulers were less kings than military officials and governors subordinate to the Gajapatis, whose houses only succeeded in converting dependent rule into autonomous royal authority after a number of generations in power. The disappearance of the central Gajapati power in the sixteenth century decisively furthered this development. *Sirdār*s thus became *rājā*s after several decades—in other words, military commanders became little kings. This recalls the process of the '*nāyaka*-ization of little-kingly domains', instituted by the early Suryavamshis, and the process of the 'royalization of the administration' that developed soon afterwards.

Among the royal houses of south Orissa listed here, there are also many whose origins are not explicitly linked with installation or recognition by the Suryavamshis. Although we cannot here go into the question of the origin of south Orissan royal houses case by case, the data presented hitherto nevertheless allow a general distinction to be made between those little kingdoms that were installed by the Suryavamshis and those that were not. It can be seen that the territories of the first group were situated on the coast and that they directly controlled the important north-south route between central Orissa and north Andhra Pradesh. To the second group, on the other hand, belong those dynasties whose territories lay, at least in part, in the mountainous, jungle-covered hinterland of the Eastern Ghats: Athgarh, Ghumsur, Dharakot, Bodogoda, Sheragada, Sanakimedi, Badakimedi, Surangi, Jarada, Parlakimedi, Butrasingi and Mandasa.

The focus of the present work is the last-named group of kingdoms, which I characterize with the term 'jungle kingdom' in order to distinguish them from the little kingdoms of the coast. The intention in making this distinction is not to create a rigid and hence artificial break with the little kingdoms of the coast of Ganjam, since the common features between the two are too many and the transition between them too gradual.[75] However, south Orissan kingdoms in the hinterland are

[75] Thus, on the coast too there were forests, bamboo jungles and chains of hills offering refuge, and most of the little kings on the coast possessed well-concealed forts, not far from their residences, that were difficult of access.

characterized by a number of peculiarities, which makes it necessary to establish the jungle kingdom as a specific sub-category of the little kingdom and to examine it separately.

My use of the epithet 'jungle' is also intended to draw attention to a gap in research on little kingdoms and to bring a sub-category of the little kingdom into the discussion. By doing so, I am aware that the metaphor of the jungle may lead to 'orientalisms' of all sorts; indeed, that it formed for a long time, as Inden has shown (1990, Ch. 3), one of the key metaphors in the hegemonic Western discourse on India. In the next section, therefore, in which I present important data concerning the little kingdom of Jeypore as a paradigm of the jungle kingdom, it will also be my concern to provide the concept of the jungle with content, and to show that it fundamentally belonged to the political ideology and religious world of India itself.

5. Jeypore: paradigm of a jungle kingdom

The territory of the kingdom of Jeypore[76] was almost identical with the area occupied in modern times by the district of Koraput in south-west Orissa. With an area of about 10,000 square miles, Jeypore was the largest of all the little kingdoms of south Orissa, and was only matched by Parlakimedi in political significance. In the 'permanent settlement' of 1803, Jeypore's tribute was set at 16,000 rupees. The Jeypore Suryavamshis traced their origin back to a prince by the name of Vinayaka Deo who, according to local tradition, came from a branch of a Rajput family from Jammu or Kashmir in north-west India and took over the kingdom from the last ruler of the Shilavamsha dynasty in 1453. Of all the kingdoms of south Orissa, Jeypore was the only one whose core area lay exclusively in the mountainous region of the Eastern Ghats: the other jungle kingdoms of the sub-region lay merely at the foot of the Eastern Ghats, in the outcrops of this chain of mountains, or had only a part of their territory in the hills, also known as the *māliahs*.[77]

[76] Until the middle of the seventeenth century the royal residence was in Nandapur, so that the designation 'Nandapur kingdom' is also met with from time to time.

[77] See Senapati (1966, 2) and Behuria (ed. 1965, 1). The statistical information in this section refers to Koraput district at the time of the 1961 census. These figures allow comparison with the state of affairs in the Jeypore kingdom, though the size of the population in the former kingdom was probably smaller.

Four geographical zones can be distinguished within the kingdom of Jeypore, which in general correspond with the sub-divisions of the modern district.[78] If one travels by bus or car from the south Orissan coast into the Ghats, one arrives in the first geographical zone, occupied by the two sub-divisions of Gunupur and Rayagada, which cover about 3,000 square miles and in 1960 had around 400,000 inhabitants. The landscape of this first zone is marked by the two fertile valleys of the Nagavali and Vamshadhara rivers. These flow down from the north-east corner of the district, which lies 500 metres above sea level. Meandering through Rayagada and Gunupur at 150 metres above sea level, the rivers make their way further down the Ghats, through the present-day Srikakulam district, into the Gulf of Bengal. In thus crossing Koraput, they pass through an area marked by rough mountains reaching up to a height of 1,600 metres and by extensive forests. The Niamgiris or Niam Hills, the homeland of the Dongria Kondh, which lie near Bissamcuttack, stand out especially for their massiveness, inaccessibility and scenic beauty.

Near Rayagada, a steep mountain pass snakes up to a high plateau about a thousand metres above sea level and upon which the early royal residence of Nandapur and the present-day administrative centre of Koraput are situated. This plateau, which broadly corresponds to the Koraput sub-division and can only be reached via steep passes to the east and north-east, that is, from the coastal region and the Gunupur-Rayagada plateau, covers about 2,000 square miles and is home to approximately 300,000 inhabitants. The Indravati, Kolab and Machkund rivers, together with their branches, flow through this second geographical zone in a western and southern direction. On the eastern edge of this high plateau is a chain of mountains whose peaks reach a height of 1,800 metres.

Some kilometres west of Koraput town, a narrow mountain road leads down to the former royal residence of Jeypore. This lies at the southern end of the third geographical zone, a plateau occupied by the Nowrangpur sub-division, about 700 metres above sea level, which, together with parts of the Gunupur and Rayagada sub-divisions, forms the district's 'grain-basket'. To the north and west this flat sub-division, crossed only occasionally by chains of hills, borders on the Kalahandi district of Orissa and on the districts of Raipur and Bastar, which belong to the federal state of Madhya Pradesh. This zone has an area of about 3,200 square miles and a population of around 700,000 people.

[78] See Map 6.

If one travels from Jeypore town in a south-westly direction via a steep pass descending 300 metres, one reaches the last of the four geographical zones of the former kingdom, the Malkangiri sub-division, which is about 2,300 square miles in area and has around 150,000 inhabitants. On the eastern boundary of this sub-division, which runs roughly in a south-westerly direction, are to be found the last high outcrops of the Eastern Ghats and, parallel to them, the valley of the Machkund river. The rest of this extensively jungle-covered zone is flat, with chains of hills only occasionally breaking the monotony. The high plateau itself gradually sinks from barely 350 metres above sea level in the north-east to some 150 metres above sea level in the extreme south-west.[79]

Density of population is highest in the Nowrangpur sub-division, at 220 inhabitants per square mile, followed by the Koraput and Rayagada sub-divisions, each with 150, and the Gunupur sub-division, with 128. Most thinly settled is Malkangiri, with 62 inhabitants per square mile. Of the 1.5 million inhabitants of Koraput district identified in the 1961 census, a good 61 percent were classed as 'Scheduled Tribes' and 12 percent as 'Scheduled Castes', the latter also counting among their number many former tribal groups or segments thereof that have come to be integrated into the caste system at the lowest end. In many respects the distinction between 'tribes' and 'castes cannot be detected in the lifestyle of the people, and the transitions between these categories are gradual. All together, we find in Koraput a proportion of population groups that can be characterized as 'tribal' that is extraordinarily high for both Orissa and for the whole of India.[80] These groups are often described as *ādivāsi*s or 'aboriginals' in publications dealing with the tribal population of the sub-continent. Although this term, with its suggestion of 'original' (*ādi*), is itself not unproblematic, in the absence of a better alternative I intend to use it, together with the equally controversial 'tribal' and 'tribe',

[79] Further information on the geographical and demographic situation of Jeypore/Koraput can be found in Behuria (ed. 1965, 1-5), Bell (1945, 1-20), Maclean (ed. 1982, 390; ed. 1987, 60-4) and Senapati (1966, 1-38).

[80] See *Census of India* (1961a, 255-7). The proportion of Scheduled Tribes in Orissa is around 25 percent. As already mentioned, this percentage increases the further one goes from the coast and fertile river valleys into the hills, which suggests a process of expulsion by in-migrating, militarily superior 'Indo-Aryan' groups. Even in the hinterland the better situated and agriculturally more fertile areas are mostly occupied by Oriya Hindus.

without quotation marks in what follows, though I do not wish to deny the relevance of the tribe–caste problematic.[81]

The most important *ādvāsi* groups living today in the district of Koraput are as follows:[82]

1. Bhottada. In Koraput there are 234,000 members of this tribe (250,000 in the whole of Orissa). Most live in the Nowrangpur sub-division.
2. Bhumia. The 75,000 members of this ethnic group live predominantly in the Nowrangpur sub-division.
3. Bondo. Around 6,000 Bondo live in the hills of the Malkangiri sub-division.
4. Gadaba. Approximately 57,000 Gadaba live, predominantly, in the Koraput and Nowrangpur sub-divisions.
5. Gond. 88,000 Gond live in Koraput district (600,000 in the whole of Orissa; five million in all India). Most are to be found in the Koraput and Rayagada sub-divisions.
6. Jatapu. More than 18,000 members identified, most of whom live in the Koraput sub-division.
7. Kondh. In Koraput district there are about 370,000 Kondh (about a million in the whole of Orissa) living mostly in the Rayagada and Gunupur sub-divisions.
8. Kondha-Dora. Of the more than 16,000 Kondha-Dora (17,500 in the whole of Orissa), most live in the Koraput sub-division.
9. Kotia. In Koraput district there are 13,500 members of this ethnic group (19,000 in the whole of Orissa) living mostly in the Malkangiri sub-division.
10. Koya. Of the around 87,000 Koya most live in the Malkangiri sub-division.
11. Omanatya. The barely 19,000 members of this ethnic group live mainly in the Nowrangpur sub-division.
12. Parenga. Most of the 9,600 Parenga live in the Koraput sub-division.

[81] On this problematic, see the overview in Urhahn (1985).

[82] Here, I must content myself with a brief list of individual ethnic groups and the most important social, political and cultural characteristics they have in common. The general information comes from the census of 1981. Because of the extraordinarily high rate of growth in the decades before this census was taken, the absolute figures given here must be reduced by some 20 to 30 per cent in order to arrive at a picture of the population size of these ethnic groups at the start of the twentieth century. In relation to the Oriya Hindus, however, the proportion of the tribal population of the kingdom in the past may have reached over 60 per cent.

13. Paroja. Most of the 247,000 Paroja (267,000 in the whole of Orissa) live in the sub-divisions of Nowrangpur and Koraput.
14. Sora. The 46,000 members of this tribe (370,000 in the whole of Orissa) live predominantly in the Gunupur sub-division.

The ethnic groups listed above belong to two larger linguistic groups, namely the Munda branch of the Austroasiatic language family (Bondo, Gadaba, Parenga, Sora) and the Dravidian language family (Bhottada, Bhumia, Gond, Jatapu, Kondh, Kondha-Dora, Kotia, Koya, Omanatya, Paroja). They are characterized by certain common features in their social and political organization. Thus, most of these ethnic groups are based on exogamous, totemic patriclans, which are not infrequently combined into larger, equally exogamous clan groups.[83] In addition, many ethnic groups are divided into endogamous halves or moieties. Generally, the most important corporate group is the village, governed in a form of dual authority by a headman (*nāik*) responsible for 'wordly' questions and a priest (*pūjāri*, *disāri*, *jāni*). The positions of these individuals pass from father to son, though a successor must possess personal ability as well as hereditary rights. A third person usually joins these two as an assistant and messenger (*chalan*, *barik*). He normally belongs to the low caste of the Dom or Pano. In many of the ethnic groups named above, there is a superordinate corporation (*desh*, *muṭṭhā*) consisting of several villages whose assemblies or *panchayat*s are governed by a common headman (*patnāik*, *bhatanāik*). There are no organs or institutions at a higher level of organization that would endow these ethnic groups with a corporate nature, as a tribe, in politico-jural affairs.

At the centre of the religious life of most of the ethnic groups named above is the 'earth goddess', who is honoured on a village basis under names like 'Thakurani', 'Hundi', 'Dharani' and many others. This goddess is represented by a large stone placed either at the edge or in the middle of the village. The village assemblies often take place in proximity to this stone and new village headmen take their oath of office in front of the goddess. Of the yearly festivals (many of which are connected with seasonal changes, changes in agricultural activities, and the desire to guarantee or increase the fertility of humans, animals and crops), the *caitra parva* in March to April is the most important. During this festival, the earth goddess is honoured, the first ripe mango fruits are ritually

[83] One important exception are the Sora, who recognize patrilineages four to five generations deep, but who have no system of exogamous, totemic clans.

consumed and all the men of the village go hunting. The *caitra parva* is also marked by music, dancing and other expressions of *joie de vivre*.

There are differences between individual ethnic groups regarding the degree of their 'acculturation' or integration into the Hindu caste system, its values and behavioural prescriptions, and regarding the extent and intensity of their contact with the Hindus living in the district. Thus, the Paroja, Gadaba and Kondh often live in towns and small markets together with the members of other ethnic groups or castes and fall under the influence of their culture and way of life, while the Koya and Bondo, for example, live withdrawn in their mountains and forests, only rarely stepping outside the isolation of their natural and social environments. Elwin characterizes this difference as follows: 'The aboriginals of Ganjam and Koraput, like those all over India, fall into two distinct classes—the true highlanders who have retained much of their own culture and live a full and happy life in the hills, and the plainsmen who have slowly drifted down from their mountain heights and have largely assimilated the outlook and practice of their more sophisticated neighbours' (1946, 1). One District Gazetteer of 1966 seeks to do justice to these different degrees of assimilation by identifying three *ādivāsi* categories, namely 'real primitive tribes', 'tribes in transition' and 'assimilated tribes'.[84]

If one looks at individual tribal societies in their own right, in many cases it can be seen that different sections within an ethnic group may be at quite different stages of integration and assimilation. Thus many of the Kondh and Sora communities that are scattered all over Orissa could be categorized as 'tribes in transition' or 'assimilated tribes', while other sub-groups of these ethnic groups, especially the Lambalanjhia Sora and Dongria Kondh, would have to count as 'true highlanders' or 'real primitive tribes' in Elwin's or Senapati's schemes respectively. These differences between or within ethnic groups also find expression in the self-understanding of many *ādivāsi* groups. Thus, the Omanatya regard themselves as higher and purer than their tribal neighbours, which is expressed in the fact that they will not take any food from the Bhottada or Bhumia. In many ethnic groups there is the already mentioned division into endogamous moieties, of which one usually counts as 'big' or 'great' (*baḍa*) and the other as 'small' or 'little' (*sāna*). The 'big' moiety is regarded as the more original, senior and prestigious one, a circumstance which its members express among other things through their greater stress

[84] See Senapati (1966, 97-8).

on Hindu prescriptions concerning purity and food taboos and through their refusal to marry members of the other moiety.[85]

Apart from the great rivers and mountain chains already mentioned, the four geographical zones of the kingdom of Jeypore described at the start of this section also had numerous other hills, mountains and smaller rivers. In addition, in 1960, even after a good century of systematic deforestation, 70 percent of the area was still covered with forests of usable timber or bushy, impenetrable jungle. Of these nearly 7,000 square miles of forest, 1,700 square miles were officially identified as 'reserved forests' or 'protected forests'.[86] Passes into the different zones from outside the kingdom and between the four high plateaux were made more difficult by natural barriers and even today are only passable with difficulty. However, the modern traveller who regards spending long hours in a crowded bus, which laboriously works its way up the snaking passes, as arduous should realize that many of the roads that today allow one to cover the roughly 250-kilometre stretch from Berhampur to Jeypore in twelve to fifteen hours were good enough only for ox-carts towards the end of the nineteenth century.[87] Until then, British military officers and officials had to allow several weeks just as travelling time when they set out on their yearly 'hill tours', which were only undertaken in the favourable (that is, dry and cool) months from November to March. According to one official of that time, 'There is not a mile of road in the district along which you can drive a gig or a pig'.[88] The people on the

[85] An overview of the tribal societies in Koraput is provided by, among others, Behuria (ed. 1965, 26-30), Carmichael (1869, 87-109), Elwin (1946), Francis (1907, 86-98), Padhi (1992), Parkin (1991, 25-32), Pfeffer (1982), Sahu (1942), Senapati (1966, 79-140), Sinha (ed. 1987), Thurston (1909, passim) and in *Tribes of Orissa* (1990). Among the monographs on individual ethnic groups should be mentioned Bailey (1960), Banerjee (1969), Boal (1982), Elwin (1950, 1955), Nayak (1989), Patnaik and Patnaik (1982), and various publications of the Scheduled Tribes and Scheduled Castes Research Institute of the Government of Orissa, including their journal, *Adivasi*.

[86] See Behuria (ed. 1965, 6-9) and Senapati (1966, 23-7). The 1961 census declared around 60 percent of the surface as consisting of forest. The massive deforestation that has been carried out, especially since the end of the second world war, renders the metaphor of the jungle I have invoked increasingly fragile since, despite a series of laws for the protection of trees, illegal deforestation continues unabated.

[87] See Behuria (ed. 1965, 9-15) and Senapati (1966, 221-44).

[88] Quoted in Behuria (ed. 1965, 9).

coasts generally regarded the climate in the hills as unhealthy, the area as malaria-infested. Many soldiers coming from the outside and other individuals visiting the *māliah*s, whether Indians or foreigners, had to pay for their stay in the hill region with their health or even their lives. And the numerous wild animals, above all tigers, which were to be found there well into the nineteenth century, were feared not only by the natives.

From all the seats of the imperial powers, whether the Gajapatis in central Orissa, the Vijayanagara kings in south India, the Golkonda *shāh*s, Hyderabad *nizām*s or the Marathas of the Deccan, the British in Madras or their respective governors on the coast of north Andhra Pradesh, Jeypore could only be reached with difficulty. And precisely because of this remote location and the difficult natural environment of the kingdom itself, the Jeypore Suryavamshis could act relatively autonomously, at least internally. Certainly, the great powers occasionally staged punitive expeditions, such as those carried out by units of the *shāh*s of Golkonda at the end of the sixteenth century or by British troops in 1775, but not infrequently these ended with great losses or yielded only temporary and limited success.[89] At best, formal recognition of the attacking imperial sovereign could be wrung from the *rājā*s of Jeypore, though this also implied a recognition of the little-kingly status of these jungle kings, as in the treaties concluded with the Golkonda *shāh*s in 1661 and the British in 1795. Not till after 1863 could the British control the mountain area around Jeypore to a degree which this colonial power had already been exerting elsewhere for many decades. Characteristically, the lower lying plateau around Gunupur and Rayagada, which was easier to reach from the coast, came under the direct control of the colonial power more than a decade before the other zones of the kingdom.

The other jungle kingdoms of south Orissa were also in a relatively protected position with regard to any incursions by great powers, simply because of their remote location and the densely forested nature of large areas of their territory. However, they were more vulnerable than Jeypore, since they were not as withdrawn into the protection of the mountains and forests. Thus, by 1836, after several years of military campaigning, the British were able to conquer Parlakimedi and Ghumsur and to bring them

[89] It was reported of a Maratha war party that crossed the mountain region of Jeypore from the north-west in the direction of the Godavari delta around 1750 that 'more than one half of the invaders fell a sacrifice to the noxious air of the hills in effecting their passage, and the remainder, feeble or disheartened, rather than hazard returning the same way, adopted the desperate resolution of making a prodigious circuit through unfrequented routes' (Bell 1945, 27-8).

under their direct control.[90] However, the many difficulties that the British encountered in doing this, especially in Ghumsur, were an important reason why the colonial power for a long time hesitated to subject Jeypore to similar direct police and jural control. In 1839, therefore, the hill region was first made subject to special laws as an 'agency tract', which allowed the highest British administrator of the district, the collector, great executive and judicial powers united in the same person. This special arrangement for the hill region and its inhabitants continued, though in a weakened form, as a 'partially excluded area' until 1952.[91]

Frustration over their inability to control the hill region and over its health- and life-threatening rigours is vividly expressed in many statements by British administrative officials and in their policy. Thus, for example, Thomas Munro, in his capacity as Governor of Madras, reflected in 1822 that one must allow the 'hill chiefs' of the Northern Sircars greater tolerance than the kings of the coast, 'lest we should be compelled to use force and involve ourselves in a petty warfare against banditti in a pestilential climate among hills and jungles'.[92] Shortly after the British had taken over the direct administration of Jeypore in 1863, a British military officer reported on the new hill station as follows:

> No officer in the northern division will come up unless compelled to do so. Neither the Assistant Agent nor Superindentents of Police ever stay a day longer than they are absolutely obliged to do, and the consequence is that work is carried on anyhow, and the only wonder is that it has been possible to keep matters going at all. [...] no decently qualified person will accept the post of sub-magistrate, which entails a broken constitution and enforced retirement at the end of six months. (Quoted in Francis 1907, 262)

In 1864 a police inspector described the difficulties in introducing a policing system in the kingdom as follows:

> The country is utterly inaccessible. There are no means of procuring pack carriage, and the service is of a description which requires that bodies of Police may be moved with rapidity, and supplies kept up with certainty. [...] I have directed the local officers to see if they can purchase elephants. [...] Attention must at once be turned to

[90] See Russell (1856).

[91] On the administration of the *māliah*s of south Orissa, see Maltby (1918, 11-14), *Report of the Partially Excluded Areas Enquiry Committee* (1940), Taylor (no date) and Senapati (1966, 70-1).

[92] Quoted in Francis (1907, 57).

> roads. The country is absolutely without these. It is generally a jungly, and in some parts a hilly country. The beds of the rivers and hill streams are deep and difficult to cross; wide paddy bottoms are met with everywhere, and are almost impassable during the many wet months of the year. (quoted in *Selections* 1864, 87-8)

The following statement on the area occupied by the Kondh dates from around the turn of the century:

> ... a newcomer must pass through a trying ordeal of repeated attacks of high fever before he can find rest. His constitution by that time is thoroughly broken down; he looks half his former self and despairs to regain his vigour and spirit as long as confined in this dreadful hole [...] the ordinary Oriya of the plains regards service in it as almost equivalent to a death sentence. (O'Malley 1908, 77).[93]

The jungle kings of the hill region had also been accorded a special position in the political ideology and practice of the various great kings, who preceded the British as overlords of the Orissan little kingdoms. Thus, in the fourth-century AD inscriptions of the Gupta king Samudragupta, the area of the present-day Kalahandi and Koraput districts, is described as 'great forest country' (*mahākāntāra*), the kingdoms situated there as 'forest kingdoms' (*āṭavī-rājya*) and one of their rulers as 'Tiger King' (*vyāghrarāja*).[94] Later royal dynasties of the region clearly indicate their forest origins or some other connection with the hill region in their names, for example, the dynasty of the Shailodbhavas or 'rock-borns' (*śila-udbhavas*) or that of the Shilavamshis (the 'rock dynasty').[95] The fact that towards the end of the seventeenth century a Pusapati ruler received the honorary title of *manne sultān* or 'Sultan of the Forest'[96] shows that the special position of the jungle kingdoms of the sub-region, which had been recognized in practical matters as well as ideologically by great kings in all periods, continued under the Mughals.

93 Many similar statements could be added here. I intend to deal in a separate publication with the 'Heart of Darkness' mood which is evident in many of the Hill Tour Reports and in other reports by British colonial officials who, plagued with frustration and sickness, were stationed in the hills.

94 See Kulke (1979a, 9).

95 See Berkemer (1993, 261).

96 See Berkemer (1993, 259).

It should be noted in passing that the institution of the jungle kingdom always played an important role on the all-India stage, even in periods of strong central power. Thus, a Dutch traveller describes the powerful Mughal ruler Jahangir (1605–1627) as 'king of the plains only' (cited in Wink 1986). A couple of decades later, an Italian traveller estimated the number of *rājā*s and *zamīndār*s in the Mughal empire that were living in the jungle at more than 5,000. It is clear that these jungle kings deserve to be attributed more than just a passive role or an autonomy realized only in isolation: for the great kings and even for the claims of imperial power, they represented constant irritation and a permanent threat. There were countless examples of rebelling governors and kings who escaped the discipline of the great power by fleeing into friendly jungle kingdoms, and imperial armies on expeditions were always in danger from surprise ambushes by jungle kings and their irregulars, experienced in guerrilla warfare, which could cause considerable losses in men and treasure. And the military services of the jungle kings as well as their notorious insubordination were deliberately deployed as part of the strategic intrigues between the Mughals, Marathas, Rajput clans, great kings, little kings and other power-seekers. In the Mughal empire too, therefore, India's jungle kings were important agents in the politics of rebellion, which marked the multi-centred Mughal empire and other Indian kingdoms.[97]

From time to time, armies acting on foreign jungle territory sought to counter the strategic advantage of their opponents by undertaking the arduous, debilitating and time-consuming work of 'jungle-cutting', that is, by cutting the sides of the path in front of them or by clearing a besieged jungle fortress of the trees and bushes surrounding it. Other authors mention that in times of peace, many rulers sought to advance the internal colonization and integration of tribal population groups through large-scale donations of fallow ground or forested land to Brahmans. This method had also been recommended by Kautilya in his *Arthaśastra*.[98]

The histories of some of the little-kingly dynasties of south Orissa clearly show that the little kings who were installed by imperial rulers played a role comparable to that of the Brahmans (often in association with them) when it came to the clearing of the jungle, and the expulsion or pacification of its inhabitants, or the extension of surplus-producing

[97] See Wink (1986, 39; 190-9). Gordon (1979) provides further evidence of the strategic role of jungle fortresses in the Maratha kingdom.

[98] On the points in this paragraph, see Kulke (1982), Panda (1985, 147-8), Pfeffer (1978), Sharma (1965, 32-4) and Shulman (1984).

land. Another practice, more effective than the rather laborious 'jungle-cutting' or the never-ending battles with tribal guerrillas, was to incorporate tribal armies into the imperial armies. Besides good pay and the granting of emblems of honour, these 'wild' warriors were tempted by the possibility of being integrated into the middle spectrum of the caste hierarchy. Kulke (1976) describes this sort of Hinduization as '*kshatriya-ization*'.[99]

The wilderness, its rulers and inhabitants also play important roles in the corpus of classical Indian literature, philosophy, art and religion, which is only indirectly influenced by considerations of power relationships and strategic politics.[100] In Sanskrit terminology, for example, we find the important conceptual opposition between *vana* (forest) and *kṣetra* (settled country), which Sontheimer defines as follows:

> By *kṣetra* I mean inhabited, well-settled space with regular plough agriculture, the village in such space...and the holy centres connected with them. [...] By *vana* I mean 'wild space', 'forest' or 'jungle' which harbours the 'hermitage', the tribals, the *saṃnyāsī* and the *āśrama.* [...] The dichotomy of *vana* and *kṣetra* is not mutually exclusive, but it is rather complementary or a continuum similarly as the continuum from tribe to caste. Related to this is the opposition between tribal religion and what has been called 'codified Hinduism' ... (1987, 127-8)[101]

Medieval Tamil literature contains the notion of five landscapes, of which the most marginal ones, the 'desert' (*pālai*) and the 'wooded mountain region' (*kuriñci*), have great symbolic significance.[102] Other studies on Indian concepts of wilderness, jungle or forest make clear the tension-charged relationship between 'wild' landscapes, together with their inhabitants (humans, animals, demons and deities) and their settled and

[99] On the points in this paragraph, see Stein (1969; 1980, 146). The role of the Maravars and other marauding warrior bands is also problematized by Bayly (1989), Dirks (1987) and Shulman (1985) at various points in their works.

[100] In India's classical epics jungle inhabitants are often described by the generic name 'Savaras'.

[101] See also Sontheimer (1989, 201-3). Kulke (1992) regards *kṣetra* as the ritually charged territory of a deity rather than as cultivated and settled land in Sontheimer's sense. What is important for Kulke is the complex relationship between *kṣetra* and *kśatra*, that is, between a spiritual and a wordly territory, rather than that between *vana* and *kśetra.*

[102] See Shulman (1980a, 288-95; 1981) and Sontheimer (1987, 121-7).

'civilized' counterparts. The 'civilized' self is made possible and constituted by a poetically construed 'alien' other.[103] In the *Mahābhārata* and the *Rāmāyaṇa* we also find the motif of the king living in the jungle for a time as a renouncer. Both the Pandava brothers and Rama were only able to return triumphantly to their kingdoms and to rule over their domains as true kings through the experience of living (and surviving) in the jungle, their heroic mastery of the savage forces of nature and the cosmos, and by overcoming many other tests.[104] Ancient rituals of royalty, especially the anointing of the king (*rājasūya*) and the horse sacrifice (*aśvamedha*), played symbolically with the idea that true royalty was only achieved by a ritual passage through the jungle, which was also imagined as the conquest of the wilderness and its forces.[105] These passages into the jungle are also expressed in the annually recurring *dasarā* festival at the end of the monsoon, in which Rama's departure from the royal city of Ayodhya is ritually re-enacted.[106]

Nothing in the picture sketched so far changes fundamentally in taking the step from the so-called 'Great Tradition' to the 'Little' Tradition. In many popular ballads, songs and orally transmitted traditions in India, from the time of the middle ages up to the present day, ancient and classical models reappear in changed forms. One example is the theme of the king's son (*rājaputra*) or crown prince (*yuvarāja*) who, excluded from his inheritance by a resentful father or brother, withdraws into the jungle, from where he starts (usually successfully) the search for a kingdom of his own (*bhūmiyāvat*).[107] The widespread theme of the king who, sickened

[103] See Falk (1973), Hara (1973) and Malamoud (1976).

[104] See Biardeau (1981), Ruben (1962) and Shulman (1985, 214-22; 293-5).

[105] See Heesterman (1957b; 1971; 1978; 1979). Elsewhere (1985, 6) he writes: 'In his unremittingly repeated circuit, the king joins two opposite and complementary worlds, the peaceably settled community (*grāma*) and the wilds (*araṇya*), where the consecrated warrior band has its being. In this way, the king (or would-be king) vindicated his power and authority over both worlds.' In Heesterman (1978, 233), the dialectical role of the king being torn this way and that between wilderness and civilization is emphasized. Falk introduces her study of the problem as follows: 'There seems to have been a complex relationship between wilderness and kingship, an institution squarely at the center of settled activity. It appears that a king had to have some kind of transaction with the wilderness and the beings that inhabited it to acquire or hold his kingship' (1973, 1).

[106] See Kane (1958, 188-94).

[107] See Claus (1978, 7-10) and Kolff (1990, 61-85).

by power struggles and intrigue, withdraws into the wilderness in his old age as an ascetic, is another indication that further insights might be obtained by examining the complementary roles of king (whether ageing or a crown prince) and ascetic.[108] Another figure who in many respects is complementary to the king in myth and history is that of the bandit or outlaw operating from within the protection of the forest.[109] When one considers the common aspects of a life led (at least temporarily) in the wilderness that connects these status groups, it immediately becomes clear that other roles, such as those of the soldier, the travelling merchant and the wandering holy man, must be added to the multifaceted picture of the king living in the jungle, whether temporarily or permanently.[110]

The conceptual distinction between wilderness and settled territory also has great relevance for village and tribal rituals as, for example, in the cult of south Indian village goddesses. Their festivals are often characterized by a symbolic marking of (and, in long parts of the ritual, inability to cross) village boundaries, as well as an effort to identify inauspicious forces within the village, in order to thrust them out into the wilderness on a cart loaded with sacrificial gifts.[111] The classical motif of the king withdrawing into the wilderness also finds approval and form in the oral traditions of the tribal population of Jeypore. To end this section, here is an example reported by Thurston (1909, Vol. 2, 245):

> The Gadabas account for the dress of their women by the following legend. When Rāma, during his banishment, was wandering in the forests of Dandaka, his wife Sīta accompanied him in spite of his entreaties to the contrary. It was one of the cruel terms of his stepmother Kaika that Rāma should only wear clothing made from jungle fibre, before leaving the capital. According to Hindu religion, a virtuous wife must share both the sorrows and joys of her

[108] On the relationship between the king (householder) and the hermit who has withdrawn into the forest, and also warrior ascetics, see Burghart (1983), Dumont (1960), Heesterman (1981), Kolff (1990, 137; 198), Lorenzen (1978), Marglin (1985, 20) and Sax (1991, 19-20).

[109] The *rājā* of Chikiti once remarked on this theme: 'We were all *dacoits* (bandits)'. The roles of king and bandit, which supplement and partly flow into one another, are described in Berkemer (1993, 256-7), Dirks (1987, 94-6), Gordon (1969, 406; 425), Shulman (1980; 1985, 340-400) and Waghorne (1989).

[110] See Bayly (1992, 35-73), Chakravarti (1990), Kolff (1990, 95; 126; 183; 199), Mishra (1994) and van der Veer (1994, 43-4).

[111] See the description in Bayly (1989, 35-6) and Whitehead (1976).

lord. Consequently Sīta followed the example of Rāma, and wore the same kind of clothing. They then left the capital amidst the loud lamentation of the citizens. During their wanderings, they met some Gadaba women, who mocked and laughed at Sīta. Whereupon she cursed them, and condemned them to wear no other dress but the cloth made of fibre.

6. Closing remarks

Using the paradigm of Jeypore, the institution of the jungle kingdom as a sub-category of the little kingdom has been characterized in terms of two elements. First, the territories of the jungle kingdoms were situated in forest and hill areas which were accessible only with difficulty from the centres of power, and internally they were characterized by an impenetrable and, especially for outsiders, dangerous environment. Secondly, the population of jungle kingdoms contained a high proportion of tribal groups, whose specific culture helped decisively to shape the political, religious and social life within the jungle kingdom, even after a Hindu take-over of rule. In addition, the close intimacy of these *ādivāsi*s with their difficult natural environment provided any king able to win their active loyalty with a strong ally against invaders from the outside.

The accounts given in the previous section should, nonetheless, warn us not to treat the categories 'jungle' or 'jungle inhabitant' too strictly as natural constants. 'Civilizing' the wilderness and its inhabitants was possible and, from the point of view of any great king, most desirable on grounds of economics and military strategy. Success in taking such measures depended, amongst other things, on the great king's ever-changing capacity to control little-kingly powers. In one period of shifting power relations, the central power might be strong enough to carry out extensive 'jungle-cutting', while in another period local potentates who had become strong again might deliberately let estates lie fallow and become overgrown with protective bushes, bamboos and forest.[112] The mere existence of a jungle and the size it reached was, therefore, not determined by the forces of nature alone. Although it may appear a paradox at first sight, to a certain extent the jungle was a product of politics, as its size was the complex result of competing claims to power. The

[112] See especially Fox (1971, 65-9, 102-3), who has worked out these cycles for north India.

'civilizing' of the wilderness and the 'junglification'[113] of the cultivated landscape represented conflicting but also supplementary *political* processes. Similarly, the process of the Hinduization of tribal populations is usually accompanied by a process of the tribalization of the population of the lowlands, and especially of the Hindu agents of colonization (governors, Brahmans, jungle kings, merchants, soldiers etc.) and their relatives found in the hinterland. The current *yuvarāja* of the former royal house of Jeypore, Shakti Vikram Deo, once said in this connection: 'After coming to Nandapur we set up a tribal system, just to please them, so the tribals accepted us as their rulers. We adopted a lot of rituals—the sacrifice of an animal with an axe. So, our enemies knew, the next battle is in the jungle.'[114]

On the one hand, with respect to their great-kingly overlords, the jungle kings had great interest in the preservation and expansion of the jungle because this, together with its inhabitants, could be exploited in terms of military policy. On the other hand, it should not be overlooked that the jungle kings, who in south Orissa were mostly Hindus from the outside, themselves had great interest in increasing the clearing of the jungles and in consistently expanding their agricultural base to yield an increasing surplus. The Hinduization of tribal subjects so as to better integrate them into a politico-religious and economic system shaped by Hindu values also determined the jungle kings' policies. In the struggle between clearing the jungle and letting it flourish, as well as between Hinduizing and tribalizing the social environment, it was therefore not only the balance of power between the great-kingly centre and its little-kingly satellites that was decisive. The policies of the jungle kings themselves were determined by contradictory considerations regarding these conflicting though also, in a complex way, supplementary processes.

I hope that by now it is clear that in India's history, politics, religion, literature and popular imagination, the complex relationship between royal authority and jungle/wilderness had and still has great practical, imaginative and symbolic significance.[115] Kingly authority in India seems

[113] 'Jungle' comes from the Sanskrit *jaṅgala*, 'arid, sterile, desert', (Hindi *jaṅgle, jaṅglī*).

[114] Personal interview, 28.12.1990.

[115] At the beginning of the 1991 election campaign, Lal Krishnan Advani, leader of the Hindu fundamentalist BJP, posed with a bow and arrow in his hands as Rama shortly before he went on expedition. See van der Veer (1994, 1; 4-6; 72).

to have arisen in, and out of, the wilderness, as is suggested by the Indological works of Falk, Heesterman and Shulman, which are mostly concerned with literary sources, as well as by the ethnohistorical works of S. Bayly, Dirks, Kolff, Kulke, Wink and others. At this point we should again recall the interplay between the often complementary characters of the ascetic, the old king, the prince eager for action, the hermit, the soldier, the wandering holy man, the bandit and the merchant, which often merge into one another. The king living permanently in the jungle—that is, the jungle king, who is the focus of this study—should be added to this series. Hence, the fact that jungle kings and their kingdoms have been accorded little attention in research on India up to now is also astonishing because the importance of 'the king and the wilderness' crosses disciplinary boundaries and links them.

CHAPTER III

THE EARLY HISTORY OF THE JEYPORE SURYAVAMSHIS

1. Introduction

According to the family chronicle, Vinayaka Deo, the founder of the royal dynasty of Jeypore (initially Nandapur), came to power in AD 1443. Members of the house of the Suryavamshis,[1] to whom the family chronicle ascribes a venerable and ancient Rajput origin, remained at the head of the kingdom for five turbulent centuries, until the annexation of the kingdom by the state of Orissa in 1950.[2]

The present chapter is devoted to the early history of the royal dynasty of Jeypore and covers the period from Vinayaka Deo's ascension in Nandapur to the end of the sixteenth century.[3] Here my main focus will be directed, in the traditional Rankian sense of historiography, to the question of '*wie es eigentlich gewesen ist*' or 'how it really was'. In this attempt to reconstruct 'actual' history, however, it is not my intention to subscribe to an antiquated historiographical understanding of the epistemological opposition between *res factae* and *res fictae*, that is, between the writing of history and of poetry. This would be a misguided undertaking in view of the fundamental questioning of the epistemological status of historical documents in themselves, which historians and anthropologists can hardly ignore following the development known as the 'linguistic turn'.[4] While in 'postmodern' approaches text and context are often seen as being conflated into one, the recently revived interest in the cultural or social logic of texts makes the search for the social and

[1] The dynasty is also known as 'Sankara' and 'Jayavamsha'. See Singh Deo (1939, 8) and Berkemer (1993, 339).

[2] See the genealogy of the Jeypore Suryavamshis in the Appendix (Figure 1).

[3] An earlier article on this theme, which has been thoroughly revised and expanded for this chapter, can be found in Schnepel (1992). See also Schnepel (1994b).

[4] In anthropology Clifford (1988), Geertz (1973a, 1990) and Clifford and Marcus (eds. 1986) are the most important references for a 'postmodern' approach influenced by literary criticism, while among historians White (1990; 1994) has been the spokesperson.

historical realities underlying them legitimate and feasible again.[5] What is important, however, in any 'post-postmodern' project of reconstructing realities through texts is the realization that the 'clues' to be found in the texts which convey access to historical, cultural, social and other realities are opaque, multivocal and ambiguous in character, and determined by conflicts of interest. It is also necessary to bear in mind that the texts being examined have their own 'idea' of history, which corresponds only in a limited sense to a historian's striving for facticity. This indigenous idea of history shapes the form and content of historical documents quite fundamentally, so that the traditional distinction between myth, legend and history as genres marked by different degrees of fictionality seems obsolete. In what follows, I shall therefore endow quite often neglected or disdainfully treated types of the source, such as local histories or oral traditions, with a more prominent status in their capacity as witnesses to the past.

While in the following section I shall introduce the sources that have been available to me in reconstructing the early history of the Jeypore Suryavamshis, section 3 is devoted to determining the possible origin of this dynasty and to the early period of its seizure of power. Section 4 is an interpolation discussing the problem of 'Rajput' identity, while section 5 deals with the period in which the kingdom in question consolidated its power. In doing so, some of the events and historical developments in the wider regions of Orissa, south India and the Deccan, which affected Jeypore's history, will again be mentioned, though this time decisively from the view point of local history. Section 6 completes the picture from a theoretical point of view.

2. Sources

For the jungle kingdom of Jeypore/Nandapur in its early period, there are no inscriptions, eye-witness reports, foundation charters or other documents of the sort which have usually provided traditional historiography on India with data and clues. For this reason alone, any reconstruction of Jeypore's actual history in the fifteenth and sixteenth centuries is difficult and problematic, and 'creative imagination' (Collingwood 1986) indispensable anyway for historians, is required in even greater measure.

One of the most important sources available to me has been the *Jayapura Raja Vamsyavali* or *Family Chronicle of the Jeypore Kings*,

[5] For example, see Chartier (1994), Conrad and Kessel (1994), Greenblatt (1994), Hunt (1994) and Spiegel (1994).

written in 1938 by R. Nanda Sarma in his role as the '*darbār* poet' of Jeypore.[6] Sarma belonged to the sixth generation of a Brahman dynasty which held the office of the royal family priest (*purohita*) of Jeypore since the late eighteenth century.[7] In his poetically composed reconstruction of historical events, he refers to palm-leaf manuscripts and ancient legends of the region (Oriya *purāṇas*) as sources. Furthermore, in 1939 Singh Deo, a lawyer and related by marriage to the royal family, published a book entitled *Nandapur: A Forsaken Kingdom*.[8] Singh Deo, too, states that his historical reconstruction is based to a considerable extent on the evaluation of old manuscripts that he has found in the possession of different Brahman scholars, including Sarma. The concrete written evidence that Singh Deo refers to in the course of his discussion, unfortunately, consists only of official manuals, district gazetteers, reports and other products of British colonial writing: none of the 'primary' sources he mentions are directly cited in *A Forsaken Kingdom*. The earliest official government publication is Oram's *Report on Nandapuram* of 1784,[9] followed by Carmichael's *Manual of the District of Vizagapatam in the Madras Presidency* of 1869[10] and Francis's *Madras District Gazetteers: Vizagapatam* of 1907.[11] Later gazetteers and other official publications do not add anything fundamentally new to the picture of the early history of Jeypore as handed down in these earlier sources.[12] In the gazetteers too, local traditions and manuscripts are mentioned as sources of information, though without being specified or quoted.[13] The Indian journalist and lay historian, Vadivelu, also leaves unspecified the sources on Jeypore's early history he mentions in his work *The Aristocracy of Southern India*, first published in 1903.[14] In the foreword

[6] Sarma (1938).

[7] This 'family history', written in Sanskrit in the form of a poem, was translated into English for me by Dr G. Nando, the author's great nephew, who today lives in Jeypore as a Sanskrit scholar and teacher. Dr Nando also helpfully took part in some of my investigations and excursions on site.

[8] Singh Deo (1939).

[9] Oram (1784).

[10] Carmichael (1869).

[11] Francis (1907).

[12] For example, see Bell (1945, 21-5) and Senapati (1966, 57-60).

[13] For example, see Francis (1907, 263).

[14] See Vadivelu (1984, 65-83).

to his eulogistically composed book he merely writes: 'I interviewed almost all the noblemen who figure in this book, ransacked their records, and culled out as much information as I thought would be useful to me' (1984, i).

During my own research in Jeypore and in the state archives of Orissa, Andhra Pradesh and Tamil Nadu, I was not able to find any of the older palm-leaf manuscripts so often referred to as evidence. Indian colleagues pursuing research on Jeypore's history also told me of their equally fruitless efforts to find these sources. We should not doubt at this point that these older manuscripts actually existed and were consulted. However, it is to be feared that the periodical airing and care of the documents has been neglected in recent decades and that as a result these sources have fallen victim to termites and the 'ravages of time'. Thus, the only documents that afford access to the early history of the Jeypore royal house are second-hand reports from the late nineteenth and early twentieth centuries. Here, it should also be stressed that the authors who probably consulted sources from the palace most closely, namely Sarma and Singh Deo, were obliged to the royal house in different degrees. Their writings are, in part at least, less concerned with 'actual history' than with 'believed history'.[15]

The legitimation and glorification of the royal authority of the Jeypore Suryavamshis, which appear in the works of Sarma, Singh Deo and Vadivelu, will also have been integral to the sources they used. These sources, too, would have been a synthesis of actual events and of idealization or legitimation. The mixing of fact and fiction in the emic sources—precisely what historians of India so often complain about—should not be seen as expressing a bad or consciously falsified historiography. Rather, we encounter here a type of historical writing which complies with the standards and interests of academic historiography, with its craving for *Ur*-texts and factualizing statements, only to a very limited extent. Thus, the value and greatness of Sarma's chronicle is seen in Jeypore itself as being expressed in the fact that 116 different meanings can be attached to the last verse (*śloka*) of the poem (verse 437). This is an example of the intention of a family chronicle like the *Jayapura Raja Vamsyavali* according to emic criteria. The form has as much meaning as the content. For the author the aim was, apparently, not so much a scientific recording of facts as the polyvalence and 'multi-existentiality' of a text that, to some extent, led an independent existence and invited commentary.[16]

[15] On this difference, see Koselleck (1979, 278-84). See also below, Figure 2.

[16] On the 'idea of history' contained in ancient Indian sources, see Thapar (1978a) and Berkemer (1998). Dirks (1987, 55-9) discusses the historical validity of local

Hence, any discussion which aims at historicity must seek to convey the ideological content of the emic sources and to trace the complex relationship of this ideology to the 'realities' lying behind the text. This applies to the panegyric versions of the early twentieth century, as well as to earlier sources on which they are based and about which we can only have indirect knowledge.

Sarma's and Singh Deo's works should be seen against the background of the 'enlightened' late colonial ritual policy of Ramachandra Deo IV (1920-1931) and Vikram Deo IV (1931-1951). This policy followed a widespread trend in India at the time to legitimize royal rule through the production of dynastic histories proclaiming royal greatness and an ancient line—a trend which can also be seen as a 'native response' to the politico-ritual spectacle of the British *darbār* (or state reception) held in Delhi in 1911.[17] The fabrication of uninterrupted family trees and dynastic histories going back into the mythical past was a flourishing practice by India's royal houses in the late eighteenth and early nineteenth centuries. Some of the sources on which Sarma, Singh Deo, Vadivelu and the gazetteers are based, especially the 'family chronicles' or *vaṃśāvalis*, probably come from that time. Here we are dealing with the period between 1770 and 1820, in which the transformation of the East India Company from a trading company into the colonial government was completed. In the course of this transformation, there took place an ever-increasing routinization and rationalization of the colonial administration, one basic element of which was the systematic acquisition of knowledge about the colonized Indian 'Other'.[18] The factualization of statements about India was also of a historicizing nature and was directed especially at the accumulation of knowledge about the numerous *rājās* or 'little kings' who exercised local powers and stood between the colonial regime and the rural population. This historicizing aspect of British colonial search for knowledge about the ruled was also an expression of a widespread romantic as well as scientific endeavour, which Rocher fittingly

histories and chronicles, advising us 'to examine any given text (or tradition) in its own terms before we ask (or simply classify) in what sense it is or is not "historical"' (ibid., 57). Berkemer (1993, 13) seeks to grasp the local histories of the ruling houses of Kalinga by recourse to Cohn's distinction (1961) between a 'traditional past' and a 'historic past'. On the use of oral traditions in historical research, see also Claus (1978, 1-2).

[17] On the *darbār* of 1911 and its effects on the ritual and ideological practice of Indian royal houses, see Cohn (1983).

[18] On this point, see, especially, Appadurai (1993) and Ludden (1993).

characterizes as 'the British Orientalists' infatuation with the ancient' (1993, 229). Elsewhere she writes about the practical, administrative and legal effects of this infatuation: 'A feature of orientalist scholarship that had a profound impact on government was its promotion of the distant past as normative' (ibid., 242).

The royal houses and land owning families of India greeted this colonial need for knowledge, which reached a provisional compilatory height in the *Fifth Report* of 1812 (into which Oram's report on Nandapur of 1784 was also incorporated) with mistrust, and they correctly regarded it as politically motivated. This mistrust existed even where administrative motives were accompanied by a genuine interest in historical knowledge, as in the case of Colonel Mackenzie and his Indian co-workers, who collected the greatest body of manuscripts on the local histories of south India up to the present day.[19] However, Indian rulers also used colonial interest in their histories to manipulate questions concerning their traditional right to possess land and to privileges of other sorts in their favour. These questions became increasingly relevant in front of administrative tribunals and courts in the course of the land reforms and census activities of the nineteenth century.[20] In this way, with the help of the Brahmans, they 'found' or 'created' documents, family trees or *vaṃśāvali*s, which identified them as 'ancient and prestigious' and were intended to endow them with legitimacy in the eyes of the British.[21]

In their histories, often composed in the decades around 1800, royal houses and their Brahman historians not infrequently appealed to older charters and other documents actually in their possession, which 'remembered' historical events and the transfer of rights. The writing and thus 'fixing' of selected historical events and dates on copper plates and palm leaves, or in temple, palace or rock inscriptions, represents a

[19] The documents in the Mackenzie Collection, collected in the decades around 1800, concentrate mainly on south Indian kingdoms, though they also cover areas up to northern Andhra Pradesh, that is, up to the boundaries of Jeypore. The Government Oriental Manuscript Library in Madras, however, has no sources referring directly to the history of Jeypore in the Mackenzie Collection. On Mackenzie, see also Berkemer (1993, 48-50), Dirks (1989b, 45-9; 1993), Kulke (1987, 146-9), Mahalingam (1976) and Wilson (1882).

[20] On the role of census activities in the process of colonial acquisition of knowledge, see Cohn (1987) and Dirks (1989b, 49-50).

[21] The various claims to be of Rajput descent were often not only 'believed' by the British: in colonial historiography itself some such fabrications were sometimes made or actively supported. See Banerjee (1928, 287-90).

practice going back into antiquity, in which Indian rulers' proclamatory interests received expression. The specific ideological content of these older sources can, therefore, only be understood against the background of the prevailing politico-ritual conditions of these more remote periods of history, in which aspects of ritual sovereignty stood in the foreground of any interest in 'tradition'.

The documents on Jeypore's early period available to me are, therefore, complex in nature, belonging to, and combining the 'texts' of, different historical periods, each with its own different idea of history, need for legitimation and ideological framework. Although the information contained in them basically belongs to the *ideological* history of the kings of Jeypore, nonetheless, in this part of the work, it will be consulted for its historical content. The following discussion, which can only proceed on the basis of meagre sources and in accordance with their different degrees of probability, thus, seeks to reconstruct not so much 'how it really was' as 'how it might have been'.

3. The origin of the Jeypore Suryavamshis

There are many claims and hypotheses concerning the origin of the Jeypore Suryavamshis and concerning the circumstances which are supposed to have led to Vinayaka's take-over of power in Nandapur in the fifteenth century. The Jeypore family chronicle represents Vinayaka Deo as the second son of a royal house of Rajput descent long established in Kashmir.[22] Oram claims, however, that the Nandapur Suryavamshis were the descendants of a 'servant and a favourite to an ancient king of Jagannaut'.[23] Carmichael, too, in the *Vizagapatam District Gazetteer*, regards the claim of the Jeypore royal house to a Rajput origin as a 'legend', and he also assumes, referring to 'a more sober account' (probably, that is, Oram's report), that the Jeypore dynasty owes its origins to a member of the court of the Suryavamsha Gajapatis.[24] In the family chronicle of the Eastern Gangas, the *Gaṅgavaṃśānucaritam*, written in the middle of the eighteenth century, however, the origin of the Jeypore kings is traced back to the imperial Gangas. The last Ganga Gajapati, Bhanudeva IV, is supposed to have withdrawn to the south after being overthrown by Kapilendra Deo, where he settled in a place called Gudari,

[22] See Sarma (1938, verses 1 to 106), as well as the versions of Vadivelu (1984, 70) and Singh Deo (1939, 9).

[23] See Oram (1784, 18).

[24] See Carmichael (1869, 284).

in the modern district of Gunupur. From there, according to this chronicle, the Ganga family were later able to seize power in Nandapur.[25]

Corresponding to these different legends of origin and migration, we find different representations of how Vinayaka Deo found his way to the hills of Nandapur from north-west India (or central Orissa) and conquered the throne. According to the Jeypore family chronicle, Vinayaka Deo, being the second-born, was excluded from succession to the royal office of his father. In his despair, he is supposed to have set out on a search for a kingdom of his own, which initially led him to Benares as a pilgrim. After he had fasted there for 21 days, Shiva appeared to him in a dream and revealed the existence of the Nandapur kingdom, over which he, Vinayaka, was destined to rule. The legend continues:

> The faithful devotee wended his way south, and after several difficulties, reached Nandapur, where he repaired to the temple of Sarveswar [Shiva] and prayed to the Deity for the fulfilment of the object of his mission. The very night the God appeared in a dream to the king of Nandapur and advised him to give away his only daughter in marriage to the Jammu prince who was then staying in his temple. The king woke from his dream and at once went to the temple, when, to his great surprise, he found the Prince of upright gait and noble bearing, though travel-spoiled. The latter narrated the story of his visit. The king was greatly pleased with everything he heard, and taking the Prince to his palace, made him his son-in-law, and entrusted to him the government of his kingdom. (Singh Deo 1939, 10).[26]

If one follows the reports of Oram and Carmichael, however, the founder of the Jeypore Suryavamshis first acquired a daughter of the Gajapati as his wife, after which he was installed in Nandapur as governor. The only child of the last Shilavamsha king of Nandapur is then supposed to have been taken by Vinayaka as his second wife, also strengthening his authority in the area through this alliance.[27]

As regards the historicity of these different versions, we must share Oram's and Carmichael's doubts concerning the Rajput origins of the Jeypore Suryavamshis. Certainly, from the twelfth century on, small

[25] See Mukherjee (1953, 19) and Senapati (1966, 58).

[26] See also the versions in Francis (1907, 263), Sarma (1938, verses 106-143) and Vadivelu (1984, 70-2), as well as Berkemer's discussion (1993, 211-13). On the Indo-European theme of the 'heroic son-in-law from a foreign country', which also has a bearing on Jeypore, see Sahlins (1985).

[27] See Oram (1784, 18) and Carmichael (1869, 284).

groups of Rajputs were pressing out of their homeland in north-west India, which had fallen under Muslim rule, into the middle Ganges valley. Yet, Rajput families were not able to come to power in the grand style for a long time to come. Their bases of power were isolated and their local dominance, which was based on continually changing alliances with entrenched power elites and on never-ending military activity, was often merely fleeting. It was only in the eighteenth century, with the waning of Mughal power, that the widespread establishment of 'neo-traditional' Hindu kingdoms by Rajput clans in the middle Ganges region and in some areas of central and western India could occur.[28]

Against this historical background, it is not likely that the kingdom of the last Shilavamshis in the hills of Nandapur became the site of a Rajput take-over of power already in the fifteenth century—not even in the sense of the action of an individual. However, what could reach southern Orissa via central Indian kingdoms and acquire meaning there was the model character of Rajput royal rule. As Sinha (1962) shows, the development of state forms of rule in many tribal societies in central India originally operating on a clan basis was 'very largely a story of Rajputisation of the tribe' (ibid., 36). Here, Sinha hits on the important distinction between Rajput infiltration actually carried out and the 'stimulus diffusion of an idea' (ibid., 71).[29]

As Sinha explains further, the employment of renowned Brahmans, brought in from the outside, was the basic prerequisite for the adoption of a Rajput model of rule by local power elites in central India. In the context of Indian politico-religious life, such priests could be brought into a kingdom by means of generous land grants. Under the spiritual guidance of their new gurus, the members of ruling families who were striving to rise in the social scale then cultivated ritual life and court etiquette in harmony with Brahmanical ideas and prescriptions. Among the innovations in ritual, ceremonial and daily behaviour were the adoption of Brahmanical life-cycle rituals, the patronage of Hindu idols, temples and festivals, the introduction of vegetarianism and avoidance of alcohol, a prohibition on the remarriage of widows, the building of palaces, the keeping of concubines and—coming back to the present point—'making up, with the help of Brahmans, a fictitious genealogy establishing mythical connection with the illustrious Rajput clans of north-western India' (Sinha 1962, 49).

[28] On this, see, especially, Bayly (1992, 17-20).

[29] Berkemer, too, argues in this context that it was 'not people, but ideas, [that] underlay this process of diffusion' (1993, 78; my translation).

The claim set out in the Jeypore family chronicle that Vinayaka Deo was of Rajput origin, thus, does not refer to a historical event in the fifteenth century but represents a later construction in the ideological history of the kingdom. Vinayaka's noble birth, the pilgrimage to Benares, the divine selection in Shiva's temple, the further divine intervention in the form of a dream that appeared to the last Shilavamsha king, as well as the latter's willing acceptance of Vinayaka as his son-in-law and successor—all these successively introduced themes form a 'charter' which was probably only produced in written form under early colonial rule. Only then did this charter acquire political relevance in legitimizing, and raising the reputation of, the king of Jeypore and his house vis-à-vis the British colonial power.[30]

Despite its late origin and ideological character, one should not simply set aside the family chronicle when it comes to reconstructing the early history of the kingdom and contemplating the origins of the Jeypore Suryavamshis. Some historical knowledge can be gleaned from the *Jayapura Raja Vamsyavali* by comparing it with a legend concerning the origin of the Suryavamshi Gajapatis, which was not far removed in either time or space. Let us recall the historical situation in central India at that time. The founder of the new ruling dynasty, Kapilendra, came from a family that had already served as *nāyaka*s under the Gangas in the south of their empire. Initially, Kapilendra's rule was strongly contested by expelled members of the Ganga court as well as by other *rājā*s in the region, who harboured their own ambitions for Gajapati status or wished to preserve their independence. Kapilendra, therefore, had to find additional religious legitimacy with the help of the priests of the Jagannath temple in Puri. As mentioned earlier, Jagannath had already developed

[30] As already mentioned, the widespread production of *vaṃśāvali*s and genealogies proclaiming Rajput descent is probably to be dated to the period between 1770 and 1820, when early colonial interests provided a stimulus to such productions. This dating also seems likely for Jeypore, because in this period a series of politico-ritual changes took place in the kingdom (for example, the employment of a new dynasty of royal gurus or the building of a new palace), to which a Rajputizing character in Sinha's sense can be attributed. Probably, then, from the newly installed *purohita* dynasty of that time descended not only, six generations later, the author of the *Jayapura Raja Vamsyavali*, but also the author of an earlier palm-leaf version of the family chronicle. On the Rajput ideal and the Rajputization of the royal houses of Orissa, see also Banerjee (1928; 1930/1, vol. 2), Berkemer (1993, 78-81), Biller (1968, 177-8), Cobden-Ramsay (1982, part 2), Kulke (1979a, 95-6; 1987, 146 note 30), Mazumdar (1925), Mohapatra (1962) and Roy (1926).

into the state deity of the kingdom under the Gangas and into the most important source of legitimacy for the Gajapatis. However, under Kapilendra Deo this function of the god of Puri acquired a new quality: while Kapilendra's predecessors merely counted as Jagannath's earthly representatives, the priests of Puri proclaimed the first Suryavamsha Gajapati to have been personally chosen and nominated by Jagannath. The chronicle of the Jagannath temple[31] reports that, in a dream, Jagannath came to the last Ganga Gajapati and ordered him to proclaim a young beggar he would meet in the Vimala temple the next day as his successor. This youth, Kapilendra, was found in accordance with the prophecy and nominated Gajapati.[32]

And here we see the heuristic value of a comparison with the origin and migration legend of Jeypore: As with the Jeypore tradition of the divine selection of Vinayaka, in the Gajapati legend we find a panegyric written for the legitimization and transfiguration of rule. In seeking a historical basis through the process of comparison, it emerges that in both cases the new kings are represented as 'intruders', as actors arriving from the outside and, without possessing any 'hereditary charisma' or 'charisma of blood', removing established but weakened dynasties. (In the context of Hindu rules of succession, the motif of a missing male successor symbolizes a reproductive and dynastic crisis as well as a political one.) Moreover, divine interventions, manifested in dreams, are proclaimed in both cases. In this way, the hereditary charisma is replaced—and outbid—by a personal, not yet routinized form of charisma. In both cases, moreover, the chosen ones appear in such shabby state upon their discovery—one is marked by his long journey, the other appears as a beggar—that their elevation as kings seems all the more impressive.

However, there is a significant difference between the two versions. Kapilendra's actual origin is disparaged, in that, though the son of a significant local magnate, he is degraded in the Gajapati chronicle into a young beggar or cowherd, while in the *Jayapura Raja Vamsyavali* Vinayaka is given a prestigious origin as a Rajput. As Dash (1978b) argues, the social disparagement of Kapilendra seems to indicate the Gajapatis' great dependence on the priests of Puri. In contrast, the legendary elevation of Vinyaka's origins might lead to the conclusion that the seizure of power in the Nandapur hills took place without priestly

[31] This chronicle is known as *Māḍalā Pāñji* and was compiled around 1600.

[32] On this see Dash (1978b, 209-12), Kulke (1978c, 204-6; 1979a, 70-3) and the *Kaṭakarājavaṃśāvali* (verse 59) in Tripathi and Kulke (eds. 1987, 59).

partisanship. On the other hand, it is precisely the emphasis with which Vinayaka is presented as a divine choice and a venerable aristocrat that indicates a lack of legitimacy of the traditional sort.

It can be concluded from all this that Vinayaka Deo came to the kingdom as an outsider without sufficient hereditary charisma to mark him as the legitimate heir to the Shilavamshis or at least as an aristocrat. Some legitimacy was acquired later through his marriage to Lilavati, the only child of the Shilavamshi king, some through the fabrication of his prestigious Rajput lineage. Above all ideological strategies, however, reigns that of divine selection.

If the Jeypore family chronicle basically represents the justification, in a later historical period, of a rule which initially lacked traditional legitimacy, does this, historically, make the other hypotheses of the origin of the Jeypore Suryavamshis more likely? I recall the claim in the *Gaṅga-vaṃśānucharitam,* that the kings of Jeypore were the dynastic descendents of the imperial Gangas, who had been deposed in central Orissa. In this case the question arises why a dynastic link with the royal line of the north-west Indian Rajputs had to be fabricated. The 'Great Eastern Gangas' were themselves a venerable royal house and, at least in south and east India, with a great reputation and with important family and political links to other royal houses in the macro-region. Given such an origin, the Jeypore Suryavamshis could have claimed a more believable dynastic origin which lacked nothing in terms of prestige. There is also the question why a supposed 'post-Gajapati' Ganga royal house in late medieval Nandapur should have evoked the theme of divine selection by Shiva. The Gangas of the eleventh century and later periods were certainly devoted Shaivites, but we should suppose that they would promote not Shiva but Jagannath, whom they themselves had been pushing into the politico-religious limelight for many centuries, as the *deus ex machina.* All in all, it is more likely that the old, forfeited Gajapati splendour and Jagannath would have been called upon as witnesses to the greatness of the line.[33]

Must one, therefore, decide in favour of the 'sober accounts' of Oram and Carmichael, according to whom Vinayaka emerged from the courtly circles of the new Suryavamshi Gajapatis and was installed by them? The thesis of a new royal line in the Nandapur hills as a feudal offshoot of the Gajapatis imposes itself, since, under Kapilendra and his successor Purushottama, many of the little kingdoms of the region were given new governors. As already mentioned, among the little kingdoms of Ganjam,

[33] Such a strategy was used by the little kingdom of Parlakimedi.

many royal houses trace their origins to this period. Why should a new ruling family in Nandapur not have come to power in this way too? And, indeed, the thesis of imperial appointment entered the writings of the gazetteers etc. and became 'official', so to say. The *District Gazetteer* of 1966 even assumes family links between the Jeypore Suryavamshis and the Gajapatis: 'It is not unlikely that the Nandapur kingdom was conferred by Kapileswara Deva, the first Suryavamshi Gajapati, to one of the scions of his family as a mark of favour' (Senapati 1966, 59).

However, for various reasons the theory of the imperial installation is not any more convincing. Why, for example, did Jeypore's royal family not evoke family or other ties with the Gajapatis of central Orissa in their family chronicle? Such a relationship would certainly not have lacked legitimation and prestige. And why, with such close relationships with the rulers of the Gajapati kingdom, was it not Jagannath, a much better known god in these matters in Orissa, but Shiva who was presented as the divine guarantor of the take-over of power in Nandapur? The absence of any mention of the pilgrimage site of Puri in the Jeypore family chronicle is especially striking when one remembers that the theme of a Rajput prince going on a pilgrimage to Puri with his pregnant wife can be found in the origin myths of many royal houses of central Orissa, West Bengal and the Deccan. On the return journey, according to these legends, the wife gives birth to a child by the roadside. The child is left behind and raised by common people, but later attains royal dignity at the place of his birth. Throughout the region, therefore, linking the origin of a royal dynasty with a pilgrimage to Puri and thus with the Gajapatis was a common theme.[34] In the Jeypore chronicle, on the other hand, Vinayaka goes on a pilgrimage not to Puri, but to Benares, the holy city of Shiva, from where, in obedience to the vision in his dream, he goes directly to Nandapur, without diverting via Puri, and without mentioning the Gajapatis or Jagannath.

Even if one interprets the lack of links with the Gajapatis and their imperial god in the Jeypore origin myth as a late ideological construct which the jungle kings used retrospectively to express their independence from the earlier overlords, there are reservations concerning a theory of imperial appointment. This is so because the widespread idea of the traditional Indian state as a hierarchically organized structure corresponds to the situation in fifteenth-century Orissa only to a limited extent. It would be to misunderstand the character and range of the power the

[34] On this type of origin or migration myth, see Sinha (1962, 39-40, 60-1, 75), McLane (1993, 130-1) and Roy (1912, 136-40).

Gajapatis exercised if one were to attribute to them the capacity to install members of their court or their own family in such a remote area as the jungle kingdom of Jeypore. This type of power—which must be distinguished from the Gajapatis' privilege in legitimizing a little king ritually, from their right to demand tribute and from their military ability to expel a recalcitrant king by force on occasion—probably existed with respect to many little kingdoms in the coastal region. However, one must question the direct influence of the central power in the hilly hinterland of southern Orissa for reasons of military strength alone. It is especially questionable because Vinayaka's first appearance comes at a time in Orissan history in which one imperial royal house had just been replaced by another one and in which the new great king, Kapilendra, had still not established his power on the coast, let alone in the hills. Any hypothesis positing the Jeypore royal house as the foster child of a strong central state must, therefore, be questioned not only theoretically, i.e., with reference to outdated notions of the nature and origin of the state in India, but also in the light of the concrete historical situation which allowed Vinayaka to come to power in Nandapur.

Compared with the *vaṃśāvali*s of south Indian kingdoms, it is also striking that in the Jeypore chronicle the idea of a gradual evolution from 'bandit' into 'chief' and 'little king' receives no expression. This theme, found in many south Indian chronicles, of the genesis and maturing of little-kingly rule is understood to be the consequence of a series of services and heroic deeds performed for the 'great king'. The development of a structural relationship between the robber/chief/little king on the one hand and the great king on the other is central to these tales.[35] In the Jeypore family chronicle, however, this type of relationship is of no significance: Vinayaka was chosen by God, and service to the Gajapatis played no role in his attainment of little-kingly status. Hence, once again, we find the Jeypore kings and their historiographers stressing their independence from the Gajapatis and so, from the emic perspective, an imperial nomination is declined.

In the legends of origin of many little kingdoms of south and central India, it is argued that their royal houses were originally old and established groups operating on a clan, caste or tribal basis. It is often reported that the local authority of these groups was transformed into royal power through internal developments.[36] Since 'great-kingly sanction' and 'tradi-

[35] See Berkemer (1993, 256-8), Dirks (1987, 78-96; 239-43) and Shulman (1980; 1985, 366-73).

[36] Sinha speaks of 'tribal-derived kingdoms'. To what extent the Nandapur kingdom in earlier times was the product of such an internal development from a

tional local power' represent themes pursued in the reports of other Indian kingdoms with great self-assurance, one can not explain their absence in the Jeypore chronicle as being only ideological in character, that is, as being the expression of a self-consciousness stressing autonomy against any overlord. The fact that neither themes are evoked suggests that the royal house of the Jeypore Suryavamshis indeed had no traditional basis of authority in the kingdom and that it did not actually belong to any of the social groups rooted in the locality before coming to power.

Where, however, did Vinayaka come from, if he was neither a Rajput from Kashmir nor a descendant of the Gangas, nor a scion of the Suryavamshi Gajapatis nor an upstart local tribal chief or caste headman? Once again, one should take seriously the social logic of the family chronicle, though without overstretching its historicity. Let us see what Singh Deo reports of the events *following* Vinayaka's marriage to the king's daughter Lilavati and his ascension to the throne:

> Vinayaka continued to rule over his country for some time but troubles soon arose and, unable to overcome them, he repaired to his native country of Jammu. On the way he came by an unexpected God-sent help from a very rich and influential merchant named Lobinia, who placed at his disposal a large army of cavalry and infantry with 10,000 cattle for transport. With this equipment Vinayakasingh Deo returned to Nandapur, put down the turbulent elements there, and placed himself firmly on the throne. (Singh Deo 1939, 10)

The 'turbulent elements' clearly convey a different picture from that of the peaceful take-over of the throne by a heroic son-in-law divinely sent from a foreign country. In the legend, the contradiction is resolved diachronically: internal difficulties that may well have existed before and during the take-over are only mentioned as occuring after he mounted the throne. Moreover, the report indirectly confirms the assumption that the central power of the Gajapatis was not present in the Nandapur region at that time: again no role is ascribed to the Gajapatis, not even with Vinayaka's re-attainment of power.

In this episode we hear, for the first time in the chronicle, of a militarily well-organized group of merchants who is presented as a decisive factor in the struggle for power. There are few studies of the merchant castes, which at that time linked the trading centres of the

---

tribal or caste basis is another question, one which cannot be gone into here. The appearance of the concept of 'rock' or *śila* in the name of the Shilavamshi dynasty (1353-1443) that preceded the Suryavamshis may indicate a tribal origin.

Deccan with those of the coasts of Andhra Pradesh and Orissa with their caravans. There is also little research concerning the exact course of the routes they took. However, the presence and influence of powerful groups of warrior merchants, who knew how to secure their caravans and local bases along the trade routes in military style, is documented beyond doubt as an important element in the politics of this period and macro-region.[37] The legend of Vinayaka's meeting with Lobinia not only confirms the impact of warrior merchants on the kingdom of Jeypore and its vicinity, it also underlines the fact that merchants did not hesitate to intervene directly in political struggles for power and, in doing so, even to install a king. In seeking historicity here, the further intervention of an 'unexpected God-sent help' must therefore be questioned. Vinayaka's meeting with Lobinia probably did not take place by chance and the military intervention of the warrior merchant was not as context-free and unconditional as local tradition suggests. In my interpretation of the emic text, Vinayaka may have previously established commercial and alliance relationships with Lobinia and other merchants, which he exploited militarily when his rule was endangered. Alternatively, Vinayaka himself may have been a member of a powerful group of warrior merchants who were well acquainted with the political and military situation in the former Shilavamsha kingdom and were both ready and able to influence conditions of power there actively in their own interest.

Summing up, therefore, one can say that hypotheses concerning Vinayaka's seizure of power appear conclusive only when one ascribes two characteristics to the founder of the Jeypore dynasty: a) that he was an outsider (not a local upstart); and b) that he was someone well acquainted with political conditions in the area who could mobilize support on the spot (rather than having been an imported Gajapati governor or a divinely sent foreigner without local backing). These two seemingly contradictory characteristics, being an outsider and yet pos-

[37] Among the authors who have studied the participation of artisan and merchant castes in Indian politics are Appadurai (1974), Bayly (1992), Beck (1970), Chakravarti (1990), Hall (1980), Mines (1984), Stein (1980, ch. V; 1991, 224-6) and Subrahmanyam (1986, 365-75). Carmichael (1869) and Francis (1907) mention at several places in their works the merchant groups known in Orissa as *brinjāri*. Francis follows the family chronicle when he writes: '[Vinayaka] recovered his position with the help of a leader of the Brinjaries' (1907, 264). Panda (1986, 41) refers to medieval Kalinga inscriptions in which merchants bear the title *mahāsenāpati*, the designation of a military leader of the Gajapati kingdom. Information on Orissan trade routes can be found in Acharya (1955/6) and Panda (1986, 122-3).

sessing local knowledge and power, are reconciled if we see Vinayaka as a member, or close ally, of one of the groups of warrior merchants who crossed the region with their caravans but who may also have lived there permanently at selected places. This hypothesis is supported by a fact reported in all the different versions, for example by Vadivelu: 'In token of gratitude to the merchant prince whose help was most opportune, Vinaik Singh Deo used in his signature Chatuni (a rope used by the merchants for tying cattle). This mark has from that time forward been used by all the succeeding kings' (1984, 72). Francis, too, mentions the fact that 'ever since then, in grateful recognition, his descendants have appended to their signatures a wavy line (called *valalradu*) which represents the rope with which Brinjáries tether their cattle' (1907, 264).[38]

The Jeypore royal family, therefore, embellished a central medium of their ritual self-representation, the official royal seal, with an imprint borrowed from the mercantile world. They did this, however, not so much through gratitude for services rendered out of friendship, but because they themselves came from this milieu or at least had close social and political contacts with warrior merchants before attaining power. For Sarma, too, Vinayaka's meeting with Lobinia was less a matter of chance: 'To tranquilise the onerous situation he took another stride. With some of his followers he went to Raipur in Chhattisgarh State and met one Labani, a contemporary wealthy merchant of Raipur. He greeted the king with royal hospitality. The king revealed the seditious activities of his tribal subjects and sought the help of the merchant' (1938, verses 135-6). According to this report, Vinayaka thus knew exactly where he could seek help against an internal uprising, here interestingly described as 'tribal', and Lobinia (alias Labani) knew who he was dealing with. Moreover, the exact identification of the place in Sarma's report also suggests that this merchant had his family seat in the central Indian region of Chhattisgarh.

Only later did the Rajput origin, sun emblem and Suryavamsha family title become the most important components of royal self-display, with which the reputation and legitimacy of the house, corresponding to the contemporary paradigm of rule, were to be elevated. In this later process of ideological renewal, which I would situate in the period between 1770 and 1820, the actual origin of the house and historical events from the foundation period were not so much erased as reinterpreted and revalued. Despite this transformational process, however, there remain enough indications of 'how it might have been'.

[38] See also Sarma (1938, verse 138) and Singh Deo (1939, 10). On the use of 'signa' among different occupational groups and castes in Orissa, see Roy (1933, 330-1).

4. The problem of 'Rajput' identity

Many writers who have concerned themselves with the problem of Rajput origins and the 'Rajputization' have been unable to free themselves from the assumption that the term 'Rajput' describes a closed, endogamous status group based on ethnic and/or genealogical criteria.[39] A great deal of the discussion focuses on the question (not by any means just an academic one) whether, with respect to any given group, we are dealing with 'true' Rajputs or only 'pseudo' or 'spurious' Rajputs. Even my own account, which questions the claims of the Jeypore Suryavamshis to a Rajput origin, has up to now followed this line of thought.

Kolff (1990) has cast doubt on this view of things in his study of the 'military labour market' in Hindustan from 1450 to 1850. According to him, the term 'Rajput', literally 'son of a king', did not originally designate an endogamous caste but was a generic title for a number of relatively open groups originating in military service (and reputation). In keeping with more recent theories of ethnicity and the formation of group identities, in which it is not so much encapsulated social units as discursive practices and their social as well as political logic that are the focus of analysis, Kolff argues that 'India's multiplicity of identities represented as many integrative concepts, as many communities of memories and expectation' (ibid., 70). Concerning the Rajputs of the pre-Mughal era he writes: 'In the nineteenth century some Rajputs were spoken of as spurious, i.e. as not answering to the then generally accepted genealogical or ethnic criteria of historical identities. I no longer accept these rigid criteria and suspect that in the ranks of these armies social identities could be achieved in a manner that was diffuse and dynamic' (ibid., 66-7).[40]

For Kolff, the formation of closed, elitist Rajput clans represents merely a later historical development whose origin is located in the military and politico-ritual situation of the Mughal empire under Akbar (1565–1605). Thus we learn:

[39] Apart from the authors mentioned in footnote 30, the studies of Chattopadhyaya (1976), Fox (1971), Tod (1920 [1829-32]) and Ziegler (1978) should be noted.

[40] Without doubt the *kṣatriya varṇa* or 'warrior caste', to which the Rajputs belong, is the most open of the four *varṇa*s. Kolff's criticism, however, is directed more widely when he suggests: 'We are far removed from the world of caste and "ascribed" status that for so long was regarded as central to the social history of India' (1990, 67). For a critique of essentializing views of the Indian caste in general and the equally problematic labels of 'clan', 'tribe' and 'race', see Kolff (1990, 181-99).

> During the sixteenth and seventeenth centuries, the top layer of Rajputs … tended to close ranks and to articulate new norms of Rajput behaviour. Bards had always encouraged their Rajput employers to assume aristocratic self-images closely linked with myths of origin that established their status as *kṣatriya*s and traced back their genealogies to, for instance, the great dynasties of ancient Indian history. But now the political power and social status of the more successful lineages tended to be legitimised exclusively in the language of descent and kinship. This idiom, of course, was deeply rooted in the traditions of Indian royalty, but from the sixteenth century onwards, the political opportunities of the Mughal court and the emphasis the Mughals themselves placed on genealogy gave it a new vigour and largely pushed into the background the more ancient character of the Rajputs as an open status group. The tendency to interpret Rajput history in genealogical terms was later inherited by Tod and other British Indian administrators. (Kolff 1990, 72)

However, this genealogically grounded exclusivity represents, for Kolff, only half the truth, since outside Rajasthan the original Rajput phenomenon has lasted into the modern period. He portrays this 'little' Rajput tradition, which stands outside the rigid orthodoxy of the 'new Rajput Great Tradition' (ibid., 73), using words which refer to Hindustan, but which are also appropriate for the jungle kingdom of Jeypore:

> There one finds, until late in the nineteenth century, on the farther edges of recognised Rajputhood, a large number of clans with traditions of service and fighting who were no longer recognised as fit marriage partners by the aristocracy. They were the so-called 'spurious' Rajputs, whose 'rajputisation' never seemed fully achieved. (ibid.)[41]

Hence, it appears that the attributes 'true' and 'pseudo' in connection with the ethnic category 'Rajput' are the result of sixteenth-century political and ideologico-ritual processes. Against the background of these considerations, the Jeypore Suryavamshis can be considered to be just as much legitimate Rajputs—in the original meaning of the word as part of the little tradition—as the noblest lineages of Rajasthan or even Mewar, while the origins of these latter, viewed more closely, can hardly be traced back historiographically further than the fourteenth century in many cases without becoming fictive. Thus, many of these 'true' Rajputs, rich in prestige and influence up to the present day, deserve no more than the description 'pseudo' if one uses the characterization 'Rajput'

[41] On this, see also Kolff (1990, 110).

consistently in the sense of their own bardic traditions and their marriage practices as well as in the understanding of colonial and traditional historical writings.

The Jeypore tradition in which Vinayaka, excluded from succession to his father's throne and unsatisfied with his lot and full of a thirst for action, proceeded to search for a kingdom of his own, does not really represent, in this view of things, an attempt to create an actually non-existent glorious origin retrospectively. Rather, it is a genuine expression of a 'little' tradition, widespread in India in pastoral, migratory circles, of an adventurous young man who leaves his home and family and enters foreign territory in order to seek honour, land and followers, thus *earning* the title 'Rajput' through courage, the arts of war and persistence, regardless of whether he originally set off as a soldier, migrant worker, pack-animal trader or actually (and ideally) as a king's son by *birth*. Hence, the question is not whether the Jeypore kings were 'true' or 'pseudo' Rajputs, but whether their 'Rajputish-ness' was based on 'blood' or on merit. The latter seems to be the case.

5. The consolidation of power

Like his Shilavamsha predecessors, Vinyaka Deo had himself installed on the 'throne of the 32 steps' in Nandapur, known as *vikrāmarka* and still in existence today as a memorial. After suppressing the revolt mentioned earlier, he was able to apply himself to consolidating his power internally and extending the borders of the old Shilavamsha empire. In doing this, he succeeded in making a number of little kings tributary to him as far as Guntur District in present-day Andhra Pradesh. After 33 years of rule, Vinayaka Deo died and was succeeded by his son Vijaya Chandra (1476-1510), who consolidated the achievements of his father by successfully suppressing the revolts of renegade governors and tributary little kings.[42]

Vinayaka's and Vijaya's periods of rule coincided chronologically with those of the first Suryavamsha Gajapatis, Kapilendra Deo (1435-1466) and Purushottama Deo (1467-1497). Like the two Gajapatis, the first Jeypore Suryavamshis were initially occupied mainly with consolidating their rule over the population of their realms and quelling rebellious governors at the borders of their kingdom. Later, they also extended their realms southwards trying to bind the newly acquired areas, with their *rājās*, to their kingdom securely. Naturally, this extension of power took place on a smaller scale than in the case of the Gajapatis, who

[42] See Singh Deo (1939, 11) and Sarma (1938, verse 132).

managed to establish one of the largest Hindu empires of their time. In their relationship with the Gajapatis, therefore, Vinayaka and Vijaya Chandra could not afford to risk direct territorial conflicts, and their parallel extension towards the south may well have been restricted to the hilly hinterland of the Eastern Ghats. Moreover, the kings of Nandapur also attempted to subdue some of the kingdoms lying between the Gajapati-dominated coast and the hills of their own jungle kingdom, where these kingdoms controlled strategically important access points into the hills.

The Jeypore family chronicle reports an antagonistic meeting between Gajapati Purushottama and Vijaya Chandra, which I would like to discuss on the basis of the respective legends of Puri and the Kimedi kingdoms. This meeting is said to have taken place during one of Purushottama's military expeditions to the kingdom of Kanchipuram, a segment of the transregional Vijayanagara empire, and is remembered in the so-called *Kāñchī Kāverī* tradition of the Gajapatis.[43] The trigger for Purushottama's campaign given in this legend, which is still very popular in Orissa, is romantic in nature. Purushottama wanted to marry the daughter of the king of Kanchipuram, Princess Padmabati, whose hand had already been promised him by her father. However, his prospective father-in-law withdrew his agreement after being told that Purushottama had acted as a 'sweeper'. This concerned the already mentioned *cherā pāhamrā* ritual at the yearly car festival (*ratha yātrā*) for Jagannath, in the course of which the king, to express his personal devotion, sprinkles Jagannath's car with water and then sweeps it with a long golden broom. Apparently offended by this ritual, the king of Kanchipuram, a Shaivite, withdrew his approval for the marriage of his daughter. Purushottama took this rejection as a personal insult and an affront to the highest god of Orissa. He, therefore, set out to take the princess by force, though his first campaign to do so ended in defeat. His subsequent pleas and prayers for divine support were heard by Jagannath, who encouraged Purushottama, in a dream, to take up the fight again, and the god entered the battle personally with his divine brother Balabhadra. Jagannath's active help manifested itself to Purushottama, again on the way to Kanchipuram, when a milkmaid by the name of Maniki wanted to cash in a ring which Jagannath, who had hurried in front of the army disguised as a knight, had left behind as a deposit for

[43] On Purushottama's rule and the *Kāñchī Kāverī* legend, see Berkemer (1993, 202-6), Dash (1978b, 212-19), Hunter (1872 vol. 1, 320-1), Kulke (1978c, 206-8; 1979a, 73-4), Mukherjee (1953, 48-63), Rajaguru (1968-72 [vol. 2], 72-5) and the *Kaṭakarājavaṃśāvali* in Tripathi and Kulke (eds. 1987, 85-8).

some curd. Kanchipuram was taken, Padmabati abducted and, after some hesitation, taken as wife by Purushottama.

Two similar legends circulate in the little kingdoms of Parlakimedi and Badakimedi. In the first tradition we meet Hamvira, Kapilendra's oldest son, who, angered at being cheated of the succession to the throne by his younger brother Purushottama, is said to have withdrawn to south Gudari, where he founded the Parlakimedi kingdom. The legend reports that, before his expedition against Kanchi, the goddess Manikeshvari requested Puroshottama, in a dream, to make peace with his brother. This reconciliation had the fortunate consequence that Hamvira's military support contributed decisively to the fall of Kanchipuram. In the Badakimedi tradition, Svarnabhanu, another of Kapilendra's eighteen sons, fell in love with the daughter of the sage Kapila, who worshipped the goddess Manikeshvari. Unfortunately, a Vijayanagara king stole this girl called Manikyabati from the hermitage with the aim of giving her as a wife to the ruler of the Bahmani Sultanate. However, Kapilendra defeated the Vijayanagara king and the girl was married to the lucky Svarnabhanu, who now also became the king of Badakimedi. The sage Kapila gave his daughter a statue of the goddess Manikeshvari as a wedding gift, which she worshipped regularly henceforward.[44]

If one compares the three versions, the following picture emerges. In the Gajapati version of the *Kāñchī Kāverī* legend, the deity Jagannath is central. It is a particular act within his cult, the *cherā pāhamrā* ritual, which triggers the conflict with Kanchipuram. Jagannath then intervenes personally, though he plays no role in the two Kimedi versions, in which events revolve around the goddess Manikeshvari. Either she intervenes by appearing in a dream, or her worshipper and human representative, Manikyabati, must be saved (and married).[45]

In the Jeypore version of the *Kāñchī Kāverī* legend, too, to which we finally turn, it is a goddess, not Jagannath, who is central. It is reported that following his successful expedition against Kanchipuram—for which the Jeypore chronicle gives the date 1479—Purushottama returned with a

[44] The Kimedi legend is discussed by Dash (1978b, 216-17) and Rajaguru (1968-1972 vol. 2, 73-5). See also Berkemer (1993, 202-6) and the *Bodokimedi Family History*.

[45] Comparing the Kimedi tradition with the *Kāñchī Kāverī* tradition of the Gajapatis, Dash (1978b, 217) sees indications of the Gajapatis' early Shakta leanings. As a consequence of their becoming Vaishnavites, Dash argues, the goddess Manikeshvari was transformed into the milkmaid Maniki, a figure who can be identified with Radha.

rich booty through the wooded hinterland of Nandapur. Here, Purushottama's men, who were unfamiliar with the area and who had lost their way, were ambushed by Vijaya Chandra, who succeeded in stealing one of the Gajapati's elephants. In the booty was also a golden sculpture of the goddess Durga, which was installed with much ceremony in Nandapur as the state deity of this jungle kingdom.[46]

Without being able to go into detail here concerning the historicity of these legends, some conclusions on the historical situation of Nandapur at the time can be made by comparing the four *Kāñchī Kāverī* versions. In all four versions the focus is on ritual concerns (partly linked with romantic motifs), on the basis of which the only two Hindu great kings in the macro-region at that time come into conflict with one another. In the Kimedi traditions, the structural opposition between Orissa and Vijayanagara leads—in the style of the processes of fission and fusion known from segmentary lineage societies—to solidarity between the Gajapati and his little kings. In the Parlakimedi version, two hostile brothers (Purushottama and Hamvira) are reunited after the intervention of the goddess Manikeshvari. In the Badakimedi version, father and son (Kapilendra and Svarnabhanu) join hands to recover Manikyabati, the young devotee of Manikeshvari. In both cases the little kings later install the goddess as their tutelary deity. In this way a ritual counterweight to the Gajapatis' Jagannath cult is set up, though its significance should not be exaggerated, for the Gajapatis themselves counted as worshippers of Manikeshvari and, thus, were not hostile to her cult.

In the Jeypore tradition, the ties between the Gajapati overlord and little king appear in a less harmonious light. Certainly, to begin with, little king and great king stand united in opposition to the great king of Kanchipuram. Central to the legend, however, is the clash between great and little king, which ends in the theft of a sculpture of the goddess Durga. Once again, therefore, in the family chronicle of the Jeypore royal house we encounter an expression of its independence from the Gajapati overlords. The two Kimedi versions also stress independence with respect to the Gajapatis, though only in their status as subordinate allies (and relatives). In contrast, the ignominy that Vijaya Chandra is supposed to have inflicted on Gajapati Purushottama expresses *both* independence *and* equality of status.

Taking into account the historical as well as geographical situation, it must again be emphasized that the kingdom of Nandapur lay not in the

[46] See Sarma (1938, verses 147-55), Singh Deo (1939, 11) and Vadivelu (1904, 72) as well as Chapter VI, Section 2 of this edition.

immediate area of influence of the Gajapatis, but on the south-west periphery of their great kingdom, which could only be controlled with difficulty. However, south-east of the Nandapur hills was the Godavari delta, an area hotly contested in the late middle ages between Orissa, Vijayanagara and the Bahmani sultanate. Rarely could the fertile delta of this river be controlled long term by one of the great kingdoms alone. Even after Kapilendra's and Purushottama's successful expeditions to the south, their rule was never consolidated in this delta, which Panda (1985) fittingly describes as 'a bone of contention'. Now, while the power of the little kings in this zone remained insecure because of the smouldering struggles and constant changes of overlord, the continuing crisis of the coast had rather a strengthening influence on the exercise and consolidation of rule by the jungle kings of Nandapur. For, on the one hand, Nandapur was not directly affected by the conflict: it was the rice basket of the Krishna-Godavari delta, not the jungle kingdoms, with their meagre agricultural surplus and their only partly controllable tribal groups, that constituted the great kings' interest. Thus, on economic grounds alone, the little kings of Nandapur remained relatively unmolested by great-kingly claims to superiority or demands for tribute. On the other hand, the border kingdom of Nandapur possessed great military and strategic significance as an ally that could offer the imperial armies safe conduct, supplies, military help and refuge. It was, therefore, in the interest of the great kings to win this jungle kingdom as an ally, a fact which increased its standing, political influence and treasury.

All in all, it may be assumed that while the kingdom of Nandapur under Vijaya Chandra had an alliance with the Gajapati empire under Purushottoma, regular military support on an obligatory and tributary basis could be neither demanded nor enforced by the Gajapatis. When Nandapur did provide active support, it was probably offered voluntarily and on an ad hoc basis; and any aid was tied to concrete demands on the side of the little king, including a share in the war booty, even if this share, as in the present case, had to be obtained by force.

After Vijaya Chandra's death in 1510, his son Bhairava Deo took over the throne of Nandapur. Bhairava ruled till 1527 and, thus, he was a contemporary of Gajapati Prataparudra Deo (1497-1540), the son of Purushottama. Under Prataparudra the Gajapati empire, which once stretched from the western Ganges delta up to the Kaveri delta thanks to the victories notched up by Kapilendra and Purushottama, began to fall apart.[47] Certainly, the exercise of sovereign power by the Gajapatis had

[47] In the south, the effectively controlled sovereign area of the Suryavamshi Gajapatis stretched up to the Pennar river (about 150 km north of present-day

always been restricted to the coastal region and the most important river valleys, even in periods when there were no strong external enemies threatening the empire. However, when, at the beginning of the sixteenth century, the Gajapati empire was attacked virtually simultaneously on its furthest borders to the north and south, it was doomed to collapse. In 1509 an army of the Bengali dynasty of Hussain Shah attacked Orissa from the north when Prataparudra was on campaign in the extreme south of his empire. Prataparudra could only meet the threatening Muslim invasion in the north with great military effort, which required his lengthy personal engagement on the spot. Internal power struggles also saw to it that the empire's ability to resist was weakened. The power vacuum that had arisen in central Orissa through Prataparudra's absence was used by his minister, Govinda Vidyadhara, to organize a palace revolt and to rise against the Gajapati in alliance with Hussain. The military campaigns in the north and internal power struggles ultimately led to Orissa becoming militarily vulnerable in the south. After three campaigns between 1512 and 1516 Krishnadeva Raya, who came to power in 1509 as the ruler of a re-invigorated Vijayanagara empire, succeeded in inflicting severe defeats on Prataparudra in the Krishna-Godavari delta. As a result, the area south of the Krishna river was permanently wrested from the Gajapatis.[48]

The diminishing power of the Gajapatis in the south was, naturally, not without consequence for the Nandapur kingdom as one of the southern 'gatekeepers' of the empire. Bhairava Deo is said to have shown himself a loyal follower of Prataparuda. In the siege of the strategically important fortress of Kondapalle (north of the Krishna river)—which was maintained with great commitment but ultimately fruitlessly by numerous princes loyal to the Gajapati for many months in 1515-16—Bhairava was probably one of Pratapuradra's active comrades-in-arms and among the *sāmanta*s taken prisoner by Krishnadeva Raya.[49]

The Gajapati empire finally collapsed when Bhairava's son and successor, Viswanatha Deo (1527-1571) was in power. After his defeat at the hands of Krishnadeva Raya, Prataparudra had withdrawn to his

---

Madras) for a time under Kapilendra and Purushottama. Military successes up to the Kaveri delta further south remained sporadic and took the form of raids rather than territorial conquests.

[48] On Prataparudra, see Dash (1978b, 219-21), Kulke (1978c, 208; 1979a, 76-7), Mukherjee (1953, 72-99), Sastri (1955, Ch. XII) and Subrahmanyam (1957, Ch. V).

[49] See Singh Deo (1939, 6-7; 118-20), Senapati (1966, 56) and Subrahmanyam (1957, 107-9).

Mahanadi core area where, until his death, he concentrated on the internal consolidation of that part of the empire that remained to him and devoted himself to his religious interests. After Krishnadeva Raya's death in 1529, the Qutb Shah of Golkonda, who had become independent with the fall of the Bahmani sultanate, managed to incorporate the area north of the Krishna river up to Simhachalam (near present-day Visakhapatnam) almost without resistance. Gajapati Pratapuradra was followed by his two sons, who, after ruling for only two years, were both murdered in 1542 by Govinda Vidyadhara. Until the end of his rule in 1549, Govinda, for his part, was occupied with resisting the further advances of the Qutb Shah in the south of the empire. Internally, too, following the double regicide, his rule was not at all secure: some of the little kingdoms of the empire broke with him and even turned against him militarily. In particular, a putsch by a member of the powerful Bhanja dynasty, which ruled several little kingdoms in north and central Orissa, forced Govinda to concentrate his forces on internal affairs: the fight against Golkonda in the south had to be given up as lost. After Govinda's death three weak Gajapatis followed in quick succession, their power increasingly eroded by palace intrigues, the revolt of rebellious royal houses and the increased military pressure of external enemies. As a result, the Gajapati empire fell in 1568.[50]

While north and central Orissa came under the direct rule of the Afghan sultanate of Bengal, the history of the region south of Lake Chilika continued to be influenced less by the situation in central Orissa than by the policies of the different powers that dominated south India and the Deccan. The extension of the power of Vijayanagara and Golkonda in the first half of the sixteenth century resulted in the fall of some of the fortresses allied to Nandapur on its southern and eastern borders, which removed important access points into the hills from its control. However, the integrity of the jungle kingdom's core area remained largely untouched. Only in the extreme south-west tip, around Motu and Malkangiri, did temporary incursions by units belonging to Vijayanagara and Golkonda occur.

For the jungle kingdom under Viswanatha Deo, these changes initially meant that the coastal and delta regions bordering Nandapur fell for a long time under the control of two new great powers, which it was essential to deal with and, if possible, come to terms with. However, for a long time Hindu Vijayanagara and Muslim Golkonda were too hostile to one another and too occupied in militarily and administratively consolidating

[50] For the end of the Gajapati empire, see Berkemer (1993, 207-11), Kulke (1979a, 77-9; 87-8) and Mukherjee (1953, 108-22).

their rule in their newly won territories in the plains to pose any acute danger to the powerful jungle kingdom. Rather, for the Nandapur kingdom under Bhairava and Viswanatha Deo (i.e. from 1510 to 1571), the period was one of relatively great internal autonomy. An indication of Nandapur's increasing power and fame can be found in the *History of Quli Qutb Shah*, which Briggs incorporated into his translation of the *Tarikh-i-Ferishta*, where one 'Vusnad Dew' is mentioned as 'Gujputty, who possessed the countries of Bengal along the sea-coast as far as the confines of Tulingana' (1990 vol. 3, 219). Assessed historically, this statement is not tenable, though the fact that Viswanatha Deo is mentioned in Islamic sources at all and then as a significant opponent of the powerful Golkonda Sultanate, or is even described as a Gajapati, indicates his strong position within the alliance of Hindu *rājā*s who were opposing the Golkonda shah in the Godavari delta in the mid-sixteenth century.[51]

Two developments in the Nandapur kingdom under Viswanatha Deo deserve special mention. First, Viswanatha transferred his royal capital from Nandapur to Rayagada, about 130 kilometres to the north. Compared with Nandapur, Rayagada, still a lively market town today, lies some six hundred metres lower, on the first high plateau of the Eastern Ghats. Nestled in the open valley of the Nagavali river, the town is at the intersection of different trade routes within the district. In addition, it lies on an important route linking the Deccan with the east Indian coast, along which the railway line between Visakhapatnam and Raipur in Madhya Pradesh runs today and which may well have been used in Viswanatha's time by the Brinjaris or warrior merchants for transregional trade. The move from Nandapur to an economically more advantageous residence may be a further indication of the mercantile origin of the Jeypore

[51] In Grant's 'Political Survey of the Northern Circars' of 1786, too, which was integrated into the *Fifth Report* of 1812, there is mention of one 'Wistna Deo or Gajeputty, a powerful prince of Orissa, having united under his sceptre all the ancient family domains, from the confines of Bengal to those of Telinga in the south' (Grant 1786, 141). Singh Deo, the panegyrist of the Jeypore kingdom, seizes on this point when he writes: 'Thus we see how powerful a Nandapur ruler was with his domains that extended from Bengal to the Telingana country in the south, which contained in its fold innumerable feudatories that paid homage to the seat of Nandapur in those days' (1939, 16). Mukherjee displays a cooler head: 'The statement that he was the king of the sea-coast of Telingana and Orissa has no basis in history' (1953, 89), though he admits that 'the chiefs of Nandapur probably seized a portion of the West Godavari district after the death of Prataparudra' (ibid.).

Suryvamshis. The family chronicle also mentions the construction of a water reservoir under Bhairava Deo, suggesting the conclusion that a systematic development of agriculture took place at that time. The move to Rayagada also indicates a change in the way wealth was accumulated: instead of raids and warlike expeditions, in the sixteenth century agriculture and trade appear increasingly as routinely exploited sources of income.

Although the move from the hills of Nandapur into the Nagavali valley meant shifting the royal capital into an economically more advantageous area, it also made the nerve centre of the kingdom more vulnerable. Rayagada was more easily accessible from the coast and less protected by natural defenses. Archaeological evidence proves the existence of an extended clay fortress in Rayagada at that time—indeed the town itself, as the name suggests (*gaḍa* = 'fort'), was basically a fortress.[52] The overall military and political situation was, therefore, by no means secure, and an architectonic attempt was made to make Rayagada more advantageous. As for the balance of power between the transregional kingdoms of the macro-region, the shifting of the royal capital from Nandapur to Rayagada reflected the changed situation in the wider area of eastern India: the new residence was more distant from the now dominant Vijayanagara kings and the Golkonda shahs and nearer the core area of the weakened Gajapatis.

The second noteworthy change under Viswanatha Deo was ritual in nature. Already, at the beginning of the sixteenth century, the Vaishnavite prophet Chaitanya (1486-1533), whose teachings were marked by his devotion to Krishna, had obtained a great following in central Orissa.[53] After initial hesitations, Gajapati Prataparudra is said to have patronized the prophet and his disciples, probably also with the aim of creating a counterweight to the now overpowering influence of the Jagannath priests from Puri. After his departure from Puri in the second decade of the sixteenth century, Chaitanya's southern migration led him and his disciples through the Nandapur hills or at least through one of the foothills. The personal appearance of the prophet in southern Orissa, therefore, came in the time of Bhairava Deo, though it was only under Bhairava's son, Viswanatha, that Chaitanya's influence contributed to a far-reaching

[52] The remains of the fortress of Rayagada, which was only fully destroyed by the British at the end of the nineteenth century, still dominate the pattern of the town. See Carmichael (1869, 239) and Singh Deo (1939, 16-7).

[53] On Chaitanya's impact on Orissa, see Kulke (1979a, 17, 76-7) and Mukherjee (1953, 100-7; 1978).

change in the ritual policy of the Nandapur kings. Shaivite forms of religiosity, which had been patronized up to then, were increasingly giving way to Vaishnavite tendencies. The fact that Viswanatha founded a number of Vaishnavite temples in the Nagavali valley should not be taken merely as an indication of his great piety. Rather, it was also an attempt to win the trust of the tribal and semi-tribal population through a more temple-oriented ritual policy and to integrate them more fully into his area of influence both socially and culturally. The *bhakti* piety that characterized Chaitanya's teaching could easily accommodate the psychological and emotional needs of the simple rural dwellers, since it provided them with direct access to Hindu deities, without the all-too-restrictive mediation of the Brahmans or strict Brahmanical precepts concerning purity.[54]

In imitation of Krishna (in his form as lover of the milkmaids or *gopīs*), Viswanatha himself is said to have had 116 wives, who sought death by burning (*satī*) after his demise. To this day, the place of their death is a memorial and regularly functions as the site of ritual activities. Despite the change of direction towards Vaishnavite forms of belief, however, tribal, tantric and shaktic elements remained dominant in the religion of the kingdom. To this day, a temple dedicated to a tribal goddess within the old fortress is the centre of rituals for the inhabitants of Rayagada and its environs.[55]

[54] On Chaitanya's influence on the religious life of the jungle kingdom, Singh Deo remarks: 'The new Vaisnavic cult of Chaitanya had its usual effect on the *Saivic* and the *Shakta* cult then prevailing in Nandapur. It was propagated throughout the kingdom, the remnants of which are still visible in the shape of the present Jeypore family ladies accepting initiation from the Vaishnava Goswamis ... In the town of Jeypore itself, we find a monastery or *mutt* in the name of *Chaitanya* in which the two images of *Gour* and *Nityanand* are worshipped as incarnation or *Avatara* of Krishna. There are other Vaisnavic temples such as "Radha Madhava", "Radhạ Kanta", "Rasik Siromani" or "Rasik swar" which are still maintained by the Devasthanam Department [temple administration] of the Jeypore Raj. There are numerous Vaisnava disciples or *Yajmans* living in the Jeypore zamindary... Viswanatha Deo ... made the Vaisnavic cult as the state religion of Nandapur in his reign' (1939, 14; see also ibid., 4-5; 15; 138-40). While Vaishnavite forms of Hinduism started under Viswanatha, the breakthrough of the Radha-Krishna cult of the Chaitanyaites in Nandapur, as in the rest of Orissa, probably only took place in the seventeenth century as a consequence of the impact of Chaitanya's disciples and wandering mendicant monks.

[55] Mukherjee's assertion that 'the chiefs of West Orissa continued their allegiance to their tutelary goddesses, whereas the zamindars of Ganjam and Jeypur accepted the Chaitanya faith and their subjects followed their examples' (1978, 318), is not

6. Closing remarks

In concluding this chapter, I would like to summarize the historical findings presented so far and place them within the broader context of the macro geopolitical region formed by Orissa, Andhra and the Deccan.

It can be observed that up to 1434, in the last decades of the rule by the Ganga Gajapatis, the little kings of the region had a relatively large number of inscriptions made in the temple of Simhachalam. At that time, this temple was the preferred platform for the proclamation of royal rule in the south: even the predecessors of the Suryavamshis of Nandapur, the Shilavamshis, are represented in this temple by five inscriptions. This allows us to conclude that the little kings of the region were able to rule relatively independently during the decline of the Gangas and that they used the waning of the central power to consolidate their positions economically and for their own expansion. However, following Kapilendra's take-over in 1434 and the gradual re-invigoration of the central power, military confrontations soon arose between the new Gajapati and the little kings of Ganjam and northern Andhra (or Kalinga), who sought to defend the independence they had won under the Late Gangas and in the confusion ensuing upon the change of regime. In particular, the area around Mahendragiri, on the present-day border between the districts of Ganjam and Srikakulam—whose control was strategically important for the securing of the coastal strip, which is narrow at this point—repeatedly became the site of fierce struggles between the Gajapatis and the little kings. As already mentioned, Kapilendra and Purushottama emerged victorious from this trial of strength, altering the power situation within the great kingdom in their favour by replacing many little kings with officials of the centre, or at least restricting their functions and reducing them to the status of tributary governors.

No inscription by the little-kingly Suryavamshis of Nandapur has been found in Simhachalam. But it should not be assumed that Kapilendra's and Purushottama's successful subjugation of the little kingdoms of the coast also extended into the hills of Nandapur. The first Nandapur kings—Vinayaka, Vijaya Chandra and Bhairava—perhaps at times cooperated with Kapilendra, Purushottama and the early Prataparudra. The position of the jungle kingdom of Nandapur must, however, be distinguished from that of the coastal kingdoms. In Nandapur, the reinvigorated central power of the Gajapatis did not lead, as with most little kingdoms on the coast, to a decline in, let alone loss of, little-kingly power.

---

entirely correct. As we shall see in Chapter V, tribal tutelary goddesses also remained of great politico-ritual importance down the centuries for the little kings of south Orissa, and their cult could and did exist alongside Krishna worship.

Certainly, the strength of the Gajapatis obstructed possible claims by Nandapur to the coastal regions, but it also enabled the jungle kingdom to extend its power into the eastern and southern foothills of the Eastern Ghats, parallel to the conquests of the Gajapatis in the south.

The fall of the Gajapatis was initiated by the attacks of Hussain Shah in the north and Krishnadeva Raya in the south, and sealed by the Qutb Shahs extending their rule into the Godavari delta. The last nail was struck in 1568 by the Bengali conquest of Cuttack. Thus the position of the Nandapur Suryavamshis, in the wider network of power, was also changed in its turn. Following Pratapuradra's decisive defeat against Krishnadeva Raya in 1516, the Gajapati withdrew from the south and the Nandapur *rājā*s of the time, Bhairava and Viswantha Deo, were able to consolidate their positions internally. In the three decades following Prataparudra's death in 1538, in which palace intrigues and external attacks increasingly eroded the central power and finally made it fall apart, a power vacuum arose in the south of the empire, which Viswanatha was able to use to consolidate his rule among the little kings of the sub-region of south Orissa/Kalinga. It has been pointed out how Viswanatha is even described as 'Gajapati' in Ferishta's (Brigg's) history. Singh Deo, who on this point is all-too willing to allow Ferishta to go unchallenged, also asserts that 'Vishwanatha Deva ... succeeded Pratapa Rudra Deo Gajapati as Gajapati of Orissa' (Singh Deo 1939, ii).

Singh Deo's further statement that the rulers of Nandapur of that period willingly described themselves as '*Nauna* Gajapatis'[56]—roughly 'Gajapati-like' or 'the equal of the Gajapati'—is more valuable in assessing 'how it might have been'. Elsewhere, Singh Deo writes: 'The kings of Nandapur after the death of the Gajapati-monarch Prata Parudra Deva declared themselves as Gajapatis of Orissa and introduced in their own palaces every custom and every exalted royal practice of the royal house of Puri' (ibid., 141-2). This suggests that the Nandapur kings' proclamation of equality to the Gajapati did not imply the take-over of actual territorial power and political overlordship but simply the fact that they had already ceased to recognize the Gajapatis of central Orissa as their nominal overlords before the Gajapatis' final collapse. Hence, the evocation of a '*Nauna* Gajapati' status by the Nandapur kings represented an attempt to appropriate the title of Gajapati and the *ritual* sovereignty over the other little kings of the region.[57] Singh Deo emphasizes precisely the

[56] See Singh Deo (1939, 15).

[57] Besides Nandapur, the *rājā*s of Parlakimedi also tried to acquire the status of ritual overlord of Orissa.

take-over of the courtly culture of Puri as one of the things the rulers of Nandapur strove for. In this respect, the Nandapur kings may well have been able to establish their *ritual* overlordship of the geopolitical area of southern Orissa and northern Andhra, but not beyond. Therefore, the description 'Southern Gajapatis'—by which, according to Singh Deo (ibid., 140), the Jeypore Suryavamshis were also known—is historically appropriate, though only if one is using it to refer to ritual status, not to the power-political weight of the jungle kingdoms in question.[58]

Thus, the rise and fall of the central Gajapati power led to repeated changes among the little kingdoms of coastal south Orissa ranging from 'non-existence' to 'governorship' to 'little kingdom'. The position of the jungle kingdom of Nandapur was, however, less strongly and less directly influenced by the changes in power of the Gajapatis. Certainly, in this peripheral area of the great kingdom the power vacuum that existed in the first phase of Kapilendra's rule provided an important prerequisite whereby the new little-kingly dynasty of the Jeypore Suryavamshis was able to come to power in the clash and interplay between the 'old nobility' (Shilavamshis), 'tribal groups' and 'warrior merchants'. However, here we are most probably not faced with individuals who were installed by the new imperial Gajapatis. Nandapur's position, therefore, shifted less between 'non-existence', 'governorship' and 'little kingdom' than between the status of little king, independent king and great king who himself presided over a *sāmantacakra*. However, the Gajapati splendour of the imperial overlords could never be fully attained.[59]

Nor did this overall situation change fundamentally in the next century. In 1565, a confederation of Islamic sultanates in the Deccan succeeded in decisively defeating the Vijayanagara empire at the battle of Talikota through which, together with the fall of Cuttack in 1568, Golkonda rose to be sole ruler of the Godavari Delta and the coast of

[58] Berkemer also comes to the conclusion that the Jeypore Suryavamshis did not possess the status of an imperial power de facto, but that they very likely counted as the 'cultural and ritual centre of the Orissa tradition and its followers in the south of the former Gajapati empire' (1993, 215; my translation). He even assumes that 'probably it was precisely this reserve in the matter of power politics that enabled the Jayavaṃśa family to maintain their status as legitimizing overlords in the plains up to the eighteenth century and in the hills of Koraput even today' (ibid.; my translation).

[59] In this attempt to identify different degrees of independence, I am following Dirks, who suggests '[thinking] about political and social relations in terms of a logic in which there is a continuum between such poles as dependence and independence, inclusion and separation' (1987, 47).

Kalinga. Already, before the death of Viswanatha, the indecisive power situation in the areas east and south of Nandapur, which ensured freedom of manoeuvre for the jungle kingdom, had shifted in favour of one single power. According to Muslim chronicles the Golkonda shah succeeded in forcing Viswanatha's son and successor, Balarama Deo (1571-97), to pay tribute. In this way, the ruler of Golkonda acquired, at least nominally, the position of overlord of Nandapur though payments of tribute were, in fact, made very irregularly. The repeated military confrontation between Golkonda and Jeypore, which was triggered in the following century mostly by the bad payment record of the Jeypore Suryavamshis, never led to the complete subjugation of the jungle kingdom or to the removal of its ruling dynasty.[60]

[60] On Nandapur in the period between 1571 to 1687 (the fall of the Golkonda sultanate), which cannot be discussed here, see Bell (1945, 24-6), Berkemer (1993, 216-37), Sarma (1938, verses 179-85), Senapati (1966, 60-3), Singh Deo (1939, 17-63) and Vadivelu (1984, 72-4).

CHAPTER IV

TRADITION AND INSUBORDINATION IN JEYPORE: THE CASE OF BISSAMCUTTACK

1. Introduction

In this chapter I would like to examine the nature of the relationship between the king of Jeypore and the governors or chiefs of the different estates within his kingdom, especially those at its borders. I shall be concentrating, particularly, on the estate of the *thātrāja*s of Bissamcuttack lying in the north-east of the Jeypore kingdom, whose history can be used paradigmatically to illustrate certain ethnohistorical aspects of politics and ritual in the hinterland of southern Orissa. However, I am less concerned with reconstructing Bissamcuttack's 'actual' history than with analysing the discourse that took place between king and *thātrāja* and with the conflictual relationship of the two protagonists in the colonial context.

By way of introduction, it can be stated that Bissamcuttack represented just one of several semi-independent estates within the little kingdom of Jeypore. Furthermore, in the seventeenth and eighteenth centuries, there also existed a whole series of neighbouring little kingdoms subject to, or at least aligned with Jeypore, which controlled the strategic passes into the kingdom from the coast. The most important estates within Jeypore were Bissamcuttack, Gunupur, Kalyansingpur, Kashipur, Malkangiri and Nowrangpur, most of which lay on the borders of the kingdom. Among the 'satellites' in the foothills of the 'galaxy' of Jeypore, whose foundation is ascribed to Viswambhara Deo I (1627-1676), were Salur, Cemudu, Golkonda, Kurupam, Merangi, Palkonda, Pachipenta, Poram, Andra, Bondapalli and Madgule.[1] I intend to deal more extensively with the internal organisation of Jeypore and its *sāmantacakra*, some of which survived into the modern period, at a later date. Here, merely the names and the assertion that the histories of many of these estates and *sāmanta*s

[1] Transition between the two categories mentioned here, i.e. 'estates' and 'little-kingly satellites' was fluid. Information on the different estates and satellites of Jeypore can be found, *inter alia*, in *Abolition of Estates* (1958), Behuria (ed. 1965, 66-8), Berkemer (1993, 215, 266-8, 325), Francis (1907, 247-308), Senapati (1966, 63-4, 405-29) and Vikram Deo Varma (1948a).

was comparable to the history of Bissamcuttack, must suffice. In short, the case of Bissamcuttack, with which I am concerned in what follows, is not an isolated one: the estate itself was only one of many components forming a larger political-administrative system but its history is paradigmatic of the history of other estates and satellites.

2. The Bissamcuttack estate

In order to arrive at an idea of the size of the Bissamcuttack estate, reference can be made to data relating to the administrative units of the modern Koraput District.[2] In the *Koraput District Gazetteer* of 1966, the *thānā* of Bissamcuttack is said to have an area of 418 square miles and a population of 61,795.[3] As additional information, 475 villages are listed in the *Final Report on the Major Settlement Operations in Koraput District* for the same administrative unit.[4] The *thānā* of Ambadola, bordering Bissamcuttack to the north, is recorded in the *Gazetteer* as having an area of 179 square miles and a population of 23,208 in 268 villages.[5] In the *Final Report*, 329 villages are listed as belonging to Ambadola.[6] Today, the two *thānā*s together form the *tahsīl* of Bissamcuttack which, with a total area of 597 square miles, corresponds approximately to the area formerly controlled by the Bissamcuttack *thātrāja*s. However, the *Gazetteer* of 1945, written before the land survey in the course of the 'major settlement operations', records an area of 823 square miles and a population (in 1941) of 74,610 for Bissamcuttack *tāluk*.[7] The *tāluk* was an administrative unit initially created in 1864; it was renamed *anchal* in 1953 and *tahsīl* in 1957.[8] In using the term *tāluk*, therefore, Bell is also including the modern Ambadola *thānā*. Nonetheless, the general information in the two *Gazetteers* of 1945 and 1966 indicates a difference of 226 square miles, which is due either to the inaccuracy of early estimates or to the fact that changes occurred between the census years of 1941 and 1961 as a consequence of administrative reforms. In the *Gazetteer* of 1907,

[2] See here Map 6.

[3] See Senapati (1966, 6, 406).

[4] Behuria (ed. 1965, 403-15).

[5] See Senapati (1966, 6, 405).

[6] See Behuria (ed. 1965, 432-40).

[7] See Bell (1945, 159).

[8] See Behuria (ed. 1965, 70).

which is the earliest of the three, it is stated, without giving sources, that the estate of the Bissamcuttack *thātrāja*s consisted of eight sub-sections (*muṭṭhā*s) with a total of 500 Kondh villages owing 40,000 rupees in taxes to the *thātrāja*.[9]

The Bissamcuttack region lies some 500 metres above sea level, the greater part of its population living in the valley of the Vamshadhara river. However, there is also a series of rough mountain ranges among which should be mentioned the Niamgiris or 'Niam Hills', the homeland of the Donghria Kondh, with peaks rising up to 1600 metres. Despite the many mountain ranges and jungles, the area is suitable for agriculture and is the source of tobacco. The Bissamcuttack *tahsīl* forms the northern part of the modern Gunupur Subdivision, which, together with the Rayagada Subdivision, also forms the north-east plateau of the kingdom, which is geographically separated from the rest of Koraput District. As already mentioned, a steep pass, difficult to travel even today, links the two high plateaus at Rayagada.

The town of Bissamcuttack itself lies at the foot of the Niamgiris, approximately at the geographical centre of the Bissamcuttack estate. The 1945 and 1966 *Gazetteers* record its population as 1961 and 2844 respectively. The name 'Bissam-cuttack' can be translated as 'poisonous fort', a description which, in the *Gazetteers*, is usually traced back to the malarial climate of the area.[10] As the seat of the *thātrāja*s, it was already the socio-cultural, economic, military, ritual and political centre of the area before it became the capital of the modern administrative units of Koraput District known as *thānā* and *tahsīl*. If tradition is to be believed, the fortress was built at the beginning of the seventeenth century by the second ruler of the *thātrāja* dynasty. According to local information, the term *thāt* means 'army' or 'band of warriors'. In official reports, *thātrāja* is often translated as 'commander of the troops'.

As far as the area, population, income and military power of their estate was concerned, then, the *thātrāja*s of Bissamcuttack presided over a not inconsiderable part of the kingdom of Jeypore. Even if one accepts the lowest of the figures given above as valid, Bissamcuttack was roughly equivalent in size to the important Mohuri kingdom in Ganjam, and Mohuri was only exceeded in size by the two established and important kingdoms of Parlakimedi and Ghumsur. In addition, from the point of view of Jeypore, the Bissamcuttack estate was located in an area relatively difficult of access. Moreover, it was difficult to control, since the

[9] See Francis (1907, 234).

[10] See Francis (1907, 232).

rough mountainous terrain of the Niamgiris offered the *thātrāja*s a quick refuge at any time. Moreover, a large part of the population consisted of the warlike Kondh, owing loyalty to the *thātrāja* rather than to the remote *rājā* of Jeypore. Thus, for the administration and military security of the kingdom of Jeypore, there existed in the *thātrāja* of Bissamcuttack an important but also powerful local magnate, continually aiming, as we shall see, at autonomy from the king.

One of the earliest British references to Bissamcuttack occurs in Oram's *Report* of 1784, in which this colonial official mentions in passing 'Vissumkotah under a Rauze or rajah called Tat Rauze, who holds it of Nandapuram and owes him military service'. Oram adds, disparagingly, 'It has a small mud fort of little consequence' (1784, 20). In 1795, the deed given by Madras to the king of Jeypore setting out his rights and duties under colonial rule was headed as follows: 'A Cowle granted by the Right Honourable Lord Hobart, President and Governor in Council of Fort St. George and its dependencies, to Ramachandra Deo, Zamindar of Jeypore, Rayagada, Izemcottah [!], Narrainpatam, Gundapuram and Singapuram.'[11] In his report of 1803, drawn up for the 'permanent settlement' of the Jeypore *zamīndārī*, the official, Alexander, begins by regretting that because of Jeypore's remote location and unhealthy climate only inexact information could be collected. However, he knew enough to be able to report that the 'districts' of Bissamcuttack and Gunupur were not directly under the control of King Ramachandra Deo II ruling in Jeypore. Bissamcuttack, according to Alexander, formed 'a separate zamindary held by a Tat Raz, who pays an annual Jamabandi [tribute] of Rupees 3344' (cited after Carmichael 1864, 287). In the 'Deed of Permanent Property Grant' of October 1803 between Lord Benwick, Governor of Fort St. George, and Ramachandra Deo II, 'Vissuncoth' is mentioned in a list of the different 'parganas of the Jeypore Zamindari'.[12]

This lack of agreement among British officials in assessing the politico-jural status of Bissamcuttack at the time of the permanent settlement reflects the ambiguous status of the estate, and it resurfaces in the legal conflicts between the kings of Jeypore and the Bissamcuttack *thātrāja*s in the years to follow. To summarize the various assessments: Oram first speaks of a *rājā*, then of a *thātrāja* owing Jeypore military service; the deed of 1795 includes Bissamcuttack among a number of other estates subject to Jeypore; Alexander calls Bissamcuttack first a

[11] See *Cowle* (1795).

[12] See *Deed* (1803) and Behuria (ed. 1965, 227).

'district', then a 'separate Zamindary'; and in the 1803 deed, Bissamcuttack is mentioned as one of 31 administrative units (*parganas*).

In the forties, fifties and sixties of the nineteenth century, the Bissamcuttack estate is repeatedly mentioned in the annual *Hill Tour Reports* of British officers. Given the high proportion of Kondh in its population, the estate was one of the centres for human sacrifice, called *meriah*, practised by this ethnic group. Bissamcuttack, therefore, represented an important stopping point for officials of the 'Meriah Agency', charged with stamping out this practice on their tours of inspection. Thus, Colonel Campbell reported of his stopover there in November 1851: 'In the house of the Tat Rajah, I discovered a youth that had been purchased by him for sacrifice, and who had undergone all the ceremonies preparatory to his immolation to the god of battles "Manicksoro" in the event of his coming into collision with the troops of his superior of Jeypore' (cited after Carmichael 1864, 327). In later reports, however, the services performed by the *thātrāja* of the time as intermediary between the *meriah* officers and the Kondh are emphasized. It seems that, within a short period, the *thātrāja* effected a radical change from being himself a patron of human sacrifice to being a committed opponent assisting the British against this custom. On one occasion, his services in this respect were even rewarded with the gift of a double-barrelled shotgun.[13]

An 'official' history of Bissamcuttack appears for the first time in Francis's *Gazetteer* of 1907.[14] Almost identical versions, each some two to three pages long, were printed in later government publications, in which new data mostly refer only to the period between the old and new publication.[15] Although these treatises aim at reconstructing Bissamcuttack's history accurately, they can also be found to reflect strongly the colonial perspective with its own metaphors and paradigms.

The following discussion is mainly based on documents relating to conflicts between the '*mahārājas*' of Jeypore and the *thātrājas* of Bissamcuttack that were brought before colonial institutions and courts between 1877 and 1926.[16] There are some 800 documents on this subject in the Orissa State Archives in Bhubaneswar, listed under the rubric of

[13] See Francis (1907, 202, 234); Campbell (1864).

[14] See Francis (1907, 232-5).

[15] See Bell (1945, 159-61); Behuria (ed. 1965, 65-6) and Senapati (1966, 406-8).

[16] The title of '*mahārāja*' was accorded by the British to some of the kings of Jeypore in the second half of the nineteenth century as a mark of honour, without this altering in any respect their politico-jural position as *zamīndārs*.

'Koraput District Records' (KDR), which itself consists of several thousand documents. Of the documents relevant to Bissamcuttack I was able to view and evaluate some two hundred, after making a selection on the basis of the brief information contained in the catalogue.[17]

To make sense of these documents, we must understand their historical background. In 1863, for the first time, the British took the administration of civil and criminal cases throughout the kingdom of Jeypore under their direct control. However, the subdivisions of Gunupur and Rayagada (and thus also the Bissamcuttack estate) had already been withdrawn from the direct control of the king of Jeypore a few years earlier. Following these radical changes, the king had freedom of action only in matters relating to the administration of his own estates and regarding the collection of taxes owed to him. Fundamentally, the jungle king of Jeypore had been turned into a landowner and tax collector, although his politico-ritual position and the functions as well as representative tasks associated with it, in which he was of use to the British, were not curtailed.

With the introduction of British administration into the Jeypore hills, the knowledge of the colonial government concerning the kingdom and its individual sub-units, like Bissamcuttack, necessarily increased. Simultaneously, the conflicts between king and *thātrāja* were no longer confined to them alone or conducted in a 'traditional' manner. Rather, from the middle of the nineteenth century, the conflicts were pursued before, and with, a third party, namely the colonial rulers, within the politico-jural framework they had established. And these conflicts were now carried out through the medium 'file'. Thus, in the context of colonial jurisdiction, a 'war of papers' began to replace the ritual abuses, political threats and military feuds of earlier periods. It is the documents emerging from this sort of confrontation—complaints, petitions, appeals, statements taken on oath, opinions, memorials, etc.—that provide the material for this chapter.

No text is ever neutral. Texts are always consciously created cultural and political constructions written by particular persons and institutions at specific times. The content of texts can, therefore, only be grasped by including in one's interpretation the competitive situations and interests within which they arose and were negotiated. In this sense, texts are the 'platforms' of multi-faceted and contradictory historical realities (and the plural form needs stressing); they possess, as Spiegel (1994) argues, a 'social logic'. If, then, texts are the products and representations of social,

[17] In most cases, I consulted the official translations made at the time from Telugu or Oriya into English, which were often attached to the original documents.

political, cultural, economic, demographic, historical and other realities, this also means that they can provide us with valuable clues for the reconstruction and interpretation of these realities. Such a view means abandoning the 'postmodern' view that there is no reality behind the text, in the sense that text and context basically merge into one another. But this does not mean going back to a naive 'pre-postmodern' point of view because, when looking at texts for the reconstruction of those realities which have brought them forth and to which they themselves were integral, it must be emphasized that texts never provide a direct path to, or a mirror-like reflection of, these realities. They are as diffuse, polyphonic and contestatory as the realities themselves.

We also have to bear in mind that texts are not simply passive stores of clues leading us to particular realities in a complex way but that they construct, reconstruct, influence and change these realities themselves. They themselves possess agency or, to use Greenblatt's term, 'social energy'. Social energy, according to Greenblatt, is 'associated with repeatable forms of pleasure and interest, with the capacity to arouse disquiet, pain, fear, the beating of the heart, pity, laughter, tension, relief, wonder' (1988, 6). If one adds 'belief in legitimacy' to Greenblatt's list, then this concept can usefully be applied to the texts discussed here. Attention must also be paid to the contests, negotiations and strategies that are used to acquire and 'circulate' (as Greenblatt phrases it) this social energy.

The focus of interest in this chapter is, therefore, less on reconstructing 'how it really was' in the late-colonial conflict between the king of Jeypore and one of his governors as they waged their 'war of papers'. What is more important is to work out how events, tradition and history are differently selected, interpreted, valued and even created in the written discourses of the different parties. The attempt will be to see how each actor in the context (or better, in different, simultaneously existing contexts, which often cannot be reconciled with one another) of specific historical constellations of power and cultural logics creates his or her own history; how, to paraphrase Sahlins (1985), events become what the interpretation makes of them.

Hence, the texts we are dealing with are not taken as pure and simple representations of realities, in fact, as manifestations of power struggles and of conflicting views or interests, they are often deliberate misrepresentations.[18] They have arisen from and themselves participated in actual conflicts and struggles which, for the participants, were matters of influ-

[18] On the politically and historically loaded understanding of 'representation', see Ahmad (1991) and Chartier (1992a).

ence, authority, honour, power, order, money, rights, prestige, rule and sheer survival, or which concerned *Weltanschauung*. In the documents discussed here, we shall see that it is different notions of 'tradition' and 'insubordination' which influence the multi-vocal and conflicting negotiations and strategies that are carried out both *in* the texts and *through* them.

3. Celebrating Queen Victoria

In June 1877 Goodrich, the 'agent to the governor' stationed in Visakhapatnam, filed a report on the development of a conflict (still not concluded when he was writing) between the Jeypore king and the *thātrāja* of Bissamcuttack. This conflict forms the thematic focus of this section and Goodrich's letter stands as the central text (for reasons of representation, not for its actual significance) around which discussion of the other sources will revolve.

In the first three points (out of 21) of his report, Goodrich summarizes the situation *before* the rise of tension as follows:

> 1. The death of Sri Narendra Tat Raj of Bissemkatak occurred early in 1876. He had three sons.
>
> 2. The absence of the Maharaja at the time prevented any immediate settlement of the succession but at Bissemkatak the eldest son of the late Tatraj was regarded as his father's successor.
>
> 3. I instructed Captain Blaseland after the Maharajah's return to inform me of any steps that might be taken for the investiture of the heir of the late Tatraj and I advised him that the matter was one which should be settled without unnecessary delay. I understood from him that the Maharajah intended to invest the eldest son of the late Tatraj at the coming Dasara feast which was the time at which such investitures are usual. (KDR 2212)

Around 1876-1877, therefore, the traditionally bilateral relationship between the *mahārāja* of Jeypore and the *thātrāja* of Bissamcuttack became a triangular one, with the arrival of a new actor on the scene, the British colonial government. This new actor was represented by the agent or highest administrator in the district, Goodrich; by his military commander in Jeypore, Blaseland; and later, by the senior assistant agent, Melville, as well as the assistant agent, Willock, both of whom were responsible for the hill region. The king of Jeypore at this time was Ramachandra Deo III who ruled from 1860 to 1889, while the deceased *thātrāja* of Bissamcuttack was Narendra Thatraj I. His son, whose accession was the cause of dispute in 1877, was Ramachandra Thatraj II.

Some important points can be made straight away. In Bissamcuttack it was taken for granted that the eldest son of the deceased should inherit the estate and position of *thātrāja*. At this time, the king of Jeypore, too, appeared to have stuck to the principle of succession by primogeniture. However, from his point of view succession could not be automatic. Rather, to the king it is constitutive of the legitimation of the new office-holder that he is formally recognized and appointed by the king. In Jeypore, the *dasarā* festival is seen as the appropriate occasion for this ceremonial transfer of the office and the rights and duties that go along with it. The delay in appointing the designated *thātrāja,* thus, may well have resulted initially only from the necessity of bridging the period between Narendra's death in the spring and the *dasarā* festival in autumn 1876. To the British, as the third party, this indigenous procedure of succession by the oldest son and his formal appointment by the *mahārāja* at *dasarā* was quite acceptable. The only thing that caused them concern was the loss of time. As they knew from other cases in their Indian empire, and from the history of their own royal family, a long inter-regnum and a lack of clarity concerning the rules of succession do not serve peace and order or the 'tranquillity' that is implored in many documents. Actually, in spring 1876, at the time of Narendra's death, there was still no indication that in the summer of 1877 the agent would be writing a long report on the unresolved conflict, going back to events that took place at the end of 1876 and the beginning of 1877. What had happened? Or, better: How did the various parties report the case?

In a letter dated 21 January 1877, Ramachandra Deo III informed senior assistant agent Melville that the *thātrāja* had been 'released' from the administration of Bissamcuttack estate. He also told Melville that his own tax officials (*amīns*) from Rayagada and Gunupur had been ordered to take over the administration of Bissancuttack. Snubbed in respect of his own powers of office, the colonial official summoned the *amīns* to appear before him on 31.1.1877 and (assuming he was acting against a possible danger to the peace of the area) forbade them to carry out the royal order. The agent in Visakhapatnam approved the action of Melville retrospectively. In a letter of 3.2.1877 he let the *mahārāja* know that he could only resume an estate or raise its taxes after the British had given their permission. For this, an application had to be made to the responsible colonial authorities.[19]

[19] On this, see KDR 2212, para 5-7.

In his reply of 18.2.1877, the *mahārāja* explained his actions as follows: 'That estate was leased out on condition of performing service but was not given on permanent zamindary tenure.'[20] In his view the case belonged to the category of tax affairs that were directly under his control and not to the civil or criminal law controlled by the British. The *mahārāja* went on to state: 'It has been the practice in our zamindary to attach and keep under amani [direct administration] jahagirs and mokhasas given to anybody when they behave contrary to our wishes, or when the grantee dies, and to renew the grant with fresh conditions when they seek our mercy.' An indigenous tradition is thus invoked against the law of the British. It is also striking how, in the passage cited, owners of estates and lease-holders of different types—holders of *jāgīrs* and *mukhāsās*, as well as the *thātrāja*—all become 'grantees', making them seem very humble in comparison to the king who in the said letter refers to 'our wishes' and 'our mercy'.

The view, expressed in this letter, that conditions of tenure have to be negotiated afresh after the death of each beneficiary, became significant when Ramachandra Deo points his attacks directly against the *thātrāja*. We learn from a brief historical interpolation by the king that Bissamcuttack had first been given to a certain Ramachandra as *mukhāsā*, quite explicitly 'on condition of performing service'. But the king also had to admit that this Ramachandra 'did not render service.' Concerning Ramachandra's son and grandson, we learn: 'Kristna never enjoyed the taluq, nor did he receive the title of Thatraja. Afterwards his son, Narendra Thatraj, served us faithfully and well; he was granted the taluq on conditions of rendering us service with 700 paiks [soldiers] and paying 1500 per annum.' Thus, the king introduced three generations of *thātrāja*s, the first of whom held the estate and the title of *thātrāja* but did not render service; the second remained entirely without royal legitimation; and only the third received the estate and the title of *thātrāja* personally from the king, rendered proper service and paid regular tribute. After *mahārāja* Ramachandra Deo also referred in the letter to the practice of regular increases in tribute along with an increasing clearance of jungle territory, he went on to stress: 'In this manner the sists [dues, taxes] were raised from time to time and removals and reappointments were made, but the taluq was never given permanently.' And: 'The title of thatraja also was conferred on particular persons specially but was never hereditary.'

The emphasis in the king's letter is on the fact that, in the past, estates and honorary titles were only given to individuals and linked to the

[20] The quotation is from KDR 2245.

payment of taxes as well as to the performance of specific services which were fixed anew on each occasion. He, then, comes to the crux of the matter, which is that the designated successor had been summoned to Jeypore with the accounts of the estate but had not presented himself before the king. Still more serious was the fact that the *thātrāja* had neglected to take part in a ceremony held on 1.1.1877 in Jeypore celebrating the proclamation of Queen Victoria as Empress of India (which had taken place the year before). Following these instances of insubordination, the second of which may well have made British officials far from neutral observers of the affair, the *mahārāja* decided to manage the estate without the *thātrāja*: 'He being thus disobedient we resolved to remove him from our service and take over the management of the taluq.' Ramachandra Deo then again evokes the legitimacy of tried and tested practices: 'It has been the practice obtaining in our samasthanam [kingdom] to resume lands, villages, and taluqs given on service when the grantees do not regularly render service, and amalgamate them with our zamindary.' And the following judgement is pronounced: 'We do not think it proper to give the taluq even with enhanced sist to a person, who being our servant, had left the palace, setting our orders at defiance.'[21]

The position of the Bissamcuttack faction regarding these developments can be discerned from two letters. In the first of these, dated 20.2.1877 and sent by the designated successor, Kshatrava Todramal Ramachandra Thatraj (as he styled himself), to the senior assistant agent,[22] he explained—no doubt realizing the precariousness of the situation—why he had not attended the ceremonies for the Empress of India: 'We had been in attendance at Jeypore with 800 paiks for a month before the day of the durbar [ceremonial reception].' Since this ceremony took place on 1.1.1887, we can conclude that the designated *thātrāja* had not been in Jeypore at the time of the *dasarā* festival in October 1876, at which he should have been appointed. It is probable that a conflict is being concealed here by both parties, since the *mahārāja*'s complaint to the colonial government referred to the *thātrāja* having stayed away, not from the *dasarā* festival but only from the ceremonies in honour of Queen

[21] In this context it should be recalled that for Weber the regular duty demanded of a governor, of visiting the ruler's court or camp, represented an essential characteristic of patrimonial rule. In addition, in the transition from the automatic succession of the governor to the principle of a fresh appointment on each occasion, Weber saw signs of the transition from a patrimonial to a bureaucratic form of rule. See Weber (1976, 605) and Bendix (1977, 352).

[22] See KDR 2251.

Victoria. The *thātrāja* explained his absence as follows: 'The Maharaja sent word to come and see the festivities with common folk and from among them, but that we should not enter the Durbar hall where he presided.' This was an open attempt on the part of the *mahārāja* to diminish the status and dignity of one of the most powerful estate holders of his kingdom. The *thātrāja* was asked to observe the ceremonies from among the common people, like a spectator of plebeian rank, whereas, in his own view at least, he should have been granted a privileged position in the ceremonial hall of the palace. This demotion could only lead to one thing: 'He having refused to receive us and having ordered us to see the festivities from among the common folk we only refrained from going there.' Even though, at the end of his letter the designated *thātrāja* declares submissively, 'We never set at naught the orders of the Maharajah who is our master', the ritual humiliation left a lasting impression.

In another letter, dated 23.2.1877,[23] the *thātrāja*'s administrator (*dīwān*) protested to the *mahārāja*'s administrator:

> Todramal Rajasri Ramachandra Thatraj Bahadur, Zamindar of Bissemkatak, recently went to Jeypore with 800 men in obedience to your written orders; and we all remained there for two months. We returned as we were unable to visit Sri Sri Sri Maharajah's lotus feet and suffered for want of money owing to the prolonged stay with a large number of men.

Apart from the fact that the length of the stay in Jeypore varies in the different sources (which, however, makes no difference as far as the absence from the *dasarā* festival is concerned), a generally more conciliatory tone is noticeable: driven by necessity, the *thātrāja* had to leave Jeypore with his 800-man strong band of fighters, without being able to pay homage to the lotus feet of the *mahārāja*. However, reasons why the *mahārāja* did not receive them and reasons for the conflict that might have arisen from the previous year's *dasarā* ceremony again were not discussed. In addition, the *thātrāja*'s administrator stressed that his lord would appear in Jeypore again at any time desired and the letter is accompanied by the tribute for the previous year. However, it should be noted that, for all the show of submissiveness, the not-yet-appointed successor, still a minor, was also styled *rājā*, *thātrāja* and *zamīndār*, leaving no doubt of how, in Bissamcuttack, his position in the conflict in question was viewed.

Though the letters shed some light on the events in Jeypore on 1.1.1877, much remains dimly hidden behind the rhetoric and official

[23] See KDR 2250.

representation. It can be guessed that other events, especially those which may or may not have taken place on the occasion of the *dasarā* festival, remain deliberately excluded. Also, other reasons or motives which may have played a role in the origin and development of the conflict are not placed on record. Thus, in the arguments put forward by both parties, the not inconsiderable increase in annual taxes from 5,000 to 7,000 rupees, demanded by the *mahārāja* (revealed in other sources), plays hardly any role. It also looks as if the *māhāraja* was pulling the strings, while the *thātrāja*, still relatively inexperienced in political manoeuvres and only gradually becoming aware of his weaker position, reacted clumsily. The position of agent Goodrich around this time indicates some uncertainty on the side of the British concerning how to assess the matter: 'The claimant presented himself at Jeypore … and from whatever cause failed to arrange matters with the Maharajah. Some haggling overtures went on but I am not informed as to what actually occurred, nor I believe was Mr. Melville informed when he visited the place in December.'[24]

What emerges from the above is that, at the end of 1876 and beginning of 1877, a struggle for power was taking place between two adversaries within the kingdom of Jeypore. The stage for this conflict was the royal capital with its ceremonial hall, and its enactment took the form of ritual. Yet, this bilateral struggle for power had to be carried on in the presence of a third party, the colonial government whose verdict, the contesting parties knew, would ultimately be decisive. As a consequence, the stage for the enactment of the conflict shifted from the royal palace to the colonial administration and its courts, and the medium through which the conflict was carried on was no longer ritual but written text. Or, more precisely, the indigenous actors stepped on to another, differently structured stage on which they reproduced the conflict through letters and petitions not, however, as a copy of the original, but new in content and form. The events were freshly selected, translated into the world of colonial understanding, and reinterpreted for the British. Thus, for example, in the letters some of the king's past actions were raised to the dignity of long-established practices and traditions possessing a lawful character, while the *thātrāja*'s hard-fought positions were presented in his letters as if they were matters of fact, as if they were established titles and names. Even with respect to the actions themselves, there is a shift in the direction of a colonial conceptualization of things: the dramatic high point of the conflict shifts from the traditional ritual framework in which power struggles were traditionally staged, namely the *dasarā* festival, to

[24] KDR 2212, para 4.

what for the British was a more familiar context, that of a ceremony in honour of Queen Victoria. In a nutshell, even in the indigenous discourse Victoria replaced Durga, and a ceremony in her honour replaced the *dasarā* festival.

Now, the British colonial government was, of course, more than just a spectator in the drama rearranged for its benefit and particular understanding. It possessed hegemony over the unfolding discourse and ultimately helped shape the form, content and outcome of these events as an agent. This becomes clear from a further exchange of letters which took place in the early months of 1877 between Goodrich and Ramachandra Deo III. In one letter,[25] the king again stressed that the increase in land wrested from the jungle and made over to farming in the course of time justified an increase in taxes. He argues that since the building of a police station by the British in the hill region, 'Every danger has disappeared and much happiness prevails.' In this 'happy' situation, he concluded, the number of soldiers maintained by the *thātrāja* could be reduced drastically to one hundred, and these should be deployed mainly to keep order at religious festivals and other ceremonies. In the opinion of the king of Jeypore, this would reduce the internal expenditure of the *thātrāja* (for the upkeep of policemen and soldiers); the taxes he owes to the king could be increased correspondingly.

From the king's point of view, therefore, the *thātrāja* looses the most important basis of his legitimacy. His function as the highest organ of order in the north-eastern part of the kingdom is represented as being invalid; hence, according to the king he should be degraded to the position of a local master of ceremonies in the service of the king. What is being signalled in addition, however, is the king's readiness to negotiate the new conditions on which the *thātrāja* might be acknowledged.

In answer, Goodrich repeats that the approval of the collector (personified by himself) is necessary for any change in conditions. However, he also declares his readiness to act as an intermediary in settling the dispute.[26] Yet, in June 1877 (to come back to the key text of this section), Goodrich no longer saw any way out of the difficult situation that did not involve the courts. As he wrote to Madras:

> The case will probably come before my Court as a Civil Court and the issue of fact and law will be somewhat as follows as they appear from the written representations of the parties. 1. Has the family of the late holder held the taluq at a fixed rate of money rent? 2. Did

[25] KDR 2242.

[26] See KDR 2243.

> conditions of service attach to the tenure? 3. If so, has there been a failure to render such service? 4. If so, what is the effect of such failure? 5. In this and (if there be) in similar tenures, has the heir of the last holders succeeded as of right? … or 7. Has the Raja appointed whom he would so ever? 8. Has any Nazzar [gift] been paid by the successor on investiture? The above covers most of the points likely to arise if the case be tried by the ordinary laws of the Agency tracts, i.e. the law in force in 1839 as limited and explained by the Agency Rules. The disposal of the matter as of an ordinary Civil Suit is attended with no special difficulty. (KDR 2212, para 10, 11)

Thus, there was confidence on the part of the agent that the law, that is, the special law introduced by the British for the hill regions or *māliah*s, could quickly be made effective if the indigenous parties could not agree amongst themselves. However, on the British side, there were other considerations also: 'The question is however of a political nature and it needs to be considered whether there are grounds for asking that it be settled as such and not referred to a Civil Court.' Hence, the representative of the British Empire did not only determine the type of law under which the said case should be treated, he also considered its political implications. Goodrich explained his thoughts in this regard as follows:

> It is a matter of ascertained knowledge that the late Tatraj of Bissemkatak has during his long life held command of the best organized body of militia in Jeypore. It is believed that his bounden service was to furnish 700 paiks (match lock men) whenever called upon. During this present year immediately on receiving news of the outbreak in the Bodogoda Malia of Ganjam I sent an express to my Senior Assistant who was on the frontier to call out a small body of these men in case they might be wanted and as always they turned out with alacrity. In Ganjam where the Police force was disciplined in part before assuming charge of the hills and carefully brought into a state of discipline afterwards such auxiliary forces as the paiks might perhaps be dispensed with. Where this process has been omitted as in the case of the Jeypore Police the militia of the country is from time to time needed on Government service. (KDR 2121, para 12, 13, 14)

In the official's assessment, then, the situation in the hill regions of southern Orissa is not as peaceful and happy as the *mahārāja* was trying to suggest. The traditional forces of Bissamcuttack, already dismissed by Ramachandra Deo as of no use or at best as a highly restricted ceremonial guard, were seen by the agent as an absolutely necessary ad hoc supplement to the police forces in the hill regions. It will have been noticed that the British government was itself laying claims to the services traditionally owed to the *mahārāja*. For Goodrich, they represented, in an interesting reinterpretation of things, 'government service'. The *mahārāja*'s arguments were, thus, doubly turned upside down. Indeed, according to Goodrich, the king no longer needed the military service of the *thātrāja*, not because they were dispensable as such but because he was no longer the main source and protector of order in the region. The landowner acting under the protection of the British—and the *mahārāja* of Jeypore at this time was legally nothing else—was certainly allowed to increase his income. Whether, however, he was allowed to abolish services and convert them into taxes was questionable.[27]

It should be clear by now that the case revolved around how the different parties assessed the nature of the services owed by the *thātrāja*. None of the parties disputed the fact that, fundamentally, the *thātrāja*'s legitimacy was based on his providing services. They all identified these services as the provision of an army of 700 to 800 men whenever required as well as at the *dasarā* festival in Jeypore every year. While the *mahārāja* no longer saw the necessity of these troops, or at least saw it as greatly reduced, which in turn allowed him either to abolish the position occupied by the *thātrāja* entirely or to impose additional taxes on him, the *thātrāja* argued against charges of his failing to render services, which had been brought up as grounds for giving him notice. In his various letters, he did not question his basic duty to provide troops when required, but only complained of the financial burden arising out of his staying several weeks in Jeypore. It should be noted that the Bissamcuttack *pāik*s did not form a standing army. Rather, most of their livelihood came from farming small parcels of land around Bissamcuttack. In staying so long in Jeypore, this natural basis for their provision was removed and the *thātrāja* was obliged to cover the maintenance of his soldiers from his own resources. With 800 men to be provided for over two months, this was not an inconsiderable burden.

Last but not least, the agent saw the necessity of retaining the Bissamcuttack army as a 'task force' in the hill regions of Koraput and Ganjam, which in his view had still not been sufficiently pacified. We should note here that already in 1877 this contradicted the broader policy of the colonial government in the Madras Presidency, which was striving to reduce the size of indigenous armies in the service of kings, little kings and *zamīndār*s as much as possible. This may explain the agent's repeated references to the especially precarious situation in the *māliah*s. In addi-

[27] See also KDR 2212, para 15-19.

tion, he introduced a new element into the discussion regarding the character of the services to be rendered (invoking an existing legal verdict from the province of Bengal): following the replacement of the *mahārāja* as the highest power in the area, the said services were now to be provided to the British. A decision as to whether the services would still be required and, if not, how and with what they would be redeemed, was a matter reserved for the new rulers alone.

The further history of the conflict of 1877, with its many turns, is quickly sketched. In February, assistant agent Willock visited Bissamcuttack and advised the *thātrāja* to come to an agreement with the *mahārāja* out of court. The *thātrāja* then asked Willock for help in arriving at a settlement. The assistant agent reported this to Captain Blaseland, the military commander in Jeypore who, in a letter of 22 April, informed him of the conditions under which the king was prepared to grant the estate. At this time, Ramachandra Deo III merely intended to give the estate to Ramachandra Thatraj II for life, not as a hereditary property; in addition, the fixed taxes (*kaṭṭubaḍi*) were to be raised from 5,000 to 20,000 rupees. Before these harsh conditions could reach the *thātrāja* and push him back into a hard position, Goodrich intervened by asking both parties to put their respective positions in writing and summoning them to Visakhapatnam on 4 June. However, the *thātrāja* regretted that he could not make this date and instead went to Parvatipur, the seat of the senior assistant agent, Melville, to tell him that he preferred to reach an out-of-court settlement. He also asked Melville for permission to go to Jeypore, where he wished to work out a solution in person with the king, who had invited him there. However, while the *thātrāja* was on his way to Jeypore, news reached him that a hearing had been arranged for 30 June in Parvatipur. The *thātrāja,* nonetheless, asked for a postponement and for permission to settle the matter with the king in person and out of court.[28]

This out-of-court, 'bilateral' arrangement was then arrived at. In September of the same year the king wrote to the agent: 'Ramachandra Thatraj, son of the late Thatraj, having come to our Court and entreated us very submissively in various ways, we fixed an annual Jammabundy [tribute] of Rs 15,000 on the Bissamcuttack taluq and kept the same under him.'[29] The sum agreed was, thus, considerably more than the 7,000 rupees initially being demanded at the end of 1876. The *mahārāja*'s threat to resume the estate, thus, achieved its aim. In order to seal the agreement in the manner customary to the region, two signed documents, a *paṭṭā* and

[28] See KDR 1777.

[29] See KDR 2402.

a *muchilikā*, were exchanged between the king and the governor, in which the two parties ratified the conditions as negotiated. Only the *muchilikā* document signed by the *thātrāja* is available to me, but this no doubt just repeats and accepts the conditions laid down in the *paṭṭā*.[30] In it, the *thātrāja* repeatedly professes his loyalty to the king, whom he calls his 'commander' (*sircār*): 'I shall render loyal and faithful service to the Sircar.' In addition, he confirms the right of the king to act at his discretion in case of the non-fulfilment of the agreement: 'If I should act contrary to this, I am bound by the orders of the Sircar that may be issued at pleasure.' The *thātrāja* also accepts the tax rise mentioned above, and that the sum was to be paid in two instalments of 7,500 rupees each in February-March ('full moon of the month of Phalguna') and at the *dasarā* festival. The number of *pāīks* to be provided by the *thātrāja* was reduced to 500. Despite the considerable increase in tribute and the recognition of the personal services he owed to the king, the *thātrāja* could also regard the 1877 agreement as a success. The size of his *kaṭṭubaīi* payments was fixed, and—what was most important to him—the estate was recognized as a hereditary property with the words, 'enjoying the Bissemkatak takuk hereditarily'. With the subsequent recognition of these conditions by the British authorities, the festival in honour of Queen Victoria in the Jeypore Hills ultimately ended in a *Pax Britannica*. Yet how long would this peace last?

4. Conflicting 'cargo cults'

The disagreements of 1876-1877 were not the first. In 1851, for example, the antagonism between king and *thātrāja* found expression in the latter preparing a human sacrifice to equip himself better for the battle against the army of Jeypore. During the reign of Narendra, too, there appear to have been problems in 1865 caused by absent or delayed payments of tribute.[31] Even after 1877, not long after the reconciliation mentioned above, the conflicts continued. For example, the *District Gazetteers* of 1907 and 1945 report about Ramachandra Thatraja in identical words: 'He was given a patta allowing him to enjoy the estate in perpetuity on these terms, but for some years refused to pay anything or go to the Dasara' (Francis 1907, 234; Bell 1945, 160). In the 1966 *Gazetteer*, the 'some years' becomes 'never till his death' (Senapati 1966, 408). The

[30] See KDR 2405.

[31] See KDR 2240; 2241.

question of how often Ramachandra Thatraja appeared in Jeypore with his men at *dasarā*, if at all, cannot be ascertained from the documents available to me. All that is certain is that there are many letters of complaint from the king concerning his insubordinate governor from the early 1880s to the *thātrāja*'s death in 1889.[32]

The British too, kept an eye on the Bissamcuttack estate, in whose 'tranquillity' they had a growing interest, and on which they continued to collect further information. The so-called *Hill Tour Reports* played an important part in this process of colonial knowledge accumulation. So far as I can determine, Bissamcuttack's 'official' history appears for the first time in the report of an inspection tour carried out between winter 1882 and spring 1883.[33] Admittedly, Turner, the military officer who wrote the report does not mention his sources but it can be assumed that he was relying mainly on local information acquired in Bissamcuttack, which he visited during his tour.

Only one point from Turner's *Hill Tour Report* will be taken up here, one which makes clear why the Bissamcuttack estate acquired such strategic importance for the British. As Turner states at the start of his report, 'It is proposed to construct the Vizianagaram-Raipur railway throughout its length.' This passing reference requires some explanation.

Plans for a railway line linking the Deccan with the coast of Andhra were first hatched in 1881. However, the project could only be completed in 1932, following many unforeseen difficulties and the loss of much human life. Military considerations certainly played a part in the original plan, for the line was intended as an important connection between the Madras Presidency and the Central Provinces. However, economic considerations also had great weight during this period of relatively stable colonial rule. In the 1907 *Gazetteer*, for example, we find the following comment: 'Connected with the new line is the question of the construction of a harbour at Vizagapatnam ... for the export of the produce of the Central Provinces which is expected to pour down the sea' (Francis 1907, 145). These early assessments of the economic usefulness of the route proved valid. Visakhapatnam is still one of the most important ports on the east coast of India and the railway line acquired, and still possesses, great economic importance. However, its economic significance does not lie simply in the transport of goods from the Deccan to the

[32] See KDR 2038; 2255; 2256; 2262; 2275; 2277; 2284; 2298; 2304; 2322; 2325; 2326; 2327; 2331; 2339; 2341; 2350; 2351; 2374. From the government's side, KDR 2287; 2288 and 2293 are concerned with this problem.

[33] See KDR 2254.

ocean ports of Andhra. The opening of the line also introduced a new period of trade with and within the sub-divisions of Rayagada and Gunupur. The north-east of the jungle kingdom of Jeypore, until then remotely situated, acquired some links of its own with the trade of the wider world through the railway connection. Among the goods imported into Bissamcuttack between 1955 and 1959 were sugar, salt, groundnut oil and kerosene. The export in this period (the only years for which I have figures, but which can still allow conclusions to be drawn regarding the structure of the trade in general) were cereals, manganese ore, betel leaves, wood, skins, tobacco, fruit, oilseeds, turmeric, rice and other agricultural crops and natural resources. Trade in some of these products within the sub-region also intensified.[34]

A report of 1935 by a malaria expert of the railway company enumerates the difficulties encountered in carrying out the project:

> The route of the Raipur-Vizianagaram Railway was originally surveyed by the now defunct East Coast Railway in 1883-86. Two years were spent on reconnaissance before a practical route across the Eastern Ghats was discovered, two years more in actual survey. The records of this party are lost, but it is known that they suffered very severely from malaria. In 1897, a further survey by the same railway … was undertaken. The party broke down from malaria 99 miles from Vizianagaram, just south of the summit of the pass at Satikona [near Bissamcuttack town], after traversing barely 40 miles of the hyper-endemic zone. In 1907 yet another party of Bengal-Nagpur Railway essayed a resurvey, but likewise broke down after achieving only two miles further than their predecessors of ten years before … When, therefore, actual construction was authorised, it was obvious to the railway administration that malaria was going to be a most potent factor in the forthcoming operations … Of the 242 miles to be built from Raipur to Parvatipur, only the first thirty and the last forty were found to be in non-malarious country but the highest incidence of the disease lay between mile 147 … and mile 223. (Cited from Senapati 1966, 387-8)

It will come as no surprise that this stretch, infected most by anopheles mosquitoes, was essentially in the so-called 'poisonous fort' area of Bissamcuttack. The expert set out in detail the anti-malaria measures introduced. In order to indicate the enormous scale of the operation, he wrote: 'The Panama canal, the largest engineering work, on which anti-mosquito measures had been taken before, is only 46 miles in length' (ibid., 388). He added: 'It was … obvious that unless malaria could be

[34] On these data, see Senapati (1966, 218-20).

controlled the massing of imported, non-immune labour for building the railway was going to result in a disaster of the first magnitude' (ibid., 389). Regarding the indigenous population, he comments: 'The problem of malaria in the district is one of increasing difficulty. Before the railway came, the villagers grew rice enough for their own needs. Now they grow for export. Where perennial irrigation is available, fields are now cropped continuously, and new fields are always being levelled up' (ibid., 392).

Thus, for the Bissamcuttack estate, the socio-economic changes induced through the railway, of which British colonial officials had at most an inkling in 1882, were considerable. To this should be added the changes that occurred in the indigenous population's experience and conceptualization of space and time due to the introduction of the railway into the area.[35] In addition, the negative ecological and climatic effects resulting from the unrestrained felling of trees can only be given marginal mention: wood was exploited on a massive scale, first in the construction of the railway and then as an export good realizable for the first time due to the greater carrying capacity of the railway. It should also be noted in passing that, besides the railway, there were other improvements in the sub-region's infrastructure. From the middle to the end of the nineteenth century, a number of roads into the Ghats and within the hill region were built or considerably improved under British supervision. While earlier only pack animals could be used for transport in the Eastern Ghats, in the last third of the century ox carts could also be used.

All these were slow and limited means of transport compared with the railway. And in contrast to porters, pack animals, ox carts and even contemporary trucks operating on bumpy paths and roads, the railway was the only means of transport that was under state administration and control. It did not serve, and could not be stopped by, any local ruler. The British operating company alone could determine its coming and going, as well as where it stopped on route and the type of cargo it carried.[36]

Let us return to the eighties and nineties of the nineteenth century. This excursion into the history of the Raipur-Visakhapatnam railway should make clear that at a time when two indigenous parties were flooding the British with petitions concerning an internal conflict, the colonial

[35] Similar changes are investigated for nineteenth-century Europe by Schivelbusch (1989). Koselleck (1979, 11) studies more generally the effect of the increasing speed of travel on forms of behaviour and the experience of time.

[36] I am using the term 'cargo' rather than the more usual terms 'freight' or 'goods' in order to draw attention to the ideational and occasionally even cultic dimensions of the problem.

administration had 'greater' plans for the area. Would not the conflict between a former potentate of the jungle kingdom of Jeypore, who had been reduced to the position of a landowner, and his insubordinate governor appear insignificant to them? At that time British officials were still crossing the unhealthy, mosquito-infested region in arduous marches lasting weeks and with great loss of health and life. Their tours were meant to demonstrate colonial presence to the local people, at least occasionally, and to prevent human sacrifice and infanticide (both of which had been eradicated with such effort in earlier decades) from breaking out again. Yet, soon, the British hoped, steam locomotives would be pulling wagons bulging with cargo up and down the hills and not only provide economic benefits for 'Her Majesty' the Queen, but also bring 'civilization' (as the British knew it) to the population of the region.

Yet, in the continuing conflict between *mahārāja* and *thātrāja*, a cargo of a different type was involved. In 1889 the king of Jeypore, Ramachandra Deo III, and the *thātrāja* of Bissamcuttack, Ramachandra Thatraj II, both died. As chance would have it, neither of these long-term adversaries left behind an heir who had already attained majority and could assume office immediately. Vikram Deo III, the designated successor to the *mahārāja*, was fifteen years old at the time of his father's death and thus excluded (under the rules laid down for Agency Tracts) until 1896 from mounting the throne. The kingdom of Jeypore came under the supervision of the Court of Wards and H.D. Taylor, a member of the Indian Civil Service, was appointed manager in Jeypore. Until the prince was enthroned (which was in 1895 for astrological reasons), Taylor ran things in such a way that by the time the office was transferred he had accumulated one million rupees in savings for the estate. The education of the young prince was entrusted to J. Marsh, a 'renowned scholar'. Vikram Deo III accepted the western education he received even in respect of his character and became an 'enlightened' Anglophile monarch up until his death in 1920. Already in 1896 we find the colonial government endowing him with the title of *mahārāja* as a recognition of his merits. In 1906 he was accorded the honour of being introduced to the Prince of Wales (the future King George V) in Madras. In 1911 he was knighted and in 1917 a British governor, Lord Pentland, visited Jeypore for the first time. While earlier monarchs of Jeypore had built temples and supported Brahmans, Vikram Deo III spent a lot of money on community projects like hospitals and schools. During the first world war he donated more than 100,000 rupees to the Madras war chest and presented the British with a fighter worth 25,000 rupees, which carried the name 'Jeypore'.[37]

The oldest son of Narendra Thatraj II of Bissamcuttack was only eight years old at the time of his father's death so that his succession was not due until 1903. Here too, therefore, an opportunity existed for the British to place the administration of the estate under their own supervision until the designated successor had reached majority. And here too, the interregnum could have been used to exercise educational influence over the youth and to guide the affairs of the place into orderly ways. Yet, British administrators and teachers were not employed in Bissamcuttack. Instead, during this period, a Brahman called Valiveti Venkata Krishnayya became the most influential person in Bissamcuttack. From 1892 to 1903 he functioned as the guardian of the *thātrāja* and afterwards, until 1922, as 'Agent and Mukhtyar [lawyer] of the Bissemkatak Estate', as he frequently styled himself in his various letters. Krishnayya became one of the key figures in the developments and disputes in the following years.

Despite the death of the two arch-enemies of 1877 and despite the influence of the British on the administration of the estates and on the education of the designated successors, the conflict between the *mahārāja* and the *thātrāja* was in no way laid to rest. In the period following Vikram Deo's accession to the throne in 1895 and before the *thātrāja*'s take-over of office in 1903, letters were exchanged between the king of Jeypore and British officials concerning yearly payment by the *thātrāja* to the *mahārāja* of 1,500 rupees.[38] This was the tax known as *nazar* which, in the present case, was a kind of compensatory payment made by the *thātrāja* for his non-appearance at the yearly *dasarā* festival. It can be seen from the documents available that even during the minority of the designated Bissamcuttack *thātrāja*, the *mahārāja* insisted that he either appear personally or pay the stipulated compensation. In his reply to an enquiry by the *thātrāja* of 15.10.1904, the new agent to the governor, R.H. Campbell, explained this *nazar* payment as follows:

[37] On these points see Bell (1945, 133) and Senapati (1966, 278). The Court of Wards was an important institution of colonial administration, not only in freeing the estates it ran from time to time from debt and in subjecting them to administrative reform, but also in exercising educational influence on future office-holders and in 'anglicizing' them. On this see Henningham (1990, 31, 37, 63-70), Metcalf (1979, 229-36, 286-8) and Yang (1979).

[38] See KDR 2274; 2284; 2285; 2286; 2287; 2288; 2293; 2294; 2295; 2301; 2314; 2315; 2316; 2317; 2318; 2330; 2346; 2347; 2348; 2362.

> It was proposed and sanctioned by the Board of Revenue in 1890 that as a substantial acknowledgement of the service nature of your estate and in lieu of your attendance with 500 paiks at the Dasara Durbar at Jeypore, an annual nuzzar of Rs. 1,500 should be paid on the occasion of the Dasara Durbar. This arrangement continued till the Estate was made over to you in last July. (KDR 2359)

Thus, again, more than just money was at issue here. The payments of 1,500 rupees, however painful they may have been to the *thātrāja* financially, represented in an even more disagreeable way the 'service nature' of the estate, and they sealed it.

Matters began to escalate when the *thātrāja* attained majority and assumed office on 20.7.1903. On 17.8.1903, Vikram Deo III sent a letter described as *hukūm* or 'order' to the *thātrāja*:

> You are hereby ordered to be present in Jeypore on the 27th September next, and to be in attendance on us on the occasion of the Dasara Durbar to be held here this year, for the discharge of any duty that might be imposed upon you as that is one of the forms of service you are required to render us as a service holder under us. (KDR 2365)[39]

The *thātrāja* did not obey this order but, following the practice of previous years, sent the 1,500 rupees. However, this time the *mahārāja* refused to accept the money. He gave his reasons in a letter to the agent dated 25.11.1903.[40] First Vikram Deo complained that the *thātrāja* (who had lived on the coast during his minority) had gone directly to Bissamcuttack on assuming office without, as was customary in his view, going first to Jeypore, paying *nazar* to the king, receiving a sari and obtaining a new *paṭṭā* document with new conditions of office. Vikram Deo admitted that 'it was arranged by the Court of Wards acting for the Madras Government that the minor might be excused attendance at the Dasara during his minority on payment of a fine of 1,500 Rs. yearly', adding: 'The arrangement ... was only intended to continue during the time of his minority.' In a letter of 17.2.1904,[41] the *mahārāja* again complained about the young man in the north-east of his kingdom: 'The thatraja of Bissem katak has not as yet observed the usual formalities in acknowledging me as his Feudal Chief nor has he remitted his sist.'

[39] See also KDR 2359; 2360; 2367.

[40] See KDR 2363.

[41] See KDR 2227.

The agent initially replied to Vikram Deo III on 17.3.1904[42]: 'I am not prepared to enter into the somewhat delicate questions regarding your right to resume the Bissamcuttack Estate or enhance the rent.' In July 1904, however, he intervened in the smouldering conflict by inviting the *thātrāja* to meet him in the town of Salur at the foot of the Ghats, so that they should go together to the *dasarā* festival in Jeypore.[43] The *thātrāja* replied that he was unable to meet this request.[44] At the beginning of October the same year, the king sent another order (*hukūm*) to his governor in Bissamcuttack, asking him to appear at the *dasarā* festival in Jeypore on 10 October with 500 *pāīks*, but to no avail.[45]. The young *thātrāja*, encouraged by his Brahmanical *dīwān* Krishnayya, decided upon open rebellion. In a letter dated 26 November 1904, Krishnayya wrote to the *mahārāja* in the name of his lord:

> 1. Maharajah, I am in due receipt of your so-called hukum … of the 4th October 1904, calling on me to attend your Dasara Durbar of this year with 500 Paiks …
>
> 2. The Bissemkatak estate is not held on service tenure as you seem to imply. It is an independent zemindari, which has only to pay the Jeypore Zemindary a fixed, unchanging and unchangeable Kattubadi of Rs. 2200 as Permanent Settlement Records.
>
> 3. I have, therefore, remitted Rs. 2200 … which I request you will be pleased to accept and formally acknowledge. (KDR 1791)[46]

In this letter not only is the agreement of 1877 between Ramachandra Deo III and Ramachandra Thatraj II swept aside, but all the other contracts that had been negotiated since 1689 (as we shall see) are also declared null and void. According to the argument of the *dīwān*, the Permanent Settlement between the British colonial government and the *mahārāja* of Jeypore had fixed Bissamcuttack's status as an independent estate and the payment of 2,200 rupees to the Jeypore king for all time to come.

The *mahārāja*'s *dīwān*, P.V. Pantulu, also a Brahman, replied to this letter sharply in the name of the king. In a letter of 31.12.1904, he

[42] See KDR 2227A.

[43] See KDR 2487; 2376.

[44] See KDR 2367; 2370.

[45] See KDR 2375.

[46] See also KDR 2373.

reproached the *thātrāja* at length over his failings from the time he had assumed office in July 1903.[47] The *dīwān* complained about the tone of the *thātrāja*'s November letter and vehemently rejected the *thātrāja*'s claim that Bissamcuttack was held as an independent *zamīndārī* and not as a 'service tenure' under the *mahārāja*. The *thātrāja* was then warned that 'you have rendered yourself liable to forfeiture of your tenure of the estate at the will and pleasure of the Maharaja.' However, one also learns that the *mahārāja* granted the *thātrāja* 'one more opportunity to make amends for your past conduct, as ... you have been probably misguided by bad advisers who have taken advantage of your youth and inexperience.'[48]

Let us now examine the period between 1877 and 1904 quickly, before moving on, with the contesting parties, into the colonial courtrooms in the next section. In 1877, the ceremony for the Empress Victoria formed the main backdrop for the performance of the political drama, offering the British a kind of illustration and initiation into the nature of the conflict. In the years that followed, however, the tensions were again dealt with on the stage on which such disputes had traditionally taken place in Jeypore (and in many other Hindu kingdoms throughout India), namely the *dasarā* festival. In this context, it is not without significance that in July 1904 the British agent intended to go to the *dasarā* festival in person. The reason for this was probably not just to make the visit of the young *thātrāja* to the *mahārāja* easier. Rather, in a report which the agent sent to Madras in 1905, other motivations are mentioned.[49] There, a detailed list of those governors of the kingdom who appeared in Jeypore at the festivities in 1904 (and of those who did not) is provided, from which it emerges that the Bissamcuttack *thātrāja* was not the only absentee. Another important point made in the report is that the Board of Revenue in Madras provided the not inconsiderable sum of 5,000 rupees to hold the festivities. In conclusion, the report reveals the mentality of the shopkeeper: 'The festival was carried out in the customary manner but at greatly reduced expenditure.'

[47] See KDR 2372.

[48] The British too, attributed much of the insubordination shown by Bissamcuttack to Krishnayya's bad influence. Thus, the *Administration Report* of 1905 (KDR 2768, Appendix D) says of the *thātrāja*: 'His obstinacy is due to the bad advice of a man called Valivati Krishnayya, who was a guardian to the Thatraj when he was a minor and who has a great influence over him ... I am afraid that a long and expensive Law suit is inevitable.'

[49] See KDR 2380.

Clearly, a certain cognitive penetration of the political significance of the *dasarā* festival can be recognized on the part of the British and this knowledge is translated in political practice as the colonial government established itself as a generous sponsor and thus as the most important patron of the festival after the king. During this period British officials also began to play a direct part in the ceremony, for example, by going through the city at the head of the procession on elephants. At the same time the ambitious plans for a railway through the region continued to be pursued, even though the great breakthrough would have to wait a little longer.

So far we have encountered two different metaphors of power and prestige. For the British it was the railway, while for the indigenous actors it was the *dasarā*-festival. The difference between these two becomes clearer if we compare the spatial dimensions and the cargos that are involved in each.

The railway, a dominant symbol of the unrestrained forward thrust of industrial-imperial power and colonial expansion, incorporates the dream of a straight, smooth iron rail ploughing its way through all natural barriers and unevenness, on which (and also in harmony with) a steadily moving machine runs tirelessly to and fro.[50] Apart from soldiers, the cargo carried by this machine does not consist of human beings. Transporting passengers initially took second place to transporting goods, through which the wealth and economic power of the empire would be increased.

While the railway only crossed the kingdom of Jeypore on its periphery, without having a starting or an end point in the kingdom itself, the movements connected with the *dasarā* festival are of a quite different order. Subjects from all parts of the kingdom set out for its politico-religious (and roughly geographical) centre by foot or pack animal. The king sits at the centre of this centre, on his throne in the *darbār* hall of his palace. He did not call those marching towards him and when he demanded active movement, it was in the form of an order and in response to gross disobedience. Essentially, however, he receives people, possessing attraction like a magnet drawing humans. Ideally, he always possesses this charisma of the centre. However, it is ritually formed and symbolically heightened at certain points of time determined by the goddess Durga and by ecological time.

Time running in a circle and the mythical acts of a goddess, therefore, create the framework within which the king of Jeypore periodically

[50] On this, more generally, see also Shivelbusch (1989).

presents himself as the centre of his kingdom and has himself confirmed in this position by his subjects. The yearly *dasarā* festival, driven by a dynamic very different from that of the steam engine, sets a great number of star-shaped movements in train, which are also physically arduous for the participants, movements from fields and hills, valleys and forests, which all merge into the 'great road' (*baḍa daṇḍa*) of the royal capital. Here, the innumerable rough marches unite into a single stream running in a north-south direction and ending in a show of homage in front of and, for some, within the palace. The cargo thereby being transported consists, first, of the numerous sacrificial animals being brought along, or rather in the lives of these animals. Other gifts, such as jungle fruits, cloth or money, are also taken along and presented to the king, who responds with splendiferous counter-gifts—seen in economic terms, he makes a loss. However, the real gifts are the participants themselves, who offer themselves and, as with the animals they have brought along, ultimately their lives to their ruler for the coming year. Through their appearance in Jeypore and through the gestures of submission they make in front of the throne, they proclaim their political loyalty and military availability for the coming year as in previous years. The cargo coming to Jeypore is, thus, of a politico-religious, not an economic nature. It represents unity, military strength, regeneration and growth and not, like the cargo on the railway, wealth.[51]

Thus, once a year at *dasarā*, all the different parts of the kingdom of Jeypore, with the king at the centre and the holders of estates at its periphery, were arranged into a group picture. The Bissamcuttack estate became noticeable within this total picture of the kingdom, though only through the absence of the *thātrāja* and his 500 *pāik*s. Casually expressed, a jewel in the crown was missing. At the same time, Bissamcuttack re-appeared in another picture, in a differently constituted vision, namely the landscape puzzle of the colonial railway operator, in which it represented a difficult, but central point along the planned route.

5. (Re-)constructed histories

After Vikram Deo III had failed to move Narendra Thatraj II to march to Jeypore and take part in the procession along the *baḍa daṇḍa*, and with three years' payments still outstanding, the king went to court in 1905. His complaint was to move through several courts and involve many summons until 1926.

[51] The symbolism of *dasarā* is treated in more detail in Ch. V, section 3.

In this connection, one important thing was that a 'History of Bissamcuttack' was sketched out in some of the documents submitted to the court. While the Bissamcuttack side distinguished itself in this respect, the British also produced their versions, which adopt a more sober tone. As for the *mahārāja*, historiography was of concern to him only in respect of the wider historical context in which the local history of his kingdom and especially that of Bissamcuttack was embedded. What was common to all these 'histories' was that they were produced not to satisfy a scientific historical interest but to win arguments before a court, influence judgements or establish guidelines for future administration.

Given the situation regarding sources, the Bissamcuttack versions stand at the centre of my analysis here. The most important source comes from the pen of the *dīwān*, Krsihnayya, and dates from 1905.[52] However, this document was written in the name of the *thātraja*, who was accorded authorship as a 'memorialist' or 'humble memorialist'.[53] In this text ('Memorial' in what follows), the history of Bissamcuttack, from the origins of the estate to the assumption of office of Narendra Thatraj II in 1903, forms the narrative framework. However, the author deviates repeatedly from the chronological narrative structure in order to turn to lengthy explanations regarding the significance of this or that historical event for the decision of the court. The author added another document to the 'Memorial', which he called 'History' (so called in what follows).[54]

[52] See KDR 2485.

[53] The document itself contains no information concerning when it was written. In a 'Supplemental Memorial' of 21.11.1905 (KDR 2491), however, reference is made to an original 'Memorial' of 20.9.1905, which in all probability is KDR 2485.

[54] One document available to me from the government archive (KDR 2168), unfortunately, has no date or information on the author, but is headed 'History' and, thanks to the cross-reference in KDR 2485, can be identified as the history mentioned therein. Like the 'Memorial', this document must be dated September 1905. The chronological classification is complicated by the fact that a 'Chronological List of Bissemkatak Thatrajas', which refers to the 1907 *District Gazetteer*, is added at the end of the History. This suggests that the 'Memorial' and 'History' documents available to me are not originals but official copies made on the occasion of the hearing held before the Madras High Court in 1915. The chronological list was probably written years later (I assume around 1910, in which year other documents were also drawn up in connection with this hearing) by a British author. Other memorials and reconstructions of the history of Bissamcuttack, which can only be mentioned in passing here, are archived under KDR 1805; 1995; 2022; 2382; 2385 and 2493.

The historical sketch in this is more extensive than that found in the 'Memorial'. All in all, the author probably saw the necessity of writing a history with a more scientific touch than the pleading 'Memorial' possessed, in order to support his politico-jural claims. At the end of his 'History' he, therefore, stresses that 'The above, though meagre, is yet an accurate history' (KDR 2168, para 23).

In this section, I shall let myself be guided by the chronology of events as they are developed in these two texts. In doing so, the focus will first of all be on providing a detailed investigation of the strategies and arguments implicitly woven into the historical sketch. The explicit statements which take up the legal disputes more directly will form the focus of the discussion in the next section.

The 'Memorial', which is addressed to the highest official in India, that is, 'To His Excellency, The Viceroy and Governor General of India', describes the origins of Bissamcuttack as follows:

> 1. The present Bissamkatak estate … was formed out of a jungly, barren and unhealthy tract of country owned by one Malla Mahunty, an ancestor of the memorialist.
>
> 2. The Embryo estate thus formed was subsequently developed and improved by Beruku Mahunty and Krishna Chendra Patro, the son and grandson respectively of the said Malla Mahunty. The then Zemindar of Jeypore which was nearest to Bissamcuttack fearing the growing power of Beruku Mahunti, made a friendly alliance with him and conferred upon him the title of Patro …
>
> 5. The above state of things continued till 1689 A.D. when the then Zemindar of Jeypore who was in strained financial circumstances owing to mismanagement of his estate … applied to Krishnachendra Patro … for an annual contribution … Krishnachendra Patro realising the insecurity of his position on account of a want of a patta from the ruling power and fearing that he would be disposed of his estate … expressed his willingness to render all possible help. A settlement was accordingly entered into between the parties by which the title of Thatraj was conferred on Krishnachendra Patro, who in return agreed to pay an annual sum of Rs. 2,200 on condition of acknowledging in writing a permanent and hereditary title to the estate held by him. This was at once given effect to by the grant of a copper plate patta. (KDR 2485, para 1; 2; 5)

In this passage, we encounter the theme of the cleared jungle, a motif found in the origin myths of many little kingdoms in south Orissa, where it is often stressed with the words, 'He cleared the jungle'. However, in these legends the original 'jungle condition' of these cleared lands is rarely, as in our document, equated with a no man's land claim. Instead, in the myths of many little-kingly dynasties in Ganjam, the motif of clearing the jungle does not serve to legitimize the claim to the land on the part of the little king. Rather, what is always mentioned there is that the great king installs the myth's hero as governor over the cleared land in recognition of his deeds. Thus, in these foundation myths, the cleared land appears as an integral element of the great kingdom, and the founder of the little-kingly dynasty is not really legitimized by the act of having cleared the land but only by the recognition of his position on the part of the great king.[55]

A small but decisive variation in this motif can be seen in the Bissamcuttack version. Here, a picture is sketched of an unhealthy, infertile jungle region, which should be regarded as the property of the ancestor of the *thātrāja*s of Bissamcuttack: 'owned by one Malla Mahunty', as it says. In the 'Memorial' no other legitimation is offered for the right of possession, which therefore appears to be inherent in the nature of the jungle itself. To a large extent, the jungle has the status of a virgin, unoccupied land, lying ready for appropriation by the brave and determined. The originally unexploited, unowned, indeed dangerous and unhealthy land was taken into possession through the act of being settled, and this 'embryo estate', according to the memorialist, developed into a considerable independent estate in the generations that followed. With this small rhetorical change, therefore, the indigenous theme of the clearing of the jungle is 'translated' for the world of colonial understanding: an adventurer and entrepreneur discovers uncultivated land, appropriates it and, together with his successors, subjects it to agricultural exploitation. The theme of land clearance is transformed into the 'go west' or 'last frontier' theme as known in western imperialism.[56]

This view of things, naturally, stood in stark contrast to that of the king of Jeypore, which we have already read about in certain documents relating to the 1877-conflict. Here, in no sense did the clearing of the jungle create any right to the land for the *thātrāja*: on the contrary, it was taken by the king as a justification for increasing tribute.

[55] See Berkemer (1997).

[56] This view of things also amounts to a denial of any 'history' before the coming of Malla Mahunty. Without wishing or being able to go into the early history of Bissamcuttack here, it may just be mentioned that Bissamcuttack, like Gudari, is repeatedly mentioned in the chronicles of the imperial Gangavamshis and Suryavamshis as a refuge for dispossessed kings or their descendants. See *Bārabāṭi Vīrakṛṣṇadev* (1816), Behuria (ed. 1964, 82) and Berkemer (1993, 247-9, 280-4).

For the memorialist, at this early period in the history of the Bissamcuttack estate, the role of the king of Jeypore was initially just that of a neighbour. Only in the second generation did he give up the role of the uninvolved neighbour and enter into a 'friendly alliance' with apparently equal partners, mainly, so it is argued in Bissamcuttack, out of anxiety concerning the entrepreneur's growing influence. The fact that the memorialist mentions the politico-ritual act of conferring the title of *pātro* by the king of Jeypore to the *thātrāja* at least expresses the recognition on the part of Bissamcuttack of a hierarchical relationship with Jeypore. According to the 'Memorial', in the third generation, under Krishna Chandra, an agreement was reached in 1689 because he required legitimation from above and also because at this time it was Bissamcuttack who feared the military power of the other party. The agreement, which provided for the title of *thātrāja* being conferred in exchange for a yearly tribute of 2,200 rupees, was apparently concluded in harmony by both sides. However, it is suggested that unsatisfactory financial conduct was the basic motive for the king's behaviour. In the 'Memorial', as far as the agreement of 1689 is concerned, the possibility of providing military services and the appearance of the *thātrāja* at *dasarā* are vaguely expressed only when Krishna Chandra's 'willingness to render all possible help' is mentioned. In addition, it is emphasized that Krishna Chandra only accepted the agreement because the king of Jeypore recognized his estate as permanent and hereditary. The agreement of 1689 is said to have been recorded on a copper plate.

In the 'History' appended to the 'Memorial', these statements are reiterated, though with some additions and alterations in content. Thus, the author remarks in his introduction to the 'History' that Bissamcuttack 'is inhabited by a mountainous race of Khonds, whose notoriously inborn nature of turbulence and lawlessness has been greatly crushed down by the administration of the benign British Government' (Kor 2168, para 2). This points to a different assessment of the nature of the jungle since, while in the 'Memorial' the jungle appears as unsettled land belonging to no one, the presence of original inhabitants is now mentioned. Though, because of their anarchic nature (before the 'benign' appearance of the British government), these are hardly seen as people possessing a right to the land.

The foundation of the Bissamcuttack estate in the middle of this different type of jungle is represented as follows:

> The original founder of the Zemindary was one Mallu Mahunty, by caste a Srishti Kurnam (a highly warlike race in those days), who emigrated from Parlakimidi in the early part of the 17th century … Mallu Mahunty started his life as a trader in Bissemkatak and a few

> of its surrounding villages, and in a couple of years or so gained the confidence of the Khonds completely, who being impressed with his assiduity and prepossessing appearance and manners, elected him as their headman. He was therefore no longer a bustling trader going from door to door and from village to village, but a man of some rank and influence, to whom people from all parts of the neighbourhood poured in with petty presents in the shape of grain and other articles of produce, with a view to obtaining good advice and for settlement of disputes among themselves. These presents gradually took the shape of occasional nuzzars signifying a silent acknowledgement of the superiority and authority of the recipient. (KDR 2168, para 3).

As soon as the jungle is seen as peopled, the implicit 'theory of the foundation of the kingdom' becomes complicated. While, in the 'Memorial', Mahunty is simply in possession, in the 'History' his social background and place of origin are given. Mahunty, we learn, belonged to the *karnam* caste about whom Carmichael reported: 'They are the writers of the country, and with the Brahmins are the only educated people in it. In hill zamindaries people of this caste exercise great influence' (1869, 119).[57] The distinction made later by Francis between valley and hill *karnams*, according to which *karnams* 'in the low country are usually accountants with a reputation for undue subtlety, but in the hills are a martial people' (1907, 233), pervades all subsequent government publications. The author of the 'History' agrees with the official British characterization of the hill *karnams* as martial, though qualifying it with the words, 'in those days'.

According to the 'History', Mahunty initially acted on the level of economics. The 'History', thus, stresses the entrepreneurial mentality of the founder of the estate, though this time his activities did not take place in the realm of agriculture but in that of trade. The explorer and discoverer of new horizons is replaced by the expanding merchant. This merchant developed (if the 'History' is to be believed), almost without his own volition and on the express wishes of the indigenous inhabitants who were impressed by his personality and sought his advice, into a local chief and *zamīndār*. His function as a recipient of gifts acquired a politico-ritual character, not an economic one.

In this passage concerning the history of the Bissamcuttack estate in the early seventeenth century, a picture is sketched of a charismatic foreigner's acquisition and exercise of power in a jungle peopled by quarrelling and anarchic humans—a picture which, it was probably

[57] See also (ibid., 64).

hoped, might be seen as a parallel to the history of the East India Company. Here, amongst other things, historical writing seems to have been undertaken with an eye to British understanding and appreciation. This 'mirroring' function of the writing of local history continues:

> The sphere of his influence and authority having thus expanded, Mallu Mahunty left no stone unturned to maintain his position by all means possible. He being by virtue of his birth a man of enterprising character, thoroughly initiated into the tactics of the martial science, at once formed a well organised force of armed men in order to protect himself and his newly formed dominion which he was master of without the knowledge of any one to whom it might have rightly or wrongly belonged. In the course of a few years he could command a militia consisting of no less than one thousand men and managed to continue in unmolested possession of his self-acquired estate till his death. (KDR 2168, para 4)

Like the East India Company, therefore, the founder of the Bissamcuttack estate did not rely on his inborn capabilities as a charismatic entrepreneur and peacemaker alone, but supplemented these by setting up a powerful military force. In this reconstruction of the early period of the Bissamcuttack estate, the king of Jeypore is conspicuous by his absence. Mahunty, it is stressed, made himself the master of a 'self-acquired' estate 'without the knowledge of any one to whom it might have rightly or wrongly belonged'.

As far as developments up to the 1689 agreement under Krishna Chandra are concerned, the 'History' embellishes the more fundamental points made in the 'Memorial', and there are more sideswipes at the king. Concerning Mahunty's son Beruku, for example, we are told: 'He was no less judicious than his father and in a short time countless men from many other hill villages flocked to his standard' (KDR 2168, para 5). Concerning the Kondh, we learn: 'There is not the least doubt that before the advent of Mallu Mahunty these mountaineers were absolute masters of the soil, owing nobody authority and paying nothing either in money or in kind to anybody' (ibid., para 6). And of the king of Jeypore, it is reported: 'The Jeypore Maharaja … had never been bold enough to enter into the contest with the savage Khonds' (ibid., para 7). According to the author, the king, 'being fully aware of the utter futility of attempting to get rid of the formidable neighbour', tried to win Beruku's friendship because, using him as a middleman, at least a small sum of tax could be realized, instead of nothing at all. In addition, strategic motives are mentioned: 'Bissamcuttack with its well-organised militia would be a barrier against frequent incursions and invasions of the Maharattas and other powers from outside, which the Jeypore country was then prey to' (ibid.). For

Bissamcuttack's rulers, again, the need for greater political legitimation is mentioned as a reason for approval of the pact.

Regarding the agreement of 1689, a translation of the copper-plate inscription is cited, in which, among other things, is stated: 'We have granted you the country of Bissemkatak of our Jeypore Zemindary with all its lands, both waste and cultivated and jungles on your agreeing to pay us the sum of Rs. 2,200 as Jamabandi every year and enjoying it hereditary to yourself, your sons, your grandsons and descendants' (ibid., para 8). To which is added the comment: 'The above named Patta absolutely transferred to Krishna Chandra Thatraj and his heirs the right and title to the country ... The grant is not for a single life but for enjoyment in perpetuity from heir to heir' (ibid., para 9).

As we shall learn later, the existence of the copper plate and the authenticity of the text submitted to the court were subject to certain doubts. However, if we accept that the translation is genuine, then things are clearly laid out to the advantage of Bissamcuttack. For according to the 'History', the Bissamcuttack estate was an 'absolute grant', not a 'service tenure', and it had been granted not for a single lifetime, but 'in perpetuity'.

The founding of Bissamcuttack and the agreement of 1689 were not the only factors with which the Bissamcuttack side tried to make and support its politico-jural point. However, after 1689 Krishnayya's historical reconstructions in the 'Memorial' and the 'History' dry up. He briefly mentions Pitambara and Samburaj, the two succeeding *thātrāja*s of the dynasty, as steady payers of tribute. He then concerns himself mainly with the history of Jeypore and with the Permanent Settlement of 1803. After the 1689 agreement, this settlement of 1803 is the next historical event whose interpretation was to acquire great significance in the legal proceedings of the early twentieth century between the *mahārāja* and the *thātrāja*. Since, it was legal and not historical questions which were the focus of Krishnayya's comments with regard to 1803, we shall defer his views in this respect to the next section and resume here, with him, our look at the history of Bissamcuttack after the Permanent Settlement:

> Some years after the Permanent Settlement Ramachandra Thatrajah succeeded ... Samburaj Thatrajah. Owing to mismanagement, he soon hopelessly fell into arrears to the Jeypore Estate. He therefore proceeded to Jeypore to have the matter settled personally with the Maharajah. An unpleasant incident, which occurred at the time of his visit to the Maharajah, turned the tide of the Thatrajah's fortune. The Thatrajah, according to the prevailing custom, made obeisance to the Maharajah as a mark of respect. The Maharajah's son, Vikram Dev, who was present there at the time expected the same

> mark of respect from the Thatrajah. Accordingly the Maharajah and his son expressed their wish to the Thatrajah, who flatly refused to do obeisance to any person other than the Maharajah, as it was wrong in principle and against custom. Matters at once assumed a serious aspect, and the Thatrajah had to return to Bissamcuttack without an interview on the subject matter in hand. (ibid., para 15)

This passage provides us with the genesis of the decade-long conflict between the two parties, sketching out something like a prototype of the event of 1877. In both cases the *thātrāja* visited Jeypore, only to leave the royal capital again in conflict with his overlord because of a dispute over a ritual. In the case of the 'unpleasant incident', which is said to have led to his early departure, respect was shown to Ramachandra Deo II (1781-1825) but not to the crown prince. As in 1877, the conflict originated in the area of etiquette, namely in the demand for an unwarranted demonstration of respect towards the king's son. At this point it should also be mentioned that it was under Ramachandra Deo II that the 'golden' statue of the tutelary goddess of the kingdom, Kanaka Durga, was set up in Jeypore for the first time; earlier it had been kept in Nandapur.[58] The 'invention' and celebration of the *dasarā* festival as conducted in Jeypore up to the 1940s is, therefore, to be located historically in this period. And it was probably not by chance that the conflict between the two adversaries took place at the same time as the origin of the *dasarā* festival of Jeypore.

What this conflict and the 1877 conflict have in common is that though financial differences only are mentioned, it is questions of status that stand at the forefront of the dispute. The 'History' does not specify what was meant by the phrase 'to do obeisance'. However, in a note of Turner's,[59] I found an indication that what was at issue was an action described as a *vandanam*. Now the term *vandana* describes that part of the *upacāra* services of the *pūjā* in which the worshipper takes his leave of the deity at the end of the ceremony, paying homage with a bow and using pleasant words. We are, thus, reminded of Dirks's description of *pūjā* as 'a root metaphor for political relations' (1987, 289).

Let us now move further and look at another, longer extract from the 'History':

> 15. Some time after the above incident, the Thatrajah who was hopelessly getting into arrears resolved to make another attempt to seek a friendly interview with Maharajah Ramachandra for the

[58] See here, Chapter VI.

[59] See KDR 2254.

settlement of his affairs … He accordingly proceeded to Jeypore, and no sooner had he visited the Maharajah than he was made a State prisoner, probably at the instigation of the Maharajah's son, Vikram Dev. The Thatrajah died a prisoner in Jeypore.

16. When the news of Ramachandra Thatrajah's imprisonment reached Bissemkatak, the people at once elected his son Krishna Chandra Thatrajah to the Gadi [throne]. Soon after his assumption of office Krishna Chandra Thatrajah sent some of his best men to negotiate with the Maharajah for the release of his unfortunate father, but by the time they reached Jeypore, Ramachandra Dev Maharajah died and was succeeded by his son Vikram Dev. The ambassadors of Bissemkatak, who were devoutly attached to Ramachandra Thatrajah wanted to try their luck with the new Maharajah, but this interview proved equally disastrous. The moment Vikram Dev heard of the assumption to the Gadi by Krishna Chandra Thatrajah at Bissemkatak, he declared open hostilities with the Thatrajah, which fact was immediately carried into Bissemkatak territories, and the Thatrajah, ever mindful of his father's imprisonment and the growing animosity of the Maharajah, fled at once with his family, including his son young Narendra Thatrajah, to Parlakimedi, thence, to Salur, Merangi and at last reached Singapore where he died in 1842.[60]

17. From about 1824 to 1842 the Bissemkatak Zemindary was under the management of Jeypore officials, whose conduct was intolerable. But the Pathros of Bissemkatak could not shake off the yoke, and Ramachandra Thatrajah was in prison and his son Krishna Chandra Thatrajah who was raised to the Gadi had fled the country. On the death of Krishna Chandra Thatrajah, the Pathros took the very first opportunity to run at once to Singapore and invite his son, young Narendra Thatrajah, who unlike his father, was possessed of martial habits to return home and ascend the throne of the Zemindary, which had been in a state of utter anarchy, oppression and corruption for many years. This he did at once, with the help of his Pathros and loyal subjects; but no sooner had this information reached the ears of Vikram Dev Maharajah through his Amins who had been driven away from Bissemkatak, than he sent out armed men to dethrone the Thatrajah. This force was completely defeated and driven out. A second time, however, the Maharajah wanted to try his fortune with redoubled vigour, smarting under the defeat he had first sustained; but this time also he failed,

[60] 'Singapore' was the semi-independent estate of Kalyansingpur, which bordered Bissamcuttack.

> the bravery of the Pathros and their loyalty to the Thatrajah having resolutely withstood the opposition. A third time also the Maharajah collected an enormous force from every nook and corner of his dominions and marched against Narendra Thatrajah, but the heroism of the latter's gallant subjects, always true to his cause, was so fully and successfully brought into play that the Maharajah had to make his way home, one and all of his men having been killed and burnt. (KDR 2168, para 15-17)

In this reconstruction, Maharaja Vikram Deo II (1825-1860) is branded as presumptuous, unjust and quarrelsome, the author of the 'History' perhaps being aware that Vikram Deo II had a very bad reputation with the British, too. To a large extent, the *ancien régime* and the period of non-interference by the colonial government ended with him, not least because of the reports concerning his despotic rule, which, at that time, were continually reaching the coast. At any rate, in the Bissamcuttack reconstruction, Vikram Deo II's bad image is again confirmed. As crown prince he is said to have shown inappropriate arrogance to the then *thātrāja* of Bissamcuttack; then he imprisoned Ramachandra Thatraj I, who had come to Jeypore a second time with good intentions;[61] he then expelled from Bissamcuttack the prisoner's son and heir, who died in exile. The new *thātrāja*, Narendra Thatraj I, was more determined than his father to oppose Vikram Deo II. Directly after his return he was attacked by the king whose assaults, however, he could ward off successfully. In the 'Memorial' the quarrels between the *thātrāja* and the *mahārāja* are located between 1842 and 1848.[62]

A second point emphasized in the 'History', apart from the despotic character of the *mahārāja*, is that the people of Bissamcuttack, particularly the chiefs or *pātros*, gave full support to the *thātrāja*. According to the writer, immediately after Ramachandra's imprisonment his son Krishna Chandra was practically raised to the throne by the people. And when this rather dejected soul died in exile, the *pātros* recalled his martially disposed son at the first opportunity and elected him *thātrāja*. The emphasis on the unconditional loyalty of the *pātros* and the inhabitants of the estate, which also found expression on the field of battle, makes the despotism of the *mahārāja* seem all the more striking. However, it should also be mentioned that at the time when the 'History' was being written

[61] In 'the' Memorial, the length of Ramachandra Thatraj's imprisonment is given as fourteen years, i.e. from 1824 to 1838. See KDR 2485, para 24; Turner also mentions fourteen years (KDR 2254).

[62] See KDR 2485, para 24.

and submitted to the colonial courts, that is, the beginning of the twentieth century, a number of *pātro*s of the Bissamcuttack estate went to court against Narendra Thatraj II (grandson of the Narendra Thatraj I whom the *pātro*s had raised to the throne) to obtain greater independence; for they no longer wished to provide the *thātrāja* with soldiers for the *dasarā* festival.[63] Thus, by repeatedly stressing the loyalty of the *pātro*s and their active role in installing the then *thātrāja*, the writer is aiming not only at Vikram Deo II, but also at the rebellious *pātro*s, whose insubordination is contrasted with the loyalty of their forefathers.

The temporary truce between Vikram Deo II and Narendra Thatraj I is described as follows in the 'History':

> After having thus unsuccessfully attempted three times to subjugate Bissemkatak, Vikram Dev fully realised the futility of physical force in deposing Narendra Thatrajah and attempted to contest his rights, if any, in the Courts of Law. A protracted litigation seems to have been conducted between the parties in the courts of the several Agents to the Governor … The Thatrajah was advised by the Agent to the Governor to arrange matters peacefully with the Maharajah, who was also similarly advised. Both parties came to an amicable settlement, the Thatrajah agreeing to pay an annual nuzzar of Rs. 300 in addition to the Rs. 2,200 of the original Jamabandi, but no patta was given, nor muchilika taken. (KDR 2168, para 17)

The new pact basically left the position of 1689 untouched. The increase of 300 rupees a year was described not as tribute (*jamabandi* or *kattubadi*) but as a *nazar*, and thus has a ceremonial, voluntary character. In addition, the lack of a contract (*paṭṭā*) strengthens the continuing validity of the 1689 agreement. The achievement of this 'verbal compromise' is dated to 1854 in the Memorial.[64]

The account then links the fate of Bissamcuttack to an internal power struggle in Jeypore by referring to the sharpening of a conflict that had been smouldering for years between Vikram Deo II and his son, later Ramachandra Deo III but still a minor in 1855.[65] We learn from the 'History' that Ramachandra's mother begged military assistance from the *thātrāja* of Bissamcuttack, who willingly sided with the opposition to Vikram Deo. Narendra Thatraj I marched at the head of a thousand

[63] The 'insubordinate' *pātro*s were those of Ambadola, Jagdalpur, Kutragada and Pukili. Information on their court cases can be found in KDR 1995; 2103; 2198; 2258; 2306 and 2768, and in Behuria (ed. 1965, 65, 68-9).

[64] Francis (1907, 233) shifts this event to 1851.

[65] See KDR 2168, para 18.

soldiers to Gunupur where the crown prince, Ramachandra Deo III, was staying with his men. In recognition of his readiness to help, Ramachandra Deo is said to have honoured the *thātrāja* with the gift of an elephant and other valuable presents on this occasion.[66]

With the *thātrāja*'s provision of soldiers and the subsequent handing over of gifts to him by the crown prince—actions which symbolize the political sovereignty of both giver and (at a lower level of the hierarchy) recipient—these two protagonists mutually defined and legitimized each other. Ultimately, a truce was brokered between father and son, and the crown prince had to postpone his ambitions for the throne until 1860. However, the bond between the future *mahārāja* and the *thātrāja* had been forged. In this context, a letter of 1877 from Ramachandra Deo III, in which Narendra Thatraj I is praised, may be recalled.[67] It should also be remembered, however, that following Narendra's death in 1876, his son Ramachandra Thatraj II (just as with his great-grandfather some fifty years before) fell into the king's disfavour and left Jeypore without permission and without matters being settled.

Up to 1860, the 'History' sketches the genesis and development of the conflict between *mahārāja* and *thātrāja* not as a structural conflict between two office-holders, or even two offices that transcended individuals, but as a conflict between Vikram Deo II on the one hand and three *thātrāja*s—Ramachandra Thatraj I, Krishna Chandra II, Narendra Thatraj I—on the other. Matters improved temporarily only after Vikram Deo II was replaced by his son Ramachandra Deo III. And yet the reign of Ramachandra Deo III was not without incident:

> Years rolled on; and the Zemindary of Jeypore passed into the hands of Ramachandra Dev about the year 1860. Four years later, that is in 1864, Balaji Viswasrai Garu, Dewan of Jeypore, who had for some time past been carefully watching the affairs of Bissemkatak … proceeded to that place on his own motion and, without the knowledge of Ramachandra Dev, interviewed Narendra Thatrajah, and successfully prevailed upon him to execute a muchilika of Rs. 5000, by falsely representing to him in the name of Ramachandra Dev that Jeypore was involved in large arrears to Government and could not pay the Pelshcush any longer without more substantial assistance from Bissemkatak. (KDR 2168, para 20)

As far as the agreement concluded in 1854 between the *mahārāja* and *thātrāja* is concerned, the continuing validity of the agreement of 1689

[66] Turner also mentions a turban (KDR 2254).

[67] See KDR 2245.

could still be justified, given the failure to exchange the *paṭṭā* and *muchilikā*. However, the changes introduced in 1864, which were not inconsiderable given the doubling of the existing tribute, were laid down in writing through the exchange of *paṭṭā* and *muchilikā* and could, therefore, no longer be dismissed as an oral agreement without basis in law. But in the 'History', the new agreement with the increase in tribute is traced back to the cunning of the *dīwān* of Jeypore, acting independently of the *mahārāja*, by which the somewhat naïve Narendra is said to have been deceived. In addition, in this agreement neither an obligation for military service nor for an appearance at *dasarā* are mentioned. These hotly contested and central issues in later conflicts are only mentioned in the 'History' for the first time in connection with the agreement of 1877.[68] Here, it must be remembered that in a letter of 1877, Ramachandra Deo III saw the service nature of the Bissamcuttack estate already fixed in the agreement of 1864. According to the *mahārāja*, what counted was the fact that 'That estate was leased out on condition of performing service' (KDR 2245). And: 'He (Narendra Thatraj I) was granted the taluq on condition of rendering us service with 700 paiks' (ibid.).

We can skip the period between the years 1877 and 1904, since this period has already been treated extensively. Let me just point out that the memorialist states that while the *thātrāja* had paid the increased tribute regularly during this period, he had 'never rendered service of attendance with the Paiks alleged to have been stipulated in the patta' (KDR 2168, para 21). Thus, the service nature of the estate was also called into doubt for the agreement of 1877.

The Bissamcuttack version of the history of this estate and its ruling dynasty stops at certain points or events in history. Significant is, initially, the question of the founding of the estate and then the agreement of 1689. According to the memorialist, the agreement of 1803 between the British and Jeypore fixed the legal status of Bissamcuttack as an 'absolute grant' only indirectly, though it did so permanently. Only limited relevance is granted to the three agreements made after 1689 (in 1854, 1864 and 1877), especially as far as the service nature of the estate is concerned. For the period after 1824, the memorialist sketches a history of permanently inflicted injustice. Thus, at the end of the 'Memorial', the author writes of the 'shabby treatment meted out by Jeypore to the ancestors of the memorialist' and of the 'injuries and sufferings inflicted on Bissemkatak Thatrajahs' (KDR 2485, para 30, 31).

[68] See KDR 2168, para 21.

Krishnayya's claim, already mentioned, that his 'History' is an 'accurate history', can only be accepted in part. Nonetheless, it is certainly the most detailed history of Bissamcuttack. Turner's history, in his *Hill Tour Report* of 1882,[69] looks modest by comparison. According to his description, the history of the dynasty of the Bissamcuttack *thātrāja*s only begins with Krishna Chandra Thatraja under *mahārāja* Ragunath Krishna Deo (1686-1708), that is, two generations later than stated by the Bissamcuttack memorialist. Thus, according to Turner, from the start the Bissamcuttack *thātrāja*s appear more obviously as persons appointed or at least legitimized by Jeypore than as independent entrepreneurs. The first official version of the history of Bissamcuttack from the point of view of the government, printed in the *Gazetteer* of 1907, is nothing more than a faulty copy of Turner's report.[70] As already mentioned, the *Gazetteers* of 1945 and 1966 basically reproduce the version found in Francis, into which other copying errors have crept.

Even if the Bissamcuttack *dīwān*'s account does provide the most detailed history of Bissamcuttack, the 'Memorial' and 'History' should not be measured against the yardstick of an academic historiography oriented towards the reconstruction of 'actual' events. The interests that guide the author are not the presentation of historical details or diachronic developments. Rather, it is concrete legal questions arising from the conflict with the *mahārāja* that are his focus. The author never loses sight of this cognitive focus, neither in his selection of historical events, nor in the style of his formulations, nor when he weaves opinions and legal comments into his historical discourse. He is a *bricoleur* seeking to use more or less secure historical data to support a politico-legal point of view.

6. From procession to litigation

After 1905 the king of Jeypore and the *thātrāja* of Bissamcuttack appeared before various tribunals within the colonial judicial system. The course of their litigation, stretching over two decades, in which the earlier variable and context-sensitive negotiations and mediations would now be codified and recorded under the premises and conditions of the colonial legal system, will be briefly sketched here.[71]

[69] KDR 2254.

[70] Francis (1907, 233) makes Ramachandra Thatraj I's fourteen-year imprisonment one of fourteen months.

[71] The 'context-sensitivity' of pre-colonial judicial proceedings in Hindu kingdoms is emphasized by Appadurai (1981, 68-71) and Lingat (1973).

The first case submitted by the *mahārāja* was decided by the agent to the governor entirely in favour of the *thātrāja*. The agent denied the right of the king to 'resume' the Bissamcuttack estate at will. In addition, the *thātrāja*'s arrears of payment were calculated on the basis of 2,200 rupees a year. This judgement was partly reversed in an appeal made before the Madras High Court in 1915. According to the judgement of this court, the estate was still not resumable by the *mahārāja*. Furthermore, though the service nature of the *thātrāja*'s position was recognized, only symbolic importance was attached to it. However, the *mahārāja* got the sum of 15,000 rupees, laid down as tribute in 1877, accepted as valid. Despite this partial victory, Vikram Deo III entered an appeal, which, however, was unsuccessful, since in 1918 the Privy Council confirmed the High Court's decision. In subsequent years the *mahārāja* returned to the courts again with complaints concerning arrears of payment and non-fulfilment of services on the part of Bissamcuttack. After Vikram Deo's death in 1920, his successor, Ramachandra Deo IV, pursued the case further.

In the meantime, however, Narendra Thatraj II died in 1913, leaving no male successor, though he tried to forestall the end of his dynasty by adopting the third son of the *rājā* of Parikud, a little kingdom on the coast.[72] At the time of the *thātrāja*'s demise, however, the adopted child was only two years old. In the coming years, therefore, the disputes were carried on between the *mahārāja* of Jeypore on the one hand and the *dīwān* Krishnayya plus two widows and a daughter of the deceased on the other. The fact that the Bissamcuttack parties quarrelled amongst themselves over many issues and were not able to present a united front considerably weakened their position. In 1926, a settlement was put forward by C.A. Souter, the new agent, under the terms of which the Bissamcuttack estate was to return to the *mahārāja*, who was to forego settlement of the steeply rising arrears on the part of Bissamcuttack and pay 240,000 rupees to the *thātrāja* as compensation. The enforcement of the settlement was postponed until the designated *thātrāja*, Govinda Chandra, reached majority in 1933 and agreed to accept it.[73]

The developments sketched above can be characterized as 'from procession to litigation'. The negotiation of conflicts was transferred out of the domains of ritual and war and into the domain of colonial law. In this sense, the excessive litigation of the Jeypore kings, not only against Bissamcuttack, was not only a continuance of war by other means but

[72] This controversial adoption is much debated in KDR 2058, 2060 and 2061.

[73] See KDR 2058; 2060; 2061 as well as Bell (1945, 161).

also a continuance of ritual: a kind of ritual litigation, adjusted to changed historical circumstances through which the former processions and rites of submission and humiliation were transformed and replaced.[74]

One letter to the *mahārāja* of Jeypore of 1909, which contains the note, 'Lawyers will not come to the Hill Tracts due to its malarious

[74] Price (1979, 212 and 230) characterizes the many cases of ruinous litigation by *zamīndār*s throughout the Madras Presidency of the time as follows:

> In the developing political systems of imperial rural south India, the Anglo-Indian court system provided new weapons and arenas for local conflict and shows of influence and strength. A local leader demonstrated the capacity to mobilise and organise loans, lawyers, witnesses, legal and procedural expertise, government officials and a variety of faction followers and dependants, providing a variety of services. Litigation, often characterised as the main activity of zamindars and their managers, offered the opportunity for enemies to be vanquished with the marshalling of new kinds of forces …
>
> All of the activities of zamindari litigation demanded cash, in large, accumulating amounts. There were costs for stamp paper fees, for documents, translation fees, copying charges, support of witnesses during court attendance, processing charges, petitions, other fees of petitioning … Even for district level pleadings, major lawyers from Madras would be hired and would travel to the district town for consultation before the court appearances and during court proceedings.

Cohn (1959, 568-9) describes a comparable situation in the Bengal Presidency:

> Almost from the establishment of British courts in India, it was apparent to the British that there were serious faults in these courts. It took years for disputes to be resolved, and there were too many appeals from lower courts. Use of forged documents and perjury in the courts became endemic. It was evident that the courts did not settle disputes but were used either as a form of gambling on the part of legal speculators who were landlords or merchants and who turned to the courts to wrest property from the 'rightful' owners or as a threat in a dispute. There is apparently no quicker way of driving an opponent into bankruptcy than to embroil him in a law suit … It is likely that most of the cases that went into courts were fabrications to cover the real disputes.

The impact of the colonial judicial system on traditional politics in India is also dealt with by Breckenridge (1976), Cohn (1965), Dirks (1986), Frykenberg (1963, 129-30), Fuller (1988), McLane (1993, 112-21) and Washbrook (1981).

climate',[75] indicates why the unending court cases were of necessity accompanied by a movement of the protagonists from the hills down to the coast. The usual place where the king and his local chief now encountered each other was no longer the residence of the king or, in case of military conflicts, the Bissamcuttack jungle. The legal experts and colonial courts were located in the administrative centres of the agent and the governor, and the courts—from the court of the special assistant agent in Parvatipur via the court of the agent in Visakhapatnam to the High Court in Madras—moved further away from the hills the higher they got. Besides the litigation that led the jungle kings of south Orissa to the coast, there were also at this time a number of economic, political, cultural and social reasons. Without wishing to go into these in more detail here, it can be stated that during this period, the *mahārāja* of Jeypore and other little kings of south Orissa felt increasingly obliged to move closer to the centres of colonial power by coming to the coast themselves or at least maintaining close family members or other representatives there. Even today, the successors of many little kings of south Orissa, including the family of the former kings of Jeypore, live in occasionally quite magnificent dependencies built at the start of the twentieth century in Visakhapatnam or Madras.

The transition from procession to legal hearing as the main arena for the negotiations and rituals of submission, and the simultaneous movement of litigants out of the remote hills of the tribal hinterland, was also accompanied by the transformation of the former jungle kings into judicially knowledgeable tacticians and politicians of the modern type. For example, among the documents in the Orissa State Archives, I found a letter of December 1910 in which R. Cambray and Co., booksellers of London, replied to the *mahārāja* of Jeypore's wish 'to acquire a complete set of Indian case laws and other important standard legal books'.[76] Certainly, this is only an anecdote, though it throws a characteristic light on the changes taking place in the interests and personalities of that period. The last *thātrāja* of Bissamcuttack, Govindra Chandra, personified these changes even more clearly. After accepting the settlement in 1933, the entire *thatrāju* family left the hills and settled down on the south Orissan coast. Thereafter, Govindra Chandra applied himself energetically to the wider politics of Orissa, spending the rest of his short life (he died in 1939 at the age of 28, leaving behind no heirs) actively

[75] See KDR 1774.

[76] See KDR 1887.

assisting in the formation of the new province of Orissa. He was, amongst other things, an elected member of the Orissa Legislative Assembly.[77]

I would now like to examine the judicial aspect of the conflict between Jeypore and Bissamcuttack by looking more closely at the position(s) of the British judges. To begin with, let us recall the insight, achieved especially by Dirks, that the granting of tax-free or tax-reduced land was an important and integral element of the gift-centred politics of Hindu sovereigns in India from the middle ages to the modern period. From Mughal times, these estates, whose size could vary from a few parcels of agricultural land to several hundred villages, were usually known by the Arabic term *inām*. Among the beneficiaries were such different corporations and persons as gods, temples, monasteries, priests, royal relatives, outstanding soldiers, palanquin-bearers, palace staff, village scribes and other local functionaries who performed various ritual, military, administrative or policing services.[78] The king of Jeypore and the other little kings of south Orissa were no exception in respect of such gifts of land, as the percentage of villages given away as *inām*s often reached 20 percent or more of the total number of villages.[79]

In Jeypore, there were three main types of *inām*: (a) *dāna*s (donations) to religious institutions or functionaries; (b) *mukhāsā*s to relatives of the

[77] See Bell (1945, 161).

[78] The central political function of the granting of *inām*s (which remained largely misunderstood by the British, due to their interpretation of the phenomenon purely in terms of economics and tax law and which, exactly because of this lack of understanding, was also the object of endless litigation) is described by Dirks (1987, 126-7) as follows:

> The inam ... was a particular privilege, and entitlement to a special status, a royal relationship. The rights and privileges of inamdars included rights to titles, offices and honors; rights to command groups of people; as well as the right to offer particular services to an overlord in a hierarchical political and social system. In other words, the inam, as both gift and entitlement, was a basic ingredient of the social and political relations of the little kingdom, in which it became one of the principal means for the creation and maintenance of the local structure of privilege.

Further details on the question of *inām*s under colonial law can be found in Baker (1976), Dirks (1979, 177-9; 1986; 1987, 117-38 and 324-58), Metcalf (1979).

[79] See Ch. II, sect. 4, above. There were, in Jeypore kingdom, 272 'major' *inām*s, consisting of a whole village or several villages and their lands, and 224 'minor' *inām*s at the start of the twentieth century.

king or other individuals of rank and merit (comparable to the *jāgīr*s of other regions in India); and (c) service *inām*s of lesser importance ('ordinary service grants'). The estate of the Bissamcuttack *thātrāja*s fell under the category of *mukhāsā inām* and, like the less prestigious ordinary service grant, was tied to the performance of specific services. In contrast to the holders of ordinary service grants, however, the Bissamcuttack *thātrāja*s and other *mukhāsādār*s of south Orissa were, as an administrative official in the middle of the nineteenth century noted, 'men of high position and influence ... whose service tenure is of an honorary and almost nominal nature'.[80] The taxes of the *ināmdār*s were called *kaṭṭubaḍi* or *jamābandī*; English jurisdiction saw these as 'quit rents' in contrast to the normal taxes on land ('land revenues'). Possession of an *inām* estate was normally heritable only by the oldest male successor in the oldest male line of the original beneficiary. If there were no descendants in this category, the donation automatically returned to the king.[81]

In the course of the 'permanent settlement' agreements of 1803 with the most important *zamīndār*s or landowners, account was also taken of the numerous *inām* properties in the Madras Presidency.[82] For in section 12, Regulation XXV of the Madras Permanent Settlement Regulation of 1802, the 'reversionary right' with respect to the *inām*s was removed from the *zamīndār*s and given to the British. As a result, individual *zamīndār*s no longer had the right to resume previously alienated *inām*s for failure to perform services, lack of a successor or other reasons, nor the right to raise the quit rents of the alienated estates. Moreover, following the permanent settlement the *zamīndār*s were prohibited from making any further donations of land and thus from establishing new *inām*s. Where this did happen anyway (as in most cases), the loss of income was borne entirely by the donator, since the decrease in receipts could not be deducted from the 'permanent' tribute (*peśkaś*) to be paid to the British. In the 'ancient *zamīndārī*s' of the 'Northern Sircars' of the Madras Presidency, which included the districts of Visakhapatnam (including Jeypore) and Ganjam, the *peśkaś* usually consisted of two-

[80] See Gopalaiya (1862, 149).

[81] Information on these points can be found, amongst other places, in *Abolition of Estates* (1958), Behuria (ed. 1965, 61-5), Bell (1945, 140-1), Carmichael (1869, 224-30), Francis (1907, 169-71, 273), B.C. Padhi (1985, 38-78), Senapati (1966, 283-4) and Vikram Deo Varma (1948a, 21-2).

[82] See *Deed* (1803).

thirds of the total income ('assets') of a king, minus the most important taxes and tolls, which subsequently went to the colonial administration.[83]

As far as Jeypore was concerned, the 'permanent settlement' of 1803 and its earlier version of 1795,[84] with their relatively low tribute agreements, were 'political settlements'. The taxes to be paid by the king to the British, first of 25,000, then of 16,000 rupees, were based merely on broad assessments of the size of the kingdom's estates (which were only measured cadastrally in 1938-1964). And these assessments were relatively favourable because of the assistance rendered to the British by Ramachandra Deo II during the 1794 'rebellion' of the king of Vizianagaram.[85]

However, the legal position of the *ināms* within the kingdom remained largely ambiguous and ultimately unresolved in both documents. Certainly, Hobart's *Cowle* of 1795 and the agreement of 1803 both guaranteed the king of Jeypore the right to receive the tributes of the *ināmdārs*, for the tribute owed by Jeypore to the British was officially fixed by including the quit-rent payments of the *ināms* within the 'assets' of the king. In both agreements, however, Ramachandra Deo and his successors were deprived of their reversionary right. Thus, for example, in the *Cowle* document we read: 'You will continue all Inams ... to the fixed Mamool [custom].' And clause 4 of the *Deed of Permanent Property* of 1803 decrees: 'This permanent assessment of the land tax on your zamindari is exclusive of ... all other alienated lands paying a small quit rent (which quit rent unchangeable by you, is included in the assets of your zamindari).' Thus, according to the agreement of 1803, the right to *ināms* was transferred to the British, though the *ināmdārs*' payments continued to go to the king, who at least theoretically passed them on as part of the tribute owed to the British. However, the agreement does not specify if the services were henceforth to be owed to the king or the British. The ambiguity of Bissamcuttack's position was increased by the

83 Information on the regulation of the *inām* affairs in the two northern districts of the Madras Presidency can be found in Behuria (ed. 1964, ch. X; ed. 1965, ch. II), Bhaduri (1976), Maclean (1982) and *Selections* (1948, 138-49).

84 See *Cowle* (1795).

85 In the introduction to the *Cowle* document is stated, 'In consideration of, and as a reward for, the steady attachment you have manifested to the Company's Government and your recent prompt obedience to their orders ... and offering your assistance in quelling those disturbances which have been excited by evil-minded persons throughout the Vizianagaram Zamindari ...' (Cowley 1795, 223).

fact that it was named in the appendix to the *Deed* as one of 31 equal administrative units (*parganah*) belonging to Jeypore.

On the British side it was hoped that the agreement of 1803, which made the *ināms* de jure subject to the British but left them de facto in a relationship of dependence with respect to the king, would win them some time. A clearer regulation regarding the *ināms* in the jungle kingdom which, around 1800, acted largely independently as far as internal political and administrative affairs were concerned, was to be postponed to a time in the not too distant future. In Jeypore we, thus, find a situation encountered in many parts of the Presidency at that time, described fittingly by Frykenberg (1977) as a 'silent settlement'. Yet, as developments in the next century were to show, the hope of an early settlement of *inām* conditions in Jeypore proved false.

In 1819 Thackeray, a member of the Board of Revenue, described Jeypore as 'a wild tract of hill and jungle, inhabited by uncivilized and indeed unconquered barbarians: their climate and their poverty have secured them from conquest. No great native Government ever seems to have thought this tract worth conquering. It has been left as a waste corner of the earth to wild beasts and Conds. Nobody seems even to know the boundary. This tract has never been explored: there is a blank left here in the maps' (cited after Francis 1907, 171). In 1858 an *inām* commission was set up for the whole of the Madras Presidency since, due to the continuing land donations of the *zamīndārs*, the latter had become increasingly indebted and in many places the situation was threatening to get out of control. The commission examined the legal validity of all *ināms*, allowing rights of possession to be retained by *ināmdārs* who could show fifty years of unbroken tax payments, even where there was no deed of gift (*sanad*). As a consequence the commission allowed those properties whose legitimacy had been recognized but whose services were no longer seen as appropriate to the times, to be converted into private properties (particularly, properties linked to military and police duties of the 'ordinary service' and *mukhāsā* types).[86] Henceforth, these *ināmdārs* had to pay a quit rent laid down in accordance with the size and type of *inām*, or else they acquired their properties through a one-off payment. Ultimately, with their 'settlements' and 'enfranchisements' the British were striving to demilitarize the region, which seemed unavoidable to

[86] 'Charitable *ināms*', that is, *ināms* tied mainly to ritual services whose communal use was recognized, were usually left untouched. This was to cause both judicial and administrative problems, as Appadurai (1981), Presler (1987) and Sontheimer (1964) show.

them following the 'rebellion' of 1857. They also wanted to turn kings and 'feudal' lords into landowners who would think in terms of agricultural economics in the style of the English gentry. A complex institution like the *inām* property, which united social, political, ritual and economic aspects into an integral whole within itself, was thus ripped out of its social context and seen merely from the economic and politico-jural points of view.

In 1862 the *inām* commission visited the districts of Visakhapatnam and Ganjam. Here, however, the final regulation of the *inām*s within the 'ancient *zamīndārī*s' encountered some typical difficulties, as the following extracts from the reports of the *inām* commissioner, G.N. Taylor, make clear.[87] 'There is, however', wrote Taylor, 'one question in regard to which the decision and orders of the Government are necessary, viz., the treatment of the jagir or mukhasa tenures in the ancient zamindaris of this district. Discussions have arisen from time to time as to whether the reversion of these tenures belongs to the Government or to the zamindars, but the final settlement of the question is still in abeyance. The subject is one of considerable importance.' Further, the commissioner makes it clear that the doubts concerning the legal position of the *inām*s within these *zamīndārī*s were due to the fact that the calculations of the different government commissions which preceded the permanent settlement and on which the tribute had been based, had not been carried out in a unitary manner. In many calculations, the *zamīndār*s' incomes were calculated by adding the full amount of the income of the *inām*s they had alienated to their assets, although actually the *zamīndār*s only realized a limited amount from these estates (namely, the *kaṭṭubaḍi* or quit-rent payments made by the *inām*s). In other calculations, the assets of these kings or *zamīndār*s were based only on the quit rents they realized from the *inām*s.

The basis adopted for calculation of tributes in 1800 seemed to be unclear to Taylor in 1862. However, in his explanations he repeatedly assumed that the total income of the *inām*s which had been alienated through donation (and not only their *kaṭṭubaḍi*s or quit rents) had been included in the assets of the king and thus also in the customary two-thirds of this sum that counted as tribute. Moreover, the fact that many *zamīndār*s had listed the total income of their *mukhāsā inām*s under their assets in the information they themselves had given to the British around the turn of the century, while in the case of *dāna*s or religious foundations only the *kaṭṭubaḍi*s had been mentioned, was interpreted by Taylor to mean that the kings had continued to regard the *mukhāsā* estates as land

[87] See Taylor (1862, 138-43).

subject to their own law, even following the act of donation. According to Taylor in 1862, however, so far the Board of Revenue had assumed that tribute calculations under the permanent settlement had been made by including the quit-rent payments of the *mukhāsā inām*s only. But since the income that the *ināmdār*s realized from their properties had probably been included in the *zamīndār*s' assets according to Taylor the reversionary right and other rights to the alienated properties also belonged to the *zamīndār*s. The basis of the calculation of the size of the tribute of different kings or *zamīndār*s was, thus, less a question of a theoretical or financial than of a politico-legal nature, and was decisive for the assessment of the status of the *inām*s within the *zamīndārī*s that had been given a permanent settlement.

As a further argument in favour of the view that *inām*s should continue to be subjected to the overlordship of the *zamīndār*s, Taylor referred to the fact that only a quarter of the *inām*s of Ganjam District listed during the permanent settlement had reappeared in a list of *inām*s of 1852, the rest supposedly having gone back to the different *zamīndār*s in the intervening half century. With respect to the question of the *inām*s, therefore, Taylor saw some kind of customary right at work in the *zamīndārī*s of Ganjam and he stressed that 'any interference with these villages after a permissive enjoyment for lengthened periods would occasion much dissatisfaction, and the Government sacrifice little in foregoing their doubtful reversionary interest.' As far as Jeypore was concerned, the situation in this jungle kingdom was even less clear than the already hazy situation in Ganjam: 'For the settlement of the inams in the zamindari of Jeypore, the Government will observe that there are no accounts whatever and no reliable information upon which the enquiry could be conducted. I propose, therefore, at any rate for the present, to avoid all interference with this estate.'[88]

About thirty years later, during H.D. Taylor's administration of Jeypore from 1889 to 1895 the first concrete attempt was made by the British to examine the legitimacy of all the *inām*s of the kingdom and establish the extent of the lands alienated. However, even after Taylor's efforts, the situation remained unclear and it was decided to wait until the

[88] The deputy collector of Visakhapatnam district suggests something similar when he writes about Jeypore: 'Hitherto there has been no interference whatever with the inams in this immense tract of country, which is remote from Government observation and control, and for the present at least, it appears to the Commissioner undesirable to disturb the existing state of matters by an enquiry into inam titles' (Gopalaiya 1861, 151).

designated king had come to the throne before taking concrete steps to tackle the *inām* affairs. The next move, in 1907, was to charge a government official to undertake further inquiries into the *inām*s of Jeypore. Again, the result remained unsatisfactory because the king refused to cooperate. Some years later another government commission was set up, which suspended its work in 1919 without having transferred a single *inām* estate to private ownership or dissolved it, as had happened in great parts of the Madras Presidency in the meantime.

7. Closing remarks

In comparison with west European kingdoms of the middle ages, the relationship between the king of Jeypore and the *thātrāja* of Bissamcuttack might be well described as 'feudal' without, however, intending to propagate the model of the feudal state for Jeypore. It recalls what was one of the most important feudal relationships in Europe, that of the military vassal linked to his lord through a personal oath of loyalty, whose services were rewarded in the form of a fief.[89] Moreover, the disputes described in this chapter between *mahārāja* and *thātrāja* find a correspondence, especially with western Europe around 1100, in what can be regarded as a structural conflict between the value of personal loyalty and the ability of the lord to resume fiefs on the one hand, and the vassals' attempt to make their properties heritable on the other.[90]

All in all, however, comparing Indian 'feudal relationships' with those in the Europe of the middle ages has only limited use because of the many differences that exist. Not least, a more thorough comparison would require a more accurate working out of the differences in respect of the different sorts of religious prototypes or models of loyalty and submission with which the Christian worship of God and the Hindu *pūjā* respectively endowed political relationships. Ultimately, such a comparison only makes sense when the specific nature and dynamics of Indian 'feudal relationships' are described and analysed in detail with reference to concrete examples; many studies up to now have remained rather abstract in focusing on the structure and principles of organisation. In my discussion of a specific situation in a jungle kingdom in the hinterland of south Orissa during the colonial period, it has not always been easy to illuminate the hazy political and legal situation which appeared unclear even to the responsible officials of the time who were on the spot. Nonetheless,

[89] See, for example, Bloch (1961, Chs XI and XII).

[90] See, for example, Bloch (1961, Chs XIV, XVI, XVII).

the foregoing description allows me to arrive at some conclusions concerning the political and legal aspects of the conflict between Jeypore and Bissamcuttack, and concerning the changes that took place during this conflict under colonial hegemony.

Let us return to the 'History' (resuming the thread in 1905),[91] in which Bissamcuttack emphasizes the fact that 'those [alienations] made *for a long time prior to the Permanent Settlement and held on valid title paying a small rent or Jamabandi to the Zemindar for a long series of years without variation*, were recognised by Government, and at the Permanent Settlement only the rents, if any, actually derived therefrom by the zemindars were included in the assets of the Zemindary for fixing the peishcush' (emphasis in original). Further, reference is specifically made to clause 4 of the Permanent Settlement of 1803, in which the Jeypore king recognizes the status of the *ināms*' quit rents as 'quite unchangeable' and that 'the Zemindar of Jeypore has no right whatsoever to interfere with Bissamcuttack ... in any respect except receiving the quit-rent of Rs. 2,200.' Bissamcuttack, and the neighbouring estate of Gunupur, whose fate was also thrown into the scales, are described as 'absolute and permanent alienations paying a small and non-changeable quit-rent'. The fact that these estates were not treated as autonomous *zamīndārīs* at the time of the permanent settlement was explained as follows a hundred years later:

> Bissemkatak and Gunupur were equally entitled to be separately settled and registered at the time alike with the other Zemindaries ... yet the peaceful and non-contentious disposition of the then Zemindars on the one hand, and the want of sufficient information, and of adequate means to enforce their power on the part of the Government officials on the other, conspired to leave Bissemkatak and Gunupur unsettled and unregistered.

In another document, the jungle nature of the estate is cited as a reason for its non-recognition as a *zamīndārī* in 1803:

> ... unfortunately owing to my Zamindari being situated at the extreme north of the Presidency bordering on the central provinces and possessing a climate destructive to mankind and containing huge mountains and thick forests inaccessible to outsiders, the Government Officers could not by any means communicate with my

[91] The following quotations come from KDR 2168, para 12 and 14. The arguments of the 'History' are repeated in their essentials in the Memorial (KDR 2485, para 14-21).

> ancestor … and the result is that my Zamindari has not received a fair treatment up to date. (KDR 2491, para 6)

In court minutes from 1906, the *thātrāja*, as 'defendant', refers point by point to the judicial statements contained in the complaint of the king of Jeypore—this time without recourse to history:

> The defendant does not admit that the Zemindar of Bissemkatak was ever bound to render any kind of service or help to the Jeypore Zemindar and the defendent says that in any event the service, if any, that the Zemindar of Bissemkatak was bound to render was only military service of a public nature. […] The allegation that Sri Narendra Thatraj accepted a cowl for the estate of Bissemkatak on Mokhasa tenure [1854] … is entirely false. […] The defendant denies … that the Bissemkatak Zemindar was paying 'Kattubandi' or rendering service to the Jeypore Zemindar though he might as a matter of courtesy have sometimes attended the Dasara durbar with paiks. […] The said services were of a public character and the Jeypore Zemindar ceased to have any right to them upon the assumption of authority by the British Government. (KDR 1805)

From these extracts, it is clear that the Bissamcuttack *thātrāja* followed two different strategies in his arguments: On the one hand he recognized that Bissamcuttack was an *inām* estate of the *mukhāsā* type and stressed that in the calculations made for the permanent settlement of Jeypore, Bissamcuttack's quit-rent or *kaṭṭubaḍi* payments only were included in the assets of the kingdom, which indirectly confirmed the *inām* status of the Bissamcuttack estate. However, through the fact that the *inām* status of Bissamcuttack was established and recognized in the *Deed* of 1803, the 'reversionary right' and claim to services were transferred to the new sovereign, the British. The services to be performed in connection with the estate were anyway not owed to the king personally but were 'public services' of a purely military type. The sporadic appearances at the *dasarā* festival were described as mere displays of politeness. On the other hand, the Bissamcuttack *thātrāja* repeatedly appeared before the court in the guise, and with the title, of a ruling *zamīndār*, not as a *mukhāsādār* paying a *kaṭṭubaḍi* and owing services. The failure, on various grounds, of the British to recognize the estate as a *zamīndārī* should, in his opinion, be made good by the court.

As already mentioned, in 1906 the agent's court decided wholly in favour of the *thātrāja*. The judge found that only the donation recorded on the copper plate in 1689 was valid and that the later agreements of 1854, 1864 and 1877 between king and *thātrāja* were void. In this copper plate grant of 1689, Bissamcuttack is identified as a permanent donation made by the king to the *thātrāja* without any requirement of service, a donation which did not give the king any right either to resume the estate or to raise the tax of 2,200 rupees laid down at that time. The High Court in Madras modified this judgement in part in 1915: doubt was cast on the authenticity of the copper plate produced by Bissamcuttack, and the agreement of 1877 counted as binding. What weighed heavily here was the fact that the agreement of 1877 had been a compromise willingly entered into by both sides and that the young *thātrāja* had been seeking to conclude an out-of-court settlement. The taxes were raised to 15,000 rupees a year, but the permanent hereditary character of the estate remained unchanged and its service aspect was granted little weight.[92]

The king's reaction to the High Court judgement is clear from a note of 19.2.1915 to the then agent in Visakhapatnam, Harris:

> Bissamcuttack appeal judgement delivered by the High Court yesterday. The findings are that the revenue of Bissamcuttack estate was included in the Jeypore assets at the time of the permanent settlement. Copper patta of 1689 relied on by Bissamcuttack found not genuine. Patta of 1877 granted by my father to late Ramachandra Thatraj was binding and I am entitled to get a fixed Kattubadi of Rs. 15,000 a year, but findings on resumption and service against me. (KDR 1976)

Vikram Deo III justified his further appeal as follows:

> However, I am sorry to say that, if I am satisfied with what the High Court has given me, giving up all my rights for [illegible] service, I shall be a terrible loser not only in this but also in all the service mokhasas of similar standing and status in my zamindary. Further the dussera service for which most of these are held and which the High Court did not consider as 'substantial' is considered, I am told, by the Privy Council as otherwise. (KDR 1962)

To the king of Jeypore, therefore, the judgement of 1915 was only partially acceptable. His actual goal was to have the status that the estate had been given by the agreements of 1854 and 1864 accepted as legally binding. According to these agreements the estate was not hereditary but merely granted for life to those appointed by him. In addition, in these agreements each appointed holder of the estate owed service to the king personally, especially as regards appearing at the *dasarā* festival. Further,

[92] The verdicts of the different courts are not available to me. However, certain conclusions can be drawn from KDR 1777 in which, in 1914, a lawyer summed up the previous legal positions and the most important arguments from verdicts in other Indian courts, which then entered into the judgement of the High Court.

according to the Jeypore king, if income from the estate increased, the size of the *mukhāsādār*'s quit rents should also increase, a right which had already been put into practice by the increase in tribute agreed in 1854, 1864 and 1877 from the initial 2,200 rupees to 2,500, then 5,000 and finally 15,000 rupees. If services were neglected or services were no longer being needed, the agreements gave the king the right to resume the estate or increase the tribute further.

Ultimately, then, everything revolved around the question of how the parties to the case and the institutions passing judgement regarded the service aspect of the Bissamcuttack estate, and here the *thātrāja*'s obligation to appear at the *dasarā* festival constituted the core of the argument.

The jural significance of this question can be understood more clearly by listing the four possibilities or possible fates with which Bissamcuttack saw itself confronted in the nineteenth century:

1: The British, who had the reversionary right over the estate, would classify it as an *inām* of the *mukhāsā* category and then transfer it permanently into private ownership. This outcome, which would have fulfilled the intention behind the permanent settlement and corresponded to the situation in the greater part of the Madras Presidency and which might have been put into force around 1860 through the work of the *inām* commission, was prevented by the lack of actual control that the British government exercised over the jungle kingdom at that time. Its reversionary right existed only de jure, not de facto.

2: As a *mukhāsā* estate subject to the king, Bissamcuttack would return to the king, as other *inām*s of the kingdom had done (for example, the estate of the *thātrāja* of Malkangiri in 1872). In the middle of the nineteenth century, this was prevented by Bissamcuttack's military might when Vikram Deo II tried to expel three *thātrāja*s in succession by force. After 1877, under the colonial power, the judicial and political strength of the *thātrāja*s acquired greater significance than their military potential.

3: As a *mukhāsā* estate subject de facto to the king, Bissamcuttack would continue to be held on the basis of a quit rent and a military-ceremonial service obligation. This would maintain the status quo, though with the Damocles sword of resumption by the king permanently hanging over the estate, as, for example, on the occasion of the 'Queen Victoria conflict' in 1877.

4: Bissamcuttack would be recognized by the British as an autonomous and independent *zamīndāri* legally equivalent to the kingdom of Jeypore, and as such bound to be permanently settled. Under different historical circumstances, this outcome might have been realized at the time of the permanent settlement, for in Ganjam and central Orissa at this time far smaller estates had been recognized by the British as *zamīndārīs*, and even as princely states. This possibility could still have been realized through the courts at the beginning of the twentieth century.[93]

Options 1 and 4 were clearly the ones to be pursued as far as Bissamcuttack was concerned. However, in order to convert either of them into politico-legal reality, it was especially important for Bissamcuttack to contest the obligation to be present at *dasarā*, since only then could 2 and 3 be averted, and 1 come true if the British were to classify the estate as a *mukhāsā inām* and not as a *zamīndārī*. A service obligation of a military but not a ceremonial nature was conceded and declared to be a 'public service', subject to the highest authority of that time, i.e. the British and not the Jeypore king.[94] However, in order to acquire the validity and prestige of an autonomous *zamīndārī*, a denial of both the ceremonial obligation to be present at *dasarā* and the military-service nature of the estate were required. But to achieve the *zamīndārī* status and title, another British requirement had to be taken into account, given the value they placed on tradition and customary law: the estate had to be propagated as being 'ancient and prestigious'.[95]

Two of Bissamcuttack's stratagems were designed to support a claim to a time-honoured status of this sort. One was to invoke repeatedly and emphatically the agreement of 1689. Doing so did not mean claiming a Rajput origin, but it did mean proclaiming the acquisition of legitimacy at a point long in the past and led, ultimately, to the first hearing being decided in favour of the *thātrāja*. Important, too, were the various (re-) constructions of the history of the estate that had been presented to the

[93] In this context, a donation of eighteen villages made by Narendra Thatraj to his *diwān* Krishnayya in May 1904 was not simply a reward for the decades of service performed by him. In making this donation, the *thātrāja* was acting like an autonomous *rājā*. The right of the *thātrāja* to make this grant was rejected both by the Jeypore king, who could permit no other person in his kingdom to make royal grants of estates, and the British, who in the Permanent Settlement of 1803 had already prohibited all *zamīndār*s from making further grants of land (though without much success). See KDR 1995 and 2768.

[94] As we have seen, already in 1877 the British agent Goodrich regarded the military services linked to the Bissamcuttack estate as 'government service' and 'service due to the state' (KDR 2212).

[95] At this point, we might recall the 'British Orientalists' infatuation with the ancient' (Rocher 1993, 229) and the 'promotion of the distant past as normative' (ibid., 242) on the part of the colonial government (already mentioned in Chapter III). On this, see also Fox (1971, 59).

court. In the course of the 'historiographical' discourse employed by all three parties, but especially by Bissamcuttack, a new dimension of time and legitimacy gained in significance. Instead of the cyclical time frame within which the displays of homage at the *dasarā* festival had traditionally occurred, a linear and historically more penetrating perception of time and of the validity of claims to legitimacy came to the fore in the court proceedings.

The value attached to the normative power of the old and the traditional that guided British 'historiographical' paradigms replaced the politico-ritual symbolism of the *dasarā* festival, which had so far provided the arena for the negotiation and settlement of the conflicting claims of different actors within the jungle kingdom. Hand in hand with the radical technical and industrial changes which were taking place in the region at that time, this 'politics of remembering' led to a gradual replacement of 'natural' by 'historical categories of time'.[96] Symbolically speaking, the energy of the steam locomotive pushing along its straight tracks replaced the dignity and martial power of the elephants that headed the *dasarā* procession.

The cultural logic and dynamics which traditionally informed the *dasarā* festival in Jeypore—outside the context of late-colonial political manoeuvring and judicial practices—will emerge more clearly when, in the two remaining chapters, the ritual politics of the jungle kings becomes the main focus of discussion.

[96] Here I am referring to concepts put forward by Koselleck (1979, 133-4).

CHAPTER V

TUTELARY DEITIES: THE ROYAL PATRONAGE OF TRIBAL GODDESSES

1. Introduction

The focus of this chapter is the patronage of cults of goddesses who were originally tribal and of merely local significance by the little kings of Orissa.[1] Here my discussion will be guided by the analytical distinction between types of ritual belief and practice that are designated 'tribal' and 'Hindu', respectively. Like the distinction between 'tribe' and 'caste', the identification of, and opposition between, two forms of religion linked with these social entities are not without problem. The danger is that an analytical distinction which was created for a limited purpose only will be mistaken for the thing itself, that is, Whitehead's 'fallacy of misplaced concreteness'. In addition, such concepts, being subject to reification and essentialization, may be interpreted wrongly as monolithic blocks stiffly opposing one another, while the many-sided and existent transitions and permeabilities may be excluded from the field of vision.

For the purposes of the discussion that follows, therefore, it must be emphasized, with Bailey (1961), that the distinctions made here between tribe and caste, tribal and Hindu religion, and Great and Little Traditions are not to be understood categorically. In the case of these and other oppositions, we are dealing rather with 'dimensional' distinctions made for analytical purposes, in which each opposed concept marks the extreme pole of an imaginary scale. Different social groups and 'their' forms of religion, thus, indicate varying tendencies or inclinations (of different strength) with respect to this or that pole. And in my usage, concepts like

[1] This chapter is a revised version of two articles published in 1993 (Schnepel 1993 and b). My discussion has profited especially from studies that deal with similar problems in central Orissa, namely those of Eschmann (1978a), Kulke (1976; 1978a; 1979b; 1980 and 1984c) and Rösel (1994). As regards south Orissa, I collected the data presented here mainly during a number of surveys conducted personally. Further information on the royal patronage of tribal goddesses in south Orissa can be found in Behera (1987, Ch. 8) and Rath (1987, Chs. 9 and 11). In addition, Bell (1945), Carmichael (1869), Francis (1907), Maltby (1918), Mohapatra (1986), Senapati (1966) and Singh Deo (1939) provide scattered references, without going into the subject in depth.

Sanskritization, Rajputization, Hinduization, Brahmanization, tribalization, universalization, tribal absorption, Indianization or parochialization, which have guided the discussion of this problem, characterize movements and changes between these two poles.[2] In addition, it must be made clear at the outset that these concepts merely describe sociological and historical ideal types in Weber's sense. Ideal types are not average types but represent conscious distortions and exaggerations of the most characteristic particularities of the phenomenon in question: ideal types exaggerate, but (hopefully) in the right direction.

In this sense of an ideal-typical opposition, the difference between a tribal and a Hindu form of religion may be reduced to certain characteristics which basically refer to the ways in which deities are considered to be present among humans and in which they are worshipped.[3] In popular Hinduism, deities are represented by anthropomorphic figures (*mūrti*s) accommodated in temples. Ideally, the worship of these deities, who possess regional and even pan-Indian recognition, consists of sixteen services or gifts (*upacāra*s) offered during the religious services (*pūjā*s) held up to five times daily by Brahmans priests. A major characteristic of Hindu religiosity and cults consists in the rite of viewing these images (*darśana*) and worshipping them in the *pūjā*. In contrast, in tribal cults gods and goddesses are worshipped in the form of non-iconic symbols placed out in the open. When compared to Hindu orthopraxis, services for tribal deities take place less frequently and regularly and correspond more to the actual needs of the believers than to a fixed routine; they also entail blood sacrifice as the highest gift. At its most intensive, however, the presence of tribal deities among humans is not experienced in the form of symbols but when they possess priests, devotees or other religious virtuosi. The deities are then thought to be present in living humans, an idea which somewhat surpasses the idea of anthropomorphic effigies as the bearers of deities.

[2] On the problematic of 'caste/tribe', which has occupied research on India for a long time, see Majumdar (1939), Marriot (1955), Munshi (1979), Reddy (1973), Sinha (1957; 1965; 1980; 1981), Srinivas (1952) as well as Urhahn's summary and discussion of the relevant literature (1985). Among the numerous studies that are concerned with the religious aspect of the problem, Fuller (1992, 24-8), Ramanujan (1988) and Sontheimer (1989) provide contributions of a more recent date. Gonda (1963, 1-26) deals with the problem of Sanskritization with direct reference to local goddesses.

[3] The distinction is from Eschmann (1978a, 80-5), though her more complex treatment of the theme has been simplified here.

2. The tribal goddesses of south Orissa

One of the most prominent characteristics of the religious life of south Orissa is the great significance accorded those deities of the 'Little Tradition' who are regarded as mother goddesses or earth goddesses. These deities are characterized as being strongly rooted in their respective territory, often possessing only a local and limited area of influence, which runs out at the border of a village, clan territory or other kind of settlement.[4] Within their own domains, however, they are greatly respected and feared, more than most of the other deities who are also worshipped in their territory. A successful harvest, the fertility and well-being of humans, animals and plants, but also the occurrence of drought, floods, epidemics (especially smallpox) or personal crises are ascribed to the favour or anger of these goddesses. Humans affected by great or unusual suffering turn to these goddesses, often as a last hope, not infrequently giving rise to reports of wonderful changes in their fate. As the embodiments of *śakti*, that is, of a dynamic and vital power associated with life, growth, sexuality, blood, fertility and wealth, these ambivalent goddesses reveal a character that is certainly generative and creative, but also frightening and destructive. Neglecting them can have devastating consequences, while worshipping them promises petitioners continued well-being or the rapid removal of impediments.[5]

[4] In their 'territoriality', as well as in many aspects of their cults, the tribal goddesses of south Orissa recall the *gramādevatā*s and *ṭhākurāṇī*s ('village goddesses' and 'earth queens') to be found all over India. Early studies of the cults of such local goddesses were provided by Crooke (1926; rpt. 1972) and Whitehead (1921; rpt. 1976). Many of the so-called 'village studies' provide insights into the cults of such goddess, as Fuller (1992, Ch. 6) illustrates. Bayly (1989, Ch. 1), Biardeau (1989) and Kinsley (1986, Ch. 13) have made comparative studies of the theme of the 'little' goddesses. Among the detailed ethnographic studies of local goddesses, Biardeau (ed. 1981), Hawley and Wulff (eds. 1986), Hiltebeitel (ed. 1989), Preston (ed. 1982), and the publications of Beck (1981), Brubaker (1979), Erndl (1993), Hardiman (1987), Preston (1980a) and Sax (1991) may be mentioned.

[5] Bayly, who speaks of the 'divinities of blood and power', stresses the ambivalent nature of these goddesses (in south India) as follows: 'These were deities who partook of all the passions and uncontained generative forces which coloured everyday human experience, and could therefore be appealed to in times of specific ills and afflictions. But although many of these power deities were recognized as healers and protectors, they were never wholly beneficent like some of the region's so-called "pure" or "high" gods, and they all had a fierce and malevolent side' (1989, 27). On the conflicting character of the goddesses, see

Some of these goddesses have gone through different degrees of Hinduization, manifested in different ways. At the end of these processes, the images or representations of the goddesses are still based on non-iconic objects such as stones, wooden posts or clay mounds. But these have been made human, with at least either a painted or attached face. The eyes, mouth and a protruding tongue represent the minimum or the essence of such anthropomorphizations. One indication of the original and still continuing attachment of these goddesses to the tribal world lies in the fact that Brahmans are rarely encountered in their temples as priests. However, their places of worship are nonetheless temples in the widest sense of the word since—in contrast to their entirely tribal 'sisters', who are worshipped in the open air, in caves and groves, or by the side of a path — Hinduized tribal goddesses have an abode, even though this may occasionally consist of no more than a corrugated iron roof over their heads. In addition, the priests, who are mostly from low-ranking castes or tribal groups, adapt their cultic services to some extent to the orthodoxy and orthopraxis known from the worship of great Hindu goddesses such as Durga or Kali. Thus, these partly Hinduized tribal goddesses are offered *pūjā* two to three times a day, and the most important yearly festival coincides with the Durga *pūjā*. However, the fact that the originally tribal nature of these goddesses has not been entirely forgotten can be seen, among other things, in the fact that in most cases they are not completely vegetarian, but occasionally demand blood sacrifices. Today, this mostly means goats and chickens, sometimes also pigs and buffaloes, all male. Earlier, human sacrifices were also offered occasionally. The frequency with which blood sacrifices are carried out today (usually by beheading with an axe or a sword), as well as other peculiarities such as the proximity of the killing site to the temple, vary and can be regarded as an indication of different degrees of Hinduization. Thus, at one end of the scale one finds blood sacrifices carried out frequently and directly within the sight of the goddess, while at the other end blood sacrifices are only carried out at major festivals, and then outside the temple complex. Some goddesses demand to see the head and blood of the sacrificed animal (as evidence of the actual killing, I was told), while for others the sight of a foreleg is enough.[6] In the cults of these only partly Hinduized goddesses priests as well as devotees may become possessed in front of the image of

---

also Babb (1975, 217-30), Erndl (1993, 153-8), Fuller (1992, 44-8), Gonda (1963, 42), Kurtz (1992, 20-8), Sax (1991, 23-35) and Tapper (1979).

[6] In the Sanskrit 'ideal' of the *Devī Māhātmya*, the head and some blood of the killed buffalo demon are offered to Durga.

the goddess.[7] Finally, it should be mentioned that on the occasion of great yearly festivals in honour of these goddesses, some devotees, as an expression of their devotion, inflict physical tortures on themselves, either through fire or by piercing the skin.[8]

3. Khambhesvari, Mohuri Kalua, Thakurani and Majhighariani

Let us now examine the cult of certain goddesses from south Orissa. Khambheshvari from Aska, a vibrant trading town in Ganjam, in the fertile valley of the river Rushikulya, belongs to a group of goddesses known as Stambheshvari which means 'goddess of the pillar', alluding to the fact that the images of this goddess consist overwhelmingly of wooden posts. In Aska itself we find an interesting doubling up of the material representation of the goddess: in front of the sacrificial site stands the non-iconic symbol of a wooden post, while in the sanctum opposite is a stone idol. This stone image of Khambheshvari, the focus of the *pūjā*s, consists of a body in the form of a *liṅgam*, roughly 1.20 metres high and with a diameter of about 40 centimetres. Attached to this stone is a round, vermilion-coloured head made out of a sheet of cardboard on to which three golden eyes and a mouth with a protruding tongue have been glued. For the *pūjā*, Khambheshvari is dressed in splendid silk robes and hung with garlands of flowers. I was allowed to photograph the goddess, for which the priest dressed her up especially. However, the head of the temple, who arrived later, was incensed that on this occasion Khambheshvari had not been adorned with a cardboard construction of eight arms (which was kept in the store room of the temple). A further stage in her anthropomorphization would therefore have been possible, though it apparently finds expression only on special occassions.[9]

The priests at the temple of Khambheshvari belong to the low-ranking caste of 'gardeners' (*mālī*s). The *pūjā* is performed twice daily, in the early morning and in the evening, and consists of the offering of lamps, incense, flowers, food and the sounding of a bell hung in front of the entrance. Among the gifts presented are coconuts, bananas, leaves in the

[7] See Plates 1 and 2.

[8] See *Selections* (1854). The British attempted to prohibit these customs. Even today in many places in India the degree of 'burden' borne during a festival or pilgrimage (e.g. by walking barefoot) counts as a measure of adoration and is seen as being especially beneficial in getting one's requests or wishes fulfilled. See also Sax (1991, 13, 54).

[9] See Plate 3.

shape of a trident called *belo patra*, and the red flowers of the *mandāra* tree.[10] Only rarely do animal sacrifices take place in the temple of Khambheshvari, though they are carried out on the occasion of the Durga *pūjā* in autumn and the *caitra parva* (an originally tribal festival based on the symbolism of the hunt) in spring. It should also be mentioned that a small movable figure of brass is carried around the temple or the town in a procession during these festivals and on *saṅkrānti* days. This is Khambheshvari's mobile substitute (*calanti pratimā*), which otherwise stands next to her in the temple.[11]

One legend about Khambheshvari, which Eschmann learned from a priest in the temple at Aska, illustrates the original relationship of the goddess with the jungle region and its inhabitants. It is said that Khambheshvari appeared in a dream to a man living in the forest called Khambhamuni and demanded from him that he worship her as a goddess. The beautiful goddess lived with the old man for a time as if she were his daughter, though this was regarded with suspicion by passers-by. To avoid getting a bad name, Khambhamuni revealed the true nature of the goddess, who immediately disappeared. Subsequently, Khambheshvari played practical jokes on the old man, for example, by buying bangles and having him pay for them. Once she appeared suddenly before him with a baby torn to pieces on her arm. Eventually, the old man lost his patience and slapped her, upon which Khambheshvari made it known that the time of her childish play (*bālya līlā*) was over, that Khambhamuni must die, and that from that day on she was to be worshipped at that very same spot by his son.[12]

[10] The flowers of the *mandarā* or coral tree are considered a suitable substitute for a blood sacrifice. Occasionally, garlands made from these flowers are hung around sacrificial animals before they are killed. In Sanskrit and Oriya literature the motif of a person dreaming of wearing a *mandarā* garland is common, which is an allusion to his or her death. Leaves of the *belo patra* are associated with Shiva on account of their trident-like form, which is also a reference to the frequent association of these goddesses with Shiva as partner. I thank Professor G.N. Dash for these observations. On the theme of red garlands appearing in a dream, see also O'Flaherty (1984, 22-3).

[11] *Saṅkrānti* refers to the first day of each solar month which, in the Hindu calendar, is determined by the period in which the sun remains in a particular zodiac (*rāśi*). See Kane (1958, 211-25).

[12] See Eschmann (1978a, 93). On Khambheshvari/Stambhesvari and her patronage see also Eschmann (1978a, 86-7, 92-4), Kulke (1979a, 22-5) and Rath (1987, 80-9, 105-7).

The temple of another goddess called Mohuri Kalua is situated some twelve kilometres west of Berhampur, near the Kerandi Hills. Directly behind the temple is a steeply rising hill, with a stony path leading up to its summit. After an arduous ascent, one passes through a narrow cleft to a shelter beneath three large rocks which stand together like a house of cards. In this cave is the original goddess in the form of a small, conically shaped heap of earth about fifty centimetres high. A vermilion head of cardboard decorated with golden eyes and a protruding tongue is placed on top of this earthen body and a tiara of peacock feathers fixed above the figure. *Pūjā* is offered to the goddess on the hill twice a week, on Sundays and Tuesdays. However, animal sacrifices are not made here because, according to the priest, it is too difficult to get animals up there. It is said that in order to spare her devotees the tiresome climb, Mohuri Kalua threw a vessel from the hill and at the point at which it landed the main temple now stands.[13]

The temple at the foot of the hill is of a medium size and rectangular in shape.[14] At the back are some houses in which live the priests, who come from the *bhaṇḍārī* or barber caste. To one side is a small temple dedicated to Shiva, who is regarded as the consort of the goddess. At three stalls, run by the priests at the entrance to the temple, tea, cigarettes, soft drinks, betel and other refreshments for pilgrims are sold, as well as coconuts, bananas and flowers as gifts for the goddess. The walls of the entrance hall are decorated with motifs of the goddess Kali, who has chains of human skulls hung around her neck. In the main hall of the temple, at the back, is a room separated off by a balustrade, where Mohuri Kalua is housed. The image of the goddess consists of a conical body, roughly 1.20 metre in height. Only when one looks at the figure from behind can one see that it consists of a mound of earth covered with cloth. I was told that this is an abandoned termite mound now occupied by a snake. The goddess's face is coloured vermilion and marked with large eyes, a striking mouth and a protruding tongue. A wooden structure with eight arms is fastened to her body. Next to, and in front of the goddess, are four smaller mounds of earth, the largest of which has a red head coloured. The other mounds are decorated with flowers, leaves, pieces of

[13] The motif of a vessel, made of brass, clay, copper or gold, thrown below, is common to many places in Orissa where one finds valley and hill temples dedicated to one and the same deity. See also Das (1967, 11).

[14] See Plate 4. Das reports (1978, 156) that this temple was built in 1775 in the reign of the Mohuri *rājā* Hari Hara Narendra Deo, that is, at a politically turbulent period, barely a year before the Mohuri royal dynasty was deposed by the British.

coconut and coconut milk and they also represent sacred objects, though they lack traces of anthropomorphization. To the right of the goddess stands a small bronze figure called *vijayā pratimā* or 'figure of victory', which is used as a movable representation of the goddess in processions.[15]

Pūjā is offered three times a day. When pilgrims step in front of the goddess with their gifts, a priest sitting in front of Mohuri Kalua offers candlelight, incense, flowers, leaves, coconut milk, bananas and other items in a shortened form of the *pūjā* ceremony. While this is going on, the supplicant stands reverently praying in front of the balustrade, or rings one of the many bells that hang from the roof. Some, to show their great devotion, prostrate themselves on the ground, with their faces to the floor and folded hands outstretched towards the goddess, praying and occasionally hitting their foreheads on the floor. I witnessed a woman with a basket full of gifts, being possessed by the goddess and collapsing. Those accompanying her, laid her on the ground, where she remained for a few minutes, shaking slightly. The goddess is offered animal sacrifices twice a week, mainly goats and chickens, which are killed in a rather remote grove outside the temple complex. A foreleg of the goat is offered to the goddess. Twice a week, the snake that lives in the body of the goddess (in the termite mound, that is) is worshipped by the priests behind closed doors and fed with milk. The greatest festival of the year takes place on the *saṅkrānti* day that marks the entrance of the sun into the zodiac called *meṣa* (Aries; in India, roughly April/May). On this festival, besides thousands of pilgrims, the Mohuri *rājā* personally visits the goddess. Many goats are killed and it is said that earlier Mohuri kings offered human sacrifices on this occasion.

Together with Mohuri Kalua, a look should be taken at the goddess Budhi Thakurani, the patron deity of the large trading city of Berhampur, since this goddess is regarded by many of the inhabitants of the area as another manifestation of Mohuri Kalua. Budhi Thakurani is one of the most important goddesses of the coastal region of southern Orissa. Tens of thousands of people take part in her festival, the Thakurani *yātrā*, which takes place every two or three years and lasts for several weeks. The celebration of this festival in spring (in the month of *caitra*) acquires special significance in the eyes of many, if there has been a long period without a good harvest or the country has been plagued by epidemics. The Thakurani *yātrā* offers an occasion for ritual costume, pantomimes and

[15] See Plate 5.

lively, occasionally ecstatic dancing.[16] The celebrations sometimes have the character of a ritual of reversal or a ritual of violence. These excesses are the main reason why the collector gives his approval for the holding of the festival reluctantly.

Budhi Thakurani is represented by a stone roughly forty centimetres high, on to which is placed a red cardboard mask representing a face.[17] During the Thakurani *yātrā*, she is also worshipped in the form of a lotus blossom. Many elements of the daily cult in the Thakurani temple are similar to those found in the temple of Mohuri Kalua. However, in Berhampur sacrifices are frequently made—up to several times a day. The sacrificial site is in the temple complex itself, behind a wall at the foot of a *neem* or margosa tree, which is regarded as sacred. The severed heads of the sacrificial victims, mostly goats and chickens, but in earlier times also occasionally humans, are offered to the goddess. The priests belong to the weaver caste (in Oriya *deśarāj* or *dera*; Telugu *devāṅangama*), usually in India a low, often even derided caste,[18] though in Berhampur they are influential merchants of Telugu descent. The head of a leading family of this caste, called *deśibeherā*, is regarded as the 'father' of the goddess, a fact which also finds ritual expression in the Thakurani *yātrā* and which alludes to the fact that, in the case of Budhi Thakurani, we have less a 'mother' goddess than a 'daughter' goddess.[19]

A further example of a tribal goddess subjected to the process of Hinduization is from the hill area of Koraput District. It will be recalled that under Viswanatha Deo (1521-1571), the fourth ruler of the Suryavamsha dynasty, the royal capital was moved for a time from Nandapur to Rayagada. One of the most important temples in present day Rayagada, which is dedicated to the goddess Majhighariani, dates from the time of Viswanatha, when it probably already possessed central ritual importance for the inhabitants of the area. If one makes one's way from the centre of Rayagada to this temple today, one first comes to a quarter of the town which can be identified as the old fortress area through the

[16] Among the animal forms adopted, the tiger, the vehicle (*vāhana*) of Durga, is the most popular.

[17] See Plate 6.

[18] See Jordan-Horstmann (1972); Nayak and Schnepel (forthcoming).

[19] A thorough study of the cult of Budhi Thakurani and her *yātrā* is still to be made. Some references can be found in Das (1978, 158-63) and Rath (1987, 109-10). I am grateful to Dr G.P. Chowdhury of Berhampur University for his support during my visits to the temple of the Thakurani.

remains of a wall. A few hundred metres before the temple is a large banyan tree with many small white stones lying under it. A split coconut, some scattered flowers, quite a number of *belo patra* leaves, and red and white spots painted on the large monolithic block of stone in front of the tree indicate that this is a sacred site. According to local information the stones lying scattered beneath the tree were gifts made to the goddess by *ādivāsis* who had come to the town.[20]

After crossing a railway line built in the 1930s (the one already discussed in the previous chapter), there is a well-kept temple dedicated to Majhighariani. Today, this temple is one of the most popular as well as the richest in south Orissa, with several thousand visitors daily, especially on Sundays. The flow of pilgrims is controlled by means of a ticketing and barrier system. However, the temple acquired its present size and splendour only some decades ago. It is reported that while constructing the railway line, a bridge being built not far from the temple collapsed on several occasions. According to local tradition, Majhighariani did this in order to have a bigger temple built for her by the railway company. It is not known precisely when the new temple was constructed, but an eyewitness describes the temple as being in ruins in 1930. Old photographs also testify to the immediate environs of the temple, which today are well-groomed, being overgrown and covered with many trees and bushes. Even the site of the legendary ritual death by burning (*satī*) of the 116 consorts of Viswanatha, located next to the temple, looks neglected in the old photographs. Today this is a small, fenced-off park, in which the deified wives are ritually honoured on *saṅkrānti* days.[21]

The figure of Majhighariani consists of seven white stones, the largest of which forms a head coloured in vermilion. The face is characterized by expressive eyes, black eyebrows, a silver nose, a golden mouth and a protruding silver tongue. The head is wreathed in a gold ornament in the shape of a crown and the image is garlanded with red and white flowers hung round the head. The seven stones can hardly be made out under this

[20] See Plate 7.

[21] See Singh Deo (1939, 14-17) and Francis (1907, 302). Both, the neglected condition of the temple at the start of the twentieth century and its restored splendour in the democratic age, without kings, can be traced back to historical circumstances that require further study. The revival of the cult of formerly neglected local goddesses is also reported from other parts of India, for example, by Beck (1981, 84) and Erndl (1993).

'mask'. Only when the sacred inner space is cleaned—a task that is undertaken after visiting time—are the naked stones revealed.[22]

The greatest festivals of the year at the Majhighariani temple are Durga *pūjā* in autumn and *caitra parva* in spring. Until 1890, human sacrifice is said to have taken place on the eighth night of the Durga *pūjā*. This was carried out at a stone especially set aside for it, called the 'priest's stone' (*jāni pāthara*), probably the stone with red and white spots under the tree in front of the temple.[23] Today, humans are replaced by a particular type of sheep. As this animal can be found only in remote areas, its sacrifice can be allocated to the realm of tribal culture. After the sacrifice, the blood is collected and brought to the goddess, while the body and head go to members of the sweeper caste. Even on a normal day, a large number of goats and chickens are sacrificed. In addition, coconuts, bananas, rice and other vegetable gifts are offered, if the request is a minor one or the pilgrim's financial means are not enough to permit a blood sacrifice. The priests of the Majhighariani temple come from the caste of the foot soldiers or *pāīk*s.

If, at this point, we summarize the most important characteristics of the examples considered so far, it can be seen that in cultic, iconographic and mythological respects, a great range is covered on our ideal-typical scale from the pole of 'tribal' religion to that of 'Hindu' religion. This is not only so when one compares these goddesses with one another, it is also noticeable in the total complex of practices and beliefs that pertain to individual goddesses. In a developmental interpretation, it could be argued that diachronic stages have become petrified and can now be found as synchronic elements existing alongside one another.

Thus, in the legend of her early stay in the forest, Khambheshvari corresponds to a jungle goddess or goddess of the wilderness. The motif of the killing of a baby strengthens her 'wild' image. Even though Hindu prejudices about tribal religious practices may have influenced this myth, it nonetheless points to earlier tantric-shaktic and tribal elements in the

[22] See Plate 8. My account is based on observation and on what I was told by some priests and temple administrators. I thank Sri K. Buxipatro, the managing trustee of the temple, for his help. I am also much obliged to Professor P.K. Nayak, who accompanied me to Rayagada and helped me greatly with my investigations.

[23] The *Gazetteer* of 1907 records: 'Alongside the road is a black slab called the Jani pothoro, or "priest's stone", on which human sacrifices are said to have been offered formerly. The hill people still regard it with awe and decline to touch it' (Francis 1907, 302).

cult of this goddess. Simultaneously, however, of all the goddesses presented here, Khambheshvari is the one who receives blood sacrifices most infrequently and has therefore moved furthest away from the tribal goddess demanding human sacrifice and towards the vegetarian world of the Hindu pantheon. Iconographically, the example of Khambheshvari shows us the unproblematic juxtaposition of non-iconic symbol—the wooden post—and the anthropomorphic image of the *mūrti* type, that is, the decorated stone figure. In the case of Mohuri Kalua, within the space marked off for the goddess there are three small mounds of earth subject to worship. In addition, behind the balustrade stands a somewhat larger mound of earth, shaped like a head, together with an abandoned termite mound with a head, torso and arms. In Rayagada, Majhighariani exemplifies another interesting juxtaposition of different iconographic stages. Here we find, on the one hand, stones under a tree which are not at all anthropomorphized or decorated, while on the other there is the image of the goddess herself consisting of seven white stones, endowed with a human trait by having formed a head with facial characteristics out of one stone. All the goddesses dealt with here also have a movable substitute, and in the temples of Mohuri Kalua, Budhi Thakurani and Majhighariani, the goddesses are represented by such different manifestations as a snake, a lotus blossom, or by queens who died in *sāti*. Finally, devotees are possessed in front of the images of all these deities, so that human bodies serve as divine vessels and complete the range of iconographic forms. Unsculptured stones and living humans form the extreme poles between which exist many other forms of the manifestation of the divine.

As far as the location of the temples is concerned, Mohuri Kalua symbolizes most impressively the change in location of a jungle goddess from an inaccessible place of worship to a much more easily accessible temple. However, her temple is situated in the foothills of the Kerandi range, several kilometres away from either the nearest market town or the former palace of the Mohuri *rājā*s (who came originally from a village named Mohada). If Budhi Thakurani really is another manifestation of Mohuri Kalua, this signifies a further step by the original goddess: down from the hills into the adjacent valley and out of the valley into the political and economic centre of the sub-region. In this context, it may be noted that the Thakurani temple of Berhampur is located not far away from the new palace of the Mohuri *rājā*, in a central part of the city. Thakurani's substitute is still carried first to the palace on the occasion of her *yātrā* and on *saṅkrānti* days, before the procession continues further. The proximity of palace and temple is at its greatest in the case of Majhighariani. This is also underlined by the name of the goddess, which can be translated as 'in the middle of the fort'. According to local tradition, the stones that form the basis of Majhighariani's image came out of the earth one day by themselves, precisely at the place where the temple stands today. The king only came to Rayagada later and built his fortress around the self-emerging (*svayambhū*) sacred site. However, Majhighariani is an exception as regards the location of her temple. Typically, the temples of the type of goddesses presented here are located on the edge of the village, on the threshold of hilly and jungly regions, and thus to some extent are situated in the liminal space between settled area and jungle, between civilization and wilderness. Even so, these temples are mostly branches of more original temples situated further away, their greater accessibility being expressed in myth through the theme of a vessel having been flung down.[24]

We must now consider the nature of the relationship between tribal goddesses and Hindu little kings who were originally outsiders. My visits to the residences of many little kings of south Orissa and to the temples of other goddesses not specifically dealt with here, suggest that among the little kings of the sub-region there were probably none who had not patronized one or even several of the most important goddesses in their realms.[25] There is evidence that neighbouring little kings, or others striving for power, competed over access to the sacred site of a goddess and the status of her patron to the extent of going to war over her; occasionally, they sought to destroy the image of the tutelary goddess of their opponent, doubtless in the hope of destroying an important source of his power.

The royal patronage that was extended to tribal goddesses consisted first and foremost in the building of suitable accommodation, then in the financing of their cults and great festivals, as well as of regular *pūjā* ceremonies and in the provision for priests and their families. Mostly, the resources required for the religious services and the maintenance of pro-

[24] Here is the decisive point distinguishing the goddess of the wilderness from the typical village goddess, despite other similarities. Partially Hinduized goddesses of the wilderness move from the outside, the *vana*, closer to the settled area, the *kṣetra*, although they are mostly worshipped on the edge of the village or at cross-roads, while village goddesses or *grāmadevatā*s are always situated at the centre of the village. See also Jansen (1995, 60-6) and Kosambi (1983, Ch. III).

[25] Other tribal goddesses of south Orissa who enjoyed the patronage of little kings include Vyaghradevi (the 'tiger goddess') from the east of Bhanjanagar, in the former kingdom of Ghumsur; Dhongoro Devi (the 'goddess of the hills'), near the old fortress of Jeypore; Khila Munda in Mandasa; Nilamma in the former kingdom of Parlakimedi; Balakumari in Chikiti; Dumula near Digapahandi in Badakimedi kingdom and Phulokeshvari in Sanakimedi.

fessional, though non-Brahman priests, who established themselves permanently as religious virtuosi between the devotees and the goddesses, were secured through small donations of land near the temples.[26] The kings also provided funds from the treasury or by raising additional payments of tribute or by raids on neighbouring kingdoms. For the goddesses themselves, the patronage of individuals with access to economic resources and political power meant an extension of their influence beyond their originally limited domains and a higher reputation. In their increased domains, they acquired the ritual recognition of most social groups, and not only, as before, of the inhabitants of one village or the members of one caste or tribe. Their temples became sites of pilgrimage, though the worship by local communities, from which the priests were also recruited, remained dominant. The local roots of these goddesses were never forgotten even though their appearance changed. They were given accommodation and a more human form. *Pūjā* was regularly performed, up to three times a day, mostly consisting of five or six *upacāra*s or services, namely the offering of sandalwood paste (*gandha*), flowers (*puṣpa*), incense (*dhūpa*), light (*dīpa*), food (*bhoga, naivedya*) and, less frequently, a bath (*snāna*).[27]

Blood sacrifices were increasingly pushed into the background in favour of vegetarian offerings. Where blood sacrifices were offered, they were frequently removed from the direct sight of the goddess, behind walls or outside the temple complex. Often, instead of sacrificial animals and humans, red *mandāra* flowers and different sorts of pumpkin or gourd found use as recognized substitutes. Alternatively, animals and humans designated for sacrifice were killed only symbolically, by simply striking the nape of the neck with a bough instead of cutting it through with a sword or axe. In myth, the new 'mildness' of the goddesses found expression in the fact that the killing of children acquired negative connotations and the goddesses miraculously brought children who had been killed back to life.[28] However, this abandonment of blood offerings did

[26] One often finds at the temples several families related to one another, who take it in turns to fill the office on a rotational basis, and whose members pursue other forms of employment apart from priestly activities. This practice can be seen as an intermediate stage between professional priests dedicated solely to religious service and 'part-time' priests.

[27] Here see also Eschmann (1978a, 86-8).

[28] Here see also Senapati (1966, 417-18) on the forest goddess Birukhomb, near Boipariguda in Koraput District, who is regarded as one manifestation of Stambheshvari.

not change the basically ambivalent and, therefore, also 'cruel' character of these goddesses, nor the bipolar nature of their power according to which they were able, both, to give and take life.

In general, the number of devotees and supplicants appearing before the royally protected and now more powerful goddesses rose. With them rose the numbers of both, blood and vegetarian offerings. While these gifts were consumed by priests and devotees in the form of consecrated food or *mahāprasāda* after having been offered to the goddesses, goods such as cloth, jewellery or money accumulated, allowing the stocks in the storage rooms of the temples to grow. The increased popularity of the goddesses and the greater wealth of their temples in turn led to the annual festivals organized in a more magnificent fashion, the kings not infrequently being in attendance personally and carrying out rituals. Because of the royal patronage, however, the goddesses became closely identified with their sponsors. The little kingly patrons regarded the goddesses they supported as their personal tutelary goddesses (*iṣṭadevatā*) or as the tutelary goddesses of their houses (*gharadevatā*) or families (*kuladevatā*), and sometimes the protection of one part of the kingdom was associated with these goddesses. For instance, the Bhanja royal house of Ghumsur supported the cult of Khambheshvari in Aska and regarded the goddess as the guardian of the 'southern gate' (*dakṣina dvāra*) of their kingdom. Mohuri Kalua was the house and family goddess of the *rājā*s of Mohuri and is till today worshipped as such by the descendants of this dynasty. Majhighariani was regarded as a tutelary goddess by the Nandapur Suryavamshis, at least in the sixteenth century. In these positions and functions, the goddesses afforded their patrons privileged proofs of favour by removing misfortunes or granting them protection in return for their royal support. Hence, through royal patronage the area of influence of tribal and locally rooted goddesses was extended beyond their original localities and cultic communities, but, at the same time, their most important favours were restricted to a preferred individual, their little kingly patron.

4. Markama

I now turn to an examination of one last goddess. Using the example of Markama, who will lead us back to the *thātrāja*s of Bissamcuttack, some of the points that have not been sufficiently developed in the discussion up to now can be brought up.[29]

[29] My research in Bissamcuttack was assisted greatly by the active help of, Professor P.K. Nayak, for which I thank him here. I am also obliged to Mr S.

Markama is the tutelary goddess of Bissamcuttack town and one of the most powerful goddesses of the estate, who is ascribed great effectiveness by her devotees, especially when it comes to holding witchcraft, demons or evil spirits at bay. A serious supplicant, I was assured, can be certain of a positive outcome while those who neglect Markama must expect evil consequences. Markama's temple lies in a grove somewhat outside the town. The image of the goddess consists of a large black stone with a smaller stone on top. The latter forms a red-coloured head, covered all over with silver eyes and a protruding tongue. The larger stone, which functions as the body, is usually decorated with red garments. During *pūjā* the head of the goddess is decorated with garlands of red and white flowers (made up like a splendid head of hair). During the services, burning candles, coconuts and many flowers with red, blue and yellow blossoms are placed on the ground in front of the deity; during sacrifices Markama is also decorated with many green *belo patra* leaves. Right next to her stands a sword with red and white stripes, which acts as her substitute in processions.[30] This 'stage' is surrounded by a stone structure, before whose semi-circular opening the priests perform their services. If one takes a few steps back and looks at the whole scenario, one receives the impression of looking into the open muzzle of a lion.

In order to reach Markama's dwelling in her medium-sized temple, raised somewhat on a mound of earth, one must climb ten stone steps. At the foot of this ascent are five wooden posts about a metre high, on which slight notches hint at heads and waists. Sacrificial animals which have been dedicated to the goddess are tied to these posts before being killed directly in the sight of the goddess.[31] In the middle of the sandy square in front of the temple lies a flat stone painted with twenty red spots surrounded with white to represent the human sacrifices that were carried out

---

Nayak, a teacher and local historian resident in Bissamcuttack, who has also privately published a brochure on the goddess (see S. Nayak no date), for his support. Essential information on Markama and her festivals comes from the main priest of the temple, Sri Mohana Pujari, though other priests and inhabitants of the town were also kindly prepared to provide information.

[30] See Plate 9.

[31] See Plates 10 and 11. These posts recall the *yūpa* sacrificial posts of the Vedic tradition, as well as the 'impalement stakes' (*kampam*), formed like tridents, in the temples of south Indian goddesses, who represent the subordinate male guardians/devotees of these goddesses. See Beck (1981), Biardeau (1984; 1989b). In Bissamcuttack, however, the presence of the posts is traced back to ritual practices of the Kondh.

at one time. It is said that the stone rose of its own accord after such sacrifices, in order to bury the humans who had been killed beneath it.[32] Directly next to the temple stands a smaller building at the back of which are kept firewood and other utensils. In the front, this smaller temple houses the goddess Karkama, Markama's 'wild' sister. The main priest of the temple told me of a legend according to which every day Karkama would first play with some children of the town and then devour them. Markama forbade this cannibalistic practice by chasing her sister underground with a broom and cursing her with the words, 'From now on, you shall remain in the earth, and only your feet will be worshipped'. As a result, today Karkama is represented only by a stone footprint at the point where she fled into the earth. Every Sunday and Tuesday, Markama is offered sacrifices in the form of goats, chickens and doves, buffalo sacrifices being rare today. The heads and some of the blood of the sacrificial animals are offered to the goddess and to the priest sitting in front of the image, who is possessed by her on these occasions. During the daily *pūjā*, the gifts consist of coconuts, bananas, millet, the juice of a particular tree, *mandāra* blossoms, sweets, red cloth and other items. The greatest festivals of the year are the two Durga *pūjā*s in autumn and spring. As in the case of Majhighariani, the priests of the Markama temple belong to the warrior caste of *pāīk*s.

Other temples in Bissamcuttack are dedicated to the deities Thakurani, Durga, Bhairava and Niamraja (a deity of the Dongria Kondh). Together with Markama, these deities suggest that the town has a strong inclination to tantric, shaktic and tribal forms of worship. Again, the priests in these temples, with the exception of the Niamraja temple, come from the *pāīk* caste. There are also temples dedicated to Jagannath, Shiva, Radhakrishna and Rama in Bissamcuttack, that is, to deities who represent a 'higher' level of Hinduism and are under the control of Brahman priests. As far as the distribution of these sacred sites is concerned, it can be seen that the temples to Markama, Niamraja and Bhairava are located somewhat outside Bissamcuttack, on the southern, northern and eastern boundaries of the town, while the temples to Durga and Thakurani, as well as to the

[32] See Plate 11. Human sacrifices are said to have still been carried out 'in great-grandfather times'. One of the temple priests told me: 'Before a sacrifice, the human victim was kept on a smaller flat stone to the left, where his hair was shaved and afterwards offered to the deity. Then the victim was presented to the deity; the cup of his little finger was chopped off and blood given to the deity. At the same time, while this blood was given, the central flat stone would rise. Either the man was killed on that stone, or the stone was of a box type and the victim was put inside the stone. Automatically, the box then descended back to earth.'

Vaishnavite and Shivaite deities, are situated not far from one another, in the centre of the earlier fortress area. The Jagannath temple is found directly opposite the palace, in a manner typical of the sacred topography of the royal residences of Orissa. This ritual layout is oriented, overall, to the main street (*baḍa daṇḍa*) running in a north-south direction. The erection of the fortress, roughly the size of two football pitches, at the southern end of the main street, is linked to the death of an indigenous Kondh chief. According to local tradition the man was buried alive to appease Markama, who repeatedly made the walls of the fortress collapse while they were being built and is said to have demanded a human sacrifice before allowing them to rise.[33]

Markama's cult is supported mainly by *pāīk*s, who are strongly represented in the town and who, in former times, were of great importance for the continued existence of the estate. This suggests either a take-over of the cult by soldiers coming from outside or the *kṣatriya*-ization of tribal elements of the population. Those inhabitants of the town and its environs who originate from other social groups also take part actively in the cult of the goddess, with the result that she is seen as the goddess of a territory and its inhabitants rather than of one social group only.

Markama's cult also symbolizes the great integrative force that goddesses of her type exercise on those parts of the population that are furthest removed from the socio-cultural and political influence of Hinduism. In Bissamcuttack, these are the Dongria Kondh, living in the nearby but rather inaccessible Niamgiris. I have already mentioned this subgroup of the Kondh in connection with the temple to Niamraja, the 'King of the Niam Hills'. This temple, which lies on a stream on the northern edge of the town, with a view of the Niamgiris, is merely a branch of the original cave temple up in the hills. I was told that earlier the Kondh living on the plateau of the Bissamcuttack estate were forced to make pilgrimages into the hills at festival time, in order to pay homage to Niamraja, who was worshipped in the form of a footprint. One day the god appeared in his full form and called out in anger, 'Why do these people keep coming up the mountain to worship me?' He then threw an earthenware water jug into the valley and a temple was built where it fell. In this subsidiary temple, Niamraja is represented by a small stone which is said to be a broken-off piece of the vessel that he threw down. The temple of Niamraja on the edge of Bissamcuttack, therefore, embodies the movement of a tribal deity towards the area of Hindu culture and power. In this respect, however, Niamraja's 'coming down' into the valley does not

[33] See also Mohapatra (1986, 237).

mean only that the plateau Kondh were now spared the difficult passage into the hills. More important is the fact that for the Hill Kondh, the temple in Bissamcuttack represents a point of entry and integration into the valley whenever they descend into the high plateau with their jungle produce to trade, or for festivals, elections and other reasons. Through this temple, they have become incorporated into a complex system of ritual relationships with other deities. And through this, they enter into ritual, socio-economic and political relationships with the devotees of these other deities and, ultimately, with the *thātrāja* himself.[34]

Returning to Markama, at this point we need only refer to the fact that this goddess is also regarded as Niamraja's consort, which explains one aspect of Markama's attraction for the *ādivāsi*s of the area. The following legend on this theme is current among the Dongria Kondh:

> In ancient times Niam Raja kidnapped a Dongria girl named Markama from Tanda village in the Niam hills. But at night the girl fled away and later on it was reported that she repented. Hearing the news, the king suddenly realized his fault. He built a temple near Bissamcuttack in the name of Markama. After this the king died. His grandson Gaising came to the throne. One night he dreamt that the apparition of his grandfather, Niam Raja, was telling him something. It told him to tell the Dongria to worship him in the Markama temple. (Nayak, 1989, 39).

From the tribal point of view, therefore, the origin of Markama's cult is traced back directly to the ancestor of Dongria Kondh, and Markama herself is of tribal origin. This notion of a close association between the goddess and the *ādivāsi*s meets with no response from the priests of the

[34] One aspect of this ritual system, namely the role of the Dongria Kondh in the *dasarā* festival in Bissamcuttack, is discussed in the next chapter. Nayak describes the relationship between Niamraja, the Dongria Kondh and the *thātrāja* of Bissamcuttack as follows: 'The Dongria Kondh entertain a strong belief among themselves that they are the descendants of Niamraja, the legendary king of the Niamgiri Hills. Niamraja is worshipped in the form of a deity by the *Nisika* clan. All other clans, though they do not get the opportunity to worship the deity directly in the cave of the Niamraja, worship the insignia of Niamraja in the form of the *satarbond*, the clan insignia. However, this Niamraja deity has been made historical by the *thatraja* of Bissamcuttack. At Bissamcuttack the Niamraja temple was constructed by the *thatraja* and the *Nisika* clan, the *bodo paraja*, or the eldest of all Dongria clans representing all the Dongria Kondhs, who come here twice a year along with their *satarbond* to offer worship to Niamraja. The *thatraja* gives them a buffalo, which is sacrificed in this temple by the Dongria Kondh' (1989, 123).

temple or the *pāīk* inhabitants of the town, even though the idea of Markama as one of the consorts of Niamraja is also widespread among the latter. Yet, this relationship does not signify any weakening of the ritual supremacy of the goddess or her subordination to a male deity, as is often the case when goddesses are seen as the consorts of Shiva. Rather, the motif of a goddess who is raped by a demon and/or must enter a lower status marriage appears to resonate in the idea of Markama's enforced marriage with Niamraja.[35]

The main priest of the temple related to me the following tale concerning the goddess, which provides an insight into her relationship with the *thātrāja*s. The sisters Markama and Karkama, he reported, appeared one day on the doorstep of a childless couple in the town, who adopted them.[36] Now, the adoptive parents owned a piece of land near the present-day temple. Markama and Karkama expressed a desire to settle down at this thickly forested spot outside the town. To begin with, however, the parents did not grant this wish. One day, as they were working in the fields, the sisters again made their way to the place they had chosen and, instead of collecting firewood, sat down under a large banyan tree that still stands there. Only after the parents went looking for their missing children in the evening did they find the sisters, whereupon Markama and Karkama repeated their wish to settle there. It then became clear to the parents that the sisters were really goddesses. They agreed to their wish, though also insisting that the king (i.e. the *thātrāja*) be asked his permission first. Thereupon, Markama and Karkama appeared to the king at night and revealed themselves to him in a dream. The following day, the *thātrāja* made his way to the forest, met the sisters, and allowed a temple to be erected to them on the spot.[37]

While the theme of this legend is the connection of the goddess with a particular locality and the beginning of her royal patronage, in another

[35] On this motif and its impact on the cults of south Indian goddesses, see Beck (1981) and Biardeau (1989b).

[36] The motif of the sudden appearance of a goddess, who is adopted by a man or married couple of tribal or low-caste origin and who then suddenly disappears, finally to re-appear again and demand her installation as a goddess, is already known to us from the case of Khambheshvari. As Eschmann (1978a, 91-2) shows, it is also to be found with respect to other goddesses in Orissa, such as the divine sisters Tara and Tarini near Purushottampur in Ganjam District. On the formation of this motif in India's classical corpus, see Beck (1981, 106).

[37] Characteristically, in the *pāīk* version, the temple is founded by the *thātrāja*, not by Niamraja.

tradition the focus is on the characteristics of her cult. The king, it is reported, adopted Markama as his family deity and chose a Brahman to be the priest in her temple. The Brahman performed the usual services for five or six days, during which the food given to the goddess was offered to the king after the *pūjā* as consecrated food (*mahāprasāda*). One day, the Brahman turned his back to the goddess and received a kick in the backside from her so that he fell and lost consciousness. Meanwhile, the king, waiting in his palace for the consecrated food, learned of the priest's fall only after sending a messenger to the temple. Markama appeared to the king at night in a dream and instructed him to release the Brahman from his duty and appoint her adoptive parents as her priests.[38] She also stipulated that Brahmans should only be used for three services, namely to perform the fire ritual (*homa*) on the seventh night of the Durga *pūjā*, and to place the sacred thread around Markama on full-moon days of the months of *śrāvaṇa* (July/August) and *pauṣa* (December/January). Another ritual change ordered by the goddess was that henceforward the king was not to receive the consecrated food, only the water in which the goddess had been bathed.[39]

Another legend reports how the *mahārāja* of Jeypore sent his soldiers against Bissamcuttack because the *thātrāja* had not paid his tribute for many years.[40] While the battle was at its height, and after many of the *thātrāja*'s soldiers had lost their lives, Markama intervened. Dressed as a milkmaid she sold the *mahārāja*'s soldiers poisoned milk, whereupon they died and the tide began to turn in favour of the *thātrāja*.[41] One of the

[38] The *pāīk* priests trace their origin back to the adoptive parents of the sisters, meaning that they stand in a quasi-parental relationship to the goddesses. The Dongria Kondh, on the other hand, being Niamraja's descendants, can be considered to be the children to Markama, Niamraja's consort.

[39] *Pādodaka* or 'water in which the feet of the deity have been washed' (Gonda 1963, 249) is quite a standard medium of divine favour in Hindu *pūjā*, like food consecrated through contact with a deity. I presume, however, that in this particular case it is less prestigious than *mahāprasāda*. In any case, in the consecrated food a possible source of income escaped the king's grasp, to the benefit of the priests.

[40] Historically, this legend probably refers to one of the five battles fought between *mahārāja* Vikram Deo II and *thātrāja* Ramachendra I in the middle of the nineteenth century.

[41] The motif of a goddess who intervenes in a battle and poisons the enemy with milk, or who overcomes them in some other way, is widespread in the traditions of Orissa. Examples can be found in Kulke (1979a, 74; 111).

mahārāja's generals then went to her temple, and shot off her head with his gun. However, the goddess avenged herself shortly afterwards by infecting him with a disease and letting him die. The *mahārāja* considered it prudent to settle his dispute with the *thātrāja* and he released him from all tributary payments and granted him the right to rule his land independently. The legend also reports that after these battles the *thātrāja* wanted to erect a new temple, safe from enemy attacks, within his fortress for the beheaded Markama. However, Markama appeared before a priest in a dream and announced that she wished to remain at her chosen place on the edge of the town. Thereupon, the king built a temple dedicated to the goddess Durga within the fortress as a substitute.

All in all, therefore, in Markama's case we find elements we have already encountered in the goddesses Khambheshvari, Mohuri Kalua, Budhi Thakurani and Majhighariani. Here is a goddess, greatly respected locally, decisively determining the fertility of the land and the well-being of the population. This goddess is accorded patronage by a power-seeker coming from the outside and stemming from a Hindu milieu, who seeks to establish royal authority over an egalitarian tribal structure. From the iconographic point of view, in the temple one finds the juxtaposition of roughly cut sacrificial stones, petrified footprints, wooden posts with small notches, and a stone goddess represented chiefly as a head. In addition, on important occasions, the stone image exists side by side with possessed humans as embodiments of the goddess. On the mythological level there is also the division of the goddess into a 'wild' manifestation and a 'civilized' one. Blood sacrifices are numerous and carried out in the goddess's immediate presence and she is offered the head and blood of the sacrificed animal. *Pūjā* is performed twice a day, and sacrifices at least twice a week, by priests from a non-Brahman caste.

Markama also vividly exemplifies the fact—and this is true of many other goddesses of her type—that cult, iconography and mythology do not entirely lose their original tribal character, despite intensive and continued patronage by Hindu kings and their Brahman supporters. Rather, the legends of Markama suggest an opposition between Brahman and tribal priests, between the temple of the tutelary goddess outside the fortress and the temple of Durga within and, finally, between Hindu king and tribal goddess. These oppositions occur in a field of meaning and action that represents not so much the transition from a tribal religion to popular Hinduism, but one which represents rather the Brahman-dominated domain of orthodox Hinduism based on codified Sanskritic traditions. In this tension-laden zone, in which Hinduization is transformed, so to speak, into Brahmanization, iconographic and mythical duplications as well as ritual divisions of labour, apparently, no longer enjoy a conflict-free co-existence. Markama's refusal to leave her temple on the edge of town and to accept new quarters in the middle of the fortress, and her 'kicking down' (in the literal sense of the word) of a Brahman in favour of *pāik* priests are only two manifestations of the fact that the patronage and Hinduization of tribal deities by kings and Brahmans can meet opposition. Clearly, there is a point beyond which non-Brahman priests and indigenous cult communities will not accept the further 'embrace' of Hindu power-holders and their Brahman priests.[42]

5. Closing remarks

The royal patronage of tribal goddesses can only be understood in the context of the establishment, consolidation and legitimation of political power by Hindu little kings in Hindu-tribal border regions or in predominantly tribal areas. It was an important means integrating tribal and semi-tribal groups into a structure of authority based on Hindu ideas and values. In this respect, royal support for indigenous goddesses was of special importance in the early stages of a newly founded kingdom. However, in the religious history of the royal dynasties of south Orissa, there are few signs of the significance of these goddesses declining in any significant measure even in the course of the following centuries. Only from the late nineteenth century did the cult of Jagannath begin to surpass the cult of the goddesses in popularity and political significance.

Naturally, royal supremacy in southern Orissa was also exercised through economic, political and administrative measures or simply through naked force. We should remember, however, that the little kings of southern Orissa were mostly outsiders accompanied by just a small band of loyal followers. With few exceptions, they had no traditional basis for their authority among the population of their newly founded kingdom. They were, therefore, looking for measures that would endow them with legitimacy and thus guarantee them an internal stability as well as the most profitable appropriation of agricultural surpluses possible. The efforts of these little kings to achieve territorial integrity and political independence also required that at least the most important fortresses, settlements and persons of the kingdom could be defended militarily. For this, the jungle kings had to make good use of the strategic advantage they obtained from the secluded location and natural inaccessibility of their realms. This was only possible through the active support of the original

[42] For other examples of the limits of Brahmanization and, today, of 'reformist' policies, see also Fuller (1992, 103-5) and Hiltebeitel (1985, 181-2).

inhabitants who knew their habitat and its dangers. It was, therefore, indispensable for internal peace and the regular creaming off of surpluses, as well as for the defence of the kingdom against external enemies, that the little kings find legitimacy in the eyes of the indigenous population and move their subjects to more than just passive acceptance of their claims to rule. The policy of the jungle kings of south Orissa was, therefore, directed more towards the 'gradual integration' of the tribal population than their 'sustained displacement' (as Kulke emphasizes against Stein, regarding the policies of kings throughout Orissa).[43]

Ritual types of action were best suited for these aims. However, the patronage of tribal goddesses with roots in a particular locality formed only a part of the ritual policies of the Hindu little kings of south Orissa. In the example of Bissamcuttack, we have already seen that temples were built and priests provided for a number of other deities. Or to give another example: in sixteenth-century Rayagada, Viswanatha was both a devotee of Krishna and a patron of the tribal goddess Majhighariani. Supporting the cults of such gods of the great tradition as Shiva, Vishnu and, with qualifications, Jagannath served not only as a demonstration of royal power internally but also satisfied the need for legitimacy vis-à-vis the outside world. In other words, it served purposes of legitimation with respect to other little kings in the region, to the great king and later, to the colonial power.

On the other hand, the generous and ostentatious patronage of autochthonous goddesses was essentially directed towards internal legitimacy, that is, towards the legitimation of the jungle kings with respect to the indigenous population. The patronage of local goddesses promised the most direct and lasting access to the trust and loyalty of tribal subjects. By patronizing indigenous goddesses, the little kings created a direct connection with the newly colonized earth and with the population integrally tied to it.[44] Underlying this were not just the earthy, material and territorial traits in the character of these goddesses. There was also the notion of the king as lord or husband of the earth, known from the classical Indian tradition and expressed in a title like '*bhūpati*', which must have had an impact when jungle king and goddess (interpreted as both the goddess of a territory and the deified territory itself) entered into a relationship with

[43] See the arguments in Kulke (1979a, 14-26).

[44] The idea of a close interweaving and mutual influence between land on the one hand and people on the other is widespread in India. See Sax (1991, 71-7, 183, 203), who cites further literature on this theme.

one another.[45] Certainly, the jungle king's domain of political power (*kṣatra*) and the ritual domain (*kṣetra*) of the locally rooted goddess remained functionally differentiated, but they formed a symbiotic unity with respect to the marriage-like relationship (embodying fertile sexuality) between the king and the goddess and her land.[46]

If one considers the motives for the royal patronage of tribal goddesses, it is not enough to point only to the *political* functions or impacts of this patronage. It needs to be stressed that the basis for this patronage lay also in the religious sentiments of the kings themselves and in their feelings of responsibility or duty. Hinduism and tribal religion are not opposed to one another as two totally different belief systems or ritual practices; rather, at many points they reveal elective affinity, similarities and zones of transition. Thus, the jungle kings were impressed also in a genuinely religious way with the tremendous effectiveness that the indigenous population accorded the goddesses, daily proof of which was not lacking for believers. The jungle kings, therefore, possessed an immediate *religious* interest in guarding themselves from the anger of these goddesses and in receiving their protection and favour. Good harvests or the keeping of epidemics at bay—of which these goddesses were the most important guarantors—were dear to the kings, not only because the increased well-being of the people made them more acceptable, but also because it was part of a king's semi-religious duties (*rājadharma*) to ensure these. However, the favour of the goddess and the well-being of the people could only be obtained through great internal devotion and the generous support of her cult. In his position as the goddess' highest-ranking devotee, patron and main sponsor of the cultic services and festivals performed for her, the king assumed an essential ritual function for his own well-being as well as for the good of the community.

In this respect, the royal patronage of tribal goddesses was based on intentions that we would call religious. The fact that the highest ritual lord in this ritually laden field also exercised political power and that, in this way, a political community emerged out of the cultic community only

[45] Vinayaka Deo also took the title of 'Nandapur Bhupati' after mounting the throne. See Singh Deo (1939, 11). On the idea of the king as 'husband of the earth', see Hara (1973), Kinsley (1986, Ch. 12), Marglin (1985, 95-108) and Shulman (1985, 64-88).

[46] Where these units were not congruent—for example, where the domain of an old-established goddess extended over the boundaries of two newly established kingdoms—it could happen that she was worshipped and protected by two or more kings (in different functions or on different occasions). For an example from central Orissa, see Kulke (1984c, 118-23).

presents a problem of interpretation if one starts out from the strict separation of religion and politics that informs western understanding—only, that is, if religion and politics are regarded as two basically different levels of action and ideology. Corresponding to the Indian point of view would be rather the picture drawn by Hocart according to which ritual and politics were originally one, with politics then developing out of ritual while remaining shaped by its ritual origin. This evolutionary view can be reinterpreted synchronically against the background of the data presented in this chapter. In the kingdoms of south Orissa, the political authority of the jungle kings possessed a fundamentally ritual character and could only be founded and maintained through a conscious recognition and practical application of this character.

The next chapter, which is devoted to the royal patronage of the great Hindu goddess Durga, will show how closely intermeshed with one another tribal and Hindu forms of religiosity were in the jungle kingdoms of south Orissa.

CHAPTER VI

DURGA AND THE DASARA FESTIVAL

1. Introduction

As seen in the last chapter, royally patronized tribal goddesses developed into liminal beings: originating from a tribal background they moved into the fold of Hindu culture—without, however, becoming completely alienated from the former or totally absorbed by the latter. In this intermediate state, they were well qualified to bridge the differences between tribal culture and Hindu culture, between the indigenous population and Hindu kings. They therefore became an important part of royal ritual policy.

At the centre of this chapter is another important element in the ritual policy of the little kings of south Orissa, namely the patronage of Durga, Kali or a similar Hindu goddess.[1] It has to be emphasized that there was no great gulf between these goddesses and tribal goddesses. Rather, royally patronized tribal and local goddesses gradually came to be associated in cult, iconography and iconology with the more orthodox Hindu goddesses of the Great Tradition. Some of them, for example, were and still are known as '*Vana* Durgas'. Moreover, there are several links between these local goddesses and elements of the Great Tradition, represented, among other things, by the *Devī-Māhātmya* text or in cultic form by the autumn festivities known as Durga *pūjā*. Markama, for example, counts in local tradition as well as in Sarala Das's late-medieval Oriya version of the *Mahābhārata* as one of Durga's stalwarts in her battle against the demons (*asuras*). A newspaper article, pointing to this early mention of Markama has been framed in glass and hung just above the stone *mūrti* of the goddess. Hence, the status of Markama as a goddess belonging to the Great Tradition is transferred from an old text into a new form of text, the newspaper article, and thereby inscribed into, and made into an element of, the present-day cult of Markama at her temple in Bissamcuttack.

The ideal-typical distinction made in the preceding chapter between tribal and Hindu forms of religion must, therefore, be relativized even further. Durga *pūjā* and the *Devī-Māhātmya* (which is not just an old text read by a few but one often recited today in ritual contexts) are in themselves the results of processes of the Sankritization of goddesses of the

[1] For an earlier article on this theme, see Schnepel (1995a).

Little Tradition. At the same time representatives of the Great Tradition continue to function as media for the continued Hinduization of India's innumerable local and tribal goddesses. The cult of these goddesses and the ways in which they are mythologically linked with the great Hindu goddesses thus exemplify a characteristic trait of Hindu religion which is often captured in the phrase 'unity in diversity': little goddesses merge with great ones and these, in turn, fragment into countless localized little ones.[2] In this respect, little goddesses continue to be Hinduized, while great goddesses continue to be tribalized and 'parochialized'.[3]

This 'unity-in-diversity' paradigm also applies to Orissa. However, it is important to also stress here the idea of the multiplicity and distinctiveness of the local goddesses against their identification with the great Hindu goddesses. This change in emphasis (and I am only arguing about placing the emphasis differently), which might be captured in the formula 'unity *and* diversity' instead of 'unity *in* diversity', seems to me to be more appropriate, at least when it comes to understanding the point of view of subaltern groups in south Orissa. From time to time, members of these groups have explicitly stressed the distinctiveness of their own local goddesses from the Hindu goddess Durga and her like. Therefore, in spite

[2] The transformation of the goddess Sati into many 'places of power' or '*śakti pīṭhas*' illustrates the latter phenomenon most strikingly.

[3] According to Marriot, the term 'parochialization' describes the downward movement of the elements of the Great Tradition and their adaptation to the Little Traditions. The integration of the components of the Little Traditions into the Great Tradition are characterized as 'universalization'. See Marriot (1955, 197-201). Some of Marriot's conclusions also apply to the situation in South Orissa: '... since universalization and parochialization have both proceeded for a very long time, we are ordinarily unable to trace the course of either process with certainty, or to decide whether a given present configuration of religious contents is the result of one, and not also the result of the other, of these two processes' (ibid., 201-2). He also characterizes the constant movements between these two kinds of tradition as a 'circular flow' (ibid.). Ramanujan (1988) characterizes the entangled nature of religious elements in India by using the term 'reflexivity'. In my opinion, however, his literary exegesis does not apply convincingly to anthropological data. The question of the distinction between Durga and the little goddesses is also discussed by Beck (1981, 96-100, 107-9) and Gonda (1963, 209-21). Kurtz (1992) discusses the problem in a book entitled *All the Mothers are One*. Eschmann (1978a, 1978b, 1978c), addressing the problem of the Hinduization of tribal goddesses in Orissa, writes: 'The process of Hinduization is ... almost paradoxically interrelated to the regional tradition in a double way. That Hindu tradition which is the frame of reference for Hinduization is at the same time its product' (1978a, 85).

of the existing mythical, iconographical, iconological and ritual associations of these local goddesses with Durga, they have seldom been completely identified with her, at least as far as their own adherents are concerned, but have always retained their distinct names and other characteristic features of their personalities. Hence, the relationship of these local goddesses, even after intensive periods of royal patronage and Hinduization, often remained one of association and never fully of identification. The 'metamorphosis of the dangerous tribal goddess into a Hindu Durga' (Kulke 1976, 10) or 'eventual identification of the aboriginal goddess with Devī or forms of Devī' (Eschmann 1978a, 94) did not take place in the cases I have examined. On the contrary, on occasion such mergers or hierarchical encompassments of the lower by the high have been explicitly rejected by the indigenous actors.

Let us recall the case of Markama, our prime example of how the absorption of tribal goddesses by kings and Brahmans was limited. Markama (and her adherents) refused to be moved into the fort and demanded autochthonous priests instead of Brahmanical ones. The fact that the *thātrāja* of Bissamcuttack built a temple for Durga in his fort instead and appointed Brahman priests to take care of this new goddess within his fort leads me directly to the main topic of this chapter.

2. Durga and the jungle kings

Most, if not all, south Orissan little kings adopted a Hindu goddess as their tutelary deity, not instead of but in addition to their originally tribal or local *iṣṭadevatās*. This patronage of a deity with a more orthodox Hindu background and wider pan-Indian or at least regional recognition was another important element in the ritual policy of the south Orissan jungle kings. Besides Durga, the most commonly adopted goddesses were Kali, Bhairavi, Camunda, and Manikeshvari, all fierce manifestations of the Great Goddess.[4] There is a new element in the royal patronage of these goddesses which goes beyond the fact that they and their cults were more 'Hindu' and less 'tribal' in character: rather these goddesses were not integrally and essentially rooted in the territories newly colonized by the kings. The 'golden' images or *mūrti*s of these goddesses, which

[4] See Plates 13 and 14. Of these goddesses, in particular Manikeshvari, who functioned as *iṣṭadevi* in many little kingdoms in central Orissa, has not received sufficient academic attention so far. Some information can be found in Berkemer (1993, 205), Dash (1978b, 216-7), Eschmann (1978a, 90), Kulke (1978a, 129-31; 1979a, 21, 111), Rajaguru (1972, 72-7) and Schnepel (1992, 181-3). See also my discussion of the *Kāñchi Kāverī* tradition in Chapter IV, Section 5.

usually conform to the iconographical norm of the demon-killing (*mahiṣasuramardinī*) Durga, were movable and as such could be brought into the kingdom from the outside.[5]

Like their tribal 'sisters', these mobile goddesses were potentially dangerous but also powerful with regard to the fulfilment of a devotee's wishes. However, their power or *śakti* derives from the statues, in which they had assumed bodily form, not from a territorial root (*mūlpīṭh*). Furthermore, their cults were not so 'down to earth' in a sociological sense when compared to the very popular and more easily approachable local and tribal goddesses. Often the temples which housed their *mūrti*s were located within the fort or next to the palace, where they were guarded and served by Brahman priests and could not be approached by anyone at any time. The powers associated with these statues turned them into powerful sources of royal legitimacy and into contested objects of political and military struggle. Fights between kings or others struggling for power were then directed less towards gaining access to a sacred territory and its goddess than towards gaining possession of a statue. Dirks characterizes this phenomenon as follows: '... the way of saying that one king has subdued another is to say that he has captured his emblems, not his lands, and that this conquest is boldly displayed. Indeed, the victor uses the emblems to embellish his own kingship, even as they are degraded and made to represent the loss of another's power' (1987, 87-8). He also speaks of 'symbolic conquest and metonymic domination' (ibid., 88).[6]

[5] The ancient motif of the demon-killing Durga is known throughout the continent. In brief, Mahisha is said to have once succeeded in conquering Indra's throne and ruling the world. Thereupon the gods, who no longer obtained their share of the sacrifice, called (or, alternatively, created) Durga in order to help them. In her fight against the demon king and his armies for the restoration of the cosmic order, the gods equipped Durga with their various attributes or weapons: Shiva's trident, Vishnu's disc, Indra's thunderbolt, Varuna's snare are some of the gifts which can often be found depicted in paintings or sculptures of the goddess. In some of her twelve hands the goddess holds a bow and arrow, as well as a sword with which she beheads Mahisha after a long and fierce fight, just when he tries to escape through the wide-open muzzle of the buffalo in whose form he had manifested himself. Frequently, Durga rides on her 'vehicle' (*vāhana*) the lion, who devours the demons (*asura*s) killed by the goddess. She pins the neck of the buffalo down to the earth with a foot and her trident. On the mythology and iconography of this goddess, see Coburn (1986; 1991), Erndl (1993, 22-30), Gonda (1963, 41) and Mitchell (1992, Plate 47).

[6] Peabody (1991) presents an interesting study of the political significance of movable statues of deities in the west Indian little kingdom of Kota. Tambiah (1985c, 327-31) also points to the important role that the possession of divine

South Orissan legends concerning such *mūrti*s often report that they had been 'stolen' or 'captured' from another person. The motif of the stolen goddess can be found expressed in a legend concerning the origin of the kingdom of Parlakimedi.[7] According to this legend, a prince called Bhima Deo went into the hinterland of south Orissa in search of a kingdom of his own.[8] A local man recognized the noble birth of the prince and inquired about the reason for his journey:

> The prince replied that he was in distress, and in quest of some country over which he might become ruler. The man carried him on his shoulders until they came to a place where eight chieftains, desirous of a prince to rule over them, were assembled in council. He was gladly received and became the head of a small tract in Kimedi, designated the country of the 'Eight Mallikas' (...) While being carried on the man's shoulders, *he made an inward vow to sacrifice him to some chosen goddess*, if he obtained his wishes. The votary on being informed of his fate, cheerfully offered himself for immolation, but the affair was deferred, the prince being for the present perplexed as to his choice of a goddess. Meanwhile the wanderer carried his arms into Kalahundy country, and subdued it. The capital … was attacked and the inhabitants forsook it. In it there was a Brahmini, a widow, who had an only daughter, whom she tenderly loved. But the girl had died, and the mother had formed an image from her jewels and golden ornaments. When the village was deserted, the widow fled and abandoned the image. In course of time the image became endowed with the gift of speech, when it gave out that the deceased girl had been deified, and was to be worshipped hereafter under the symbol of this jewelled image, and with the title of 'Manikeswari' or the 'Goddess of the Jewel'. In her the prince found his 'Ishta Devi', and to her sacrificed his victim; and when resigning Kalahundy ... he took the image with him and enshrined it in his new capital. (Carmichael 1869, 88-9; his emphasis)

In contrast to Bissamcuttack—where the acquisition of a Durga image gained significance only once the kingdom had already been consolidated and the locally most important goddess could not be appropriated any

---

images and other sacred objects acquired in the Hindu and Buddhist kingdoms of Southeast Asia. On this theme, see also Jansen (1995, 49-52), Sax (1993, 167-9).

7 This legend was recorded by Captain Frye, who lived for some time in the Kondh region as special assistant agent.

8 Historically, Bhima Deo is said to have been one of the nineteen sons of Gajapati Prataparudra.

further—in this legend the acquisition of the image is depicted as having been crucial to, even constitutive of, the foundation of a kingdom. For the prince did not end his quest after being offered the lordship by the eight tribal chiefs or clan leaders, which might have been sufficient to establish his kingdom in a purely political sense. Instead, he wandered on in search of a goddess to whom he could sacrifice and who would be his and the kingdom's tutelary deity. Only after obtaining the image of a goddess and fulfilling the vow of a human sacrifice can royal authority—this seems to be the message—legitimately be established and exercised. The legend of Bhimo Deo also shows us that by stealing the image from someone else, the prince and aspiring king not only acquired the highly desired image and the alliance of a powerful goddess, he also proved himself to be the worthy new ruler of a kingdom, having demonstrated his merit through action. The goddess, in turn, signified the acceptance of her new 'owner' by beginning to speak.

An alternative version regarding the origin of the present *mūrti* of Manikeshvari in Parlakimedi was given to me by the late S.N. Rajaguru, an acknowledged historian of Orissa and a member of the *purohita* family of the former kings of Parlakimedi. He argued that the Manikeshvari statue originally came from Mukhalingam. This town, lying about fifty kilometres from Parlakimedi, was known in earlier times as Kalinga-nagara and functioned as the capital of the Eastern Gangas before they assumed power in central Orissa in the twelfth century. Manikeshvari is said to have been worshipped by the Gangas as their family deity and they took her along with them when they transferred their royal capital to central Orissa. The kings of Parlakimedi, who regarded themselves as the dynastic descendants of the Ganga Gajapatis, are said to have acquired the statue during the reign of Jagannath Narayana Deo in the middle of the eighteenth century and to have brought it to Parlakimedi. This account by Rajaguru provides the Manikeshvari statue in Parlakimedi with a more respectable origin than the one given above.

During my visit to Parlakimedi in 1992, Manikeshvari was worshipped in the form of a four-armed Durga in a small temple not far from the present palace. There were two further Durga statues to her left and right. Sacrifices of buffaloes, goats and fish are made especially on *mahāṣṭamī*, i.e. during the eighth night of Durga *pūjā*, but also on full-moon nights and during *caitra parva*. They are carried out close to a wall of the building which houses the goddess, and a small window in this wall allows the goddess to watch. The goddess is presented with the heads and blood of the animals.

Coming back to the first story concerning Bhima Deo and Manikeshvari, we remember that it links the worship of the goddess with the ritual killing of a tribal chief. This is a widespread motif to be found all over Orissa in connection with the foundation of jungle kingdoms. Kulke sees this motif as having a base in reality and interprets the ritual killings of tribal chiefs as a 'primordial violent force to establish power' (1976, 10). To him, they are an important vehicle for the establishment of kingdoms, symbolizing the subordination of tribal chiefs to the newly arrived kings. The chiefs, who had hitherto been honoured in the form of their heads, are poignantly described by Kulke as 'martyr *iṣṭadevatā*s'. It was their fate, according to Kulke, to be quickly surpassed in their function of tutelary deities by tribal goddesses.[9]

However, further questions arise when we consider the fact, reported in most stories, that the tribal chiefs submitted *voluntarily* to their fate. Do these legends recall, as Kulke's interpretation suggests, the real subjugation and killing of tribal chiefs that were posthumously glorified into voluntary sacrifices in order to soften the aggressiveness of the act and turn the subjugated tribes into allies? Or does the motif of the chief who 'cheerfully' offers himself for immolation rather express, as I would like to suggest, a complex and (especially in its early phase) fragile juxtaposition of tribal and regal principles of authority and power? The legend certainly expresses hierarchy, as manifested by the image of the chief carrying the king on his shoulders. But it also expresses consensus, as manifested by the common veneration of a goddess, by the motif of the eight chiefs 'desirous of a prince to rule over them', and by the tribal chief's consent to being killed.

In this context, it should be remembered that in the Parlakimedi legend and in two other legends which refer to the foundation of the forts of Rayagada and Bissamcuttack, the tribal 'martyrs' are quite explicitly said to have been sacrificed on the 'altars' of goddesses (i.e. Manikeshvari, Majhighariani and Markama). Against this background, Kulke's evolutionary sequence from martyr *iṣṭadevatā* to tribal goddess and to Durga should be extended. At least in the traditions discussed here, goddess, king and tribal chief act as three simultaneous but interdependent actors in a single politico-ritual complex. The story of the killing of a tribal chief represents more than just an individual act through which regal power was constituted once and for all. This thesis is supported by the fact that, in the jungle kingdoms of south Orissa, not only tribal goddesses like Markama, Majhighariani and their like, but also Durga, Kali, Manikeshvari and other Hindu goddesses periodically received human sacrifices at the behest of jungle kings. However, in these cases the victims were

[9] See Kulke (1976 and 1984c).

less tribal chiefs than boys or male youths who had been abducted and/or bought from other hilly regions or the plains, as is also known from the *meriah* sacrifices of the Kondh. Among the reasons given for these sacrifices, which can be found in historical documents or are given in interviews, are the building of new forts, palaces or bridges, that is, activities which are intended to construct material emblems of royal authority. Also mentioned often are epidemics, the illness of a king or a member of the royal family, the installation of a new king, the preparation for a war expedition, or the threat of an attack from an enemy, that is, events which paradigmatically relate to the well-being and continuity of the kingdom.[10]

In the family chronicle of the Jeypore dynasty, we encounter yet another version of the motif of the stolen image. Vijaya Chandra, the second king of the Jeypore dynasty, is credited with the following feat (already mentioned in Chapter II in connection with the *Kāñchī Kāverī* tradition of the Gajapatis):

> Purushottama Dev launched a war against Kanchi, defeated the king, and brought his daughter, princess Padmabati, along with the image of Lord Ganesh, Lord Gopal, Lord Narayan, made of black marble stone, and Goddess Jaya Durga made of gold. On their retreat to Puri they crossed the border of Nandapur kingdom. At that time Vijaya Chandra blocked the road and forcibly snatched away the image of Kanak (golden) Jaya Durga and Lord Narayan which were carried on the back of an elephant. He installed the two images in Nandapur and performed all the seasonal ceremonies of Kanak Durga, particularly so georgeously the dasara function that fetched him good name and fame all over Bharat. (Sarma 1938, verses 147-155)

In this legend the loser is not represented, as in the Parlakimedi version, by a defeated king of inferior or at best equal status, and there is no mention of the help and sacrifice of a tribal chief. Instead, the legend narrates the theft of a Durga image by a little king from his own overlord. Hence, this legend is not about the establishment of a kingdom and the problematic relationship between king and tribal leaders/subjects, but about the relationship between little king and great king.

The *mūrti* of Kanaka Durga, we are told, was part of the booty which the Gajapati himself had captured from another great king after a battle in

[10] On the phenomenon of human sacrifice in south Orissa, see Bell (1945, 298), Boal (1982, Ch. II), Campbell (1864), Carmichael (1869, 106, 327), Francis (1907, 202, 234, 262-3), *History of the Rise and Progress* (no date), Hota (1959), Macpherson (1863), Mohapatra (1986, 237), Padel (1995) and *Selections* (1864, 18, 34).

which, it is implied, Vijaya Chandra had initially fought by the side of his overlord. It was only upon returning home from their common expedition, in the dense forest of Nandapur kingdom, that the little king and former ally turned against his superior and deprived him of the image and other valuables. Quite obviously, the theft was no trifling matter. On the one hand, the stolen image of 'Golden Durga' must also have possessed some material value.[11] But more painful to Purushottama will have been the loss of the ritual value of the image. Because Durga is known to have been the family deity of the Gajapatis up to modern times, the theft of the image represented a personal insult to the great king. Moreover, it constituted an obvious act of political insubordination or *fitna* by a little king *vis-à-vis* his overlord, who is depicted as being unable to prevent it or to exercise any punitive measures afterwards.

While the family chronicle of the Jeypore kings proudly reports this theft, as far as I can see there is no mention of it in any of the Puri chronicles.[12] Whether this points to a fabrication on the part of Jeypore or to the suppression of an embarrassing historical event on the part of the Gajapatis is difficult to determine. However, here we are more concerned with legitimizing strategies in the ritual policy of the Jeypore kings. In such a context to record a theft of a Durga *mūrti* must have been intended to express that, from an early stage in history, the royal house of Jeypore was bold and powerful enough to oppose the Gajapatis and that it possessed some kind of politico-ritual independence from them. In addition, it is mentioned that the splendour with which the annual Durga festival was enacted 'fetched the king good name and fame all over India'. These boastful statements regarding the acquisition of the *mūrti* of a 'Golden Durga' and the splendour of the festival established around it suggest therefore that in their ritual policy the Jeypore kings sought to emulate the achievements and fame of their overlords and aspired after 'greatness' themselves.

Durga has been the family goddess of the Jeypore *rājā*s ever since the capture and installation of the image in the ancient capital of Nandapur in the late fifteenth century. Hence, the foundation of a kingdom is again (as

[11] Singh Deo (1939, 11) doubts that the *mūrti* of Kanaka Durga, which at his time was still installed in the Durga temple next to the Jeypore palace, was made of gold and argues instead that it was made of an alloy of eight kinds of metals. The same opinion was expressed to me by a senior member of the royal family.

[12] The *Kaṭakarājavaṃśāvali* simply states: 'He [Purushottama] brought a statue of Lord Krishna ... as well as several other images' (Tripathi and Kulke, eds. 1987, 87).

in Parlakimedi) linked to the theft and ritual installation of a Durga *mūrti*. Over the centuries, the royally patronized cult of Durga did not diminish in significance even up into modern times. However, it could and often did exist side by side with the Jeypore kings' dedication to, and patronage of, a local or tribal goddess. At the same time, different kings of this dynasty were also the devoted adherents of religious teachings which were not particularly sympathetic to, or did not stand in elective affinity with, the shaktic or tantric forms of worship that dominated the cult of the goddesses (whether 'tribal', 'partially Hinduized' or 'Hindu' in character). Thus, Viswambhara Deo II (1713-1752) is reported to have been a great devotee of Krishna along the lines of the *bhakti* teachings brought into Orissa by Chaitanya during the sixteenth century. But Viswambhara is also said to have been greatly devoted to Kanaka Durga:

> Viswambhara Deo used to go to Nandapur daily from Narayanapatna on horses, each kept at a distance of six miles, in order to visit Kanaka Durga. The Raja never touched anything as food without having *Darsan* (visit) of the said Deity. One day there was flood in the hill streams owing to continuous rains and the Raja was detained on his way to Nandapur and could not reach the temple of the deity, and hence he had to fast for two or three days. In the course of his fast, the Deity Kanaka Durga being much pleased with his devotion appeared before him one night in a dream and ordered him to refrain from his daily journey to Nandapur and asked him to construct a small golden image of Kanaka Durga after the main image at Nandapur and continue worshipping at Narayanapatna. (Singh Deo 1939, 80)[13]

This legend opens up another perspective with regard to the territoriality of these goddesses. As we have seen, deities like Majhighariani or Markama possessed and still possess strong local roots. With movable goddesses like Kanaka Durga or Manikeshvari the matter was different. Certainly they did not completely lack in territoriality, as their spheres of influence or *kṣetra*s were considered to be more or less coterminous with the realms or *kṣatra*s of their royal patrons. But their power or *śakti* was not rooted in a locality itself. It radiated from wherever their images were located, this being dependent on who the last owner was and where exactly he had placed her, and it gradually diminished as one moved towards the periphery.[14] The patronage of movable tutelary goddesses thus allowed greater flexibility to a king's movements, and it expressed a

[13] On Narayanapatna as the royal capital, see Singh Deo (1939, 138-43).

[14] On this phenomenon, see also Kulke and Rothermund (1991, 145).

kind of royal legitimacy and range of authority which had gained some degree of autonomy from its all too narrow tribal or local base. When this happened, tribal tutelary goddesses could again lose importance and their cults be reduced to their original, locally confined sphere of influence. This was especially the case when a king gave up his residence in the *kṣetra* of a locally rooted goddess and built a fortress elsewhere.[15]

However, lack of territoriality and the greater mobility of the statues of Durga and her like did not mean that an image accompanied every shift in a king's residence. Instead, in the jungle kingdoms of south Orissa, the seat of the *mūrti* of a tutelary goddess appears to have been more permanent than the residence of the king. The story of Viswambhara's daily pilgrimage provides only one example of a situation where the king and the tutelary deity stayed at different places. In fact, in the Jeypore kingdom, the spatial separation of the goddess and the king occurred as early as the middle of the seventeenth century, when, under Viravikrama Deo (1637-1669), the royal capital was shifted from Nandapur to Jeypore. This move to a new residence some forty miles from Nandapur is said to have been made on account of a curse uttered by the goddess Kali. It is reported that after six successive kings had had only one son each, astrologers found Nandapur to be an inauspicious place. Members of the family of the former Jeypore kings gave another explanation to me for leaving Nandapur: On one occasion the eldest son and heir of a Jeypore king left the fortress in order to cremate his deceased father just outside the town, as custom demands. On returning, he was prevented by a younger son from re-entering the fortress. This version provides less a religious reason, the curse of a goddess, than a political one, the usurpation of the throne by a collateral, junior line of the royal dynasty, as prompting the move from Nandapur to Jeypore.

The fact that during Viravikrama's reign in the middle of the seventeenth century Muslim domination (the Golkonda sultanate) had already taken root in coastal Andhra and was gradually extending its sway into the hinterlands of south Orissa may well have been taken by the Jeypore kings as another indication of the inauspiciousness of Nandapur. It is therefore quite probable that there were also strategic and political reasons for transferring the royal capital further away from the coast. What is important in the context of my discussion here is the fact that the move to Jeypore is regarded, even today, as being the result of a curse by Kali, the dark and terrible side of Durga. The possession of a Durga *mūrti* (and

[15] Such a loss in significance probably happened to Majhighariani in Rayagada, which functioned as a royal capital for two kings only.

spatial proximity to it) is, therefore, ambivalent in character: it can mean power and well-being, but it might also bring about infertility, and hence the end of a dynasty, as well as death.[16]

When leaving Nandapur, Viravikrama Deo did not take the original image of Kanaka Durga with him. Like Viswambara, who had a duplicate effigy made after he was unable to cross the swollen river, we can assume that Viravikrama before him had a substitute of Durga installed in Jeypore. The story of Viswambara's daily journey to see the goddess and of his installation of a substitute image in Narayanapatna thus shows that in the long run such a situation is not desirable. This is also made clear by a story which relates an event that occurred during the rule of Ramachandra Deo II (1781-1825) and is remembered as follows:

> A hooligan named Mallaparaj carried out a coup in Nandapur with a group of revolutionaries. He was a notorious and formidable robber. To keep the golden image of Goddess Durga away from his mischief, a devotee hid it in a well. After a few days the devotee died and the image could not be recovered. The king could not find the image. At that time a learned man named Dibayasingh Nanda came from Puri to pay a visit to this place. He was adept in many occult sciences and a man of learning. He was the ancestor of the Nanda dynasty in Jeypore. By applying his Tantric skill he was able to find the hidden image of the Goddess and please the king. The king then brought the image of Durga Devi from Nandapur to Jeypore on a saddle with pomp and ceremony, sacrificing animals at different halting places en route. The king also gave three villages of Nandapur to Dibyasingh Nanda and appointed him as the chief worshipper of the deity. (Sarma 1938, verses 300-312)

In this episode about a 'coup' in Nandapur the motif of the stolen image is linked to the motifs of the threatened, hidden, lost, rediscovered and newly installed image.[17] In evoking these successively combined themes, the legend seems to convey the message that it is not enough just to steal an image, to install it as a tutelary deity and to be a far-away devotee in order to claim royal status. A proper king has to prove his

[16] Members of the family of the former Jeypore kings do not visit Nandapur even today on account of this divine curse. Only the 'enlightened' king Vikram Deo IV (1931-1951) is known to have visited the temple of Durga/Kali in Nandapur at which kings were installed in former times. He is said to have died one day later. On the curse of Nandapur, see also Francis (1907, 264).

[17] These motifs occur often in Orissan legends, especially in connection with Jagannath, as is reported at various places in Kulke (1979a). See also Chapter III, Section 2.2 above.

ability to hold on to the image and to prevent its theft from yet another party. In other words, to acquire an image *and* to keep it in one's possession—that is what makes a man a king.[18]

According to the legend, then, the Jeypore kings almost failed to prove their continuing worth as patrons of Kanaka Durga. To start with, in the legend they do not appear as keepers of authority and order in the 'kingless' town of Nandapur, as would have befitted them. For, ultimately, the theft of royal property by a 'revolutionary' and 'notorious robber' (one could also consider him as a man striving for little kingly power and following tradition by stealing a Durga *mūrti* from the present ruler) was prevented not by royal soldiers but by a lone individual. Moreover, the narrative suggests that the goddess was not being attended by a proper priest. The devotee who hid the image is depicted as a layman and, ultimately, as too weak to handle the powerful *mūrti* himself. This is suggested both by his sudden death and by the way in which the chronicler puts this simple devotee into striking opposition to the ritual expert who then appears on the scene. The narrative, therefore, initially represents the Jeypore kings as being at fault both politically and ritually and, hence, as violating their *rājadharma* in a twofold sense.

In the legend, the motifs of the threatened, almost stolen, then hidden and lost image are followed by the motifs of the rediscovered and newly installed image. For this a new protagonists is introduced in the 'plot': a man coming from the holy city of Puri who, by applying occult tantric knowledge, manages to regain the lost *mūrti*. After the rediscovery, the king corrects the dharmic shortcomings of his dynasty by appointing Dibyasingh Nanda as the chief priest of the goddess, granting villages to his family, appointing him the royal priest (*purohita*), and having the *mūrti* of Kanaka Durga installed in Jeypore.

The author of the *Jayapura Raja Vamsyavali*, in which these events were reported in 1938, was a descendant of this tantric expert. This fact will have supported the view of a prestigious Puri origin for this dynasty and of the great occult knowledge of its founder. Whether these claims are historically valid or not notwithstanding, around 1800 there certainly was a re-invigoration of the cult of goddess Durga in the Jeypore kingdom. Historically, the transfer of Durga to Jeypore took place at a time of substantial political and religious change in the kingdom. Ramachandra's father, Vikram Deo I (1758-1781), had become involved in the military

[18] Is it not an ironical twist of history and an expression of the new structures of power in modern, kingless times that the image was again stolen from the dethroned Jeypore family some fifteen years ago?

activities of the little kings of the region against the British. This resulted in the first punitive expedition by the British into the kingdom and in the subsequent destruction of the Jeypore fort in 1775. By contrast with his father, Ramachandra Deo II adopted a policy of co-operation with the colonial government, participating actively in the military activities of the British against 'rebellious' little kings and tribes in the hill region or *māliahs*. This shift of policy, combined with the fact that by the 1780s the British had fallen out with their erstwhile ally (and Jeypore's long-time arch-rival), the little kingdom of Vizianagaram, made Ramachandra the colonial power's most important ally in the *Northern Circars*. By the turn of the century, this led to Jeypore's tribute being settled at the comparatively low figure of 16,000 rupees.[19]

The security experienced under British rule led Ramachandra to the construction of a new palace 'out in the open'. The so-called 'old fort' (*purāṇagarh*) of Jeypore, destroyed by the British, had been situated at the foot of a steep mountain range, with speedy access to its (at that time) heavily forested jungles in cases of emergency; it was more a strategic jungle fortress than a palace. The new palace and its surrounding new township, on the other hand, were built at some distance from this natural shelter, in the middle of the more accessible high plateau of this area. The main feature of this new capital was the 'great street' or '*baḍa daṇḍa*' running along a north-south axis. At the southern end of this street stood the palace and a number of temples dedicated to Hindu deities such as Raghunath, Shiva and Jagannath. With the establishment of a new and more prestigious politico-ritual centre designed according to orthodox brahmanical prescriptions and containing an impressive palace and splendid temples, Ramachandra II sought to enhance and consolidate his reputation as a *dharmic* Hindu *rājā*. He presented himself as someone who fulfilled the moral duties of a proper Hindu king in that he built and patronized Hindu temples and acted as a royal donor, also inviting Brahmans into the country and granting lands to them.[20]

The ritual policy of the Jeypore dynasty at the beginning of the nineteenth century, which was characterized by a strong move towards the further Hinduization of the kingdom's social, cultural, political and religious life, was directed more at external legitimation, i.e. at gaining legitimacy as proper Hindu kings vis-à-vis other kings of the region and

[19] See Cowley (1795, 223), Senapati (1966, 69-71) and Chapter IV, Section 6 above.

[20] For an analysis of the evolution of royal town-planning and ritual policy in central Orissan kingdoms, see Kulke (1980).

the colonial power. The patronage of local and/or tribal goddesses, which was so important for the internal legitimation of royal authority, decreased in significance but did not vanish completely. As far as the royal patronage of Durga is concerned, we find that despite the introduction of new Hindu deities (with their priests) into the region and their ostentatious placement under royal patronage, the cult of this goddess was far from fading into insignificance. The very fact that she was brought to Jeypore and installed within the new palace compound, in the closest possible proximity to the king, expresses the continuing politico-ritual importance she was meant to have. This conclusion is also supported by the style in which her journey from Nandapur to Jeypore was conducted. According to the chronicle, it was a triumphant procession on horse or elephant—a rite (ride) of passage which was accompanied by a large number of impressive sacrifices on the way. And thc continuing significance of Durga in Jeypore was more than just a family affair: she became the tutelary deity of the realm (*rāṣṭradevatā*). Hence, far from being overshadowed by the cult of Jagannath, Durga remained at the very centre of the politico-ritual life of the kingdom, for the kingdom's most important ritual of the year was not Jagannath's 'car-festival' (*ratha yātrā*) during the monsoon but the intertwined sequence of *Durga pūjā* and *dasarā* in the autumn.

3. Durga *pūjā* and *dasarā* in Jeypore[21]

Durga *pūjā* represents one of the most important religious festivals in the Hindu calendar. Success and well-being in the coming year are thought to depend in no small measure on the devotees' strict observance of the most important ritual prescriptions and prohibitions attached to the occasion, while negligence of the goddess may lead to serious consequences.[22] Durga *pūjā* takes place during the first nine nights of the bright half of the lunar month of *āśvina* (September-October), so that it is often given the alternative name of '*navarātrī*' or 'nine nights'. Underlying the festival is the sacred myth of the slaying of the buffalo demon Mahishasura and other demonic powers by the goddess. Hence, Durga's roles as 'Goddess

[21] An earlier article on this topic, which has been revised and extended here, can be found in Schnepel (1996).

[22] Kane comments that 'whoever, through laziness, hypocrisy, hatred or stupidity does not celebrate the great festival of Durga has all his desires frustrated by the angry Devi; ... rewards are promised when one celebrates Durgotsava' (1958, 156).

of the Battle' and 'Restorer of Cosmic Order' form the imaginative centre of the festival. In some parts of India, including Orissa, people celebrate a second, less important Durga *pūjā* in the lunar month of *caitra* (March-April). The temporal coincidence of the two Durga *pūjā*s with the completion of the two major harvest seasons of the agricultural year suggests that originally they must have been closely connected, mythologically and ritually, with agricultural and fertility rites and with marking the change of the season.[23]

Dasarā takes place on the day immediately after the Durga *pūjā* celebrations, and the term '*dasarā*' is often used for the combined ceremonial sequence taken as a whole. However, at *dasarā* people also celebrate the successful military campaign of Rama, the hero of the *Ramāyāṇa*, against Ravana, the demon king of Lanka. There, thus, exists a religious context for this tenth day which is independent from Durga *pūjā* (and its mythology) and which is celebrated in some places as *Rāmlīlā*. *Dasarā* counts as one the most auspicious days of the year and one on which it is lucky to start a new enterprise. In earlier times, this included the king's setting out on a military campaign with his army. Some commentators ascribe a military origin to this festival while others, again, see a connection with seasonal agricultural rites.[24] These differences apart, there is not only a close temporal and ritual interconnectedness between Durga *pūjā* and *dasarā*, but also a mythological and imaginative one, for in remembering and ritually re-enacting the killings of Mahishasura and Ravana, the two ceremonies celebrate the destruction of demonical powers and the restoration of a cosmological order that had been endangered, even destroyed.[25]

To return to Jeypore, it will be remembered that according to the family chronicle, *dasarā* had been celebrated as the principal ritual of the

[23] On Durga *pūjā* as a rite of fertility, see Jansen (1995, 141-2, 150), Kane (1958, 186) and Kinsley (1986, 95 and 111).

[24] On Durga *pūjā* and *dasarā* as understood in the classical tradition, see Berkson (1995), Coburn (1991), Erndl (1993, 22-30), Fuller (1992, 108-11), Kane (1958, Chs. 9 and 10) and Kinsley (1986, Ch. 7).

[25] Even though Durga only plays a minor role in the two great Indian epics, the *Mahābhārata* and *Rāmāyaṇa*, there developed in many places in India a Little Tradition, often transmitted only orally, according to which she had an important part in the success of the Pandava brothers or of Rama respectively. This linking of the mythology and cult of Durga with these Indian epics and their heroes is expressed by the popular idea that the seventh day of Durga *pūjā* celebrates the successful intervention of the goddess in the battle of Rama against Ravana. See Jansen (1995, 151-4) and Kinsley (1986, 107-9).

kingdom from the late fifteenth century onwards. It is also reported in the chronicle that, immediately after the statue of Durga had been stolen from Gajapati Purushottama by Vijaya Chandra, it was installed in the then royal capital Nandapur. The annual *dasarā* festival held in honour of the goddess is also said to have been celebrated so splendidly that it brought the kingdom 'good name and fame all over India'. Celebrating *dasarā* in Nandapur with such splendour was a public challenge to the Gajapatis' status of overlordship. To start with, it centred around a Durga *mūrti* allegedly stolen from them, thus representing a ritual and political humiliation of the 'great king' by one of his subordinates. Moreover, around the late fifteenth century, *dasarā* was a festival which signified the ideological orientation of the jungle kings towards a southern model of kingship and, therefore, the possibility of Jeypore accepting a great kingdom from the south as overlord in place of the Gajapatis. In Vijayanagara, the only other great Hindu kingdom of the macro-region at that time, *dasarā* was the main annual ritual performance of the polity. This imperial focus on *dasarā* was emulated by many of the little kings under Vijayanagara.[26] The Gajapatis, by contrast, supported the cult of Jagannath, which had been patronized in Orissa by the imperial dynasty of the Late Eastern Gangas from the early thirteenth century onwards, turning the 'car festival' (*ratha yātrā*) of the god into their principal state ritual. The little kingdoms under Gajapati supremacy adopted a similar focus in their ritual policies. Hence, by celebrating *dasarā*, the Nandapur/Jeypore kings, apart from showing their devotion to Durga, were also making a political statement according to which they wanted to be perceived as semi-independent and/or possibly seeking the shelter of the 'umbrella' of another sovereign, namely the Vijayanagara king.

I have now prepared the ground for a closer examination of Durga *pūjā* and *dasarā* in the Jeypore kingdom and would like to concentrate on the festival as it was celebrated in Jeypore town during the nineteenth and twentieth centuries. One account for this can be found in the *Vizagapatam District Gazetteer* of 1907, written by a colonial officer named Francis:

> The great event of the year in Jeypore is the Dasara feast, which lasts for sixteen days and includes several ceremonies in honour of

[26] On *dasarā* in Vijayanagara and the little kingdoms under its sway, see Breckenridge (1977), Dirks (1987, 39-43, 90-1), Sewell (1970, 91, 228-378) and Stein (1980, 384-90). Further information on *dasarā* in other places and kingdoms of India can be found in Forster (1983, 134-8), Fuller (1992, 111-25, 139-42), Fuller and Logan (1985), Jansen (1995, 158-77, 269-71), Pfaff-Czarnecka (1990), Rao (1936), Ray (1989), Sontheimer (1981) and Toffin (1981).

> the goddess Kanaka ('golden') Durga whose temple is within the palace walls. (...) Sheep and goats are sacrificed on each of the first thirteen days of the Dasara and on the fourteenth some buffaloes as well. On that day which is known as *Bodo Uppano* ('great offerings') day, the Maharaja, dressed in white, himself visits the goddess' shrine and then holds, from a white throne, a darbar which is attended by the bollo loko (courtiers) and lampatas (servants) and others, while the senior Maharani ... does the same after him, receiving bhets (presents) from the ladies who attend. On the sixteenth, or *Sanno Uppano* ('little offerings') day, the Maharaja, who this time is dressed in scarlet, worships the goddess in the Darbar hall of the palace and holds, from a scarlet throne, a darbar at which bhets are offered. Neither of the thrones are used except at the Dasara. It is customary for the Maharaja's feudal retainers to come into Jeypore with their followers to pay their respects at this second darbar, and many of the inams and mokhasas in the estate ... have been granted on the express condition that the grantees do this annual service.
>
> On the eighteenth day, preceded by the goddess Kanaka Durga and a white flag which was captured long ago from the troops of Bastar in one of the many skirmishes which took place with that State, the Maharaja and his son, seated in ambaris on elephants and followed by the European and other officials of the place in howdahs on other elephants go in procession to the *Dasara poda* in a mango grove to the north of the town. There worship is paid to the goddess by the Maharaja and afterwards the crowd proceed to shoot a brinjal off the top of a long bamboo. (Francis 1907, 262-3)

The fact that from the 1880s, British officials participated in the festivities at Jeypore as observers (and even actors) and that they regularly sent reports to the administrative centres in Visakhapatnam and Madras suggests that Francis' report is pretty accurate. The first thing that strikes us here concerns the length of the festivities. While, as has been pointed out, Durga *pūjā* in India usually lasts nine nights with *dasarā* being placed on the tenth day, festivities in Jeypore are said to have lasted for sixteen days. This may reflect a particularly strong devotion to, and greater importance of, Durga in this kingdom. But it appears that the most important days, the eighth and tenth days of the usual sequence, fell in Jeypore on the fourteenth and sixteenth days respectively. Thus, six days of Durga worship were placed before the common temporal sequence. In order to understand this, it must be kept in mind that the beginning of this sixteen-day sequence coincided with another important date in the Hindu ritual calendar, which probably escaped Francis. According to shastric lore, in the lunar month of *āṣāḍha* (June-July) Durga falls asleep and only awakes again on the ninth lunar day of the dark fortnight of the month of *bhādrapada* (August-September) which precedes the month of *āśvina* in which Durga *pūjā* takes place.[27] This is the first day of the sixteen-day sequence described by Francis.

We also learn that two *darbār*s were held in Jeypore, one on the fourteenth (eighth) day, dominated by the colour white (symbolizing mourning), and another on the sixteenth (tenth) day of the proceedings, dominated by the royal colour scarlet. In both cases we find exchanges of gifts in the *darbār* hall. The first was limited to members of the inner circle of the royal family and the permanent court while the second, politically more important, was a fully developed state affair with officials, functionaries and 'feudal' retainers being the main participants.[28] Moreover, in both *darbār*s the king ostentatiously presented himself as the chief devotee of Durga. However, in the first *darbār* he visited her in her temple, which is within the precincts of the palace, while in the second the goddess was brought out of the temple and worshipped in the *darbār* hall itself.[29] Finally, Durga led the procession to the festival ground, where she was once again worshipped by the king even more publicly. This process of gradually bringing Durga out into the open signifies a shift in meaning. At Durga *pūjā* and *dasarā*, the goddess no longer served the function of the tutelary deity of the royal family (*kuladevatā*) but rather that of the state deity (*rāṣṭradevatā*).

Let us now concentrate on the politically vital tenth day of the *dasarā* proper. The following account of the proceedings in 1941 comes from an Indian gentleman named Sahu:

> The Dussara at Jeypore is a sight to see not only for me but for gods. (...) And Lo! What a sight! People have thronged in their thousands. From all parts of Jeypore people have come to witness

[27] See Kane (1958, 157-8).

[28] Curiously enough, the first day was known as the day of the 'great gifts', the second as that of the 'little gifts'.

[29] I could not ascertain whether in Jeypore the image of Kanaka Durga was actually placed on the throne during her worship in the *darbār* hall, as Dirks (1987, 40-2, 66) reports to have been the case in late medieval Vijayanagara. Mayer (1985, 209; 1991, 776), too, observes that during *dasarā*, as celebrated in some west, central and south Indian kingdoms, goddesses were invoked and invited to take their place on the royal throne (*gadi*), or rather in its essential part, the cushion of the throne. He emphasizes the almost physical bond that existed between the king and the goddess when the former sat on the throne during the audience of the tenth day. See also Rao (1936, 147-8).

the festival. (...) They have come with their banners, their drums and flutes and various other musical instruments. Hundreds of ceremonies have gone on for the past seven days and ceremony after ceremony is going on. The Maharajah has been fasting in the midst of it; for religious ceremony requires it. And though he has been going through such purificatory penance, so to say, he bears it calmly without any show of it on his face.

The procession begins. Elephants have been caparisoned and *howdas* are fixed. Riders pour in. A horse shies. The rider got down and several rushed in. At last the horse was taken out. The cars are moving slowly, meandering and then stopping in front of the Rajbati. Hundreds go in and out of the Palace. Hundreds are on the verandahs of the Raghunath Temple and hundreds again have come to the verandah on the first floor and hundreds again have gone to the terrace. Those who are at the top are no doubt at a more advantageous position. The police is controlling the crowd. But I must say that the hill tribes are better disciplined than the so-called educated men who are not really educated. The Maharajah Saheb will be coming. All are expecting him. Lights have been lighted throughout the Palace. The torch-bearers are coming. The elephants are lowering themselves and squatting on the ground to facilitate guests getting on their backs with the help of ladders. Noble animals, indeed. On the elephants go the District Officers and the Agency Sub-Judge of Koraput. And there are other elephants but you cannot see all or know all in such a vast gathering. And yet only thirty-two police men are managing the whole crowd. It certainly goes to the credit of the people. Well, thousands were raising their necks to have a *darsan* of the Maharajah. I tried myself but utterly failed. Yet I was not disappointed. After all you see the Rajah in the Crowd and he is the symbol of the crowd. Someone said, 'where the Chhatram [royal umbrella] is, there is the Maharajah Saheb.' There were hundreds of swords - men carrying unsheathed swords. While the procession was going on, there was sword play. Mock sword fights were also going on with much gusto and dexterity too. Hundreds of flag-bearers were also there. The Paroja women with their tufts of hair well-tucked to the right and decorated with flowers and heavy brass ornaments on both the hands ... were marching happily with their protectors. But they are bold enough to go into the crowd sometimes jostling and elbowing at other times being jostled and elbowed. Sometimes some engaging lover is catching the hand of the Paroja girl and they are marching happily talking to each other many confidential things of future hope and love. There are the Gadaba girls in threes and more, arm in arm, with their heavy and large ear-rings of iron and brass and dressed colourfully and threading their way quite manfully. While they are so free and able

> to manage themselves, women of the middle classes are timid, shy and confined in *purdah* and see little of life.
>
> I got into the crowd and saw whatever little I could. Some mischievous fellows were holding the tall, long air balloons raising them high and moving them up and down with an indecent motive and cutting their way through the aboriginal girls, two or three of them tied together and lo! what a fun! The aboriginal girls are quite able to manage for themselves.
>
> We proceed to the Dussara *padia*. There is a pandal erected and the Maharajah Saheb with the Collector of Koraput and his wife ... several others of the Estate officials and others are there now seated. Music and dance go on. Maharajah Saheb goes through the whole *gamut* of it (he has to); others are not so attentive. The roaring of the cannon at intervals during the gala show goes on and makes the dancing girls as well as others startle and shiver. The whole night the aboriginals are going on with their rhythmic dances. I wonder what frenzy has caught them. The whole procession, when it gathered in the beginning and when it proceeded, left no doubt that it was a war procession.
>
> The brinjal ceremony is yet to be performed on the Dussara *padia* and yet it is 12 o' clock in the night. I came away in a car. (...)
>
> During the Dussara days at Jeypore one man, a Yogi, though not in reality but an imitation, keeps watch day and night. He is supposed not to eat and not to sleep these seven or eight days. (…)
>
> Lastly, the Yogi, the Maharaja and the Kanaka Durga of Jeypore are all combined into one – a symbol, an inspiration of piety, purity and unity of life. Then Maharajah when he is one with the people, is Maharajah. That is why I could not locate the Maharajah in the procession, greater than which one cannot expect.
>
> The brinjal on high is shot, the end is achieved. The morning breaks, the Dussara ends. (Sahu 1942, 33-6).[30]

[30] The author, L.N. Sahu, lived in Jeypore for three years as the guest of the king. Like the then king, Vikram Deo Varma, he was a member of the 'Servants of India Society', which had a strong reformist interest in the moral and economic 'uplifting' and 'improvement' of the indigenous population. Sahu's interest in the tribal peoples of Jeypore kingdom resulted in the publication of a book in 1942, financed by the king, from which this lengthy citation is taken.

Despite its obvious personal touch and sociological shortcomings, this description contains much valuable information which will structure the discussion which follows. In order to complete and corroborate the picture, my analysis will also make use of material which I gathered myself through interviews with people in Jeypore as well as my own observations of present-day celebrations in Jeypore and, if only at random, from reports on *dasarā* festivals in other parts of India.

To start with, Sahu repeatedly comments on the size of the gathering: 'People have thronged in their thousands', and there are 'hundreds' here and 'hundreds' there. This emphasis on magnitude characterizes the *dasarā* proceedings as *the* big event of the year.[31] Moreover, the participants are described as being in an extraordinarily exalted and festive mood. People came with their banners and their musical instruments; flirting and dancing went on all night, and the author wonders 'what frenzy has caught them'. Elsewhere, Sahu speaks of the 'bacchanalian enjoyment of the people' (ibid., 1).

From Sahu's account we sense something of the strong attraction that *dasarā* in Jeypore had for the tribals of the kingdom, who here are represented mainly by the Paroja and Gadaba. Apart from this, the account provides hardly any insights into the different social backgrounds of the participants. The author simply states that 'from all parts of Jeypore people have come to witness the festival'. Only in passing does he make social distinctions, for example when he contrasts well-behaved tribals with the less well-behaved, 'so-called educated men', or self-assertive tribal women (who move freely in the crowd) with timid Hindu women of the middle classes (who have to stay at home). All in all, however, the various participants seem to mingle freely and all of them merge, in the eyes of Sahu, into one huge unified and internally undifferentiated crowd. Even the king is described as being 'one with the people', or as the author also puts it: 'You see the Rajah in the Crowd and he is the symbol of the crowd'.

Such a view of the crowd as being a large, unified, undifferentiated gathering of joyous people may reflect, on the one hand, our eyewitness's own subjective impression as much as his lack of interest in a more accurate sociological perspective. On the other hand, it probably also captures part of the spirit of the *dasarā* festival in Jeypore and of the meaning it

[31] Concluding his report, Sahu (1942, 36) regrets that the number of participants was only half of what it used to be. This decrease in numbers suggests that, by the early 1940s, *dasarā* in Jeypore was already past its zenith and was about to fade into the comparatively insignificant event that it has become in the town today.

had for many of its participants. The underlying indigenous 'corporation theory' might be characterized as implying that during *dasarā* all subjects of the kingdom, no matter what their social backgrounds, came together and melted into one big mass in which they were equal among themselves and even at one with the king. In this respect, in the former kingdom of Jeypore *dasarā* had a morally unifying and socially levelling function.[32]

There are also indications in Sahu's account that *dasarā* had something of a carnival atmosphere and that normal restrictions in morals and behaviour were transgressed, for example, when balloons were used to make obscene gestures. The generally exalted and uninhibited mood also refers to kingship as a value in itself. When it is reported that 'hundreds go in and out of the Palace', this suggests an easing of the usual restrictions as regards access to and movement within the palace and indicates a temporary lessening of the respect usually shown to the seat of royal power. It might even be suggested that *dasarā* in Jeypore also had, at least partially, the character of a 'rite of inversion' or of 'a rite of rebellion'. This assumption gains support from the depiction of the king as a rather passive figure who calmly endures his lot, undergoes penance and, for one day, lets the people have their way: 'Maharajah Saheb goes through the whole gamut of it (he has to)', and he 'bears it calmly without any show of it on his face'.[33]

[32] In his exegesis of puranic texts, Kane reaches a similar conclusion when he writes: 'This Durgā-pūjā is very cosmopolitan in character. It could be performed not only by persons belonging to the four varṇas, but even by those who were outside the pale of the caste system. Durgā-pūjā has a congregational character and is not purely religious, but has a social element in it' (1958, 157).

[33] The thesis of *dasarā* as being partly a rite of inversion and/or rebellion is supported by the following statements from the *Kālikāpurāṇa* (as cited by Kane), which refer to a ceremony known as *śabarotsava* (and hence probably tribal in origin): 'The *visarjana* (sending away) of Devī should be made with festivals in the manner of śabaras, viz. people may make merry to their heart's content by throwing dust and mud, with auspicious sports and revelry, with indulgence in words and songs referring to male and female organs and with words expressive of the sexual act. The Devī becomes angry with him who does not abuse another and whom others do not abuse and pronounces on him a terrible curse' (1958, 177). Kane also comments: 'This provision that everyone, how highsoever, was to join in the śabarotsava was probably made for emphasizing that before the Devī the highest and the lowest were of equal status and every one must join in the frolics on the 10th tithi to show that all men were equal at least one day in the year' (ibid.). On the ritualization of excessive and obscene behaviour at *dasarā*, see also Jansen (1995, 149-50), Kinsley (1986, 113, 206).

The king was the centre and main actor of the proceedings. Sahu's account conveys the impression that the many thousands of participants who had come together in Jeypore were led by a single, ultimate motive, namely their desire to see the king: 'all are expecting him' and 'thousands were raising their necks to have a *darsan* of the Maharajah'. The king occupied this 'attractive' and central position in the *dasarā* proceedings not only on account of his being the polity's head in a political sense but first and foremost by virtue of being Kanaka Durga's principal devotee and the patron of the festival's ritual actions: our sources leave no doubt as to the essentially religious character of the festival and the king's ritual function in it.

Francis's account places emphasis on the great number of animal sacrifices carried out, especially on the eighth night of the proceedings. Sacrifices were made on each of the nine nights of *navarātrī*, but the 'great eighth night' (*mahāṣṭamī*), which celebrates the night on which Durga is believed to have killed the buffalo demon, was the climax as far as sacrifices were concerned.[34] On this night many blood sacrifices (*bali*s, *balidāna*s), mainly goats and buffaloes, were sponsored by the king and carried out under his patronage. Up until the middle of the nineteenth century, there were also human sacrifices to Kanaka Durga on this eighth night. This is apparent from colonial reports and can also be deduced from the specific way goats and buffaloes were killed. Thus, Thurston reports: 'It was the practice, a few years ago, at every Dassara festival in Jeypore … to select a specially fine ram, wash it, shave its head, affix thereto red and white bottu and nāmam (sect marks) between the eyes and down the nose, and gira it with a new white cloth after the manner of a human being. The animal being then fastened in a sitting posture, certain pūja (worship) was performed by a Brāhman priest, and it was decapitated. The substitution of animals for human victims is indicated by various religious legends' (1909 [vol. 3], 379). Senapati reports: 'The legend of human sacrifice is associated with this festival but since long only animals like the goats and the sheep are offered for sacrifice. Curiously enough the flowers which adorn the animals are described as "Mariah Puspa" as a reminiscent of human sacrifice. On the sixteenth day buffaloes are also sacrificed' (1966, 140).[35]

[34] The *Kālikāpurāṇa* mentions a great number of living creatures, like turtles, various kinds of birds, goats, buffaloes, tigers and human beings, which please the goddess as sacrificial victims—as long as they are male. See Kane (1958, 164-8) and Kinsley (1986, 113).

[35] Singh Deo (1939, 13) adds that these *meriah* flowers were brought especially from Nandapur.

The buffalo was not just a useful substitute for human beings as a sacrificial victim—he was *the* victim par excellence. This symbolic role becomes clear if one remembers how closely this festival and its accompanying mythology are linked with the killing of the demon-king Mahisha. The buffalo is one of the most important forms or manifestations assumed by the demon during his battle with Durga and in which he is finally slain by the goddess. This imaginative and symbolic significance of the buffalo is also expressed in the iconography of the 'demon-killing goddess' or *Durgāmahiṣāsuramardinī*, which depicts the goddess with a foot on the neck of the demon/buffalo lying on the ground. Both, Mahisha in mythology and iconography as well as the buffalo in ritual are killed by decapitating them with a sword.[36] The buffalo, thus, ideally represents the demon-king Mahisha in general besides embodying the specific qualities and attributes associated with the demon king: like Mahisha, the sacrificial buffalo counts as demonic, silly, strong, virile and threateningly lascivious. All in all, he represents the forces of chaos and rebellion. In the mythological killing of Mahisha and the actual killing of the buffalo during the eighth night of Durga *pūjā*, these evil and inauspicious forces are expelled jointly by goddess and king, and the cosmic order is regenerated.[37]

By contrast to Francis, Sahu, an active member of a group campaigning for the abolition of blood sacrifices, restricts himself to reporting that 'hundreds of ceremonies have gone on for the past seven days and ceremony after ceremony is going on'.[38] He is more informative only when it comes to describing those ritual roles of the king that are more in line with 'refined' Hindu practice: 'The Maharaja has been fasting in the midst of it; for religious ceremony requires it'; and 'he has been going through ... purificatory penance'. Sahu, here, points to the element of

[36] In India, the sword of the king often counts as a weapon which has been handed over to him by the goddess, contains her *śakti* and thus makes possible his military success. An enemy killed in battle by the king is, therefore, comparable to Mahisha. See Jansen (1995, 107-19). In many village temples of Orissa, Durga is represented not by an anthropomorphic *mūrti*, but by a sword.

[37] On the pan-Indian phenomenon of buffalo sacrifice, see Beck (1981), Biardeau (1984), Herrenschmidt (1981), Hiltebeitel (1980; 1981; 1985), Jansen (1995, 66-8) and Sax (1991, 139-55).

[38] Between 1907 and 1942, the years the two accounts by Francis and Sahu were written, the number of animals actually sacrificed most probably decreased considerably on account of the policy of the state and efforts by Hindu reformers against this practice.

atonement and purification which is, no doubt, important as well (and perhaps even more so in his reformist times than in the nineteenth and earlier centuries). However, he does not mention the fact that the king was also the patron of blood sacrifices and that, at one point or another, he personally beheaded a goat or buffalo. Sahu, thus, ignores the king's role as sacrifier, i.e. as nominal head of the numerous sacrifices, and as sacrificer, i.e. as someone performing the actual sacrifice. This omission on Sahu's part is striking, because he will have been well aware of the classical role of the Hindu king as lord of sacrifices or *yajamāna*.[39]

However, Sahu writes in a sort of historical diversion: 'Then came the *meriah* sacrifice to propitiate this Durga. The *meriah* is now represented by another name—that of *yogi*' (1942, 36). These statements are important not only because they give an indication of earlier (human) sacrifices during Durga *pūjā*, but also because the fasting *yogi* is introduced as a replacement of the former sacrificial victim.[40] Sahu's statement that 'lastly, the Yogi, the Maharajah and the Kanaka Durga of Jeypore are all combined into one' justifies an interpretation according to which the king not only acted as sacrifier and occasionally sacrificer, but that he was also identified with the victim (buffalo demon, buffalo, human being and *yogi*) and with Durga. This brings us back to Hocart's theory of ritual according to which, in sacrificial rites, a series of imitative identifications take place through which patron, victim and deity are made equivalent to each other. Through various symbolical transformations, which aim at making 'one thing equivalent to another so that by acting on one you can act on another' (1970a, 69), the patron of the ritual (ideally represented by the king) is made equivalent to the object of the ritual, namely life.[41]

[39] Typically, the king only functions as *sacrifiant*, not as *sacrificateur*, to use Hubert and Mauss's distinction (1964) between the patron of a sacrifice and the person who actually carries it out. In a personal interview with the present *yuvarāja* or 'crown prince' of Jeypore, Shakti Vikram Deo, I was told that Jeypore kings sometimes conducted sacrifices personally, though only at important events and in the presence of selected persons. At other, more public occasions they are said to have executed a first, non-lethal strike, before the actual decapitation was carried out by a priest. As a concession to tribal practices an axe instead of a sword was used for sacrifices. Dirks (1987, 98-9) recounts a legend in which a hero's ability to behead a buffalo with a single stroke is depicted as being vital to, and even constitutive of, his assumption of royal authority.

[40] In Jeypore the female members of the royal house, too, stay on a diet of milk and fruits only during the 'nine nights'.

[41] See my discussion of Hocart's theory of ritual in Schnepel (1988, Section 4). I first encountered the idea that the Hindu king might be identified with Mahisha

One aspect that is made clear in Sahu's account is the military and competitive character of the event. With regard to the procession leading to the festival ground after the *darbār* reception, he emphasizes that 'the whole procession, when it gathered in the beginning and when it proceeded, left no doubt that it was a war procession'. He also mentions that hundreds of people were carrying unsheathed swords and conducting mock fights with them. Military emblems were displayed in the procession itself, including, as mentioned by Francis, a white banner once captured in a victorious campaign against the neighbouring kingdom of Bastar.[42] Elephants, important 'weapons' in the traditional war strategy of Hindu kings and symbols of military strength and royal dignity up to the present day, headed the procession. On the festival ground itself, cannons were repeatedly fired and a shooting competition on a *brinjal* (aubergine) was held, in all probability a local variant of the classical *digvijaya* ritual in which the victory of a king (in the manner of Rama, who carries bow and arrows) in all cardinal directions and his central position as universal ruler (*cakravartin*) were symbolically expressed.[43]

---

during Durga *pūjā* in a conversation with Georg Berkemer. As far as the identification of the king with Durga is concerned, Dirks also observes (in connection with *dasarā* in Vijayanagara) that 'the king is depicted as the principal devotee of the deity with whom he is simultaneously identified. The emblems of both are conspicuously mixed together' (1987, 41).

[42] The white flag of the procession is probably identical with the one described in the *Journal of the Andhra Historical Research Society*: 'During this festival a flag of white cloth is hoisted outside the palace and on the flag is seen a rampant lion of white cloth sewn on it. The rampant lion must be the crest of the Goddess of the family' (vol. VI, 1). Senapati mentions two other insignia of the procession, whose origins are described as follows: 'In 1661 Abdullah, a relation of the Sultan of Golconda, invaded the Jeypore hills, but as the Rajah was loyal to the Sultan, he presented Viravikrama a sword ensign and standard together with a copper plate grant conferring upon him the title of Maharaja … the two golden ensigns called 'Mahi' and 'Marad' were being used by the Maharajas during the Dashara festival' (1966, 62).

[43] Different in content, though not necessarily in its competitive nature, was a scholarly meeting which took place in the palace during Durga *pūjā* and was attended by Brahmans, academics and other scholars invited by the king from all parts of India. That such events featured, at least in recent celebrations of *dasarā* in Jeypore, is confirmed by a collage of photographs showing the participants of one such meeting in the early 1930s, which I found hanging in the palace office. For parallels in the late medieval *dasarā* at Vijayanagara, see Dirks (1987, 66).

Sahu comments on the military character of the *dasarā* celebrations as well: 'Dussara festival is a commemoration of the ancient custom of preparations for a military campaign against the neighbouring states. After all agricultural operations have been fulfilled and some produce is gathered, they were making arms and weapons ready for the warfare. This was the main object of the function. Other things have been introduced afterwards' (1942, 36). The observation that the cool and dry season after the monsoon was preferred for invasions and military campaigns is relevant and verified by many historical examples.[44] However, it is doubtful whether, as Sahu seems to suggest, *dasarā* had its origin in a military custom which was later transformed into a solely commemorative rite. Rather, Durga *pūjā* and *dasarā* were always essentially ritual preparations for military enterprises undertaken directly afterwards. At *dasarā* the fighting mentality and military order among soldiers was annually re-established and heightened, so that the festival had quite a pragmatic effect as regards military undertakings and was always closely connected with them.

The procession was led by the king and the statue of Durga, accompanied by the king's eldest son and successor (*yuvarāja*), on elephants, almost as if they were leading an army into war. They were followed, also on elephants, by holders of the highest and most powerful offices in the kingdom. In the colonial period this privileged group also included British administrators like the collector, the superintendent of police and the chief engineer. Following these fifteen to twenty elephants at the head of the procession came a military band and thirty to forty cavalrymen on horses. Then came lesser officials and landlords on foot, followed by groups of soldiers from the kingdom's various territorial parts. The flags that were carried by each of these groups on well-decorated bamboo sticks in order to mark their distinctive local identities constituted such a spectacular and symbolically important element of this tenth day that in Jeypore *dasarā* was also known as '*jhaṇḍā yātrā*' or 'festival of flags'. The procession represented an ordered, well-organized military group in which differences of status, rank and territorial identity were carefully displayed. In this sense, it was a distinct contrast with the unordered, undisciplined and undifferentiated mass of spectators. It might even be suggested that the amorphous, over-joyous disorder of the crowd into which visitors from all parts of the Jeypore kingdom had initially melted was not just contrasted with the ordered and disciplined proces-

[44] See, for example, Gordon (1979, 11-2) and Sastri (1955, 293).

sion, but itself partially transformed in character, for some of the crowd integrated into and became part of the ordered military procession.

The war-like character of *dasarā* in Jeypore was not independent of, or in opposition to, the religious function of the ceremony. In this respect, it must be stressed that on the ninth day of Durga *pūjā*, which is also known as *āyudha pūjā*, members of the various occupational groups worship the implements and tools of their trade. A rickshaw driver will conduct *pūjā* for his cycle, a professor for his pen, a farmer for his plough, etc., while kings and soldiers were expected to worship their horses, elephants and weapons with lustrations. In this context Dirks observes that '*Āyudha* means weapon or arms, thus suggesting the possible military etymology of this rite, an etymology all the more convincing because of the specific associations of the next and final day with Ksatriyas and military victory' (1987, 39). Dirks also points out that this tenth day was known as *Vijayā-daśamī* or the (tenth) 'day of victory' (ibid.). As I have mentioned earlier, mythologically this victory refers to Rama's expedition against Ravana, to Durga's slaying of the buffalo demon and, in general, to victory over the entire world of demons. But *dasarā* as a royally patronized cult also signified a more worldly kind of victory, that of the king and his warriors over the enemies of the kingdom.[45]

To return to Kanaka Durga in Jeypore, she was also known and worshipped during *dasarā* as 'Vijayā Durga' or 'Victory Durga'. It is here that the ritually demonstrated positions of the king as chief devotee of the goddess and military leader connect. Put succinctly, the king worshipped the goddess at *dasarā* not as private individual or family head but as king and military leader. Durga herself was worshipped in her role as victorious, battle-proven *rāṣṭradevatā* or state deity, not as *kuladevatā* or tutelary deity of the family. This explains her gradual emergence out into the open: from her temple into the palace and from there to the head of the procession and onto the open-air festival ground. Hence, at *dasarā* in Jeypore, ritual centrality and military power were combined in the king—and these two aspects mutually reinforced each other. On the one hand, the king gained military strength on account of his ritual role in the cosmic drama of killing the demon and due to his close association with the warrior goddess Durga. During the *darbār*, when king and goddess together sat on the throne cushion or *gadi*, their relationship can even be

[45] As Dirks explains it: 'A king who did not celebrate Vijayadasami could not anticipate victory within the year' (1987, 40). On the military character of Durga *pūjā* and *dasarā*, see also Breckenridge (1977, 86), Fuller (1992, 125), Kane (1958, 186-94) and Kinsley (1986, 106-11).

characterized as hierogamous. On the other hand, the king could only assume this role as strong patron and virile husband of the goddess because he had already proved himself to be a successful 'thief' of the *mūrti* of the goddess, as holder of military power and as head of a hierarchically ordered polity which during the festivities magnificently displayed its common will, political unity and military might.

One of the functions of *dasarā* in Jeypore was to ritually emphasize the oneness, cohesiveness and military strength of the kingdom and regenerate these annually. However, another function of the ritual proceedings of the tenth day was also to display and renew the kingdom's territorial segmentation and the way in which positions of status and rank were allocated. Paradoxical as it might sound, *dasarā* could be said to have expressed and renewed both the kingdom's moral unity and its internal political divisions. It expressed, in Dirks' words, a 'hierarchical solidarity between chiefs and kings' (1987, 29).

If we examine the internal differentiations and hierarchical orderings expressed during *dasarā*, the first and most basic social distinction was that between the king and his subjects. Another dividing line appeared when the crowd divided into mere spectators and active participants in the procession. Within the procession, internal differentiation was further accentuated: the king and powerful men led on horseback or on elephants, while the rest of the marchers, subdivided into their respective military-territorial units, followed on foot. The fact that the flags behind which these groups rallied represented the local tutelary goddesses of their territorial divisions or villages is also significant for here, too, we find a mixture of military and ritual elements. Ultimately, there was not only the subordination of all the kingdom's territorial subdivisions under one king, but also a rallying of all the local goddesses behind Durga.

Internal differentiation reached its most prominent and expressive articulation during the *darbār* on this day, which took place before the procession. First of all, it divided the subjects of Jeypore into those who were allowed into the hall of ceremony and those who had to remain outside. This inside-outside division reflected the social and political distinction between the king, landed chiefs, nobles, important military functionaries and officials on the one hand and the remaining spectators, including the rank-and-file warriors who took part in the procession but were not allowed inside the hall, on the other. As elsewhere in India,[46]

[46] For other accounts of *darbār* hall proceedings, see Allen and Dwivedi (1984, 152-65), Cohn (1983, 165-79), Dirks (1987, 39-43), Fuller (1992, 125-7), Inden (1981, 106-8, 116), Mayer (1981, 144-5), McLane (1993, 13-4, 48-52, 107-11),

proceedings in the *darbār* hall of Jeypore were highly sensitive expressions of differentiations in rank and precedence. The king entered the hall first to sit in state and '*in communio*', as Mayer (1985) phrases it, with the goddess on the throne. The participants in the ceremony then entered the hall in reverse order of their standing and they would later leave it in direct order of their standing. During the proceedings in the hall, seating arrangements and other aspects of behaviour and etiquette, such as how close one was allowed to approach the throne, how the exchange of gifts was actually effected and what the transactions exactly entailed, further emphasized the distance between the king on the throne and the participants, expressing at the same time the hierarchical rankings and status differences of the latter. In the gift-exchange effected during the *darbār* the king and the goddess, jointly seated on the throne, established themselves not only as the exemplary centre of the cosmos but also as the centre of a redistributive process, which both united those approaching the throne in a position subordinate to the centre and at the same time established status differences among them.[47]

4. A 'rebel *dasarā*' in Bissamcuttack

The structure of hierarchical relations thus made manifest was not a matter of vague speculation or public opinion but fixed by royal decree and historical precedent, prior to being displayed in the hall. Permission to enter the hall, the allocation of symbolic space within it and the various forms of ritual honours displayed during the audience reflected, in a sort of annually recurring symbolic show, the kingdom's political hierarchy, as well as the social, moral and cosmological order upon which the welfare of the kingdom and its inhabitants was thought to depend. But pro-

---

Price (1979, 210-4), Sewell (1970, 228-378), Sharma (1965, 21-6), Stein (1980, 384-90) and Toffin (1981).

47 The gifts which some of the lesser chiefs made to the king-on-the-throne were token gifts and often consisted of one rupee only or, in the cases of tribal chiefs, of jungle products, the king's return gifts being pieces of cloth. Other chiefs, however, had to pay substantial amounts of money. Bissamcuttack, as noted earlier, had to pay 1,500 rupees. Traditionally payments were made in gold, later also in the form of British notes which bore the head of Queen Victoria. Although the exchange which took place inside the *darbār* hall can be regarded as 'ritualistic' rather than 'economic' in character, it must not be forgotten that most chiefs were obliged to make one of their two annual payments of tribute on the occasion of *dasarā*. During this event there, therefore, existed a close iconnection between 'more economic' and 'more ritual' kinds of payment or gift.

ceedings during *dasarā* in Jeypore were more than just a reflection of actual relationships of power and status and more than just a histrionic display by a 'theatre state'. In practice, matters of honour and precedence were fluid and changeable, and as such they were not fixed once and for all but had to be re-established and reconfirmed on an annual basis. On account of this dynamism they were always carefully guarded and, at times, hotly disputed. In particular the king, as principal ordering authority and symbolic point of reference in relation to whom all other persons were ranked, could and indeed did use the occasion to reshuffle the order in his own interest. He could, for example, introduce someone new into the favoured ranks of *darbār* hall attendants, elevate one chief whom he trusted, and humiliate another who had incurred his anger during the past year. All this the king could do by manoeuvring and changing small, but carefully observed and highly valued matters of etiquette. He could even resort to a dramatic act of ritual ostracism by altogether barring some person of standing from attending the festivities in the *darbār* hall, as happened in 1877 to the *thātrāja* of Bissamcuttack. Hence, relations of power and the hierarchical order in the kingdom were not only reflected and ceremonially fixed during the *darbār*, but also newly mixed and redistributed.

Those who were allowed inside the hall and seated according to their status were all united *vis-à-vis* the king in their capacity as loyal subordinates. By their very attendance at the *darbār* and their display of deferential conduct towards the king, particularly through the act of gift-exchange, they all made a common symbolic statement signifying their lasting, even reinvigorated allegiance to the king. At the same time, they expressed the continued incorporation into the kingdom of the territories or groups they represented. The *dasarā* festival, therefore, displayed and renewed the king's authority, while, at a higher level, it constituted a spiritual renewal of the unity, strength and welfare of the kingdom and of the cosmos at large.

To many chiefs and officials the annual participation in the *dārbar* hall proceedings, thus, provided a welcome opportunity for a prestige-enhancing display of status and legitimacy. Demonstrating loyalty at the *dārbar* during *dasarā* not only expressed their subordination to the king's all-encompassing authority, it also symbolized, reconfirmed or established that they stood in a privileged relationship to the king and even shared in his sovereignty. The desire to obtain the king's public acknowledgement was especially great when a chief or functionary, in line with the prevailing custom of primogeniture, had already taken over his deceased father's position de facto during the past year but still lacked final authorization from the king. *Dasarā* was the main occasions for the inaugural visits of such persons. It was in the course of this festival that they first paid homage to the king, that they formally, and at times contractually, accepted the existing or revised conditions of office or tenureship and that they paid an often considerable 'nomination fee'. In turn, they were acknowledged and legitimized in their positions by the king, which he usually expressed by binding a turban-like sari around the appointee's head and (in modern times) handing over a legally binding certificate. What is more, when senior officers and important tenure-holders were issued their titles and swore allegiance, they were doing so in front of Durga as well. Hence, their acts of showing homage and swearing loyalty were made not only towards the king but also towards the kingdom's tutelary deity. Consequently, their legitimation derived from both a secular and a higher spiritual source. *Dasarā* therefore had inaugural and authorizing functions as far as key administrative and politico-economic positions in the kingdom were concerned. And again, the proceedings at *dasarā* did not just reflect and renew existing tenures and hierarchical relationships; they were also constitutive of privileges and obligations, imbuing office-holders with higher royal and divine sanction.[48]

However, chiefs who felt bold and powerful enough to strive for more independent positions, or to seek a different source of legitimation, saw in their attendance at the *Durgā-pūjā* and *dasarā* festivities in Jeypore an enforced and unwanted manifestation of their subordination. These individuals—in most cases semi-independent holders of estates and military fiefs at the kingdom's borders—preferred to celebrate their own *dasarā* festivals rather than go to Jeypore as subordinates. Historical instances of such refusals to attend are many (Bissamcuttack was not the only case) and one could say that 'ritual absenteeism' on the occasion of *dasarā* was an integral part of the little kingdom's politico-ritual dynamics.

Instances of ritual absenteeism can be observed to have increased dramatically from the mid-nineteenth century onwards, when the Jeypore

[48] This refers to the position of the king as well, because his sitting on the throne at *dasarā* and the other rites he went through were, at one level, just the annual re-enactment and renewal of his erstwhile ritual anointment (*abhiṣeka*) and installation. During my stay in Parlakimedi, I noticed that the road which leads to Manikeshvari's abode is called '*Anka* road'. *Anka* years are the years of a king's rule (sometimes of a dynasty), and the counting starts only after the inauguration ceremony in front of the goddess is completed. The street name thus indicates the close connection between royal legitimacy and divine sanction that exists in Parlakimedi and elsewhere. On the concept of *anka*, see Berkemer (1993, 131-6), Marglin (1985, 165), Mukherjee (1953, 24) and Wilson (1968).

king often had to call upon colonial courts in order to enforce a chief's attendance or to dismiss a recalcitrant absentee, whereas in earlier times he would have used military force and other means of compulsion to achieve these ends. Thus, in the case of several chiefs their attendance at *dasarā* with a fixed number of warriors and a stipulated gift was an expressly fixed service obligation. As such, it was of a compulsory nature, not an act of homage rendered voluntarily. We may here recall Francis's statement that 'many of the inams and mokhasas in the estate ... have been granted on the express condition that the grantees do this annual service' (1907, 263).[49] The refusal of a chief who was under such a service obligation to attend at *dasarā* at Jeypore constituted, from the king's point of view, an act of insubordination and a breach of contractual obligations; more fundamentally, though, it brought to light secessionist tendencies in one of the kingdom's territorial sub-units. From a rebel chief's point of view, absenting himself from *dasarā* was one of the most forceful public statements of his aspirations for greater independence, even autonomy.

A further expression of the 'secessionist' tendencies of a rebel chief, which logically complemented his ritual absenteeism, was for him to hold a *dasarā* festival of his own.[50] Often it was sufficient for a chief to adapt the tribal or local festivities already established around the Hinduized cults of autochthonous goddesses to the Jeypore model. What was important was that in their own festivals the 'rebels' assumed a central position comparable to that of the Jeypore king in his celebrations. In this way, they could ritually bind the chiefs, estate-holders and subjects of their domains to their own overlordship while preventing them from going to Jeypore and demonstrating their allegiance there.

A glimpse of how *dasarā* was celebrated in Bissamcuttack under *thātrāja* rule will illustrate these more general observations in some detail.[51] In Bissamcuttack the festivities centred around the tutelary deity,

[49] On this point, see also Behuria (ed. 1965, 57, 68), Francis (1907, 273, 303), Sahu (1942, 25), Senapati (1966, 284), as well as Chapter IV above.

[50] Senapati's list of places (1966, 467) in which *dasarā* festivals were held in modern Koraput District includes Bissamcuttack, Malkangiri, Kotpad, Nowrangpur, Rayagada, Gunupur, Gudari and Umarkot, that is, essentially those places in which powerful, semi-independent and, more often than not, 'rebellious' chiefs had their seats.

[51] The following account is based on an interview with Sri Mohana Pujari, the chief priest of the Markama temple, in October 1991. I was also able to observe the festival in Bissamcuttack during that year. Further information can be obtained from Nayak (1989, 39-40, 77, 178-86).

the now well-known goddess Markama, and not around the Durga *mūrti*, which, it will be recalled, had been installed in a temple within the walls of the fortress after the *thātrāja* had failed to move Markama out of her grove.[52] However, a temporary *maṇḍapa* or exhibition platform was erected in the centre of Bissamcuttack during Durga *pūjā*, and sword representations of Markama, Bhairava and Niamraja were worshipped there. On the seventh night of Durga *pūjā*, which was dedicated specifically to *khaṇḍa* or sword *pūjā* at the *maṇḍapa*, the centre of activities moved from the Markama temple at the edge of town to the centre.

The ritual climax was on the eighth night or *āsṭhamī rātrī*, when many Dongria Kondh, in festive dress and carrying knives, axes and clubs, came down from the Niamgiris to Bissamcuttack town. Earlier they would offer sacrifices to their respective clan deities as well Niamraja, the mythical ancestor of all Dongria Kondh. Now, in Bissamcuttack, it was their right to sacrifice five buffaloes sponsored by the *thātrāja*. For the sacrifices, the Dongria Kondh were subdivided into five groups constituted on the basis of membership of residential units.[53] First, the largest group, consisting of members of five villages, assembled beneath a large, sacred tree near the Niamraja temple. This group carried a white umbrella (*chattra*), brought from the original Niamraja temple in the mountains, in front of them. On their arrival, the *pāīk* priests of the Markama temple took the umbrella, which symbolizes royalty, and carried it to the *maṇḍapa* platform in the centre of the town, where it was honoured with *pūjā*. The priests then fetched the sword of Niamraja from the *maṇḍapa* platform and took it in procession back to the Niamraja temple, where it was normally kept. At this temple one of the *pāīk* priests touched the buffalo dedicated to Niamraja with the sword, after which the actual sacrifice was carried out. However, the animal was not killed by decapitation with a sword or axe, but in the typical Kondh way called *juro*: all the Kondh belonging to the sacrificial group rushed to the beast with their knives and axes and ecstatically hacked it to death, trying to grasp as many pieces of bloody meat as possible. Next, a sacrificial group consisting of members of nine Kondh villages assembled at the temple of Markama, where a further sacrifice of the *juro* type was carried out. Then two other groups, one consisting of members of three Kondh villages and the other of two

[52] See Chapter V, Section 4, above.

[53] Among the Dongria Kondh, residence is largely determined by membership of a patriclan. It can, therefore, be assumed that the five village groups mentioned by Mohana are identical with the clans Nisika, Wadeka, Sikoka, Kadraka and Pusika listed by Nayak (1989, 180).

Kondh villages, gathered at the Durga and Thakurani temples, where further blood sacrifices of the same type took place. Finally, a group from a Kondh village lying in the Bissamcuttack plateau valley (not in the Niamgiris) assembled at the temple of Bhairava, where a buffalo was sacrificed, not in the *juro* manner, but by beheading it with a single stroke of Bhairava's sword. On the morning of the ninth day, all Dongria Kondh moved to the palace of the *thātrāja*, where they presented him with gifts of bananas, oranges, coconuts, tobacco and other jungle products. In return, the *thātrāja* gave away red saris to the heads of clans and ritual dignitaries of the Kondh.[54]

5. Concluding remarks

During Durga *pūjā* in Bissamcuttack, therefore, there existed a ritual system, with the *thātrāja* as patron, in which offerings to the shaktic-tantric temples of the town and gift exchanges in the palace were made. Through a sort of ritual 'division of labour' the estate's *ādivāsis* were internally divided into distinct sacrificial groups. The ritual links established between the Dongria Kondh and the *thātrāja* expressed not so much subordination as mutual recognition and solidarity, in accordance with the semi-autonomous status of these mountain inhabitants. Nayak also underlines this point:

> The Dongria were presenting the king with gifts and mementoes in recognition of the greater friendship with him, who in lieu of it gave one new cloth as headgear to each of the leaders representing the clans. This was symbolic of the king's acknowledgement of the

[54] Sahu (1942, 178-82) discusses the *dasarā* festival in Bissamcuttack as celebrated in the 1930s, that is, after the loss of power of the *thātrāja* dynasty. His report shows some deviations from the account given here. For example, according to Sahu, the Dongria Kondh only arrived in Bissamcuttack on the ninth day, to make music, dance and celebrate in other ways all day and throughout the ninth night. Buffaloes were sacrificed on the morning of the tenth day, followed by an exchange of gifts with the *amīn*, as local representative of the king, at around midday. Moreover, Sahu mentions four sacrifices only, the sacrifice at the Bhairavi temple not being in his list. As for the sacrificial groups at the temples of Niamraja, Thakurani, Durga and Markama, he gives the names of ten, four, six and seven villages respectively. If one compares these villages with the list of Dongria Kondh villages given by Nayak (1989, 221-6), one sees that they all come from a single *pañcāyat* (of altogether nine Dongria Kondh *pañcāyats*), namely Kurli Grama situated directly to the west of Bissamcuttack. See also the map in Nayak (1989, 32).

> glory of the Dongria over the earth under their occupation. Acknowledgement of their glory and political importance … is of primary importance to them over any other affairs relating to the zamindar king. (Nayak 1989, 184)

However, the element of subordination found in the relationship between the king and the chiefs, evident in Jeypore, was not altogether absent in Bissamcuttack: on the tenth day, another *darbār* was held for the chiefs, functionaries, soldiers and other dignitaries of the estate who were directly subordinate to the *thātrāja*. Here, too, the governors of the large fiefs on the periphery of the Bissamcuttack estate were duty bound to appear at the *dasarā* festival with a fixed number of warriors and to hand over a certain amount of money as a ceremonial gift, receiving white saris in return. In the years in which the *thātrāja*s went to Jeypore for *dasarā*, these governors and their warriors formed part of the 500-man contingent of the *thātrāja* and contributed money for the latter's donation to the king.

As in Jeypore, the *dasarā* itself, when hundreds of people arrived in Bissamcuttack from near and far, had a festive character with dances, traditional theatre, the looking for and taking away of brides, and shooting competitions. Many elements of the Jeypore *dasarā* found a local echo in Bissamcuttack, such as the carnival-like boisterousness, the display of military power, the great number of sacrifices, and the ceremonial use of royal symbols like the sword and the umbrella. Royal ritual in general, and the *dasarā* festival of Jeypore in particular, thus provided an important model. In Bissamcuttack we are, therefore, faced with the phenomenon stressed by Dumont (1970, 160-2), namely, that in India royal functions were imitated, in a descending line, on all levels of political and territorial authority, down to the village headman.[55] The *thātrāja*, as the patron of politico-ritual events in Bissamcuttack, adopted a role in imitation of the king of Jeypore. In doing so, however, he remained rebelliously absent from the *dasarā* events in Jeypore and also set himself apart from the model with his own *dasarā* festival, even denying the model's legitimacy to some extent. At the same time, by holding his own *dasarā* festival, he increased his reputation with his immediate subordinates and the *ādivāsi*s of the nearby mountains, as well

[55] Hocart (1950, 155) also refers to the phenomenon of the 'degradation of the royal style'.

as created the preconditions for demanding their personal loyalty and military help in case of conflict with the king of Jeypore.[56]

Finally, let us remember that the king of Jeypore also celebrated his own *dasarā* festival in a 'rebellious' manner. For, according to the family chronicle of the Jeypore kings, the statue of Durga stolen from the Gajapatis was central to the celebrations in Jeypore.[57] The fact that this theft is not mentioned in the chronicle of the Gajapatis only underlines that this and other traditions cannot be measured solely by the scale of academic historiography; they are, instead, manifestations of a politics of remembrance and/or of a politics of silence and forgetting.

[56] After the dismissal of the last *thātrāja* in the 1920s, the Jeypore kings, represented by their *amīn*s, and after 1952 by the *tahsīldār*s, the local representatives of the Indian government, continued the relationship with the Dongria Kondh at *dasarā* in the manner described. Only from the 1960s, when buffalo sacrifices were abandoned under pressure of reformists, did the appearance of the Dongria Kondh at *dasarā* peter out. Today, the greatest attraction of the ritual year in Bissamcuttack is the Jagannath car festival.

[57] The ruler of the neighbouring kingdom of Bastar, in Madhya Pradesh, complained to the British colonial government that 'the Raja of Jeypore was to pay homage to him as his lord by attending every Dasara festival with three hundred peons, which conditions the Jeypore Raja strongly refuted' (Behuria ed. 1965, 57).

ILLUSTRATIONS

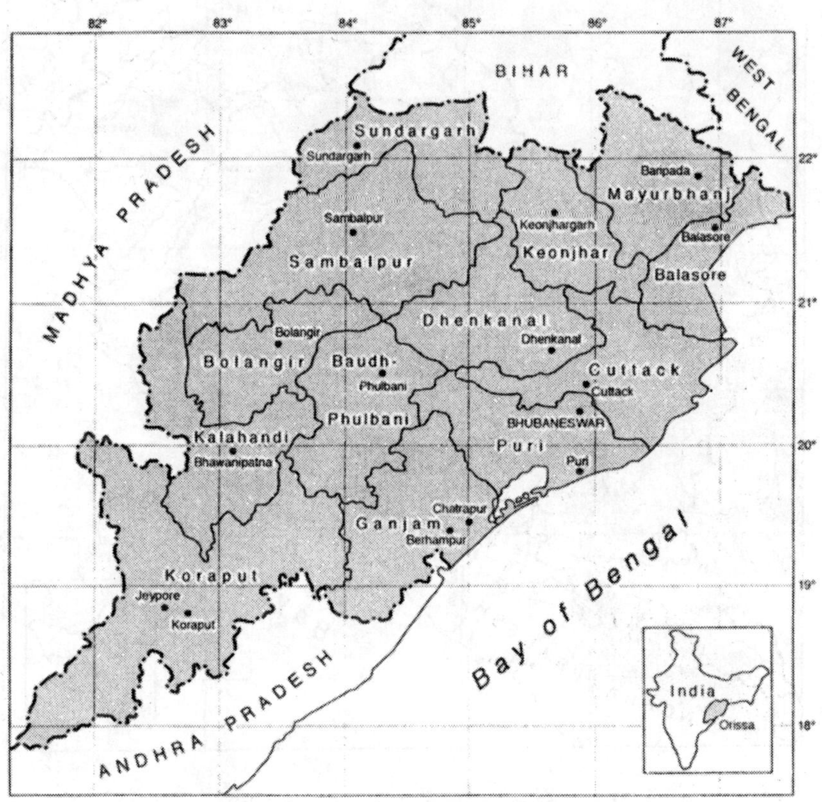

Map 1: Traditional districts of Orissa.

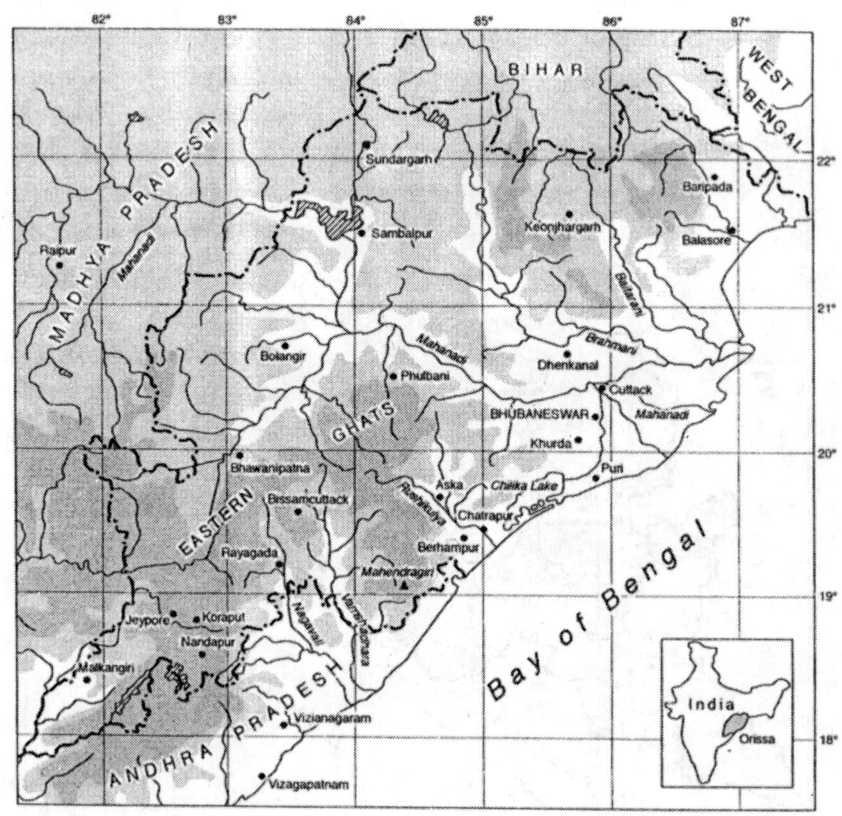

Map 2: Geographical map of Orissa.

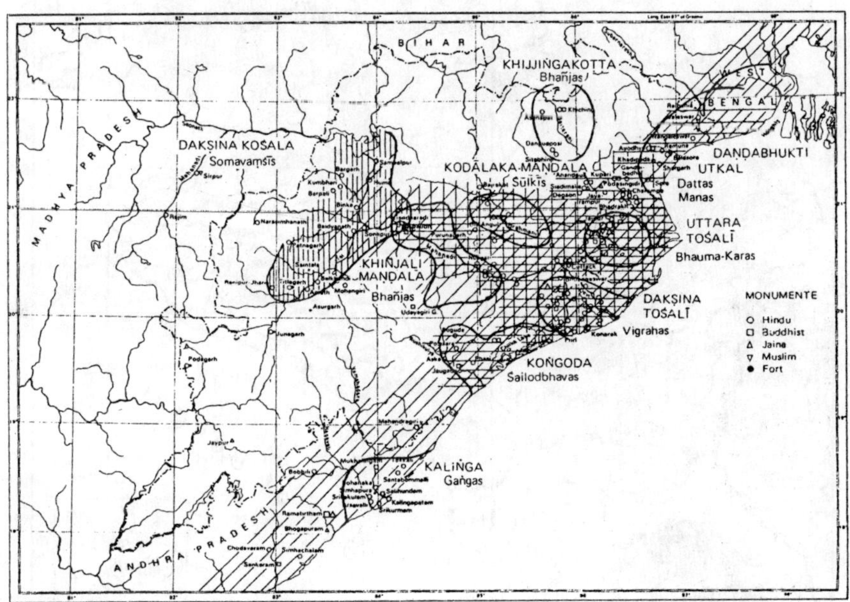

Map 3: Early nuclear areas and kingdoms of Orissa (from Kulke 1979a).

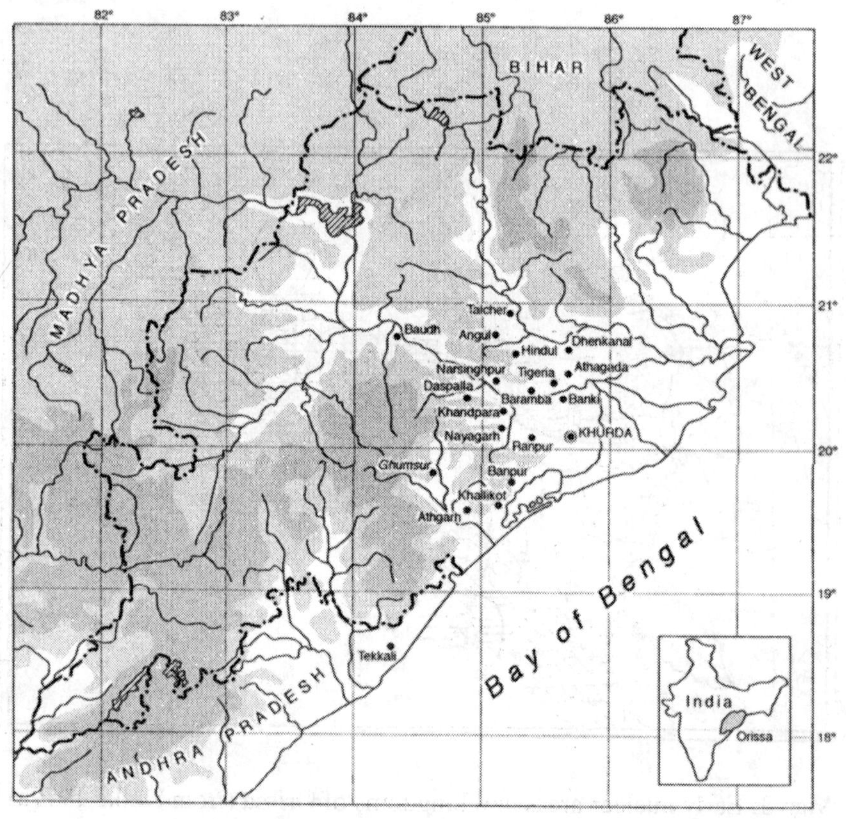

Map 4: *Gaḍajāta*-kingdoms (based on Kulke 1979a).

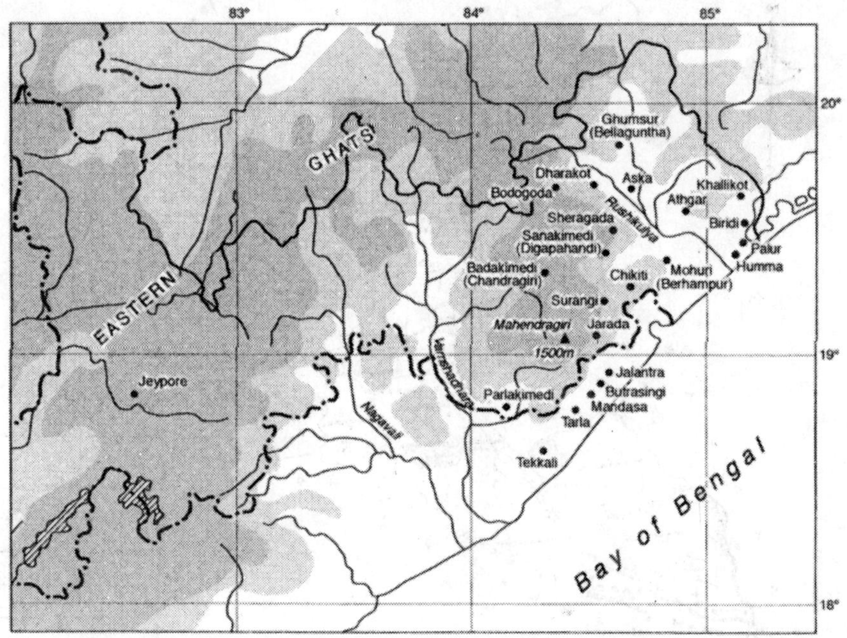

Map 5: Little kingdoms of south Orissa.

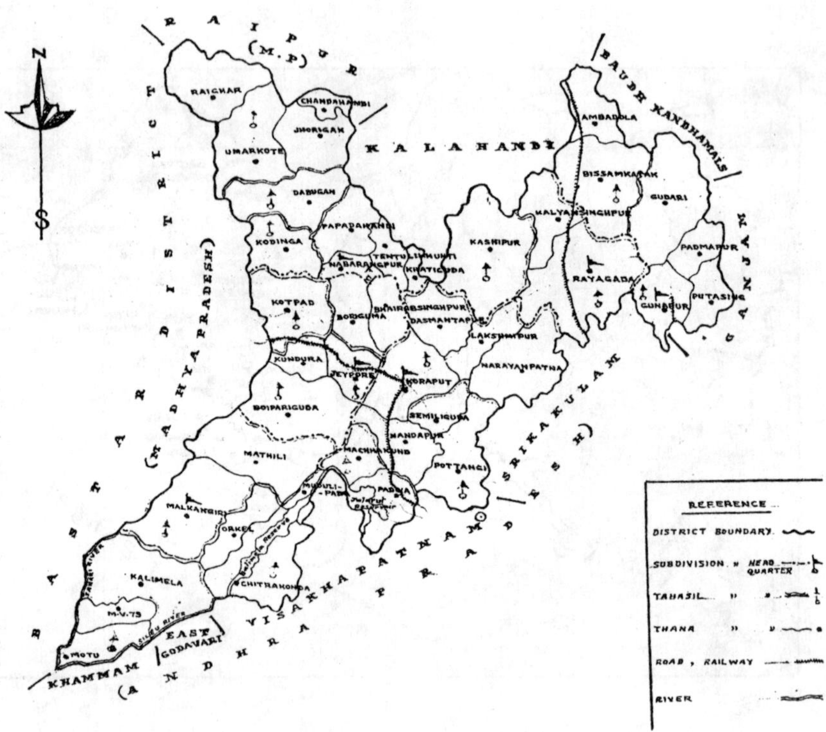

Map 6: Koraput-District.

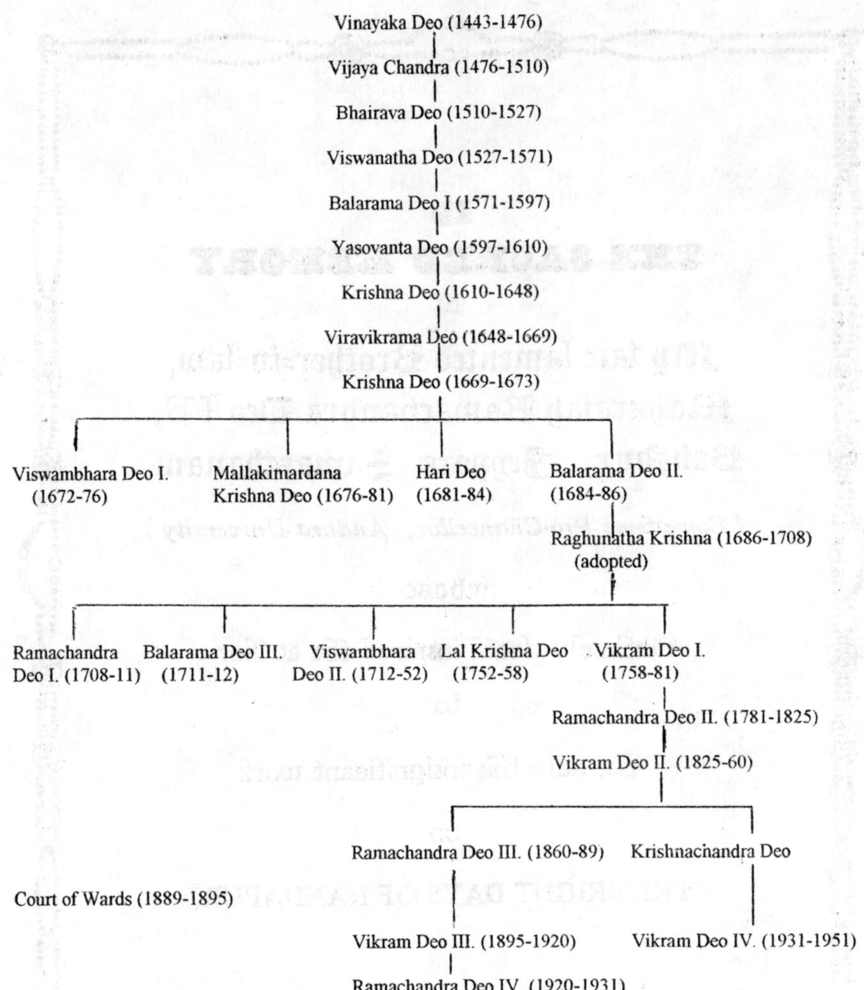

Figure 1: Genealogy of the Jeypore Suryavamshis.

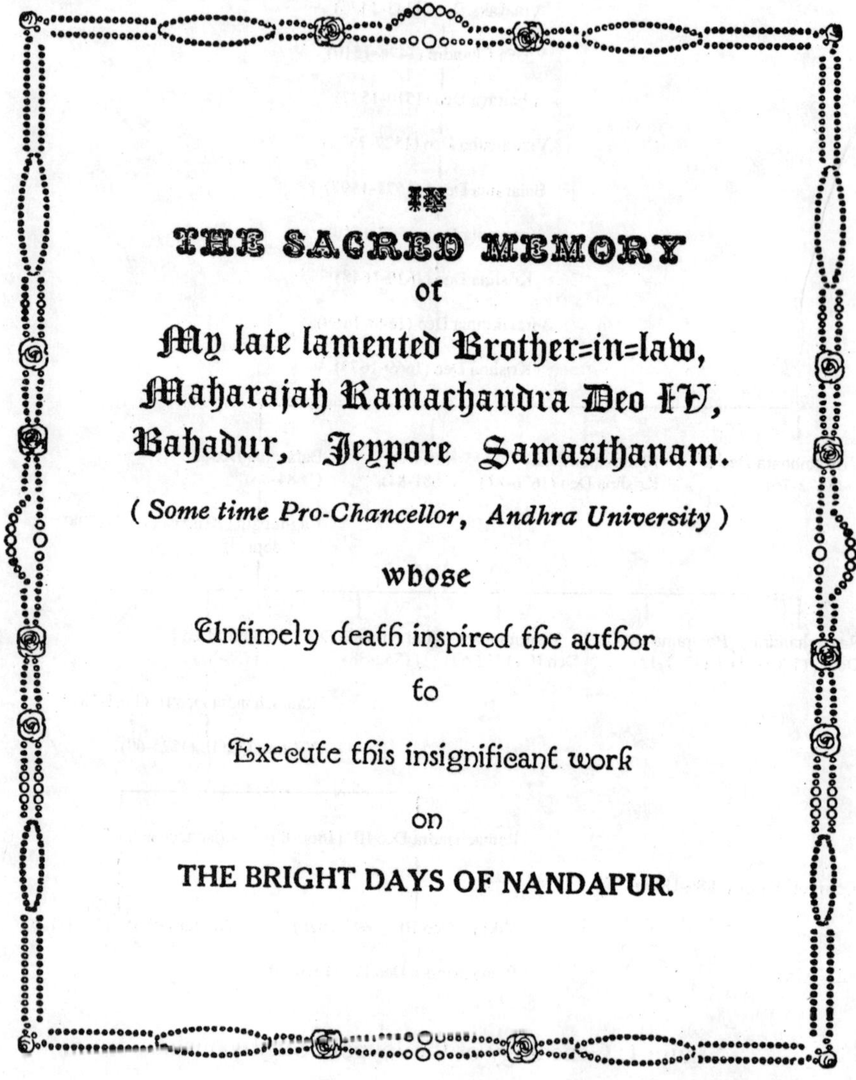

IN

THE SACRED MEMORY

of

My late lamented Brother-in-law,

Maharajah Ramachandra Deo IV,

Bahadur, Jeypore Samasthanam.

(*Some time Pro-Chancellor, Andhra University*)

whose

Untimely death inspired the author

to

Execute this insignificant work

on

THE BRIGHT DAYS OF NANDAPUR.

Figure 2: Dedication (from Singh Deo 1939).

Plates 1 and 2: Possessed priest at the Markama temple.

Plates 3 and 4: Khambeshvari; temple of Mohuri Kalua.

Plates 5 and 6: Mohuri Kalua; Budhi Thakurani.

Plates 7 and 8: Stones in front of the Majhighariani temple; Majhighariani.

Plates 9 and 10: Markama; temple of Markama.

Plates 11 and 12: Wooden posts; stone of human sacrifices.

Plates 13 and 14: Chamunda (Orissa State Museum); Manikeshvari.

BIBLIOGRAPHY

Abolition 1958. *Abolition of Estates* (Administration Report, November 1952-April 1956), Cuttack: Board of Revenue.

Acharya, P. 1949. 'Atharagada or Eighteen Forts', in *Proceedings of the Indian History Commission* 12, 282-4.

Acharya, P. 1955/6. 'Ancient Routes in Orissa', in *Orissa Historical Research Journal* 4, 43-50.

Ahmad, A. 1991. 'Between Orientalism and Historicism: Anthropological Knowledge of India', in *Studies in History* 7, 135-63.

Aitchison, C.U. (ed.) 1930 [1909]. 'A Collection of Treaties, Engagements and Sanads' (10 vols.), Calcutta: Government Press.

Allen, C. and S. Dwivedi 1984. *Lives of the Indian Princes*, London: Century Publishing.

Altekar, A.S. 1958 [1949]. *State and Government in Ancient India*, Delhi: Motilal Banarsidass.

Anderson, B. 1991 [1983]. *Imagined Communities: Reflections on the Origin and Spread of Nationalism*, London: Verso.

Anderson, P. 1974. *Lineages of the Absolutist State*, London: Verso.

Anjaneyulu, M.S.R. 1982. *Vizagapatnam District, 1769-1834: A History of the Relations between the Zamindars and the East India Company*, Waltair: Andhra University Press.

Appadurai, A. 1974. 'Right and Left Hand Castes in South India', in *Indian Economic and Social History Review* 11, 216-60.

Appadurai, A. 1977. 'Kings, Sects and Temples in South India', in Stein (ed.), 47-74.

Appadurai, A. 1981. *Worship and Conflict under Colonial Rule: A South Indian Case*, Cambridge: Cambridge University Press.

Appadurai, A. 1983. 'The Puzzling Status of Brahmin Temple Priests in Hindu India', in *South Asian Anthropologist* 4, 43-52.

Appadurai, A. 1993. 'Number in Colonial Imagination', in Breckenridge and van der Veer (eds.), 314-39.

Appadurai, A. and C.A. Breckenridge 1976. 'The South Indian Temple: Authority, Honour and Disribution', in *Contributions to Indian Sociology* (N.S.) 10, 187-211.

Appadurai, A. 1985. 'Scale and Social Formations in South India, 1350-1750', in Frykenberg and Kolenda (eds.), 51-66.

Babb, L.A. 1975. *The Divine Hierarchy: Popular Hinduism in Central India*, New York: Columbia University Press.

Bahro, R. 1990. *Die Alternative: Zur Kritik des real existierenden Sozialismus*, Berlin: Treptower Verlagshaus.

Bailey, A.M. and J. Llobera (eds.) 1981. *The Asiatic Mode of Production: Science and Politics*, London: Routledge and Kegan Paul.

Bailey, F.G. 1957. *Caste and the Economic Frontier: A Village in Highland Orissa*, Manchester: Manchester University Press.

Bailey, F.G. 1960. *Tribe, Caste and Nation: A Study of Political Activity and Political Change in Highland Orissa*, Bombay: Oxford University Press.

Bailey, F.G. 1961. '"Tribe" and "Caste" in India', in *Contributions to Indian Sociolology* 5, 6-19.

Baker, C. 1976. 'Tamilnad Estates in the Twentieth Century', in *Indian Economic and Social History Review* 12, 1-44.

Bakker, H.T. (ed.) 1992. *The Sacred Centre as the Focus of Political Interest*, Groningen: Egbert Forsten.

Ballhatchet, K. and D. Taylor (eds.) 1984. *Changing South Asia: Religion and Society*, London: University of London.

Banerjee, R.D. 1928. 'Rajput Origins in Orissa', in *Modern Review* 43, 285-329.

Banerjee, R.D. 1930/1. *History of Orissa* (2 vols.), Calcutta: R. Chatterjee.

Banerjee, S. 1969. 'Ethnographic Study of the Kuvi-Kandha', in *Anthropological Survey of India*, Calcutta.

Bārabāṭi Vīrakṛṣṇadev 1816. *Bārabāṭi Vīrakṛṣṇadev*. Orissa Research Project Manuscripts 455 (translated from Telugu by S.N. Rajaguru), Heidelberg: South Asia Institute.

Bayly, C.A. 1992 [1983]. *Rulers, Townsmen and Bazaars: North Indian Society in the Age of British Expansion, 1770-1870*, Delhi: Oxford University Press.

Bayly, S. 1984. 'Hindu Kingship and the Origin of Community: Religion, State and Society in Kerala, 1750-1850', in *Modern Asian Studies* 18, 177-213.

Bayly, S. 1989. *Saints, Goddesses and Kings: Muslims and Christians in South Indian Society, 1700-1900*, Cambridge: Cambridge University Press.

Beattie, J.H.M. and G. Lienhardt (eds.) 1975. *Studies in Social Anthropology: Essays in Memory of E.E. Evans-Pritchard*, Oxford: Oxford University Press.

Beck, B. 1970. 'The Right-Left Division of South Indian Society', in *Journal of Asian Studies* 29, 779-98.

Beck, B. 1981. 'The Goddess and the Demon: A Local South Indian Festival and Its Wider Context', in *Puruṣārtha* 5, 83-136.

Behera, D. 1984. *Freedom Movement in the State of Ghumsur in Orissa, 1836-66*, Calcutta: Punthi Pustak.

Behera, D. 1987. *The Bhanjas (The House of Upendra Bhanja) and the Khonds of Orissa*, Calcutta: Punthi Pustak.

Behuria, N.C. (ed.) 1964. *Final Report on the Major Settlement Operation in Ganjam Ex-Estate Areas, 1938-1962*, Cuttack: Orissa Government Press.

Behuria, N.C. 1965. *Final Report on the Major Settlement Operations (Koraput District), 1938-64*, Cuttack: Orissa Government Press.

Beidelman, T.O (ed.) 1971. *The Translation of Culture: Essays to E.E. Evans-Pritchard*, London: Tavistock Publication.

Bell, R.C.S. 1945. *Orissa District Gazetteers: Koraput*, Cuttack: Orissa Government Press.

Bendix, R. 1977 [1960]. *Max Weber: An Intellectual Portrait*, Berkeley: University of California Press.

Berkemer, G. 1992. 'The "Centre out There" as State Archive: The Temple in Siṃhācalam', in Bakker (ed.), 119-30.

Berkemer, G. 1993. *Little Kingdoms in Kalinga: Ideologie, Legitimation und Politik regionaler Eliten*, Stuttgart: Franz Steiner Verlag.

Berkemer, G. 1997. 'The Chronicle of a Little Kingdom: Some Reflections on the Tekkali tālūka Jamīṃḍārla-vaṃśāvali', in Kölver (ed.), 65-95.

Berkson, C. 1995. *The Divine and Demoniac: Mahisa's Struggle with Durga*, Delhi: Oxford University Press.

Bernier, F. 1914 [1710]. *Travels in the Moghul Empire, A.D. 1656-1668*, Oxford: Milford.

Béteille, A. 1965. 'Social Organization of Temples in a Tanjore Village', in *History of Religions* 5, 74-92.

Béteille, A. 1980. 'On the Concept of Tribe', in *International Social Science Journal* 32, 825-8.

Bhaduri, A. 1976. 'The Evolution of Land Relations in Eastern India under British Rule', in *Indian Economic and Social History Review* 13, 45-58.

Biardeau, M. 1981. 'The Salvation of the King in the Mahābhārata', in *Contributions to Indian Sociology* 15, 75-97.

Biardeau, M. 1984. 'The Śami Tree and the Sacrificial Buffalo', in *Contributions to Indian Sociology* 18, 1-23.

Biardeau, M. 1989. 'Brahmans and Meat-Eating Gods', in Hiltebeitel (ed.), 19-33.

Biardeau, M. (ed.) 1981. *Autour de la Déesse Hindoue* (Puruśārtha, vol. 5), Paris: Ecole Francaise d'Extreme Orient.

Biller, J. 1986. *Zur Entstehung von Herrschaft und Staat: Das Beispiel des indischen Regionalreiches von Orissa*, Freiburg: Hochschul Verlag.

Blake, S.P. 1979. 'The Patrimonial-Bureaucratic Empire of the Mughals', in *Journal of Asian Studies* 39, 77-94.

Bloch, M. 1961 [1940]. *Feudal Society* (2 vols.), London: Routledge and Kegan Paul.

Boal, B.M. 1982. *The Konds: Human Sacrifice and Religious Change*, Westminster: Aris and Phillips Ltd.

Bodokimedi Family History no date. *Bodokimedi Family History*. (Family history submitted to the District Collector of Ganjam in 1947 in support of a pending legal case.)

Boholm, Å (ed.) 1996. *Political Rituals*, Gothenburg: Institute for Advanced Studies in Social Anthropology.

Brara, N.V. 1998. *Politics, Society and Cosmology in India's North East*, Delhi: Oxford University Press.

Breckenridge, C.A. 1977. 'From Protector to Litigant: Changing Relations between Hindu Temples and the Raja of Ramnad', in Stein (ed.), 76-106.

Breckenridge, C.A and P. van der Veer (eds.) 1993. *Orientalism and the Postcolonial Predicament: Perspectives on South Asia*, Philadelphia: University of Pennsylvania Press.

Briggs, J. 1990 [1829]. *History of the Rise of the Mahomedan Power in India till the Year A.D. 1612*. (4 vols.; translated from the original Persian of Mahomed Kasim Ferishta), Delhi: Low Price Publications.

Brubaker, R.L. 1979. 'Barbers, Washermen and Other Priests: Servants of the South Indian Village and Its Goddess', in *History of Religions* 19, 128-52.

Burghart, R. 1983. 'Renunciation in the Religious Traditions of South Asia', in *Man* (N.S.) 18, 635-53.

Burghart 1984. 'The Formation of the Concept of Nation-State in Nepal', in *Journal of Asian Studies* 44, 101-25.

Burghart 1985. 'Theoretical Approaches in the Anthropology of South Asia', in Burghart and Cantlie (eds.), 1-14.

Burghart 1987. 'Gifts to the Gods: Power, Property and Ceremonial in Nepal', in Cannadine and Price (eds.), 237-70.

Burghart, R. und A. Cantlie (eds.) 1985. *Indian Religion: Collective Papers on South Asia*, London: Curzon Press.

Byres, T.J. and H. Mukhia (eds.) 1985. 'Feudalism and Non-European Societies', in *Journal of Peasant Studies* 12. (Special Issue Edition)

Calkins, P.B. 1970. 'The Formation of a Regionally Oriented Ruling Group in Bengal, 1700-1740', in *Journal of Asian Studies* 29, 799-806.

Campbell, J. 1864. *A Personal Narrative of Thirteen Years of Service among the Wild Tribes of Kondhistan*, London.

Cannadine, D. and S. Price (eds.) 1987. *Rituals of Royalty: Power and Ceremonial in Traditional Societies*, Cambridge: Cambridge University Press.

Cannetti, E. 1980 [1960]. *Masse und Macht*, Frankfurt am Main: Fischer.

Carmichael, D.F. 1869. *Manual of the District of Vizagapatam in the Madras Presidency*, Madras: Asylum Press.

Census of India 1961a. 'Census Atlas of Orissa', in *Census of India* (vol. XII-part IX-A), Orissa: Government Press.

Census of India 1961b. 'Administrative Atlas of Orissa', in *Census of India* (vol. XII-part IX-B), Orissa: Government Press.

CÉRM 1970. *Sur le 'mode de production asiatique'*, Paris: Éditions Sociales.

Chakravarti, R. 1990. 'Monarchs, Merchants and Mathas in Northern Konkan. c. 900-1053', in *Indian Economic and Social History Review* 27, 189-208.

Champakalakshmi, R. 1981. 'Peasant State and Society in Medieval South India: A Review Article', in *Indian Economic and Social History Review* 17, 411-26.

Chartier, R. 1992. *Die unvollendete Vergangenheit: Geschichte und die Macht der Weltauslegung*, Frankfurt: Fischer.

Chattopadhyaya, B.D. 1976. 'Origin of the Rajputs: The Political, Economic and Social Processes in Early Medieval Rajasthan', in *Indian Historical Review* 3, 59-82.

Chattopadhyaya, B.D. 1995 [1983]. 'Political Processes and the Structure of Polity in Early Medieval India', in Kulke (ed.), 195-232.

Chauduri, A.B. 1993. *State Formation among Tribals: A Quest for Santal Identity*, New Delhi: Gyan Publishing House.

Claessen, H.J.M. and P. Skalnik (eds.) 1978. *The Early State*, Den Hague: Mouton Publishers.

Claus, P.J. 1978. 'Oral Traditions, Royal Cults and Materials for a Reconsideration of the Caste System in South India', in *Journal of Indian Folkloristics* 1, 1-25.

Clifford, J. 1988. *The Predicament of Culture: Twentieth-Century Ethnography, Literature, and Art*, Cambridge: Harvard University Press.

Clifford, J. and E. Marcus (eds.) 1986. *Writing Culture: The Poetics and Politics of Ethnography*, Berkeley: University of California Press.

Cobden-Ramsay, L.E.B. 1982 [1910]. *Bengal Gazetteers: Feudatory States of Orissa*, Calcutta: KLM Private Limited.

Coburn, T. 1986. 'Consort of None, Śakti of All: The Vision of the Devī-Māhātmya', in Hawley and Wulff (eds.), 153-65.

Coburn, T. 1991. *Encountering the Goddess: A Translation of the Devī-Māhātmya and a Study of Its Interpretation*, Albany: State University of New York Press.

Cohn, B.S. 1959. 'Some Notes on Law and Change in North India', reprinted in and cited from Cohn 1990, 554-74.

Cohn, B.S. 1960. 'The Initial British Impact on India: A Case Study of the Benares Region', reprinted in and cited from Cohn 1990, 320-42.

Cohn, B.S. 1961. 'The Pasts of an Indian Village', reprinted in and cited from Cohn 1990, 88-99.

Cohn, B.S. 1962a. 'An Anthropologist among the Historians: A Field Study', reprinted in and cited from Cohn 1990, 1-17.

Cohn, B.S. 1962b. 'Political Systems in Eighteenth-Century India: The Benaras Region', reprinted in and cited from Cohn 1990, 483-99.

Cohn, B.S. 1965. 'Anthropological Notes on Disputes and Law in India', reprinted in and cited from Cohn 1990, 575-631.

Cohn, B.S. 1977. 'African Models and Indian Histories', reprinted in and cited from Cohn 1990: 200-23.

Cohn, B.S. 1980. 'History and Anthropology: The State of Play', reprinted in and cited from Cohn 1990, 18-49.

Cohn, B.S. 1981. 'Anthropology and History in the 1980s: Towards a Rapprochement', reprinted in and cited from Cohn 1990, 50-77.

Cohn, B.S. 1983. 'Representing Authority in Victorian India', in Hobsbawm and Ranger (eds.), 165-209.

Cohn, B.S. 1987. 'The Census, Social Structure and Objectification in South Asia', reprinted in and cited from Cohn 1990, 224-54.

Cohn, B.S. 1990 [1987]. *An Anthropologist among the Historians and Other Essays*, Delhi: Oxford University Press.

Cohn, B. and M. Marriot 1958. 'Networks and Centers in the Integration of Indian Civilisation', in *Journal of Social Research* 1, 1-9.

Collingwood, R.G. 1986 [1946]. *The Idea of History*, Oxford: Oxford University Press.

Conrad, C. and M. Kessel (eds.) 1994. *Geschichte schreiben in der Postmoderne: Beiträge zur aktuellen Diskussion*, Stuttgart: Reclam.

Coomaraswamy, A.K. 1942. *Spiritual Authority and Temporal Power in the Indian Theory of Government*, New Haven: American Oriental Society.

Cowley 1795. *Cowely Granted by the Right Honourable Lord Hobart, President and Governor in Council of Fort St. George and Its Dependencies to Ramachandra Deo, Zamindar of Jeypore, dated 12th March 1795*, reprinted in and cited from Behuria (ed.) 1965, 223.

Crooke, W. 1972 [1926]. *Religion and Folklore of Northern India*, New Delhi: Chand & Co.

Dallapiccola, A.L. and S. Zingel-Avé Lallemant (eds.) 1989. *Shastric Traditions in Indian Arts*, Stuttgart: Franz Steiner Verlag.

Dallapiccola, A.L. and S. Zingel-Avé Lallemant (eds.) 1985. *Vijayanagara - City and Empire: New Currents of Research*, Stuttgart: Franz Steiner Verlag.

Das, A. 1967. 'Karligarh: A Tribal Fort', in *Adivasi* 9, 1-12.

Das, Bhaskar 1985. *Socio-Economic History of Southern Orissa*, Calcutta: Punthi Pustak.

Das, Binod S. (ed.) 1984. *Life and Culture in Orissa*, Calcutta: Punthi Pustak.

Das, Binod S. (ed.) 1986. *Glimpses of Orissa*, Calcutta: Punthi Pustak.

Das, Bitchitrananda 1978. *History of Mohuri, 1767-1850*, Berhampur: Berhampur University (dissertation).

Dash, G.N. 1978a. 'The Evolution of Priestly Power: The Gaṅgavaṃśa Period', in Eschmann, Kulke and Tripathi (eds.), 157-68.

Dash, G.N. 1978b. 'The Evolution of Priestly Power: The Sūryavaṃśa Period', in Eschmann, Kulke and Tripathi (eds.), 209-21.

Dash, G.N. 1978c. 'Jagannātha and Oriya Nationalism', in Eschmann, Kulke, and Tripathi (eds.), 359-74.

Dash, G.N. 1998. *Hindus and Tribals: A Quest for Co-existence*. New Delhi: Decent Books.

Deed 1803. *Deed of Permanent Property Granted to Ramachandra Deo, Zamindar of Jeypore, the 21st October 1803*, reprinted in and cited from Behuria (ed.) 1965, 225-7.

Derrett, J.D.M. 1976. 'Rājadharma', in *Journal of Asian Studies* 35, 597-610.

Dewey, C. 1972. 'Images of the Village Community: A Study in Anglo-Indian Ideology', in *Modern Asian Studies* 6, 291-328.

Dirks, N.B. 1976. 'Political Authority and Structural Change in Early South Indian History', in *Indian Economic and Social History Review* 13, 125-58.

Dirks, N.B. 1979. 'The Structure and Meaning of Political Relations in a South Indian Little Kingdom', in *Contributions to Indian Sociology* (N.S.) 13, 169-206.

Dirks, N.B. 1982. 'The Pasts of a Pāḷaiyakārar: The Ethnohistory of a South Indian Little King', in *Journal of Asian Studies* 41, 655-83.

Dirks, N.B. 1986. 'From Little King to Landlord: Property, Law, and the Gift under the Madras Permanent Settlement', in *Comparative Studies in Society and History* 28, 307-33.

Dirks, N.B. 1987. *The Hollow Crown: Ethnohistory of an Indian Kingdom*, Cambridge: Cambridge University Press.

Dirks, N.B.1989a. 'The Original Caste: Power, History and Hierarchy in South Asia', in *Contributions to Indian Sociology* (N.S.) 23, 59-77.

Dirks, N.B. 1989b. 'The Invention of Caste: Civil Society in Colonial India', in *Social Analysis* 25, 42-51.

Dirks, N.B. 1993. 'Colonial Histories and Native Informants: Biography of an Archive', in Breckenridge and van der Veer (eds.), 279-313.

Drekmeier, C. 1962. *Kingship and Community in Early India*, Stanford: Stanford University Press.

Dumont, L. 1960. 'World Renunciation in Indian Religions', in *Contributions to Indian Sociology* 4, 33-62.

Dumont, L. 1962. 'The Conception of Kingship in Ancient India', in *Contributions to Indian Sociology* 6, 48-77, reprinted in and cited from Dumont 1980, 287-313.

Dumont, L. 1966. 'The "Village Community" from Munro to Maine', in *Contributions to Indian Sociology* 9, 66-89.

Dumont, L. 1970. *Religion, Politics and History in India: Collected Papers in Indian Sociology*, Paris: Mouton & Co.

Dumont, L. 1979. 'Preface' to the French edition of *The Nuer*, by E.E. Evans-Pritchard 1940, reprinted in Beattie and Lienhardt (eds.), 328-42.

Dumont, L. 1980 [1966]. *Homo Hierarchicus: The Caste System and Its Implications*, Chicago: University of Chicago Press.

Dumont, L. 1986a. *Essays on Individualism: Modern Ideology in Anthropological Perspective*, Chicago: University of Chicago Press.

Dumont, L. 1986b [1957]. *A South Indian Subcaste: Social Organization and Religion of the Pramalai Kallar*, Delhi: Oxford University Press.

Dumont, L. and D. Pocock 1957. 'Village Studies', in *Contributions to Indian Sociology* 1, 23-42.

Dumont, L. 1958. 'A.M. Hocart on Caste', in *Contributions to Indian Sociology* 2, 45-63.

Durkheim, E. 1933 [1893]. *The Division of Labor in Society*, New York: Macmillan.

Elias, Norbert 1983 [1933]. *Die höfische Gesellschaft: Untersuchungen zur Soziologie des Königtums und der höfischen Aristokratie*, Frankfurt: Suhrkamp.

Elwin, V. 1946. *A Brief Survey of the Aboriginal Tribes of the Districts of Ganjam and Koraput*, Cuttack: Orissa Government Press.

Elwin, V. 1950. *Bondo Highlander*, Bombay: Oxford University Press.

Elwin, V. 1955. *The Religion of an Indian Tribe*, Oxford: Oxford University Press.

Erndl, K.M. 1993. *Victory to the Mother: The Hindu Goddess of Northwest India in Myth, Ritual and Symbol*, Oxford: Oxford University Press.

Eschmann, A. 1978a. 'Hinduization of Tribal Deities in Orissa: The Śākta and Śaiva Typology', in Eschmann, Kulke and Tripathi (eds.), 79-97.

Eschmann, A. 1978b. 'The Vaiṣṇava Typology of Hinduization and the Origin of Jagannātha', in Eschmann, Kulke and Tripathi (eds.), 99-117.

Eschmann, A. 1978c. 'Prototypes of the Navakalevara Ritual and their Relation to the Jagannātha Cult', in Eschmann, Kulke and Tripathi (eds.), 265-83.

Eschmann, A., H. Kulke and G.C. Tripathi 1978. 'The Formation of the Jagannātha Triad', in Eschmann, Kulke and Tripathi (eds.), 169-96.

Eschmann, A., H. Kulke and G.C. Tripathi (eds.) 1978. *The Cult of Jagannath and the Regional Tradition of Orissa*, Delhi: Manohar.

Evans-Pritchard, E.E. 1940. *The Nuer: A Description of the Modes of Livelihood and Political Institutions of a Nilotic People*, Oxford: Oxford University Press.

Evans-Pritchard, E.E. 1950. 'Social Anthropology: Past and Present', in *Man* 50, 118-24.

Evans-Pritchard, E.E. 1961. *Anthropology and History*, Manchester: Manchester University Press.

Evans-Pritchard, E.E. and M. Fortes 1940. 'Introduction', in Evans-Pritchard and Fortes (eds.), 1-23.

Evans-Pritchard, E.E. and M. Fortes (eds.) 1940. *African Political Systems*, Oxford: Oxford University Press.

Falk, N.E. 1973. 'Wilderness and Kingship in Ancient South India', in *History of Religions* 13, 1-15.

Feudatory and Tributary States 1907. *The Feudatory and Tributary States of the Orissa Division and the Rules Applicable to Them*, Part 1, Calcutta: Bengal Secretariat Press.

Fifth Report 1812. *Fifth Report from the Select Committee on the Affairs of the East India Company* (vol. 2): *Madras Presidency*, Madras: Tamilnadu State Archives.

Forster, E.M. 1983 [1953]. *The Hill of Devi*, Hammondsworth: Penguin.

Fortes, M. 1945. *The Dynamics of Clanship among the Tallensi: Being the First Part of an Analysis of the Social Structure of a Trans-Volta Tribe*, Oxford: Oxford University Press.

Fortes, M. 1953. *Social Anthropology at Cambridge since 1900: An Inaugural Lecture*, Cambridge: Cambridge University Press.

Fortes, M. 1970 [1969]. *Kinship and the Social Order: The Legacy of Lewis Henry Morgan*, London: Routledge and Kegan Paul.

Fox, R.G. 1971. *Kin, Clan, Raja and Rule: State-Hinterland Relations in Pre-Industrial India*, Berkeley: University of California Press.

Fox, R.G. (ed.) 1977. *Realm and Region in Traditional India*, Durham: Duke University Press.

Francis, W. 1907. *Madras District Gazetteers: Vizagapatam*, Madras: Government Press.

Frenz, M. 2000. *Vom Herrscher zum Untertan. Spannungsverhältnis zwischen lokaler Herrschaftsstruktur und der Kolonialverwaltung in Malabar zu Beginn der britischen Herrschaft (1790-1805)*, Stuttgart: Franz Steiner Verlag.

Frykenberg, R.E. 1963. 'Traditional Processes of Power in South India: An Historical Analysis of Local Influence', in *Indian Economic and Social History Review* 1, 122-42.

Frykenberg, R.E. 1965. *Guntur District, 1788-1848: A History of Local Influence and Central Authority in South India*, Oxford: Oxford University Press.

Frykenberg, R.E. 1977. 'The Silent Settlement in South India, 1793-1853: An Analysis of the Role of the Inams in the Rise of the Indian Imperial System', in Frykenberg (ed.), 37-53.

Frykenberg, R.E. (ed.) 1969. *Land Control and Social Structure in Indian History*, Madison: University of Wisconsin Press.

Frykenberg, R.E. (ed.) 1977. *Land Tenure and Peasant in South Asia*, New Delhi: Orient Longman.

Frykenberg, R.E. and P. Kolenda (eds.) 1985. *Studies in South India: An Anthology of Recent Research and Scholarship*, Madras.

Fuller, C.J. 1979. 'Gods, Priests and Purity: On the Relation between Hinduism and the Caste System', in *Man* (N.S.) 14, 459-76.

Fuller, C.J. 1984. *Servants of the Goddess*, Cambridge: Cambridge University Press.

Fuller, C.J. 1985. 'Royal Divinity and Human Kingship in the Festivals of a South Indian Temple', in *South Asian Social Scientist* 1, 3-43.

Fuller, C.J. 1988. 'Hinduism and Scriptural Authority in Modern Indian Law', in *Comparative Studies in Society and History* 30, 225-48.

Fuller, C.J. 1992. *The Camphor Flame: Popular Hinduism and Society in India*, Princeton: Princeton University Press.

Fuller, C.J. and P. Logan 1985. 'The Navarātrī Festival of Madurai', in *Bulletin of the SOAS* 48, 79-105.

Galey, J.C. 1989a. 'Introduction: Kingship in the Leeway of Scholarship', in Galey (ed.), 1-29.

Galey, J.C. 1989b. 'Reconsidering Kingship in India: An Ethnological Perspective', in Galey (ed.), 123-88.

Galey, J.C. (ed.) 1989. 'Kingship and the Kings', in *History and Anthropology* 4, Chur: Harwood Academic Publishers.

Ganjam District Records (old). *Ganjam District Records: Old Series*, Madras: Tamil Nadu State Archives.

Ganjam District Records (new). *Ganjam District Records: New Series*, Bhubaneswar: Orissa State Archives.

Geertz, C. 1973a. 'Thick Description: Toward an Interpretive Theory of Culture', in Geertz 1973b, 3-30.

Geertz, C. 1973b. *The Interpretation of Cultures: Selected Essays*, New York: Basic Books.

Geertz, C. 1980. *Negara: The Theater State in Nineteenth-Century Bali*, Princeton: Princeton University Press.

Geertz, C. 1990 [1988]. *Die künstlichen Wilden: Der Anthropologe als Schriftsteller*, München: Hanser.

Geib, R. 1975. *Die Indradyumna-Legende: Ein Beitrag zur Geschichte des Jagannātha-Kultes*, Wiesbaden: Harrassowitz.

Giesey, R.E. 1960. *The Royal Funeral Ceremony in Renaissance France*, Geneve: Libraire E. Droz.

Godelier, M. 1978a. 'The Concept of the "Tribe": A Crisis Involving Merely a Concept or the Empirical Foundations of Anthropology Itself?', in Godelier 1978b, 70-96.

Godelier, M. 1978b. *Perspectives in Marxist Anthropology*, Cambridge: Cambridge University Press.

Gonda, J. 1963. *Die Religionen Indiens (vol.2): Der jüngere Hinduismus*, Stuttgart: W. Kohlhammer Verlag.

Gonda, J. 1965a. 'Gifts', in Gonda 1965b, 198-228.

Gonda, J. 1965b. *Change and Continuity in Indian Religion*, The Hague: Mouton.

Gonda, J. 1969 [1957]. *Ancient Indian Kingship from the Religious Point of View*, Leiden: E.J. Brill.

Gopal, K.K. 1964. 'The Assembly of Samantas in Early Mediaeval India', in *Journal of Indian History* 42, 241-50.

Gopal, L. 1963. 'Sāmanta: Its Varying Significance in Ancient India', in *Journal of the Royal Asiatic Society* 5, 21-37.

Gopalaiya, B. 1862. 'Reports on the Inams of the Vizagapatnam District', reprinted in and cited from *Selections* 1948, 145-51.

Gordon, S.N. 1969. 'Scarf and Sword: Thugs, Marauders, and State-formation in 18th Century Malwa', in *Indian Economic and Social History Review* 6, 403-29.

Gordon, S.N. 1979. 'Forts and Social Control in the Maratha State', in *Modern Asian Studies* 13, 1-17.

Gough, E.K. 1955. 'The Social Structure of a Tanjore Village', in Marriot (ed.), 36-52.

Gough, E.K. 1971. 'Nuer Kinship: A Re-Examination', in Beidelmann (ed.), 79-122.

Grant, J. 1786. 'Political Survey of the Northern Circars', in *Fifth Report*, 131-264.

Greenblatt, S. 1994. 'Die Zirkulation sozialer Energie', in Conrad and Kessel (eds.), 219-50.

Greenwold, S.M. 1975. 'Kingship and Caste', in *Archives Européennes de Sociologie* 16, 49-75.

Guha, A. 1974. 'Tribalism to Feudalism in Assam, 1600-1750', in *Indian Historical Review* 1: 65-76.

Gunawardana, R.A.L.H. 1976. 'The Analysis of Pre-colonial Social Formations in Asia in the Writings of Karl Marx', in *Indian Historical Review* 2, 365-88.

Gupta, G.R. (ed.) 1983. *Religion in Modern India*, Delhi: Vikas Publications.

Habib, I. 1962. 'An Examination of Wittfogel's Theory of Oriental Despotism', in *Enquiry* 6, 53-73.

Habib, I. 1985. 'Classifying Pre-colonial India', in Byres and Mukhia (eds.), 44-53.

Hall, K.R. 1980. *Trade and Statecraft in the Age of the Cōḷas*, New Delhi: Abhinav Publications.

Handelman, D. 1990. *Models and Mirrors: Towards an Anthropology of Public Events*, Cambridge: Cambridge University Press.

Hara, M. 1973. 'The King as Husband of the Earth', in *Asiatische Studien* 27, 97-114.

Hardiman, D. 1987. *The Coming of the Devi: Adivasi Assertion in Western India*, Delhi: Oxford University Press.

Hardy, P. 1986. 'The Authority of Muslim Kings in Medieval South Asia', in *Puruṣārtha* 9, 37-55.

Hardy, P. 1987. 'Islamischer Patrimonialismus: Die Mogulherrschaft', in Schluchter (ed.), 190-216.

Hasan, N. 1969. 'Zamindars under the Mughals', in Frykenberg (ed.), 19-29.

Hawley, J.S. and D.M. Wulf (eds.) 1986 [1982]. *The Divine Consort: Rādhā and the Goddesses of India*, Boston: Beacon Press.

Heesterman, J.C. 1957a. 'Reflections on the Significance of Dakṣiṇā', in *Indo-Iranian Journal* 3, 241-58.

Heesterman, J.C. 1957b. *The Ancient Indian Royal Consecration*, Den Haag: Mouton & Co.

Heesterman, J.C. 1971. 'Kautilya and the Ancient Indian State', reprinted in Heesterman 1985, 128-40.

Heesterman, J.C. 1978. 'The Conundrum of the King's Authority', reprinted in Heesterman 1985, 108-27.

Heesterman, J.C. 1979. 'Power, Priesthood, and Authority', reprinted in Heesterman 1985, 141-57.

Heesterman, J.C. 1981. 'Householder and Wanderer', in *Contributions to Indian Sociology* (N.S.) 15, 251-71.

Heesterman, J.C. 1985. *The Inner Conflict of Tradition: Essays on Indian Ritual, Kingship, and Society*, Chicago: Chicago University Press.

Hegel, G.W.F. 1961 [1848]. *Vorlesungen über die Philosophie der Geschichte*, Stuttgart: Reclam.

Hein, E. 1978. 'Temple, Town, and Hinterland: The Present Network of "Religious Economy" in Puri', in Eschmann, Kulke and Tripathi (eds.), 439-68.

Heitzman, J. 1987. 'State Formation in South India, 850-1280', in *Indian Economic and Social History Review* 24, 35-61.

Heitzman, J. 1997. *Gifts of Power. Lordship in an Early Indian State*, Delhi: Oxford University Press.

Henningham, S. 1990. *A Great Estate and its Landlords in Colonial India: Darbhanga, 1860-1942*, Delhi: Oxford University Press.

Herrenschmidt, O. 1981. 'Le sacrifice du buffle en Andhra Cotier. Le 'culte de village' confronté aux notion de sacrifiant et de unité de culte', in *Puruṣārtha* 5, 137-77.

Hiltebeitel, A. 1980. 'Rama and Gilgamesh: The Sacrifices of the Water Buffalo and the Bull in Heaven', in *History of Religions* 19, 16-44.

Hiltebeitel, A. 1981. 'Draupadī's Hair', in *Puruṣārtha* 5, 179-214.

Hiltebeitel, A. 1985. 'On the Handling of the Meat, and Related Matters, in Two South Indian Buffalo Sacrifices', in *L'Uomo* 9, 171-99.

Hiltebeitel, A. (ed.) 1989. *Criminal Gods and Demon Devotees: Essays on the Guardians of Popular Hinduism*, Albany: State University of New York.

History of the Rise and Progress no date. *History of the Rise and Progress of the Operations for the Suppression of Human Sacrifice and Female Infanticide, compiled from Official Correspondence, from the Years 1836 to 1854. Part I. The Operations of the Madras Government*, Bhubaneswar: Orissa State Museum Library, Catalogue No. 1460.

Hobsbawm, E. and T. Ranger (eds.) 1983. *The Invention of Tradition*, Cambridge: Cambridge University Press.

Hocart, A.M. 1933. *The Progress of Man: A Short Survey of His Evolution, His Customs and His Works*, London: Methuen.

Hocart, A.M. 1950. *Caste: A Comparative Study*, London: Methuen.

Hocart, A.M. 1954. *Social Origins*, London: Watts.

Hocart, A.M. 1969. *Kingship*, Oxford: Oxford University Press.

Hocart, A.M. 1970a. *Kings and Councillors: An Essay in the Comparative Anatomy of Human Society*, Chicago: Chicago University Press.

Hocart, A.M. 1970b. *The Life-giving Myth, and Other Essays*, London: Methuen.

Hocart, A.M. 1987. *Imagination and Proof: Selected Essays of A.M. Hocart*, Tuscon: University of Arizona Press.

Hoffmann, H. 1953. 'Die Begriffe "König" und "Herrschaft" im indischen Kulturkreis', in *Saeculum* 4, 334-9.

Holy, L. 1979. 'The Segmentary Lineage Structure and Its Existential Status', in Holy (ed.), 1-22.

Holy, L. (ed.) 1979. *Segmentary Lineage Systems Reconsidered*, Belfast: Queens University.

Hota, N.R. 1959. 'Human Sacrifices among the Kondh of Orissa', in *Orissa Historical Research Journal* 8, 151-7.

Hubert H. and M. Mauss 1964. *Sacrifice: Its Nature and Function*, Chicago: University of Chicago Press.

Hunt, L. 1994. 'Geschichte jenseits von Gesellschaftstheorie', in Conrad and Kessel (eds.), 98-122.

Hunter, W.W. 1872. *Orissa: or the Vicissitudes of an Indian Province under Native and British Rule*, Calcutta.

Huntington, R. and P. Metcalf 1979. *Celebrations of Death: The Anthropology of Mortuary Ritual*, Cambridge: Cambridge University Press.

Imperial Gazetteer 1909. *The Imperial Gazetteer of India: The Indian Empire*, Oxford: Clarendon Press.

Inden, R. 1978. 'Ritual, Authority, and Cyclic Time in Hindu Kingship', in Richards (ed.), 28-73.

Inden, R. 1981. 'Hierarchies of Kings in Early Medieval India', in *Contributions to Indian Sociology* (N.S.) 15, 99-125.

Inden, R. 1990. *Imagining India*, Oxford: Blackwell Publishers.

Jansen, R. 1995. *Die Bhavani von Tuljapur: Religionsgeschichtliche Studie des Kultes einer Göttin der indischen Volksreligion*, Stuttgart: Franz Steiner Verlag.

Jha, D.N. (ed.) 1987. *Feudal Society Formation in Early India*, Delhi: Chanakya Publications.

Jones, R. 1831. *An Essay on the Distribution of Wealth and the Sources of Taxation*, London.

Jordan-Horstmann, M. 1972. 'Der dumme Weber: Spotterzählungen bei den Mundas', in *Anthropos* 67, 564-85.

Joshi, A. 1967. 'The Origin of the Bhanjas of Khijjingakōtta', in *Orissa Historical Research Journal* 16, 41-53.

Kane, P.V. 1958. *History of Dharmaśāstra: Ancient and Medieval Religious and Civil Law in India* 5, Poona: Bhandarkar Oriental Research Institute.

Kantorowicz, E.H. 1957. *The King's Two Bodies: A Study in Mediaeval Political Theology*, Princeton: Princeton University Press.

Kantowski, D. (ed.) 1984. *Recent Research on Max Weber's Studies of Hinduism*, München: Weltforum Verlag.

Kelly, R.C. 1985. *The Nuer Conquest: The Structure and Development of an Expansionist System*, Ann Arbor: University of Michigan Press.

Kinsley, D. 1986. *Hindu Goddesses: Visions of the Divine Feminine in the Hindu Religious Tradition*, Berkeley: University of California Press.

Kölver, B. 1993. *Ritual und historischer Raum: Zum indischen Geschichtsverständnis*, München: Stiftung Historisches Kolleg.

Kölver, B. (ed.) 1997. *Recht, Staat und Verwaltung im klassischen Indien.* (Schriften des Historischen Kollegs, Kolloquien 30), München: R. Oldenbourg Verlag.

Kolff, D. 1990. *Naukar, Rajput and Sepoy: The Ethnohistory of the Military Labour Market in Hindustan, 1450-1850*, Cambridge: Cambridge University Press.

Koraput District Records no date. *Koraput District Records*, Bhubaneswar: Orissa State Archives.

Kosambi, D.D. 1956a. 'On the Development of Feudalism in India', in *Annals of the Bhandarkar Oriental Research Institute* 36, 258-69.

Kosambi, D.D. 1956b. 'Origins of Feudalism in Kashmir', in *Journal of the Bombay Branch of the Royal Asiatic Society* 31, 108-20.

Kosambi, D.D. 1983 [1962]. *Myth and Reality: Studies in the Formation of Indian Culture*, Bombay: Popular Prakashan.

Koselleck, R. 1979. *Vergangene Zukunft: Zur Semantik geschichtlicher Zeiten*, Frankfurt am Main: Suhrkamp.

Krader, L. 1973. *Ethnologie und Anthropologie bei Marx*, München: Hanser.

Krader, L. 1975. *The Asiatic Mode of Production: Sources, Development and Critique in the Writings of Karl Marx*, Assen: Van Gorcum.

Kulke, H. 1976. 'Kshatriyaization and Social Change: A Study in Orissa Setting', in Pillai (ed.), 398-409.

Kulke, H. 1978a. 'Royal Temple Policy and the Structure of Medieval Hindu Kingdoms', in Eschmann, Kulke and Tripathi (eds.), 125-37.

Kulke, H. 1978b. 'Early Royal Patronage of the Jagannātha Cult', in Eschmann, Kulke and Tripathi (eds.), 139-55.

Kulke, H. 1978c. 'Jagannātha as the State Deity under the Gajapatis of Orissa', in Eschmann, Kulke and Tripathi (eds.), 199-208.

Kulke, H. 1978d. 'The Struggle between the Rājās of Khurda and the Muslim Subahdārs of Cuttack for Dominance of the Jagannātha Cult', in Eschmann, Kulke and Tripathi (eds.), 321-42.

Kulke, H. 1978e. '"Juggernaut" under British Supremacy and the Resurgence of the Khurda-Rājās as "Rājās of Puri"', in Eschmann, Kulke and Tripathi (eds.), 345-57.

Kulke, H. 1979a. *Jagannātha-Kult und Gajapati-Königtum: Ein Beitrag zur Geschichte religiöser Legitimation hinduistischer Herrscher*, Wiesbaden: Franz Steiner Verlag.

Kulke, H. 1979b. 'Early State Formation and Royal Legitimation in Tribal Areas of Eastern India', in Moser and Gautana (eds.), 29-37.

Kulke, H. 1980. 'Legitimation and Town-Planning in the Feudatory States of Central Orissa', in Pieper (ed.), 30-40.

Kulke, H. 1982. 'Fragmentation and Segmentation Versus Integration? Reflections on the Concepts of Indian Feudalism and the Segmentary State in Indian History', in *Studies in History* 4, 237-64.

Kulke, H. 1984a. 'Local Networks and Regional Integration in Orissa: Ritual Privileges of the Feudatory Rājās of Eastern India in the Jagannātha Cult of Puri', in Ballhatchet and Taylor (eds.), 141-8.

Kulke, H. 1984b. 'Max Weber's Contribution to the Study of "Hinduization" in India and "Indianization" in Southeast Asia', in Kantowski (ed.), 97-116.

Kulke, H. 1984c. 'Tribal Deities at Princely Courts: The Feudatory Rājās of Central Orissa and their Tutelary Deities (iṣṭadevatās)', in Mahapatra (ed.), 13-24, reprinted in and cited from Kulke 1993, 114-36.

Kulke, H. 1985. 'Die frühmittelalterlichen Regionalreiche: Ihre Struktur und Rolle im Prozess staatlicher Entwicklung Indiens', in Kulke and Rothermund (eds.), 77-114.

Kulke, H. 1987. 'The Chronicles and the Temple Records of the Mādaḷa Pāñji of Puri: A Reassessment of the Evidence', in *Indian Archives* 36, 1-24, reprinted in and cited from Kulke 1993, 137-58.

Kulke, H. 1992. 'Kṣatra and Kṣetra: The Cult of Jagannatha of Puri and the "Royal Letters" (chāmu ciṭaus) of the Rājās of Khurda', in Bakker (ed.), 131-42, reprinted in and cited from Kulke 1993, 51-65.

Kulke, H. 1993. *Kings and Cults: State Formation and Legitimation in India and Southeast Asia*, Delhi: Manohar.

Kulke, H. 1995a. 'Introduction: The Study of the State in Pre-modern India', in Kulke (ed.), 1-47.

Kulke, H. 1995b. 'The Early and the Imperial Kingdom: A Processural Model of Integrative State Formation in Early Medieval India', in Kulke (ed.), 233-62.

Kulke, H. (ed.) 1995. *The State in India, 1000-1700*, Delhi: Oxford University Press.

Kulke, H. and D. Rothermund 1991 [1986]. *A History of India*, Calcutta: Rupa & Co.

Kulke, H. and D. Rothermund (eds.) 1985. *Regionale Tradition in Südasien*, Stuttgart: Franz Steiner Verlag.

Kulke, H. and B. Schnepel (eds.) 2001. *Jagannath Revisited: Studying Society, Religion and the State in Orissa*, Delhi: Manohar.

Kuper, A. 1982. 'Lineage Theory: A Critical Retrospect', in *Annual Review of Anthropology* 21, 71-95.

Kuper, A. 1988. *The Invention of Primitive Society: Transformations of an Illusion*, London: Routledge.

Kurtz, S.M. 1992. *All the Mothers are One: Hindu India and the Cultural Reshaping of Psychoanalysis*, New York: Columbia University Press.

Leach, E.R. 1970 [1954]. *Political Systems of Highland Burma: A Study of Kachin Social Structure*, London: Athlone Press.

Lingat, R. 1973. *The Classical Law of India*, Berkeley: University of California Press.

Lorenzen, D. 1978. 'Warrior Ascetics in Indian History', in *Journal of the American Oriental Society* 98, 61-75.

Ludden, D. 1989 [1985]. *Peasant History in South India*, Delhi: Oxford University Press.

Ludden, D. 1993. 'Oriental Empiricism: Transformations of Colonial Knowledge', in Breckenridge and van der Veer (eds.), 250-78.

Machiavelli, N. 1986 [1532]. *Il Principe*, Stuttgart: Reclam.

Maclean, C.D. (ed.) 1982 [1893]. *Glossary of the Madras Presidency*, New Delhi: Asian Educational Services.

Maclean, C.D. 1987 [1885]. *Manual of the Administration of the Madras Presidency* (vol. 1), New Delhi: Asian Educational Services.

Macpherson, W. 1863. *Lieutenant Macpherson's Report upon the Khonds of the Districts of Ganjam and Cuttack*, Madras: United Scottish Press.

Maddox, S.L. 1920. *Final Report on the Survey and Settlement of the Province of Orissa, 1890-1900*, Ranchi: Government Print.

Mahalingam, T.V. 1976. *Mackenzie Manuscripts: Summaries of the Historical Manuscripts in the Mackenzie Collection*, Madras: University of Madras Press.

Mahapatra, L.K. 1984. 'The Role of Hindu Princes in the Caste System of Orissa', in Das (ed.), 42-60.

Mahapatra, L.K. 1987. 'Ex-Princely States of Orissa: Mayurbhanj, Keonjhar and Bonai', in Sinha (ed.), 1-51.

Mahapatra, M. 1981. *Traditional Structure and Change in an Orissan Temple*, Calcutta: Punthi Pustak.

Mahapatra, S. (ed.) 1984. *Folk Ways in Religion: Gods, Spirits and Men*, Cuttack: Institute of Oriental and Orissan Studies.

Maine, H.S. 1907 [1871]. *Village Communities in the East and West*, London: J. Murray.

Majumdar, D.M. 1939. 'Tribal Cultures and Acculturation', in *Man in India* 19, 99-173.

Malamoud, C. 1976. 'Village et Foret dans l'Ideologie de l'Indie Brahmanique', in *Archive Européennes de Sociologie* 17, 3-20.

Maltby, T.J. 1918. *The Ganjam District Manual*, Madras: Government Press.

Mandelbaum, D.G. 1955. 'The World and the World View of the Kota', in Marriot (ed.), 223-54.

Marglin, F.A. 1985. *Wives of the God-King: The Rituals of the Devadasis of Puri*, Delhi: Oxford University Press.

Marriot, M. 1955. 'Little Communities in an Indigenous Civilization', in Marriot (ed.), 171-222.

Marriot, M. 1968. 'Caste Ranking and Food Transactions: A Matrix Analysis', in Singer und Cohn (eds.) 1978, 133-71.

Marriot, M. (ed.) 1955. *Village India. Studies in Little Community*. Chicago: Chicago University Press.

Marx, K. 1972. *On Colonialism: Articles from the New York Tribune and Other Writings*, New York: International Publisher.

Mauss, M. 1967 [1925]. *The Gift*, New York: Norton and Company.

Mayer, A.C. 1960. *Caste and Kinship in Central India*, Berkeley: University of California Press.

Mayer, A.C. 1981. 'Perceptions of Princely Rule: Perspectives From a Biography', in *Contributions to Indian Sociology* (N.S.) 15, 127-53.

Mayer, A.C. 1985. 'The King's Two Thrones', in *Man* (N.S.) 20, 205-21.

Mayer, A.C. 1991. 'Rulership and Divinity: The Case of the Modern Hindu Prince and Beyond', in *Modern Asian Studies* 25, 765-90.

Maynard, H.J. 1917. 'Influence of the Indian King upon the Growth of Caste', in *Journal of the Punjab Historical Society* 6, 88-100.

Mazumdar, B.C. 1925. *Orissa in the Making*, Calcutta: University of Calcutta.

McLane, J.R. 1993. *Land and Local Kingship in Eighteenth-Century Bengal*, Cambridge: Cambridge University Press.

Metcalf, T. 1979. *Land, Landlords and the British Raj: Northern India in the Nineteenth Century*, Delhi: Oxford University Press.

Middleton, J. and D. Tait 1955. 'Introduction', in Middleton and Tait (eds.), 1-31.

Middleton, J. and D. Tait (eds.) 1955. *Tribes Without Rulers: Studies in African Segmentary Systems*, London: Routledge and Kegan Paul Ltd.

Mill, J. 1858 [1821]. *The History of British India*, London: John Madden.

Mines, M. 1984. *The Warrior Merchants: Textiles, Trade, and Territory in South India*, Cambridge: Cambridge University Press.

Mines, M. and V. Gourishankar 1991. 'Leadership and Individuality in South Asia: The Case of the South Indian Big-Man', in *Journal of Asian Studies* 49, 761-86.

Mishra, K.C. 1971. *The Cult of Jagannātha*, Calcutta: Firma K.L. Mukhopadhyay.

Mishra, M.K. 1994. 'A Hero of Mahabharata in the Folk and Tribal Traditions of Central India', in *Orissa Historical Research Journal* 39, 76-91.

Misra, P.C. 1980. *History of Ganjam under the British (1707-1900)*, Berhampur: Berhampur University (dissertation).

Mitchell, A.G. 1992 [1982]. *Hindu Gods and Goddesses*, New Delhi: USB Publishers and Distributors Ltd.

Möhlig, W and T. von Trotta (eds.) 1994. *Legitimation von Herrschaft und Recht*, Köln.

Mohan, A. 1990. *Princely States and the Reform in Hindu Law*, Bombay: Tripathi Private Ltd.

Mohapatra, K. 1962. 'Historical Tradition among the Gonds of Orissa', in *Orissa Historical Research Journal* 10, 33-8.

Mohapatra, R.P. 1986. *Archaeology in Orissa: Sites and Monuments* (2 vols.), Delhi: B.R. Publishing Corporation.

Monier-Williams, M. 1981 [1899]. *A Sanskrit-English Dictionary*, Delhi: Motilal.

Montesquieu, C.L. de 1965 [1748]. *Vom Geist der Gesetze*, Stuttgart: Reclam.

Moser, R.R. and M.K. Gautana (eds.) 1979. *Aspects of Tribal Life in South Asia I: Strategy and Survival*, Bern: University of Bern.

Motte, T. 1953 [1766]. 'A Narrative of a Journey to the Diamond Mines at Sumbhalpoor', in *Orissa Historical Research Journal* 1, 1-48.

Mukherjee, P. 1953. *The History of the Gajapati Kings of Orissa and their Successors*, Calcutta: S. Mukherjee General Trading Company.

Mukherjee, P. 1978. 'Caitanya in Orissa', in Eschmann, Kulke and Tripathi (eds.), 309-19.

Mukherjee, Prabath 1959. 'Human Sacrifice among the Khonds of Orissa: A Note', in *Orissa Historical Research Journal* 8, 164-7.

Mukhia, H. 1981. 'Was there Feudalism in Indian History?', in *Journal of Peasant Studies* 8, 273-316, reprinted in Kulke (ed.) 1995, 86-133.

Mukhia, H. 1985. 'Peasant Production and Medieval Indian Society', in Byres and Mukhia (eds.), 228-51.

Munshi, S. 1979. 'Tribal Absorption and Sanskritisation in Hindu Society', in *Contributions to Indian Sociology* (N.S.) 13, 293-317.

Nayak, P.K. 1989. *Blood, Women and Territory: An Analysis of Clan Feuds of the Dongria Kondhs*, New Delhi: Reliance Publishing House.

Nayak, P.K. and B. Schnepel forthcoming. *The Caste of Fools: Stories of the Weaver in Orissan Folklore*.

Nayak, S. no date. *Victory to Mother Markama (in Oriya)*, Bissamcuttack: private publication.

Neale, Walter C. 1969. 'Land is to Rule', in Frykenberg (ed.), 3-16.

Needham, R. 1970. 'Introduction', in Hocart 1970a, xiii-xcix.

Oberdiek, U. 1991. *Kontinuität und Wandel: Die staatliche Integration der indischen Stämme*, München: Trickster Verlag.

O'Flaherty, W.D. 1984. *Dreams, Illusion and Other Realities*, Chicago: University of Chicago Press.

O'Leary, B. 1989. *The Asiatic Mode of Production: Oriental Despotism, Historical Materialism and Indian History*, Oxford: Blackwell.

O'Malley, L.S.S. 1908. *Bengal District Gazetteers: Angul*, Calcutta: Bengal Secretariat.

O'Malley 1984 [1929]. *Bengal District Gazetteers: Puri*, New Delhi: Usha Publications.

Opler, M.E. 1956. 'The Extensions of an Indian Village', in *Journal of Asian Studies* 16, 5-10.

Oram, W. 1784. 'Report on Nandapuram Zemindari', in *Proceedings* 1915, 18-20.

Padel, F. 1995. *The Sacrifice of Human Being: British Rule and the Konds of Orissa*, Delhi: Oxford University Press.

Padhi, B.C. 1985. *Studies in the History of Koraput District during the British Rule, 1803-1936*, Bhubaneswar: Utkal University (dissertation).

Padhi, B.C. 1992. *Socio-economic Conditions of the Tribal under the British Rule, 1803-1936*, Calcutta: Punthi Pustak.

Padhi, S.C. 1986. *British Relations with the Chiefs and Rajas of Orissa*, Calcutta: Punthi Pustak.

Panda, H.C. 1985. *The British Policy Towards the Orissan Princely States during the First Half of the Nineteenth Century: Angul, A Case Study*, Bhubaneswar: Utkal University (dissertation).

Panda, S.K. 1985. 'The Krishna-Godavari-Delta: A Bone of Contention between the Gajapatis of Orissa and the Rayas of Vijayanagara', in Dallapiccola und Zingel-Avé Lallemant (eds.), 88-96.

Panda, S.K. 1986. *Herrschaft und Verwaltung im östlichen Indien unter den Späten Gangas, ca. 1038-1434*, Wiesbaden: Franz Steiner Verlag.

Parkin, R. 1991. *A Guide to Austroasiatic Speakers and their Languages*, Honolulu: University of Hawai Press.

Patnaik, J. 1988. *Feudatory States of Orissa, 1803-1857* (2 vols.), Allahabad: Vohra Publishers.

Patnaik, N. 1977. *Cultural Tradition in Puri: Structure and Organization of a Pilgrim Centre*, Simla: Indian Insitute of Advanced Study.

Patnaik, N. and P.S. Das Patnaik 1982. *The Kondh of Orissa*, Bhubaneswar: Tribal and Harijan Research Institute.

Patnaik, Nareen 1991. *A Desert Kingdom: The Rajputs of Bikaner*, London: Weidenfeld and Nicholson.

Patro, N. 1981. *History of Parlakhemundi from 1767-1881*, Berhampur: Berhampur University (dissertation).

Patro, P.S.N. 1981. *Krushna Chandra Gajapati Narayan Deo. The Maharaja of Parlakhemundi*, Bhanjanagar: Smt. P.P.K. Patro.

Pattnaik, R.K. 1982. *The History of Khallikote*, Berhampur: Berhampur University (dissertation).

Peabody, N. 1991. 'In Whose Turban does the Lord Reside? The Objectification of Charisma and the Fetishism of Objects in the Hindu Kingdom of Kota', in *Comparative Studies in Society and History* 33, 726-54.

Perlin, F. 1985a. 'Concepts of Order and Comparison, with a Diversion on Counter Ideologies and Corporate Institutions in Late Pre-colonial India', in Byres and Mukhia (eds.), 87-165.

Perlin, F. 1985b. 'State Formation Reconsidered II', in *Modern Asian Studies* 19, 415-80.

Pfaff-Czarnecka, J. 1990. 'The Nepalese Durgā Pūjā Festival, or Displaying Political Supremacy on Ritual Occasions', in *Proceedings of the International Seminar on the Anthropology of Tibet and the Himalaya*, Zürich: Ethnographic Museum, 270-86.

Pfeffer, G. 1978. 'Puri's Vedic Brahmins: Continuity and Change in their Traditional Institutions', in Eschmann, Kulke and Tripathi (eds.), 421-37.

Pfeffer, G. 1982. *Status and Affinity in Middle India*, Wiesbaden: Franz Steiner Verlag.

Pieper, J. (ed.) 1980. *Ritual Space in India: Studies in Architectural Anthropology*, London: Art and Anthropological Research Papers 17.

Pillai, S. (ed.) 1976. *Aspects of Changing India: Studies in Honour of G.S. Ghurye*, Bombay: Popular Prakashan.

Pouchepadass, J. and H. Stern (eds.) 1991. *De La Royauté à L'État: Anthropologie et Histoire du Politique dans le Monde Indien*. (Puruṣārtha, vol. 13), Paris: Editions de L'École des Hautes Études en Sciences Sociales.

Presler, F.A. 1987. *Religion under Bureaucracy: Policy and Administration for Hindu Temples in South India*, Cambridge: Cambridge University Press.

Preston, J.J. 1980a. *Cult of the Goddess: Social and Religious Change in a Hindu Temple*, New Delhi: Vikas.

Preston, J.J. 1980b. 'Sacred Centers and Symbolic Networks in South Asia', in *Mankind Quarterly* 20, 259-93.

Preston, J.J. (ed.) 1982. *Mother Worship: Theme and Variations*, Chapel Hill: University of North Carolina Press.

Price, P.G. 1979. 'Raja-Dharma in 19th Century South India: Land, Litigation and Largess in Ramnad Zamindary', in *Contributions to Indian Sociology* (N.S.) 13, 207-39.

Price, P.G. 1996. *Kingship and Political Practice in Colonial India*, Cambridge: Cambridge University Press.

Proceedings 1915 [1784]. *Proceedings of the Committee of Circuit in the Vizagapatam and Chicacole Districts, dated 12th September 1784*, Madras: Government Press.

Quigley, D. 1993. *The Interpretation of Caste*, Oxford: Clarendon Press.

Quigley, D. 1995. 'The Paradoxes of Monarchy', in *Anthropology Today* 11, 1-3.

Raheja, G.G. 1988a. 'India: Caste, Kingship, and Dominance Reconsidered', in *Annual Review of Anthropology* 17, 497-522.

Raheja, G.G. 1988b. *The Poison in the Gift: Ritual, Prestation, and the Dominant Caste in a North Indian Village*, Chicago: Chicago University Press.

Raheja, G.G. 1989. 'Centrality, Mutuality and Hierarchy: Shifting Aspects of Inter-Caste Relationships in North India', in *Contributions to Indian Sociology* (N.S.) 23, 79-101.

Rajaguru, S.N. 1968/1972. *History of the Gangas* (2 vols.), Bhubaneswar: Orissa State Museum.

Rajaguru, S.N. (ed.) 1958-66. *Inscriptions of Orissa* (5 vols.), Bhubaneswar: Orissa State Museum.

Ramachandra Rao, C.V. 1976. *Administration and Society in Medieval Āndhra (A.D. 1038-1538) under the Later Eastern Gaṅgas and the Sūryavaṃśa Gajapatis*, Nellore: Manasa Publications.

Ramanujan, A.K. 1988. 'Where Mirrors are Windows: Toward an Anthropology of Reflections', in *History of Religions* 28, 187-216.

Ramaswamy, V. 1982. 'Review' of *Peasant State and Society in Medieval South India*, by B. Stein 1980, in *Studies in History* 4, 307-20.

Rana, R.P. 1987. 'A Dominant Class in Upheaval: The Zamindars of a North Indian Region in the Late Seventeenth and Early Eighteenth Centuries', in *Indian Economic and Social History Review* 24, 395-410.

Rao, B. 1928. 'The Gaṅgavaṃśāvali of Parlakimedi', in *Journal of the Andhra Historical Research Society* 2, 250-8.

Rao, C.H. 1936. The *Dasara in Mysore: Its Origin and Significance*, Bangalore: Bangalore Printing and Publishing.

Rao, M.S.A. 1977. 'Rewari Kingdom and the Mughal Empire', in Fox (ed.), 79-89.

Rao, V.N., D. Shulman and S. Subrahmanyam 1992. *Symbols of Substance: Court and State in Nayaka Period Tamil Nadu*, Delhi: Oxford University Press.

Rath, A.K. 1987. *Studies on Some Aspects of the History and Culture of Orissa*, Calcutta: Punthi Pustak.

Ray, A. 1989. 'The Cult and Ritual of Durgā Pūjā in Bengal', in Dallapiccola and Zingel-Avé Lallemant (eds.), 131-41.

Reddy, N.S. 1973. 'Caste in a Tribal Society', in *Contributions to Indian Sociology* (N.S.) 7, 156-67.

Report 1940. *Report of the Partially Excluded Areas Enquiry Committee*, Cuttack: Government Press.

Reports 1836-7. *Reports on the Disturbances in the Zemindary of Goomsoor*, Bhubaneswar: Orissa State Archives.

Richards, J.F. (ed.) 1978. *Kingship and Authority in South Asia*, Madison: University of Wisconsin Publication Series.

Rocher, R. 1993. 'British Orientalism in the Eighteenth Century: The Dialectics of Knowledge and Government', in Breckenridge and van der Veer (eds.), 215-49.

Rösel, J. 1980. *Der Palast des Herrn der Welt: Entstehungsgeschichte und Organisation der indischen Tempel- und Pilgerstadt Puri*, München: Weltforum Verlag.

Rösel, J. 1986. 'Max Weber, India and the Patrimonial State', in Kantowsky (ed.), 117-52.

Rösel, J. 1994. 'Göttinnen, Krieger und Brahmanen: Volksreligiosität und Herrschaftsbildung im Hinterland von Orissa', in Möhlig and von Trotta (eds.), 113-28.

Rothermund, D. 1970a. 'Feudalism in India', in Rothermund 1970b, 165-78.

Rothermund, D. 1970b. *The Phases of Indian Nationalism and Other Essays*, Bombay: Nachiketa Publications.

Rothermund, D. 1989. 'Review' of *Land and Sovereignty in India*, by A. Wink (1986), in *Journal of the Economic and Social History of the Orient* 32, 239-40.

Roy, S.C. 1912. The *Mundas and their Country*, Calcutta.

Roy, S.C. 1926. 'Pseudo-Rajputs', in *Man in India* 5, 152-68.

Roy, S.C. 1933. 'Some Interesting Aspects of Orissan Ethnology', in *Journal of Bihar and Orissa Research Society* 19, 319-36.

Ruben, W. 1962. *Waldabenteuer des indischen epischen Helden*, Berlin: Akademie Verlag.

Rudolph, S.H. 1963. 'The Princely States of Rajputana: Ethic, Authority and Structure', in *Indian Journal of Political Science* 24.

Rudolph, S.H. 1987. 'Presidential Address: State Formation in Asia - A Prolegomenon to a Comparative Study', in *Journal of Asian Studies* 46, 31-46.

Rudolph, L. and S.H. Rudolph 1985. 'The Subcontinental Empire and the Regional Kingdom in Indian State Formation', in Wallace (ed.), 40-59.

Russel, G.E. 1856. 'Reports on the Disturbances in Purla Kimedy, Vizagapatnam and Goomsor in 1832-6', in *Selections from the Records of the Madras Government*, Madras: Government Press.

Sahlins, M. 1961. 'The Segmentary Lineage: An Organization of Predatory Expansion', in *American Anthropologist* 63, 322-45.

Sahlins, M. 1972. *Stone Age Economics,* Chicago: University of Chicago Press.

Sahlins, M. 1985. *Islands of History*, Chicago: University of Chicago Press.

Sahu, L.N. 1942. *The Hill Tribes of Jeypore*, Cuttack: Orissa Mission Press.

Said, E.W. 1978. *Orientalism*, London: Routlegde and Kegan Paul.

Sakalani, A. 1987. *The History of a Himalayan Princely State*, Delhi: Durga Publications.

Samal, J.K. 1988. *Princely States of Orissa, 1905-1947*, Allahabad: Vohra Publishers.

Sarkar, J. 1916. 'The History of Orissa in the Seventeenth Century, Reconsidered from Persian Sources', in *Journal of Bihar and Orissa Research Society* 2, 152-65, and 3, 338-49.

Sarma, A.V.D. 1986. *Integration of Andhra and Orissa Cultures: Viewed through the Biographical Sketch of Vikrama Deo Varma of Jeypore, 1869-1951*, Delhi: B.R. Publishing Corp.

Sarma, R.N. 1938. *Jayapura Raja Vamsyavali: A History of the Solar Dynasty of Jeypore*, Madras: Vavilla Press.

Sastri, K.A.N. 1955. *A History of South India from Prehistoric Times to the Fall of Vijayanagar*, Madras: Oxford University Press.

Sax, W.S. 1991. *Mountain Goddess: Gender and Politics in a Himalayan Pilgrimage*, Delhi: Oxford University Press.

Schivelbusch, W. 1989 [1977]. *Geschichte der Eisenbahnreise: Zur Industrialisierung von Raum und Zeit*, Frankfurt am Main: Fischer.

Schluchter, W. 1984. 'Weltflüchtiges Erlösungsstreben und organische Sożialethik: Überlegungen zu Max Webers Analysen der indischen Kulturreligionen', in Schluchter (ed.), 11-71.

Schluchter, W. (ed.) 1984. *Max Webers Studie über Hinduismus und Buddhismus: Interpretation und Kritik*, Frankfurt am Main: Suhrkamp.

Schluchter, W. 1987. *Max Webers Sicht des Islam: Interpretation und Kritik*, Frankfurt am Main: Suhrkamp.

Schnepel, B. 1987a. 'Max Weber's Theory of Charisma and its Applicability in Anthropological Research', in *Journal of the Anthropological Society of Oxford* 18, 26-48.

Schnepel, B. 1987b. 'Review' of *Essays on Individualism*, by L. Dumont (1986a), in *Journal of the Anthropological Society of Oxford* 18, 289-92.

Schnepel, B. 1988. 'In Quest of Life: Hocart's Scheme of Evolution from Ritual Organization to Government', in *Archives Européennes de Sociologie* 29, 165-87.

Schnepel, B. 1990. 'Corporations, Personhood, and Ritual in Tribal Society: Three Interconnected Topics in the Anthropology of Meyer Fortes', in *Journal of the Anthropological Society of Oxford* 21, 1-31.

Schnepel, B. 1992. 'The Nandapur Suryavamshis: Origin and Consolidation of a South Orissan Kingdom', in *Orissa Historical Research Journal* 38, 170-99.

Schnepel, B. 1993a. 'Der König und seine Göttin: Ritual und Politik in Südorissa, Indien', in *Mitteilungen der Alexander von Humboldt-Stiftung* 61, 17-26.

Schnepel, B. 1993b. 'Die Schutzgöttinnen: Tribale Gottheiten in Südorissa (Indien) und ihre Patronage durch hinduistische Kleinkönige', in *Anthropos* 88, 337-50.

Schnepel, B. 1994a. 'Little Kingdoms Reconsidered', in *Occasional Papers* 5, Bhubaneswar: Department of Anthropology.

Schnepel, B. 1994b. 'Goddesses, Kings, and Tribals: Remarks on the Ritual Policy of a South Orissan Jungle Kingdom', in *Man in Society* 8, 19-36.

Schnepel, B. 1995a. 'Durga and the King: Ethnohistorical Aspects of the Politico-Ritual Life in a South Orissan Jungle Kingdom', in *Journal of the Royal Anthropological Institute (Man)* 1, 145-66.

Schnepel, B. 1995b. *Twinned Beings: Kings and Effigies in Southern Sudan, East India and Renaissance France*, Gothenburg: Institute for Advanced Studies in Social Anthropology.

Schnepel, B. 1995c. 'Review' of *Little Kingdoms in Kalinga: Ideologie, Legitimation und Politik regionaler Eliten*, by G. Berkemer (1993), in *Journal of the Economic and Social History of the Orient* 39, 69-72.

Schnepel, B. 1996. 'The Hindu King's Authority Reconsidered: Durga-pūjā and Dasarā in a South Orissan Jungle Kingdom', in Boholm (ed.), 126-57.

Schnepel, B. 1997. *Die Dschungelkönige: Ethnohistorische Aspekte von Politik und Ritual in Südorissa/Indien*, Stuttgart: Franz Steiner Verlag.

Schnepel, B. 1999. 'Ethnologie und Geschichte: Stationen der Standortbestimmung aus der britischen Social Anthropology', in *Historische Anthropologie* 7, 110-28.

Schulte-Nordholt, H. 1993. 'Leadership and the Limits of Political Control: A Balinese "Response" to Clifford Geertz', in *Social Anthropology* 1, 291-307.

Selections 1854. *Selections from the Records of the Madras Government. 7: Reports on the Swinging Festival and the Ceremony of Walking through Fire*, Madras: Government Press.

Selections 1864. *Selections from the Records of the Madras Government. 81: A Collection and Precis of Papers about Jeypore*, Madras: United Scotish Press.

Selections 1948. *Selections from the Records of the Madras Government.* New (Revenue) Series 1: *A Collection of Papers Relating to the Inam Settlement in the Madras Presidency*, Madras: Government Press.

Senapati, N. 1966. *Orissa District Gazetteers: Koraput*, Cuttack: Orissa Government Press.

Sewell, R. 1970. *A Forgotten Empire*, New Delhi: India Book House.

Sharma, R.S. 1965. *Indian Feudalism, c. A.D. 300-1200*, Madras: Macmillan.

Sharma, R.S. 1985. 'How Feudal was Indian Feudalism?', in *Journal of Peasant Studies* 12, 19-43.

Sharma, R.S. 1989. 'The Segmentary State and the Indian Experience', in *Indian Historical Review* 16, 80-108.

Sharma, R.S. 1995. 'How Feudal was Indian Feudalism' (Revised and updated version), in Kulke (ed.), 48-85.

Sharma, R.S. and V. Jha (eds.) 1974. *Indian Society: Historical Probings. In Memory of D.D. Kosambi*. New Delhi: Peoples Publishing House.

Shulman, D. 1980a. 'On South Indian Bandits and Kings', in *Indian Economic and Social History Review* 17, 283-306.

Shulman, D. 1980b. *Tamil Temple Myths*, Princeton: Princeton University Press.

Shulman, D. 1981. 'The Crossing of the Wildernis: Landscape and Myth in the Tamil Story of Rama', in *Acta Orientala* 42, 21-54.

Shulman, D. 1984. 'Die Integration der hinduistischen Kultur durch die Brahmanen: "Große", "mittlere" und "kleine" Versionen des Paraśurāma-Mythos', in Schluchter (ed.), 104-48.

Shulman, D. 1985. *The King and the Clown in South Indian Myth and Poetry*, Princeton: Princeton University Press.

Sigrist, C. 1968. *Regulierte Anarchie: Untersuchungen zum Fehlen und zur Entstehung politischer Herrschaft in segmentären Gesellschaften Afrikas*, Freiburg: Walter Verlag.

Singer, M. 1956. 'Introduction: The Indian Village. A Symposium', in *Journal of Asian Studies* 16, 3-5.

Singer, M. and B.S. Cohn (eds.) 1968. *Structure and Change in Indian Society*, Chicago: Aldine.

Singh, U. 1993. *Kings, Brāhmaṇas and Temples in Orissa. An Epigraphic Study AD 300-1147*, Delhi: Munshiram Manoharlal.

Singh, S. 1974. 'A Study in State-formation among Tribal Communities', in Sharma and Jha (eds.), 317-36.

Singh Deo, K.B. 1939. *Nandapur: A Forsaken Kingdom*, Cuttack: Utkal Sahitya Press.

Sinha, B.N. 1980. 'Orissas geographische Gegebenheiten', in E. Fischer (ed.), 17-24.

Sinha, B.N. (ed.) 1987. *Adivasi Atlas of Orissa*, Bhubaneswar: Govt. of Orissa; Dept. of Harijan and Tribal Welfare.

Sinha, S. 1957. 'Tribal Cultures of Peninsular India as a Dimension of Little Tradition in the Study of Indian Civilization: A Preliminary Statement', in *Man in India* 37, 93-118.

Sinha, S. 1962. 'State Formation and Rajput Myth in Tribal Central India', in *Man in India* 42, 35-88.

Sinha, S. 1965. 'Tribe-Caste and Tribe-Peasant Continua in Central India', in *Man in India* 45, 57-83.

Sinha, S. 1980. 'Tribes and Indian Civilization: A Perspective', in *Man in India* 60, 1-15.

Sinha, S. 1981. 'Tribes and Indian Civilization: Transformation Process in Modern India', in *Man in India* 61, 105-42.

Sinha, S. (ed.) 1987. *Tribal Polities and State Systems in Pre-colonial Eastern and North Eastern India*, Calcutta: Bagchi & Company.

Sircar, D.C. 1953. 'Some Minor Dynasties of Orissa', in *Orissa Historical Research Journal* 2, 13-20.

Sircar, D.C. 1966. 'Landlordism Confused with Feudalism', in Sircar (ed.), 57-62.

Sircar, D.C. (ed.) 1966. *Landsystem and Feudalism in Ancient India*, Calcutta: Calcutta University Press.

Smith, A. 1778. *An Inquiry into the Nature and Causes of the Wealth of Nations*, London.

Sontheimer, G.D. 1964. 'Religious Endowments in India: The Juristic Personality of Hindu Deities', in *Zeitschrift für vergleichende Rechtswissenschaften* 67, 45-100.

Sontheimer, G.D. 1981. 'Dasarā at Devaraguḍḍa: Ritual and Play in the Cult of Mailār/Khaṇḍobā', in *South Asian Digest of Regional Writing* 10, 1-28.

Sontheimer, G.D. 1987. 'The Vana and the Kṣetra: The Tribal Background of Some Famous Cults', in Tripathi and Kulke (eds.) 1987b, 117-64.

Sontheimer, G.D. 1989. 'Hinduism: The Five Components and their Interaction', in Sontheimer and Kulke (eds.), 179-212.

Sontheimer, G.D. and H. Kulke (eds.) 1989. *Hinduism Reconsidered*, Delhi: Manohar.

Southall, A.W. 1953. *Alur Society: A Study in Processes and Types of Domination*, Nairobi: Oxford University Press.

Southall, A. W. 1970. 'The Illusion of Tribe', in *Journal of Asian and African Studies* 5, 28-50.

Southall, A. W. 1988. 'The Segmentary State in Africa and Asia', in *Comparative Studies in Society and History* 30, 52-82.

Spencer, G.W. 1969. 'Religious Networks and Royal Influence in Eleventh Century South India', in *Journal of the Economic and Social History of the Orient* 12, 42-56.

Spiegel, G.M. 1994. 'Geschichte, Historizität und die soziale Logik von mittelalterlichen Texten', in Conrad and Kessel (eds.), 161-202.

Srinivas, M.N. 1952. *Religion and Society among the Coorgs*, Oxford: Oxford University Press.

Srinivas, M.N. 1955. 'The Social System of a Mysore Village', in Marriot (ed.), 1-35.

Srinivas, M.N. 1975. 'The Indian Village: Myth and Reality', in Beattie and Lienhardt (eds.), 41-85.

Srinivas, M.N. and A.M. Shah 1960. 'The Myth of the Self-sufficiency of the Indian Village', in *Economic Weekly* 12, 1375-8.

Staal, F. 1979. 'The Meaninglessness of Ritual', in *Numen* 26, 1-22.

Stein, B. 1969. 'Integration of the Agrarian System of South India', in Frykenberg (ed.), 175-216.

Stein, B. 1975. 'The State and the Agrarian Order in Medieval South India: A Historiographical Critique', in Stein (ed.), 64-91.

Stein, B. 1977a. 'The Segmentary State in South Indian History', in Fox (ed.), 3-51.

Stein, B. 1977b. 'Introduction', in Stein (ed.), 1-10.

Stein, B. 1977c. 'Temples in Tamil Country, 1300-1750 A.D.', in Stein (ed.), 11-47.

Stein, B. 1980. *Peasant State and Society in Medieval South India*, Delhi: Oxford University Press.

Stein, B. 1985a. 'Politics, Peasants and the Deconstruction of Feudalism in Medieval India', in Byres and Mukhia (eds.), 54-86.

Stein, B. 1985b. 'Vijayanagara and the Transition to Patrimonial Systems', in Dallapiccola and Zingel-Avé Lallemant (eds.), 73-87.

Stein, B. 1985c. 'State Formation and Economy Reconsidered I.', in *Modern Asian Studies* 19, 387-413.

Stein, B. 1989. *Vijayanagara* (The New Cambridge History of India I.2.), Cambridge: Cambridge University Press.

Stein, B. 1991. 'The Segmentary State: Interim Reflections', in Pouchepadass and Stern (eds.), 217-38.

Stein, B. (ed.) 1975. *Essays on South India*, New Delhi: Vikas Publishing House.

Stein, B. (ed.) 1977. *South Indian Temples*, in *Indian Economic and Social History Review* 14 (Special issue edition).

Stevenson, J.A.R. 1916. *Report on Goomsur Zemindari (Reprint of a letter from J.A.R. Stevenson, Collector of Ganjam, to the President and Members of the Board of Revenue, Fort St. George, 4th October 1836.)*, Chatrapur: Ganjam Collectorate Press.

Stietencron, H. von 1978a. 'The Advent of Viṣṇuism in Orissa: An Outline of its History according to Archaeological and Epigraphical Sources from the Gupta Period up to 1135 A.D.', in Eschmann, Kulke and Tripathi (eds.), 1-30.

Stietencron, H. von 1978b. 'Early Temples of Jagannātha in Orissa: The Formative Phase', in Eschmann, Kulke and Tripathi (eds.), 61-78.

Stietencron, H. von 1978c. 'The Śaiva Component in the Early Evolution of Jagannātha', in Eschmann, Kulke and Tripathi (eds.), 119-23.

Stirling, A. 1904 [1822]. *An Account (Geographical, Statistical and Historical) of Orissa Proper or Cuttack*, Cuttack.

Subbarao, B. 1956. *The Personality of India: A Study of the Development of Material Culture of India and Pakistan*, Baroda.

Subbarayalu, Y. 1973. *The Political Geography of the Chola Country*, Madras.

Subbarayalu, Y. 1982. 'The Cōḷa State', in *Studies in History* 4, 269-306.

Subrahmanyam, R. 1957. *The Sūryavaṁśi Gajapatis of Orissa*, Waltair: Andhra University.

Ṣubrahmanyam, S. 1986. 'Aspects of State Formation in South India and Southeast Asia, 1550-1650', in *Indian Economic and Social History Review* 23, 357-77.

Subrahmanyam, S. and D. Shulman 1985. 'The Men Who Would be King: The Politics of Expansion in Early Seventeenth-Century Northern Tamilnadu', in *Modern Asian Studies* 24, 225-48.

Tambiah, S.J. 1976. *World Conqueror and World Renouncer: A Study of Buddhism and Polity in Thailand against a Historical Background*, Cambridge: Cambridge University Press.

Tambiah, S.J. 1985a. *Culture, Thought, and Social Action: An Anthropological Perspective*, Cambridge: Harvard University Press.

Tambiah, S.J. 1985b [1977]. 'The Galactic Polity in Southeast Asia', in Tambiah 1985a, 252-86.

Tambiah, S.J. 1985c. 'A Reformulation of Geertz's Conception of the Theater State', in Tambiah 1985a, 316-38.

Tapper, B.E. 1979. 'Widows and Goddesses: Female Roles in Deity Symbolism in a South Indian Village', in *Contributions to Indian Sociology* 13, 1-31.

Taylor, G.N. 1862. 'Letter from G.N. Taylor, Esq., Inam Commissioner, to the Secreatry to Government, Revenue Department, dated Chatrapore, the 11th February 1862', reprinted in and cited from Selections 1948, 138-44.

Taylor, H.D. no date. *Memoir on the Ganjam Maliahs in the Madras Presidency*, Cuttack: Government of Orissa; Revenue Department.

Taylor, W. 1838. 'Some Additional Notes on the Hill Inhabitants of the Goomsoor Mountains, with the Translation of a Telugu Paper, Containing an Historical Narrative of Bhonja Family, Feudal Chieftains of Gūmsara', in *Madras Journal of Literature and Science* 7, 89-104.

Tekkali Zamindar, no date. *Tekkali Zamindar: The Geneulogical Account of Kadamba Jagaddeva Dynasty of Tekkali. Orissa Research Project Manuscripts* 447 (Translated from Telugu by S.N. Rajaguru), Heidelberg: South Asia Institute.

Thapar, R. 1978a. 'Origin Myths and Early Indian Historical Tradition', in Thapar 1978b, 294-325.

Thapar, R. 1978b. *Ancient Indian Social History: Some Interpretations*, New Delhi: Orient Longman.

Thapar, R. 1984. *From Lineage to State: Social Formations in the Mid-first Millennium B.C. in the Ganges Valley*, Bombay: Oxford University Press.

Thorner, D. 1966. 'Marx on India and the Asiatic Mode of Production', in *Contributions to Indian Sociology* (N.S.) 9, 33-66.

Thurston, E. 1909. *Castes and Tribes of Southern India* (7.vols.), Madras: Government Press.

Thusu, K.N. 1980. *Gond Kingdom of Chanda*, Calcutta: Anthropological Survey of India.

Tod, J. 1920 [1829-32]. *Annals and Antiquities of Rajasthan or the Central and Western Rajput States of India*, Oxford: Oxford University Press.

Toffin, G. 1981. 'Culte des Déesse et Fete du Dasai chez les Newar (Nepal)', in *Puruṣārtha* 5, 55-81.

Toffin, G. 1993. *Le Palais et le temple: La Fonction Royale dans la Vallé du Nepal*, Paris: CNRS.

Trautmann, T.R. 1981. *Dravidian Kinship*, Cambridge: Cambridge University Press.

Tribes of Orissa 1990. *Tribes of Orissa*, Bhubaneswar: Harijan and Tribal Welfare Department.

Trikhy, T. 1989. *The Southern Aboriginal Tribes of Orissa*, Berhampur: Berhampur University (dissertation).

Tripathi, G.C. 1978. 'Jagannātha: The Ageless Deity of the Hindus', in Eschmann, Kulke and Tripathi (eds.), 477-90.

Tripathi, G.C. and H. Kulke (eds.) 1987. *Kaṭakarājavaṃśāvali: A Traditional History of Orissa*, Allahabad: Vohra Publishers.

Tripathi, G.C. and H. Kulke (eds.) 1987. *Religion and Society in Eastern India: Anncharlott Eschmann Memorial Lectures, 1978-1986 (vol. 1)*, Bhubaneswar: Utkal University.

Turner, V. 1974. *Dramas, Fields and Metaphors: Symbolic Action in Human Society*, Ithaca: Cornell University Press.

Twenty-Five Questions … 1861. *Twenty-Five Questions Addressed to the Rajas and Chiefs of the Regulation and Tributary Mahals,* Calcutta: Bengal Military Orphan Press.

Urhahn, M. 1985. *Grenzen und Übergänge von Kasten- und Stammesgesellschaft in Indien*, Heidelberg: South Asia Institute (dissertation).

Vadivelu, A. 1984 [1903]. *The Aristocracy of Southern India* (2 vols.), Delhi: Mittal Publishers.

van der Veer, P. 1994. *Religious Nationalism: Hindus and Muslims in India*, Berkeley: University of California Press.

Vizagapatnam District Records no date. *Vizagapatnam District Records*, Hyderabad: Andhra Pradesh State Archives.

Waghorne, J.P. 1989. 'From Robber Baron to Royal Servant of God? Gaining a Divine Body in South India', in Hiltebeitel (ed.), 405-26.

Wallace, P. (ed.) 1985. *Region and Nation in India*, Delhi: Oxford University Press.

Walters, R. 1980. 'Signs of the Times: Clifford Geertz and Historians', in *Social Research* 47, 537-56.

Washbrook, D. 1981. 'Law, State and Agrarian Society in Colonial India', in *Modern Asian Studies* 15, 649-721.

Weber, M. 1968 [1921]. *Economy and Society: An Outline of Interpretative Sociology*, New York: Bedminster Press.

Weber, M. 1976 [1921]. *Wirtschaft und Gesellschaft: Grundriss der verstehenden Soziologie*, Tübingen: J.C.B. Mohr.

Weber, M. 1988 [1921]. *Gesammelte Aufsätze zur Religionssoziologie II: Die Wirtschaftsethik der Weltreligionen II. Hinduismus und Buddhismus*, Tübingen: J.C.B. Mohr.

White, H. 1987. *The Content of the Form: Narrative Discourse and Historical Representation*, Baltimore: Johns Hopkins University Press.

Whitehead, H. 1976 [1921]. *The Village Gods of South India*, Delhi: Summit Publications.

Wills, C. 1919. 'The Territorial System of the Rajput Kingdoms of Medieval Chhattisgarh', in *Journal and Proceedings of the Asiatic Society of Bengal* 15, 197-262.

Wilson, H.H. 1882. *The Mackenzie Collection: A Descriptive Catalogue of the Oriental Manuscripts and Other Articles*, Calcutta.

Wilson, H.H. 1968 [1855]. *A Glossary of Judicial and Revenue Terms*, Delhi: Munshiram Manoharlal.

Wink, A. 1984. 'Sovereignty and Universal Dominion in South Asia', in *Indian Economic and Social History Review* 21, 265-92.

Wink, A. 1986. *Land and Sovereignty in India: Agrarian Society and Politics under the Eighteenth-Century Maratha Svarājya*, Cambridge: Cambridge University Press.

Wittfogel, K.A. 1977 [1957]. *Die orientalische Despotie: Eine vergleichende Untersuchung totaler Macht*, Frankfurt am Main: Ullstein.

Yadava, B.N.S. 1973. *Society and Culture in North India in the Twelfth Century*, Allahabad.

Yang, A. 1979. 'An Institutional Shelter: The Court of Wards in Late Nineteenth-Century Bihar', in *Modern Asian Studies* 3, 247-64.

Ziegler, N.P. 1978. 'Some Notes on Rajput Loyalties during the Mughal Period', in Richards (ed.), 215-51.

INDEX

C

D

E

F

G

H

I

J

K